San Martin

JOSE SAN MARTIN
Portrait by Bouchet

San Martin

KNIGHT OF THE ANDES

BY RICARDO ROJAS

TRANSLATED BY HERSCHEL BRICKELL
AND CARLOS VIDELA

Introduction and Notes by
Herschel Brickell

COOPER SQUARE PUBLISHERS, INC.
NEW YORK ● 1967

Published 1967 by
Cooper Square Publishers, Inc.
59 Fourth Avenue, New York, N. Y. 10003
Library of Congress Catalog Card Number: 66-30783

Printed in U.S.A. by
NOBLE OFFSET PRINTERS, INC.
NEW YORK 3, N. Y.

Contents

Introduction

In this biography, already sufficiently popular and admired in South America, a distinguished Argentinian scholar and writer, who is looked upon as the leading authority on his country's literature, presents us with a full-length portrait of the Latin-American hero capable of being most easily understood and appreciated by North Americans.

The more romantic and dashing Simón Bolívar has been a source of prime interest on the part of biographers, especially in recent years, but his genius must in its very nature remain far more alien to our understanding than that of his fellow liberator to the south.

This is not even to hint at an invidious comparison where none is needed. These two men earned the right to their heroic titles and deserve the eternal gratitude of all those who love liberty. But it is to say that San Martín's calm dignity and lofty character have won him frequent comparison with George Washington, who was the striking embodiment of certain so-called Anglo-Saxon virtues. Bolívar, on the other hand, was pure Latin in temperament and action, and it is more difficult to find his counterpart in our own revolutionary story.

Señor Rojas' approach to his task is plainly more Latin than Anglo-Saxon. He treats San Martín as a superman, belonging to the long line of supermen or semimythical beings who are God-inspired in their search for the Holy Grail or some other symbol of a passionate love of mankind. We are accustomed to see our great men as larger than life, as they were, but nevertheless to insist that they remain within the human range. (At times our biographers have gone to the extreme of pointing out their faults lest we lose them as full brothers.)

But the mystical approach to the problem of the greatness of such a man as San Martín may help to explain a hero to us when nothing else can, and the author in the present case goes far toward establishing a right to his point of view. He deals with a life filled with unusual elements and also filled with significance for the concept of a New World, a vision and a goal revived in our own times by the current period of war.

Above all else, this man San Martín was, unlike most of the revolutionary leaders in the New World, a professional soldier. This fact ought to help us to comprehend his unflinching self-discipline, which manifested itself in his refusal to be rendered helpless by persistent and painful illnesses. It showed itself again in his relatively humane treatment of prisoners, something notable in a series of wars marked by shocking incidents among both the Spaniards and Creoles. It may have had much to do with his retirement from public life —his renunciation—at the high point in his career. It certainly helps to explain his marvelous military successes, such as Chacabuco and Maipú.

San Martín was eleven years old when he became a soldier in the Spanish Army, his father having returned to the mother country. He was no more than thirteen when he smelled powder and blood, and when he returned to Argentina in his early thirties he had had two decades of experience as a warrior. He came home aflame with the desire to see his country liberated from the Spain for which he had been fighting, and it was an opportune moment for the return of anyone who understood military science; there was need of all the skill he had acquired.

Thus when he came to the supreme test of his career, the crossing of the mighty and forbidding Andes from Argentina to Chile, opening the way for an attack on Peru, the heart of Spanish power, he knew what he was doing. But neither experience nor training nor patriotic fervor is sufficient to explain what many noted authorities have called one of the greatest military feats of all human history. A gauge of its epochal importance lies in the names always invoked for comparison. These are three, Hannibal, Napoleon and Alexander, and there is no trace of hyperbole here. The nearest feat to San Martín's was, in fact, Alexander's crossing of the Hindu Kush, and San Martín had to create and equip his conquering army before his march could begin. He conquered the Andes, and his name will forever be associated with this rugged, lofty range that has played so large a part in the history of South America.

The details of the crossing, with a well-equipped army of five thousand men, a crossing lasting upward of a month, are to be found in one of Señor Rojas' most stirring chapters. In this achievement, which very definitely broke the Spanish hold on a continent, San Martín displayed another facet of his genius, namely, his knowledge of men and his ability to choose his subordinates. His friend and companion Tomás Guido was one of these, and the two who made the conquering of the Andes possible were the former priest and mechanical genius, Luis Beltrán, and Alvarez Condorco, the invaluable scout and map maker. Beltrán, they say, did not even flinch when San Martín mentioned thirty thousand horseshoes, and his production of arms and ammunition foreshadowed our current contribution to the cause of human freedom.

Imperishable military glory came to San Martín for his Andean triumph and its direct consequences, but not even the greatest of his victories thunder more loudly in history than some of his other actions of a peaceful nature. In Santiago, when a grateful citizenry presented him with a purse as a reward for his assistance, he at once caused a public library to be established with the money. He had not the eloquent tongue or the inspired pen of Bolívar, but he left schools and libraries in his trail and summed up the whole matter by saying: "Education is the master key that opens the door to prosperity and makes a nation happy."

These are the simple words of a soldier who wielded his sword for humane ends and who could write, as he once did in a famous letter to Bolívar, with wholehearted sincerity: "I am an instrument of justice: The cause that I defend is the cause of humankind."

Considering the place San Martín rightfully occupies among the heroes of the New World and his exceptionally sympathetic character, it is surprising that much more has not been written about him in English. Anna Schoell-kopf's small volume of several years ago was known to few people, and Margaret Haynes Harrison's recent *Captain of the Andes: The Life of Don José de San Martín, Liberator of Argentina, Chile and Peru* to only a few more.

Nor is the material in Spanish particularly abundant, although there is always the definitive work of Bartolomé Mitre, *Historia de San Martín*, to which all future biographers should pay a debt of gratitude as a magnificent source book. Hence there is obviously a need for the present translation.

First published in 1933, the Rojas biography appeared under the title *El Santo de la Espada*, or "The Saint of the Sword." It was at once successful in the Argentine and widely read elsewhere in Latin America. Our attempt to put it into English was beset with difficulties, as Spanish lends itself much better to the author's mystical approach than our more prosaic and less rhetorical English. It is fair to assume that few translators with a real love of the original language of a work have ever felt anything except humility in gazing upon their attempt to reclothe an author's thoughts in alien garments. I am sure I speak for Mr. Videla as well as myself when I say that we feel, therefore, less proud than humble.

But it is wholly obvious, whatever differences of opinion there may be about the translation, that San Martín needs to be better known in the United States. For long months now he has never been far from my thoughts, and I have found him a most inspiring companion, Argentina's great contribution to New World liberty and therefore to human freedom everywhere.

HERSCHEL BRICKELL

Washington, D.C.
July 4, 1944

Prologue

THE LIFE OF General José de San Martín can be told in three stages: the first one, from 1778 to 1816, is one of learning and training; the second one, from 1816 to 1822, is one of accomplishment and power; the third one, from 1822 to 1850, is one of sacrifice and love. To those three stages correspond the three parts of this book, under the titles of "Initiation," "Achievement," and "Renunciation." The last part gives unity to the work, in discovering through external facts the inner norm of an extraordinary life.

San Martín himself, when withdrawing from Peru, pointed out to O'Higgins those three moments: "My youth was sacrificed to the service of the Spaniards; my middle age to the service of my country; I have a right to dispose of my old age." This he did as if he were outlining the plan for us to follow in writing his biography: youth, maturity, old age.

As for the psychological measures of the three stages, he himself said of the first one: "One will be what one must, or he will be nothing." Of the second, "I must follow the destiny that calls me." And of the third, "I am, and shall continue to be, in retirement from the world." These are San Martinian phrases which I have adopted as epigraphs for the three parts of the book. Illumined by this key, I believe I have discovered San Martín's mystic secret, and, in calling him "The Saint of the Sword," I define with those words the work of our protagonist, thus fixing his epic profile among those of the universal and holy leaders of men.

Such an interpretation of our personage, together with the plan adopted for the narration of his life, leads me to feel that there is something new in this book; not in its subject matter, most of which has already been made public, but in the mold in which I am recasting it, and in the order of the artistic composition.

The facts of San Martín's life help me to show what he was through what he did. I am thus writing a biography that is set in the individual perspective of psychology rather than in the social perspective of history, without excluding the myth that is inherent in every epic and which gives heroic lives a transcendent mystery.

Many American works have been printed having San Martín as their subject, or alluding to him because of their reference to events in which he had a part; and it would suffice to refer to the works mentioned by Dr. Carlos

Salas in the five volumes of his *Bibliography of San Martín*. Among them I must mention especially the monumental *History of San Martín and of the South American Emancipation*, written half a century ago by General Bartolomé Mitre, a definitive work for the composition of the story and amazing for its task of research and collection of documents. I have used those works in preparing my book, and I have taken advantage sometimes of books by travelers and the memoirs of witnesses. But the chief source for this evocation has been the *Archive of San Martín*, which the Mitre Museum published in twelve large volumes, under the direction of Don Alejandro Rosa. Letters and public papers signed by San Martín have served me as confidences from him.

San Martín was not a man inclined to intimate confidences. But there is enough material in his Archive to enable one to attempt, as I do here, a resurrection of his historical figure through a book that belongs definitely to the province of esthetic creation, although the previous information offered by historical science has been necessary in order to back up with facts everything that is said here, or to infer from the documents what is here inferred. The object has been that of restoring to the main character the plenitude of life in the flesh, by the daily anecdote; and in the spirit, to place him in the heroic category.

Despite the enormous bibliography, the personality of San Martín had become somewhat beclouded by the accumulation of political, economic, and military events described by history. What I proposed to do, instead, was to paint the personality of San Martín, the man, a purpose which suffices by itself to establish an essential difference between the books which place the accent on the individual and those which place it on the epoch. To justify the new endeavor I should need to repeat Plutarch's words in his Life of Alexander: "I do not write a 'history,' I write a 'life.'"

The military nature and the patriotic meaning of the San Martinian epic have prevented many from perceiving clearly the moral springs of conduct and the human amplitude of this armed saint's conscience. A general, although more brilliant than the other generals of the independence, and a patriot, although more disinterested than other patriots of Argentine history, these things are what we usually admire in San Martín. But there is something exceptional in him which goes beyond the character of the equestrian statues and of the chromos hung in schoolhouses. That greater vision is the one that I propose to evoke, such as I saw it through his works and his sacrifices.

It is doubtless a great honor for the Argentine Army to have had such a "general" as a patron of its arms; but if it is a mission for heroes to go on exerting their influence from immortality, San Martín, as he will emerge from these pages, comes to give timely lessons in abnegation to those who serve under the same liberating banner which he carried in triumph throughout the American continent. A shaper of soldiers and a winner of battles, that he was in eminent degree; but it is interesting to clarify the moral reasons for his conduct. His figure, without predecessors among warriors, does not belong to the Homeric tradition of Achilles or Hector, in which were formed Alexander, Caesar, Charlemagne, Frederick, Napoleon, and the American Bolívar, the last as great as they. San Martín was an ascetic with a mission of charity, and he belongs to the breed of the armed saints, prototypes of Lohengrin and Parsifal in medieval legend, knights in the divine realm, true "protectors," whose epic mysticism had not found complete realization in history before the San Martinian case; but it has Castilian precedents in King Pelayo and the Cid in history, or in Amadis of Gaul and Don Quixote in literary legend. Our hero called himself "protector" when he achieved his task. "A pure and simple soul, made a seer through piety, will bring you liberation": thus speaks the character of the Wagnerian poem.

As an Argentine patriot, San Martín also broke the mold, and it is in his own country, where he had some of his worst enemies, that, by reason of his campaigns in Chile and his disobedience on the eve of the expedition to Peru, he was considered a traitor to the cause of Buenos Aires, which was already torn asunder by the fight between unitarians and federalists. But he is not a fetish of one region alone, and his glory cannot be the object of partisan comparisons which would diminish his stature when measured in terms of the internal politics of his country, or in terms of village polemics which even today are frequent in South American history. San Martín belongs to all of independent America, for actions in behalf of society, and to the whole of mankind, for the moral mastership which makes him universal.

Today San Martín has statues in all of the principal Argentine cities; the first was erected in Buenos Aires, on the same spot of the Retiro where he began his military service, and among the others the outstanding one has been erected on the Hill of Glory, in Mendoza, facing the Andes. In 1863 Santiago de Chile unveiled San Martín's monument in Las Delicias, which the hero visited so many times. Peru celebrated the centennial of its independence with a monument to its Protector, and it has made a national museum, under the name of San Martín and Bolívar together, of the house of La Magdalena, in which both lived. Colombia honors San Martín in Bogotá, a prominent plaza adorned with an equestrian statue being called "The Square of San Martín." Venezuela has erected in Caracas, near the house of Bolívar, a statue to San Martín. The other America has placed his bust in the Hall of Nations, in Washington. All the land of the New World seems to be watched over by the effigy and the name of San Martín. In the Old World, France gave a base for a statue in Boulogne-sur-Mer for the expatriated paladin to whom she lent refuge in his old age, and to whom she gave a sepulcher on his death. There is missing today only the monument which Spain owes to this son of Spaniards, whom she educated at the Nobles' Seminary in Madrid, whom she herself commissioned a colonel in her armies, and whom she herself armed at Arjonilla, Bailén, and Albuera during the Napoleonic invasion.

When we think of San Martín, we should recall that he did not always dress in a uniform. Let us not forget that when he was leading his grenadiers along the banks of the Paraná, watching the Spanish naval squadron which he later defeated at San Lorenzo, he was not in uniform, but was wearing a poncho and a wide-brimmed hat. When he crossed the Andes with his army, he did not do it riding a magnificent mount, but astride a Cuyan mule with a *criollo* saddle. When from the observation tower of Maipú he watched with his glasses the movements of the enemy before engaging him in battle, he was also wearing a poncho and a wide-brimmed hat. When he was visited on board the schooner *Moctezuma* by the Englishman, Basil Hall, on the eve of the triumphal entry into Lima, San Martín was not in uniform: he was wearing a long frock coat and a fur cap. When he returned from expatriation in 1829 and he found the gates of his country closed to him, Colonel Olazábal found him, on board the *Chichester,* melancholically peering at the city from the river, dressed in a coarse-cloth frock coat and wearing slippers. When, in the last days of San Martín's exile in Europe, Alberdi saw him in Paris, in the home of Guerrico, San Martín was conservatively dressed in a black frock coat. All these images of the great man are as true as those of his portraits in uniform, and do not at all resemble his equestrian statues or his popular chromos. At the end of this narration we shall see how necessary it is to strip San Martín from all his occasional vestments, and even from the mortal flesh of his body and the mummified bronze of his monuments, in order to tear asunder the veils that hide his spirit.

Whatever the kind and the number of the documents used, the secret of this life of San Martín lies in having illumined the gestures and words of the personage that we evoke with the inner light of his own conscience. The warrior and the patriot having already been consecrated by the work of learned historians, it was time to stylize the silhouette of the paladin who in his career-at-arms was unique because he was a tamer of his instincts and a moralist in action. A man who had been initiated in the mystery of human passions was able to become, thanks to that, a "protector" in the mystic sense in which the masters of the spirit, who mark the epochs of history, are "protectors."

José de San Martín, the Saint of the Sword, is a unique figure of universal significance; and for that reason I write, to offer it to the world as a simple tribute of my admiration for this exemplary man, this account of his life.

PART I

Initiation

"One will be what one must, or he will be nothing."

—SAN MARTIN

———◆———

I. YAPEYU, THE NATIVE CRADLE

ON THE ARGENTINE BANK of the Uruguay River a woman sat in the shadow of ancient trees, looking at the waters of the serene stream, while the light of the dying afternoon fell upon the landscape. This still young woman held on her lap a small child, who often climbed down from the maternal knees to play in the native forest. The mother was Spanish, but the child was *criollo*,[1] born in that very spot of the New World, his skin bronzed by the sun of America, his eyes and hair both very black. The woman looked dreamily at the child, surrounded now by his native woods, and then turned to gaze at the majestic river without ever suspecting the tremendous future in store for the male that her womb had given to the world.

The child was a son of Don Juan de San Martín, and it must be told who the father was, what fortune joined him to his mother, and how the child happened to be born in this place; because all this is necessary in order to follow from the beginning the threads which, in the dark, made the pattern of a mysterious destiny.

[1] See Notes, p. 361.

The viceroyalty of the River Plate had not yet been founded when Don
Juan de San Martín, born in the village of Cervatos de la Cueza, in the
kingdom of León, came to live in Buenos Aires, then an obscure town lost in
the vast colonial empire of the Spaniards. Under the increasing prosperity of
its cattle industry and its trade, aided by the liberal rule of Carlos III, the
imminence of coming changes was already felt. Moral changes brought about
by the expulsion of the Jesuits were added to the military restlessness produced
by the invasion of Uruguay by the Portuguese from Brazil. As a consequence
of these wars, and although some regular troops garrisoned the city of Buenos
Aires, a voluntary militia was formed and Don Juan enlisted in it as a lieutenant of infantry.

The governor of the country was at that time Don Francisco de Paula
Bucarelli, Knight of the Order of Santiago and Captain General, who in the
year 1769 appointed Don Juan de San Martín adjutant major, transferring
him from the company commanded by Agustin de Aizpurúa to the place of
Juan Vásquez, which was vacant through the latter's promotion, in the volunteer corps already mentioned. King Carlos III later confirmed this appointment.

At the end of June 1770, Don Juan received from his general a peremptory
order to take ship immediately for a mission outside Buenos Aires. Subject as
he was to military discipline, Don Juan had to leave, but before going he
wanted to satisfy his scruples concerning a personal affair. For this purpose
he spoke to his comrades, Francisco Somalo, captain of dragoons, Juan Vásquez, captain of infantry, and Nicolás García, lieutenant of volunteers, and
asked that one of the three, in his absence, marry in his name a certain young
Spanish woman, also a resident of Buenos Aires, to whom he had pledged his
word.

This was agreed upon by his friends and on the morning of June 30 he
gave them power of attorney before three witnesses, explaining in the document that he had not had it drawn by a notary public because of the haste
of his departure, "and because of other just reasons which he wishes to keep
to himself." The text of the proxy stated that the wedding was to be performed
"according to the rites of Our Holy Mother Church, after the three admonitions of the Council of Trent, or without them, if dispensation were obtained";
and the proxy-giver added: "so that giving myself to her as her husband she be
received as my wife, as I receive and recognize her and which action I naturally approve and wish that it have the same validity as if it were performed
in my presence," "to the fulfillment of which I obligate my person and my
property, present or future, and I entreat the justices and judges of His
Majesty, wherever they may be, that in the fulfillment of this obligation they
hold me in the manner prescribed by law." Having taken care of these steps,
the bridegroom left, the bride being assured of the performance of his
promises.

The young woman to whom Don Juan de San Martín had given his promise was named Gregoria Matorras, a legitimate daughter of Don Domingo Matorras and Doña María del Ser, who had once lived in the village of Paredes de Navas, in Old Castile, but who were already dead. Don Juan, when he named her in his proxy, called her a "noble maiden," but it is known that this expression was used to designate simple *hidalguía*, a condition of race which in Spain excluded the Moors and the Jews, and in America the lower orders. Gregoria's father was a native of the valley of Lamco, in the mountains of Santander, a country whence came the good and old Castilian lineages, adjacent to the lands of Pelayo and the Cid. A Matorras had been one of the conquerors of the Chaco; he was an uncle of Gregoria, and perhaps he was also a relative of Don Fernando Matorras, royal lieutenant of the city of Buenos Aires, who, in 1761, had paid for sumptuous feasts to celebrate the inauguration of Carlos III, organizing, among other acts, theatrical perform- ances in the courtyard of his home. As to Don Juan, suffice it to remember that he was a lieutenant and that "clean blood"[2] was a requisite to enter the militia. His parents, Don Andrés de San Martín and Doña Isadora Gómez, were from León, and lived in Cervatos, in the episcopate of Palencia, to which the Spanish home of Gregoria also belonged, and perhaps the families had known each other in the Peninsula.

Other people bearing the same family name as Don Juan came to the River Plate in the eighteenth century; one of them, named exactly the same as our hero's father, an officer of the militia and a rich man, paid, like Lieutenant Matorras, for celebrations and dances in Buenos Aires to commemorate the inauguration of Carlos III, bringing Indians from Misiones to dance in the main square. The Buenos Aires City Council, which was then made up of the Ramos Mejías, the Lezicas, the Aranas, and among them Don Martín de Alzaga appointed in 1784 a José de San Martín mayor of the San Vicente district in the borough of Magdalena. Maybe these other San Martíns were relatives of Don Juan; but we can only affirm, both in relation to him and his bride, that they were *hidalgo* people, honorable and poor, although of no known aristocratic ancestry.

The wedding took place in Buenos Aires on October 1, 1770, Bishop Don Manuel Antonio de la Torre officiating, with Captain Somalo representing the absent bridegroom. Don Hermenegildo de la Rosa acted as notary, and witnesses were Don José de Andújar, dean of the cathedral, and the clergy- men Juan Rodríguez Cisneros and Antonio de la Torre. (The ecclesiastical dispensations and the military permission had previously been read.) Gregoria then left as a newlywed to join her husband, who was in Misiones, on the Uruguay River. A short time later Lieutenant San Martín was appointed governor of the department of Yapeyú, and there the newlyweds established their residence. They had several children, one of them a girl whom they called María Helena, and four boys: Juan Fermín, Manuel Tadeo, Justo

Rufino, and the youngest, José Francisco, who was born at Yapeyú on February 25, 1778.

The four brothers followed the military career of their father; but the youngest, José, born in a humble home in an obscure corner of America, was destined to shine later as the champion of American emancipation. Gregoria Matorras, "the noble maiden," eight years after her romantic wedding in Buenos Aires, and Don Juan, the absent bridegroom who married her, "the better to serve God," thus gave, as a blessed fruit of their love, a criollo child who came into the world in the midst of the American forest, bringing with him the fatal horoscope of glory.

At the risk of going into too much detail, let us recall some features of the natural and social atmosphere in which José de San Martín spent the first three years of his life, inasmuch as the impressions of childhood crystallize in the deepest strata of the human subconscious.

The town of Yapeyú was a mere Indian settlement established in 1626 by the Society of Jesus (the Jesuit Order), and as such it belonged to the vast system of the Guaranitic missions. Located on the right bank of the Uruguay River, where it meets the Guabirabí, it belongs now to the Argentine province of Corrientes, and at that time it was linked by land and river with Buenos Aires, administrative capital of these districts, and with all the river towns to the north, up to the Brazilian border.

The ousting of the Jesuits, carried out by Governor Bucarelli in 1767, placed Misiones (name of a province), as well as all the property of the Society, under the lay authority. The much discussed system of the Guaranitic missions, organized by the sons of Loyola, was an experiment in theocratic communism. Much of their economic structure survived after lay rule had come, although without the spiritual values of what was called the Jesuitic Empire. The decline of those towns and their ultimate disappearance caused the defenders of the Society to praise its system because of the prosperity which the padres brought about; and the enemies of the Society to blame them for the ephemeral nature of their foundation. But the truth is that the missions were destroyed by the aggressions of the Portuguese in Brazil against the Spaniards of the River Plate, and by the Wars of Independence in the Argentine littoral. The destruction of the missions through the hostility of Portugal had already started in the days of the Jesuits; but when Lieutenant Don Juan de San Martín was governor of Yapeyú, this district still had, like other regions of the same kind, its population and its riches, although the war dangers persisted. Therefore Don Juan had to attend both to war and to administration at the time when José was born.

Yapeyú was similar to the other towns in the Argentine missions because of its symmetric layout. It had a main square, in front of which was a well-built church, and at its right was the school, old residence of the padres, where

Governor San Martín had his offices and his home. The school had sixteen rooms overlooking the first courtyard and thirty rooms overlooking the second. In these rooms were distributed, with their furnishings, the school, the library, the department of archives, the pharmacy, the stores, the art, sculpture, and music rooms; besides the shops of the millers, the bakers, the cooks, the weavers, the carpenters, and the shoemakers, all of them with their respective tools.

Although in the year of the expulsion of the Jesuits the books of almost all the urban convents were taken up and carried, together with other papers, to the Fort of Buenos Aires, there remained in the library of Yapeyú, after 1780, four thousand folio and quarto volumes bound in sheepskin, comprising works of the classic humanities, of sacred history, of Spanish literature, of natural science, theology, law, medicine, many Jesuitic chronicles, and grammars, dictionaries, and collections of sermons in the Guarani language, some of which had been printed in the missions by the Indians.

The stores used to have, even then, up to two thousand *arrobas*[3] of maté in bags made of cowhide, and as many arrobas of raw cotton, besides wool that was spun, dyed, and woven by the Indians, as well as bolts of cloth and other goods from Castile, and hides, tobacco, sugar, honey, flour, lumber, dried meat, dried fruit, and similar provisions.

In the art schoolroom there were guitars, violins, drums, flutes, and various instruments which the Indians made or played, and which were used by the native orchestras organized by the priests for the church festivals, especially that of Corpus Christi, which the neophytes celebrated with "dances of Moors and Christians," popular choruses and ceremonies as beautiful as that called "of the new fire." The town church was spacious, with walls made of stone and a thatched roof, and equipped with all the ornaments peculiar to the Jesuit style, some of which, brought from other towns, have been salvaged from the ruins and have come to us; Solomonic or spiral columns, multicolored altars, images of saints, candelabra, fabrics, and heads of Indian angels between golden wings.

Behind the church and the school there was a wide fruit orchard, and in the square before there was a cross at each corner, with a tall column in the center, bearing the image of the Virgin, cut in stone. In the town proper next to the square, forty blocks of uniform buildings were the abode of the Indians, with separate houses for the widows, and among the men there were soldiers and craftsmen, subject to a discipline only slightly less rigid than at the time of the Jesuits. All of this, men and things, formed the domestic and political atmosphere in which lived Governor San Martín and little José, who was baptized in the church which later disappeared. At the door of the church, or in the square, or in the school, the little child must have received the caress of the Indians.

The jurisdiction of Yapeyú extended upon the eastern shore of the Uruguay

River, from the Ibicuy River to the Bellaco Creek, some one hundred and fifty leagues in length, and on the western bank, from the end of Corrientes up to the Brazilian domain of the Portuguese Crown. When Don Juan administered it, Yapeyú comprised sixteen ranches and twenty-five outposts, each one with its chapel and huts for the peons in charge of the cattle. Besides the lands for pasture, there were corrals where the animals could be gathered, and at the time there were 60,000 cows, 900 oxen, 400 calves, 8,500 rams and ewes, 3,780 horses, 830 donkeys and mules, 4,780 mares, 2,200 fillies of up to two years of age, 576 big colts, 1,719 small colts, 1,900 burros, sixty-one pigs, and thirteen suckling pigs. Beyond the ranches, through the faraway fields, roamed wild cattle which from time to time were rounded up and branded. The mission carried on a trade in grease, hides, and meat, both for the consumption of near-by towns and for export, paying with its proceeds the taxes collected in the name of His Majesty, or using this money for purchases of merchandise from Castile, which was brought from Buenos Aires. On the highways converging upon the town, up to forty oxcarts carried on trade, besides cattle which the Indian peons drove on foot, or which were shipped across the river to Salto Oriental and other river towns.

All of this constituted the properties which Don Juan had to administer, and which he administered very scrupulously, collecting his small salary late and unsatisfactorily. (So much so that his wife, Doña Gregoria, had once to go down to Buenos Aires to try to collect his back pay.) However, they were not short of anything, in the midst of such abundance, to feed the family, and José enjoyed during his first few years the bounty of a patriarchal establishment.

Favored by a propitious climate, the Jesuits cultivated maté and orchards and gardens in Yapeyú, as they did in other missions. When the San Martíns went to live there, there still was in existence a maté plantation of four thousand plants, and in the town's school grounds, as well as near some outlying churches, roses and jasmine prospered, with groves of sweet and bitter oranges, royal and common lemons, figs, peaches, apples, and pears; of all of which there remained, at the end of the nineteenth century, some vestiges buried in the brush. The subtropical climate favors spontaneous vegetation there. Thorn bushes, tala[4] and carob trees alternate with palms, and in the corners where the humidity is greatest reeds and ferns grow, marking the beginning of the forest, which becomes more luxuriant to the north, finally becoming a real tropical jungle in Brazil. Every few miles large grazing grounds are found, full of rich pasture for cattle. Numerous wild animals, snakes, and pumas, as well as singing birds which give its name to Uruguay ("the river of birds"), live in the forests there. Many creeks flow there into the great river whose majestic waters run between those paradise-like banks. The Uruguay River runs here between high and firm shores, and a light prominence marks the mouth of the Guabirabí River, next to Yapeyú. More than once, Doña Gregoria Matorras must have taken the small José through those orchards full of fragrant fruit, and along the riverbanks which the breeze cools in the summer afternoons, while the sun gilds the sky between the forests.

Such was the scene where José de San Martín saw the light of day and where he passed the first years of his childhood, in the rich land of Yapeyú, located in the Argentine Mesopotamia, bound by the Paraná and the Uruguay, two huge rivers which come from the interior of America and which, farther south, join to form the River Plate.

Governor Don Juan de San Martín spent there his busy days, interrupted once in a while by some Portuguese alarm or by some visit to his territory. On winter nights he stayed at home near the fire, to go over his accounts, to plan work, or to think about his children. While he was not a widely read man, he would take a book from the library once in a while, perhaps the *Herbario* by Father Montenegro, containing medical information about the native flora, which he might have needed because of the sickness of some of his children; or the *Lunario* by Father Suárez, with notices about the weather, useful for agriculture; or the *Vocabulario* by Father Ruiz Montoya, with the names which the Guarani Indians gave the things of the land; or the *Diferencia* by Father Nieremberg, with its advice about the temporal and the eternal, whose hair-raising images had been carved by the Indians; or the *Crónica* by Father Lozano, about the feats of spiritual conquests of the tribes of those regions. Other times, while the children slept, he spoke to his wife, nostalgically, about Spain, anxious to return there someday to educate his children.

The years passed, and to that corner of America the news came, through some traveler from Buenos Aires or Montevideo, of the changes taking place in the world. In 1776 the viceroyalty of the River Plate had been created, and that same year Cevallos was fighting the Portuguese in Uruguay. In 1778 (when José was born) the King of Spain gave new exemption from duties to the Port of Buenos Aires and more freedom to the trade of his River Plate colonies. From there on the institutions of America began to flourish.

In 1781 Don Juan de San Martín left his post in Misiones and went with his family to live in Buenos Aires, which was already the capital of a new viceroyalty. That year witnessed the continental uprising of Tupac Amarú[5] in vindication of the native races, which Viceroy Vértiz punished ruthlessly, ordering the Indian chieftains to be torn limb from limb and their heads shown on poles on the highways of Upper Peru. José was then three years old, and he must have heard something at home about this uprising.

In Buenos Aires, on the banks of River Plate, which receives its waters from his native Uruguay, the boy from the missions lived another four years. There he reached the age of reason; there he was initiated into the Christian doc-

trine, into sacred history, into the grammar that was taught by the schools of
that time; there he learned to read and write.

One of the first and most honest biographers of San Martín, Don Juan
María Gutiérrez, heard an old man say, who had been a classmate of San
Martín at his Buenos Aires school, "San Martín was destined to become a great
man; in school he was a very remarkable boy; if he had died without becoming
illustrious, I should have remembered him nonetheless." Such a testimony
must be believed. It suggests a precocious child, whose historical personality
did not disappoint the prophecies of the hero's school days.

Here in Buenos Aires he acquired the consciousness that all of this was his
country, and he linked forever his life to the fate of these regions and of all
America, because the child from Yapeyú, a bronzed, black-eyed boy, had been
born for continental undertakings.

'In 1785 Don Juan de San Martín, his wife, and his five criollo children
went back to Spain. Of them only José was destined to return to his native
land. He returned when his America most needed him, and he served her
with extraordinary self-sacrifice.

In the presence of such an exception and before telling the heroic story,
one's fancy takes pleasure in questioning the sphinx, although the sphinx only
answers through widely scattered symbols: "What twist of fate brought
Gregoria and Don Juan, born in León in Castile, to join their obscure lives
in faraway Buenos Aires and to marry by proxy when Don Juan left for
Misiones, following orders received from his superiors? Why, when the San
Martín family, formed in America, went back to Spain, did all the criollo
brothers remain there to serve the King and only José return to his American
fatherland to fight against the King? Why was José born in an Indian mission,
whose name, *Yapeyú*, means in Guarani language, 'that which is ripe,' 'the
fruit that has reached its ripeness,' as if the name of the aboriginal cradle were
marking, with the voice of the oracle, the future of the hero?" The sphinx
does not answer, but in casual facts it is possible to believe that coincidences
are discovered, which from an early hour often announce the future destiny
of superior lives.

It is said that some Greek mothers, in their pregnancy, used to spend hours
looking at the most beautiful statues, so that the beauty of the sacred images
would have an influence upon their beings and communicate their ideal perfection to their as yet unborn children. José de San Martín's mother did not
have before her eyes the images of Olympic gods or those of Homeric heroes;
but her naïve soul must have been moved in her pregnancy at the sight of the
Christian icons made by the Indians, while she prayed in the church of Yapeyú
for her child yet to be born. The mystic and military spirit of the double
ancestry, Castilian and Leonese (the people who fought with Pelayo and the
Cid), was already animating the child in her womb, while the maternal eyes
looked at the orderliness of the mission administration and at the life of the

tropical forest, next to the rushing "river of birds," which comes down from the heart of America to the sea, embellished with songs and flowers. All of this remained in the child's subconscious, and twenty-five years of residence in Spain could not erase it. The thought of Yapeyú was the magnet which brought him back to the place of his birth; and when in 1812 he began his military career in Buenos Aires he asked that Indians from Misiones be brought to him for his regiment.

When, drawn to his native land, José de San Martín, a grown man, returned from Spain to America and crossed the Andes with his armies to reach Lima, he won on the hillsides of Chacabuco the victory with which he started his continental campaign. At the time of his victory, the Portuguese monarchists, commanded by the Marquis de Alegrete, were invading the Uruguayan missions and destroying Yapeyú; they erased San Martín's native town with a barbarous fire. The other mission towns—Apóstoles, San Carlos, San José, San Javier, and Santa María la Mayor—were also destroyed. An Indian named Andrés Guacurarí (better known by the name of Andrecito), captain of cavalry under Artigas, resisted the invasion with other Indians. The Guarani chief had raised his hosts in a proclamation, recalling the Hebrew chieftains who saved the people of Israel from the Pharaoh's yoke, and adding that in the same manner he wanted to unite the natives of his land "under the sweet voice of liberty, which is calling them," to save them from Portuguese despotism. In spite of this Biblical invocation the Portuguese monarchists won; they ruined fifty leagues of the fertile region, they killed more than three thousand Indians, they drove away more than fifteen thousand horses, and they took with them to Brazil a great booty in gold, silver, and church ornaments. They did not spare even the children; Almeida Coelho, of the invading army, told of having seen more than one child strangled in the land where a child prodigy had been born thirty-nine years before; this child is the same José de San Martín who at the time was fighting for the freedom of the continent.

The hero born in the Yapeyú signed his first report of the Chacabuco victory on February 13, 1817; that is the same date borne by the report in which Chagas, Portuguese chief, tells of the destruction of Yapeyú. San Martín never visited, when he grew up, the place of his birth; if he had returned to Yapeyú after his glorious feats he would have found only ruined walls covered by weeds, a picture of desolation.

Juan Bautista Alberdi met San Martín in Paris in 1843 and then wrote: "I had thought he was an Indian, as he had been described to me so many times." His skin was bronzed and his eyes were black; but he was Indian only by reason of the place of his birth and through his destiny.

The devotees of the San Martinian glory have gone on pilgrimages to the point where the Guabirabí meets the Uruguay, vainly searching for relics of the illustrious cradle.

In what was Yapeyú there is today the chief town of a provincial district named San Martín; but the ancient name of Yapeyú is still a key for deciphering the mystery of the man who bore that name.

Let us bear this in mind now when we try to penetrate the secret of that man whose name was that of a saint and who was born in a mission whose Indian name means "the fruit that has reached its ripeness."

II. MILITARY APPRENTICESHIP IN SPAIN

In the middle of 1785 Carlos III, from Aranjuez, ordered that Captain Don Juan de San Martín be transferred from Buenos Aires and added to the staff of the citadel of Málaga. The same royal order granted him a salary of three hundred *reales* in his new rank. That was not enough for a family that was already numerous, nor did Don Juan, when he returned from America, possess any great property, if an exception is made of some small amounts owing to him, which for a long time he did not succeed in collecting in their entirety. Despite that, he settled in Málaga, with his wife and their children.

María Helena, the girl, kept close to her mother. The boys, as they grew up, joined the militia, thus lightening the expenses of the household. Juan Fermin and Manuel Tadeo later joined the Soria Regiment; Justo Rufino, the most worldly of the four, became a member of the King's Guard in the American Company, whose ranks were joined also by other Argentines. Meanwhile José, who was only seven years old when they arrived in Spain, entered the Madrid Nobles' Seminary, an aristocratic school founded by Philip V at the beginning of the century.

José, whose precocity, although not too brilliant, was nevertheless notable, distinguished himself for his memory, his discretion, his deep attentiveness. In the seminary he completed the elementary studies which he had begun in Buenos Aires, where he learned to read and write. In Madrid he acquired notions of natural science, geography, mathematics, Latin, French, rhetoric, music, fencing, drawing, and dancing. José did not possess any literary talent, and he never succeeded in becoming even a fair-to-middling writer. The eloquence which he sometimes succeeded in imparting to his orations or letters in his later years did not spring from classic models or from poetic inspiration, but from the concise clarity of his intelligence and the moral vigor of his character. As to the arts, he had some inclination for music, but he preferred to paint, and succeeded in doing some passable water colors: he used to say in Buenos Aires, in 1813, that if he had to make a living outside the army he could do it painting ladies' fans. The exact sciences, like geometry, objective in their figures and ciphers, were his favorite mental discipline and the ones best adapted to the manner of his genius, such as it showed itself later, both in heroic action and in his private life. This exact school training left intact the substance of his spirit, which was bound to make itself felt later in life, showing a new type of hero, different, both in his sayings and in his gestures, from all the leaders and men of war that history tells us about.

Quite different was the education of Bolívar,[1] heir to a fortune, under the teachings of Simón Rodríguez, who brought him up on the classics and the encyclopedists and accompanied him later, like a tutor and a prince, on a voyage to Europe, in the course of which the young Venezuelan, who had lost his parents, visited Paris and Rome, bringing to life, in the illustrious cities which his master discussed, the lessons he had studied in his books. Much of the lofty spirit of Rodríguez passed on to his disciple, especially in the combination of romantic feeling and classical form. Bolívar's literary style springs from his apprenticeship, when he read Vergil, Tacitus, and Rousseau. Because of this the intellectual genius of Bolívar was the epitome of the European tradition. San Martín, on the other hand, made only elementary studies; at the age of thirteen he was already taking part in battles, and so his original genius had a spontaneous flowering, without literary ornaments. The difference between these two great men appears thus well marked from their origins, because they belong to two entirely different spiritual worlds.

The little inclination that José felt toward ornamental studies, the meager fortunes of his parents, and above all his precocious vocation were the cause of his leaving the Nobles' Seminary to enter the ranks of the Peninsular Army. He was only eleven years old when, from Málaga, he requested admission as a cadet, in the Murcia Regiment. He stated in his application, addressed to the Marquis de Zayas, that "following the example of his father and his cadet brothers who are serving in the Soria Regiment, he wishes to pursue the distinguished career of the army" and that "his father is ready to provide for his upkeep according to His Majesty's regulations."

At the time, his father was still serving in Málaga and being paid his meager salary as a captain. The Count of Bornos reported favorably on this application, in Madrid, on July 9, 1789, which is the date that San Martín considered as marking the beginning of his career. Significant coincidence; that same year 1789, a few days later, in Paris, the Bastille of the kings fell into the hands of the people; and on the same day, the July 9, 1822 (sixth anniversary of the Argentine Independence which San Martín fathered), the hero entered Lima, thus crowning his career.

The military beginnings of José de San Martín took place, then, in Peninsular territory, in the service of the King; and for twenty years his was a school of continuous war, inside and outside Spain, on the sea and on land, in a single campaign of valor and promotions, worthy of the man in those days of invasions and revolutions.

His first day of battle had for a stage the Africa of the Moors, beside the lieutenant of artillery, Don Luís Daoiz, whom the French were about to shoot in Madrid on May 2, 1808. From Melilla he passed to Orán in 1791: in Orán, besieged by the enemy, he withstood fire for thirty-seven hours, until the city became a mass of rubble. José was hardly thirteen years old. A good beginning for such a soldier.

His second battle took place in the Roussillon, under the orders of General Ricardos, a magnificent tactician. Now he was fighting against the veteran armies of France, on French territory. The Spanish Army had crossed the Pyrenees to attack the enemy on his own soil. The Argentine cadet fought in the battles of Masdeu and Truilles, in the defensive actions of Torre Batera, Greu de Ferro, San Marshall, Villalonga, San Lluc, Bunyuls del Mar, and in the victorious capture of San Telmo, Port Vendres, and Collioure, advancing to the very gates of Perpignan. General Dagobert commanded the French Army. The Roussillon War ended in a Spanish defeat in the year 1795. San Martín, who fought valiantly in the ranks of the Murcia Regiment, was promoted, first to sublieutenant and then to lieutenant, upon the battlefield. José was then seventeen years old.

His third campaign was on the sea. Lieutenant San Martín, with his regiment, joined the Spanish Mediterranean Navy to fight against the British. On an English ship stood Nelson, like San Martín, on the eve of his glory. The Spanish defeat of San Vicente took place on February 14, 1797, wherein the future victor of Trafalgar and the future victor of Chacabuco fought in opposite camps. On February 15, 1798, the frigate *Santa Dorotea*, on board of which was San Martín, was attacked by the *Lyon*, a powerful 64-gun English ship of the line. The struggle was unequal and terrible. The *Dorotea* surrendered; but the gentlemanly British victor expressed to Mazaredo, the Spanish admiral, his amazement at the courage of those who lost. The young man from the Indies, who had known in the Roussillon the emotions of victory, was now acquainted with those of defeat; and he who knew in Orán the catastrophe of fire knew now that of water. The young weapons were well tempered by such alternatives.

The fourth stage took place on Portuguese land, and it had two episodes: the first, in 1801, when, at the head of a company of the Murcia Regiment, San Martín crossed the border of the Algarves and took part in the siege of Olivenza, which surrendered without a fight. The second episode occurred in 1807, after the Treaty of Fontainebleau, when he fought with the Regiment of Volunteers of Campo Mayor, under the orders of General Solano, Marquis of Socorro, who commanded an army of six thousand men, with which he captured the city of Yelves, without any blood being spilled. Between the first and the second of these harmless episodes, San Martín took part in the blockade of Gibraltar. Then came the Peace of Amiens. The Crown of Spain was at the time tangled in the politics of France, whose ally she became, and in rivalries with Portugal, which served England. San Martín had a close look into the demoralization of a regime that was crumbling and into the dynastic intrigues of kings who desecrated their thrones.

The fifth stage began with the Napoleonic invasion. He now saw the kings as captives of the Corsican adventurer, while the rebellious peoples called, not upon the king, but upon the people and the fatherland. The mayor of Móstoles gave out his laconic and beautiful proclamation: "Our country is in danger; Madrid is dying, a victim of French perfidy. Spaniards, come to her rescue." It was the second day of May 1808. In Madrid they had already executed, together with other rebels, Daoiz, San Martín's comrade at Orán, during those bloody episodes which Goya masterfully painted. Spain was in flames. The Army of Andalucía, under General Solano, Marquis of Socorro, under whose orders San Martín fought, was moving.

Throughout the peninsula the atmosphere was one of heroism; on one side Napoleon and his eagles, on the other side the Spanish people and their lions. San Martín fought with the people against the imperial invader. Cries of vengeance and independence were heard. The first popular councils appeared. Municipalities and civilians assumed the representation of headless Spain. A new spirit was flowing which before long passed to the New World. The Council of Seville urged Solano to place himself at the head of the Cádiz insurrection, while the people, in mutiny, asked the general to attack the French Fleet that was anchored in the bay. General Solano hesitated; the Cádiz crowds attacked the palace. Captain José de San Martín, officer of the day, concentrated the troops in the building and barred the gates. The people shattered the gates with gunfire and invaded the palace in a pandemonium of sword thrusts, shots, and shouts. General Solano escaped to the roof, but the mutineers caught him and tore him to pieces. San Martín learned from that occurrence a lesson he never forgot. He always carried with him, in his wallet, a picture of General Solano. He did not wish to forget either him or them: he had seen his honorable chief brutally immolated without being able to prevent it, and he had seen the face of the Gorgon, the mob, the monster, in one of her outbursts of fury.

The War of Spanish Independence continued meanwhile. José de San Martín was still in the Regiment of Volunteers of Campo Mayor. The Council of Seville promoted him to adjutant of his regiment which then joined the Army of Andalucía, now commanded by General Castaño. Dupont, at the head of the French Army, was crossing the Sierra Morena in the direction of the Guadalquivir. The Spanish advance guard went to meet him, and at Arjonilla came into contact with the enemy. On seeing him San Martín charged with twenty-one horsemen, backed by a platoon of infantry. The French waited for them in formation. San Martín ordered his horsemen into line of battle and advanced with them, sword in hand.

Entering upon the sixth stage of his career, let us stop a moment to read the report praising the feat of San Martín:

This courageous officer [said the report], paying attention only to his superior's orders, arranged his troops in battle order and attacked with so much intrepidity that he succeeded in completely dispersing the enemy, who left upon the field seventeen dead dragoons and four prisoners, who, although wounded, were taken away on their own horses, the French officer having run away and the rest of his soldiers being so frightened that they threw away even their shakos, our soldiers being able to capture fifteen horses in good condition, the rest of the animals having been killed. San Martín and his courageous troops regretted very much that the French officers were able to run away, together with the rest of the enemy soldiers; but having heard the bugle sound recall, he had to restrain his ambitions of glory. Lieutenant Colonel Mourgen ordered a withdrawal because he observed that a reinforcement of one hundred men was coming to join the enemy. In consequence he ordered that Lieutenant Don Carlos Lanzarote go with twenty horses to help San Martín on the side of Arrecife, while he himself advanced on the right with the squadron of the Queen's Dragoons commanded by Captain Don José de Torres, leaving the rest of the column under the orders of Lieutenant General Don Dionisio Bouligni, cavalry commander of the Company of Chasseurs of the Walloon Guard, with orders to take possession and protect the equipment and position so that the enemy might be held, permitting San Martín to retreat in good order. On our side only one chasseur of Olivencia was wounded, in spite of the fact that much fire from muskets and pistols was aimed at our troops. San Martín gave generous praise to all his men, particularly to the sergeant of hussars of Olivencia, Pedro de Martos, and to the chasseur of the same regiment, Juan de Dios, who saved his life in a moment of imminent danger.

This was published in the *Gaceta Ministerial,* of Seville, on June 29, 1808, six days after the battle.

As a reward for this feat San Martín was promoted captain of Bourbon Cavalry. For the first time his name was heard praised in public. The soldiers beaten at Arjonilla were those of Austerlitz and Jena. His martial action, sword in hand and on horseback, showed San Martín with the prestige of a heroic statue. Juan de Dios, who saved his life in Arjonilla (as another Juan, a man of God, would do later at San Lorenzo, his first Argentine victory), was "de Dios" (of God), and preserved him for great things.

The war was still going on when, on July 18, 1808, the Army of Napoleon was defeated at Bailén. A gold medal, with a legend written on one side and a crown of laurel over two crossed swords, was given San Martín for his courageous conduct in that new setback for the Napoleonic arms, which before had been victorious all over Europe. San Martín found himself later in the Spanish defeat of Tudela, and in 1811 San Martín triumphed again, at Albuera, over the invaders, and in that fight he was wounded by a French sword. The Spanish Army entered victorious into Madrid. The American was beginning to become an actor in the great spectacles of armed victory. San Martín was then living through the seventh stage of his military apprenticeship.

In this military whirlwind, promotion had come rapidly to San Martín. A captain at Arjonilla, he was promoted lieutenant colonel of cavalry after Bailén. On January 25, 1810, the Supreme Council appointed him adjutant to General Coupigní. In June 1811 he was transferred as commander of the Regiment of Dragoons of Sagunto, a regiment whose name commemorated the famous siege; and this was the last post which San Martín held in the Spanish Army. The following year he was to change totally the direction of his life.

Very few marks of his private life were left by San Martín after the many years of his residence in Spain. We know almost nothing about the days which he spent in Madrid and Barcelona. His parents may have transmitted to him the Castilian and Leonese traditions: the episcopate of Palencia, where they had been born, still remembered the days of the old romances, of the democratic communities, of the religious pilgrimages. To the north lies Covadonga, city of the reconquest, and Vivar, birthplace of the Cid, and the River Duero, with its heroic traditions, and La Mancha, with Don Quixote, and Compostela, with the myths of the Holy Grail and the legend of the Apostle James, an armed saint; all of it good Castilian leaven for the soul of a young fighting man.

But the days of San Martín's young manhood were spent chiefly in the south, in Andalucía, where he learned to appreciate good Spanish wines. He was wont to go to Málaga, where his father lived, and to gay Seville for military reasons. However, Cádiz was the city he frequented most. Cádiz was at the time the gate of Spain to the Atlantic, the road to America. There he gave a helping hand at the time of the great epidemic of 1803, with so much abnegation that these services were entered in his military record. There he met several comrades who were later his antagonists in the Wars of the New World; among them the future General Ordóñez was made a prisoner at Maipú. There he met young García del Río, who became later his minister in Lima and his first biographer. There he met young Don Alejandro Aguado, who was to be his protector in Paris. There he met a woman, whom we shall call Pepa la Gaditana (Pepa, the girl of Cádiz), the only feminine figure whom we see passing fleetingly across the horizon of those days.

Among the papers of the curate Don Cecilio Tagle, which Vicuña Mackenna[2] acquired in Lima about 1860, there was found a letter from a woman signed "Pepa," addressed to a Spaniard who was fighting in Peru in the year 1821. That woman, "who could only be a wench," according to Vicuña Mackenna, said to her man that should he fall prisoner, he should show that letter to San Martín and tell him her address, because San Martín had known her in Spain. Better to identify herself she added some intimate details of the days when San Martín, a member of the Cádiz garrison, was a friend of hers.

(San Martín was in Cádiz when in 1802 there passed through that city a young Venezuelan named Simón Bolívar, who was traveling in Europe with his tutor Rodríguez. They did not meet then. They met in Guayaquil, twenty years later. . . .)

During the feverish convulsions which upset Spain in the first decade of the nineteenth century, San Martín, a Spaniard from America, served the motherland with courage and loyalty. He fought against all her enemies: the Moors in Africa, the French in Roussillon, the Portuguese in their own land, the English on the Mediterranean, and finally against the legions of Napoleon. He had honestly performed his duty, defending the cradle of his elders; but now the time had come to attend to a new duty, to defend his own cradle. He had learned much in those martial convulsions. He knew how to use his arms. He had seen how kings fall and how peoples became emancipated. To his technical experience he had added a political apprenticeship. His historic conscience encompassed the vast universal drama, close to whose chief characters—Napoleon, Nelson, Wellington—he had been acting. He had won decorations; he was a lieutenant colonel at thirty; he enjoyed the estimation of his superiors. However, he was not happy. A deep crisis gnawed at the heart of this silent great man. Old links of the flesh and the soul were breaking; new links seemed to be joining in the dark to bind him mysteriously to the definitive destiny of his genius.

In 1808, when transferring from the Murcia Regiment to that of Campo Mayor, José de San Martín asked for his military record. Lieutenant Colonel Don Juan Maya, of the battalion commanded by Colonel Don Rafael Menacho, gave it to him: "The First Adjutant Don José de San Martín y Matorras, aged twenty-seven, his country, Buenos Aires, in America, his quality noble, son of a captain, his health good, his services and circumstances those which are expressed hereunder . . ."

To the mention of the promotions that we already know about, and to the mention of his bachelorhood, the record added that he had never had a furlough, and Colonel Menacho appended his judgment: "Valor, constancy, ability, and good conduct." All the chiefs under whom he served felt affection toward him: Colonel Menacho, who died in the siege of Badajoz; General Solano, who died in the mutiny of Cádiz; Generals Ricardos, Constaño, and Coupigni.

In September 1808 Marquis de Coupigni wrote San Martín, calling him "my esteemed friend," to congratulate him on his promotion to lieutenant colonel and for his decoration at Bailén; and as he knew San Martín was ill, the letter ended thus: "I regret very much that you are ill and I shall be particularly pleased to hear of your recovery." In Seville by May 1809, "feeling recovered from the dangerous illness which he had suffered,"

San Martín asked to be transferred to the Army of Catalonia, under the orders of the friendly general, following the wishes of Coupigni, who had requested to have him at his side, as his aide. The Marquis of Palacio, at Seville, authorized the transfer. The Council of Seville, which had inherited the supreme authority because of the disappearance of the Central Council, appointed him, on January 25, 1810, adjutant general.

Carlos González and José Moreno Daoiz report:

The ill health of the applicant, who is a meritorious officer and deserves every consideration, moved General Castaño to incorporate him into the Military Inspection Commission of which they are members, with the sole purpose that he may continue receiving his salary . . . but he has told us that his breathing permits him to travel and that he wishes anxiously to return to the defense of our pressing cause.

"A man who may be useful in any position," the report adds.

San Martín fought against primitive people in Africa; he challenged a cataclysm at Orán, the sea on board the *Dorotea*, and mutiny at Cádiz; he watched the violent death of Menacho, Daoiz, and Solano; he learned to cross mountains in the War of the Roussillon; he electrified the cavalry with his courage at Arjonilla; he saw cowardice in Yelves and Olivenza; he won a decoration at Bailén; he risked his life in more than one combat and was wounded at Albuera; he met the French, Portuguese, English, Spaniards, and Moors, allies or enemies. Sometimes he was defeated, and once, with his victorious army, he entered Madrid; he watched from the Peninsula the downfall of Louis XVI and the dishonor of the Spanish Royal Chamber: María Louisa and Godoy; or the treasons of the dynastic families: Carlos IV and Fernando VII; or the cowardly flight of the Braganzas: Don Juan and his Portuguese court. All of this was a part of the Napoleonic catastrophe, in the eruption of which the genius of San Martín forged his weapons and tempered his will.

A legend tells how Napoleon himself, who on a certain day was reviewing a detachment of Spanish soldiers, stopped in front of San Martín and, taking hold of a button on his uniform, read the name of his regiment: "Murcia." When he read this, Napoleon, the cosmic demon of catastrophe, looked deeply into the black eyes of the American. (If this anecdote is apocryphal, it deserves not to be.)

Such meetings do not happen in vain. The man from humble Corsica, who had arrived at the palace of the Paris kings, exchanged a look with the man from humble Yapeyú, who was to arrive one day at the viceroyal palace in the City of Kings. And therein lay the catastrophe: in that kings and viceroys were ceasing to reign, so that there could begin in the world, with the man from Corsica and the man from Yapeyú, the reign of man. But both warriors, the one from Europe and the one from America, came from

French encyclopedism, and British liberalism created a new spirit, and in those times of danger, secret societies multiplied in order to initiate the neophytes in the new ideals.

A clever man of adventure named Francisco Miranda, born in Caracas, was the pioneer in Europe of a movement which was destined to play a vital part in American independence. Miranda fought in the armies of the French Revolution with such brilliance that his name is engraved on the stones of the Arch of Triumph in Paris. Going through Europe, he became a friend of Empress Catherine of Russia and a confidant of the British minister Pitt. He thus acquired notions of democracy and linked himself with Masonic centers, adopting the methods of discipline and secrecy characteristic of the lodges in order to organize the first conspiracies, formed for plotting uprisings in the Spanish colonies.

He was thus able to organize in London the center of liberating action that was called "The Great American Reunion," through which passed the Venezuelans Simón Bolívar and Andrés Bello[1] and natives of other regions who later played a part in the rebellion of the New World. Because of the secrecy surrounding the organization, it has not been possible to find out whether the lodge was a Masonic institution; but it is evident that it worked according to the principles of Masonry, even though it was not an official branch of it and did not strictly follow its doctrine, its rites, and its rules.

A letter from the Girondine Brissot to Dumouriez, a friend of Miranda, contained the following, as early as 1792: "Spain is becoming ripe for freedom. It is necessary to make this revolution both in European and in American Spain. All this must coincide."

Miranda wrote Alexander Hamilton from London in 1798:

May Providence allow that the United States do for our compatriots of the South, in 1798, what the King of France did for them in 1778. . . . We shall profit from your wise lessons, and I am pleased to say, beforehand, that the projected form of government is mixed; we shall have a hereditary ruler called Inca, as the Executive Power. The Senate will be composed of noble families, but it will not be hereditary.

Hamilton answered expressing his sympathy for those plans of British-American co-operation in favor of the independence of Spanish America. The revolutionary work of Miranda, with ever more liberal tendencies, was continued in England; and later he himself, aided by Pitt, undertook the carrying out of his plans through the London lodge.

Organizations similiar to that of London had been created in Paris, Cádiz, Philadelphia, New York, Caracas, and Buenos Aires, with no connection among them but tending toward the same principles of revolution. Merchant ships of various powers carried from one to the other shore of the Atlantic the emissaries of this silent conspiracy that was undermining the European dynasties and strengthening the desire for independence in the American colonies. A vast speculative and operative labor was carried out in those centers. Agents of Napoleon, Pitt, and Adams were not strangers to this mysterious work. Spanish ministers like Count Aranda and noblemen like Count Puñonrostro were Masons. The Jesuits, ousted by the Madrid Royalists, were working against Spain from London, Vienna, Genoa, and other cities. The Indian uprising of Tupac Amarú, in 1781; that of "the Frenchmen" in Buenos Aires; the English invasions of the River Plate; the La Paz revolution of 1809; the attempts at liberation of the Venezuelan Miranda along the shores of his country, were portents of the forthcoming continental cataclysm.

The year 1810 sounded the decisive hour. Simultaneously Caracas and Buenos Aires organized the popular juntas, which began the epics in which the Venezuelan, Bolívar, and the Argentine, San Martín, were destined to be the chief figures. These two had passed through London before embarking upon their adventure, although without meeting each other.

While that invisible network of intrigue was being woven between America and Europe which was destined to dismember the Spanish Empire, San Martín had lived apart from it all, concentrating his energies on his military duties. But one day, in Cádiz, the year being 1808, a countryman of his, Matías Zapiola, Buenos Aires-born officer of the Spanish Navy, spoke to him of a mysterious lodge of which he was secretary and which had for its purpose the co-ordination of action looking to the emancipation of the American colonies. Cádiz was at the time a hotbed of plotting, as Alcalá Galiano remarks in his Memoirs, both for and against the interests of Napoleon.

But this lodge about which Zapiola spoke did not have any connection with internal politics of the metropolis and was made up exclusively of criollos, among whom were some Argentines: He named Carlos de Alvear, José Moldes, and Francisco de Gurruchaga. They called themselves the "Rational Knights," and some had already come into contact with Miranda's London "Reunion" or with Buenos Aires "brethren" like Pueyrredón, Lezica, and Rodríguez Peña, who were working in Buenos Aires. Their plans concerned chiefly the emancipation of the River Plate and adjacent regions, in connivance with the Venezuelans who were preparing themselves in London for a similar effort against the mainland in the Antilles, thus encompassing, from north to south, the whole of South America. San Martín thus joined the Cádiz lodge, although not without first overcoming strong scruples in the depth of his soul.

The downfall of the Peninsular dynasties, the abdication of Carlos IV, the flight of the Portuguese monarchs, and the Spanish anarchy, all this gradually destroyed in his conscience the prestige of the cause he had formerly defended, until, at the end of 1810, learning of the landing of Miranda in Venezuela and the uprising of Saavedra in Buenos Aires, San Martín made up his mind and waited for the moment of breaking forever the links that joined him to the Spanish monarchy.

In the austere conscience of San Martín this was a terrible moment. He never gave vent to his torment in pathetic confidences. He was to suffer equally painful wounds later, but without ever changing his serene expression, like that of a bronze statue. He was not an adventurer who had formerly fought for France, like Miranda, nor was he a free young man like Simón Bolívar, who had come to Europe to amuse himself after receiving a large inheritance.

San Martín had grown up in the Spanish Army since the age of eleven. He was poor, and whatever he possessed he owed to the country of his parents. His Spanish mother still lived. But the Spanish-American world had just broken in two halves, one on each side of the sea. He was to choose one and he chose America, realizing that this was to be his duty according to the inflexible destiny of his genius.

At about that time San Martín had known in Spain a noble Scot named Lord Macduff (later the Earl of Fife), who had come from Vienna to fight for Spain against Napoleon, enlisting as a simple volunteer. Between the two men a strong friendship developed, which in the course of time was to become gratitude on the part of San Martín for the services of the Scot, and admiration on the part of Lord Macduff for the great feats that his Argentine friend accomplished in America.

This Lord Macduff was a charming man. In 1817, as soon as he learned about the victory at Chacabuco, he wrote to the victor, from Edinburgh, to congratulate him: "You cannot, my friend San Martín, imagine to what extent the news of your good conduct fills me with satisfaction. Ever since my return from Spain I have been telling my countrymen, 'Patience! A man down there will surprise you all!'"

To judge by these words, the Earl of Fife must have guessed the genius of San Martín before anybody else, and foreseen his great feats. Elsewhere he compares the Chilean campaign with that of Napoleon from Rheims to Paris, which he saw "on the spot." His countrymen in London used to give him news of the good friend whom in 1817 he wished to embrace, "so that we can talk about the extraordinary events that have taken place since the days of Cádiz." (This wish was fulfilled in 1824, when San Martín returned from America.) He felt proud to have known "such a good and esteemed friend . . . winner of the liberty of America . . . such an honest man as José de San Martín . . . worthy of comparison with Washington . . . a man at the forefront as a soldier and philosopher." And indeed this definition of "soldier and philosopher" was not unfitting for our hero. We owe it to this Scottish lord, and to him we also owe the tricks that helped San Martín run away from Spain when the Argentine decided to return to his native land.

San Martín told him of his resolution to go back to Buenos Aires to offer his sword to the cause of his country, and Macduff took it upon himself to facilitate this voyage, which was destined to have transcendental consequences. The Scot was acquainted with Sir Charles Stuart, diplomatic agent of Great Britain in Spain. A false passport was necessary so that San Martín could hide his status as a Spanish subject, and, what was more important, as a military officer on active duty, since he was at the time colonel of the Sagunto Regiment. The English diplomat was the man to solve this difficulty, and he gave him the passport. With this English passport, San Martín, wearing civilian clothes, went to England, carrying in his poor suitcase the papers certifying his military career and his rank, his only assets, which he was to tender as a token of love to those Spains of the New World, where he had been born of Spanish parents.

In the last few days of 1811 San Martín arrived at the British capital, where he was joined by Carlos María de Alvear and Matías Zapiola, his brethren of the Cádiz lodge. With them was also the captain of cavalry, Francisco de Vera, the captain of militia, Francisco Chilabert, the sublieutenant of infantry, Antonio Arellano, and the lieutenant colonel of Walloon Guards, Baron Holmberg, who, although he was a Bavarian by birth, had decided, after fighting for Spain, to go to America and fight for liberty. They were all ready to undertake the journey together.

San Martín also met in London two young Argentines, Manuel Moreno and Tomás Guido,[2] who had just arrived from Buenos Aires as secretaries to Don Mariano Moreno, who had died at sea; saddened by this tragedy, these young men felt a little crestfallen, notwithstanding their newborn patriotic hopes. They both told him of the events that had taken place on May 25 of the previous year, and they made reference to the symptoms of a split which was already undermining the independence party. All this increased San Martín's desire to leave as soon as possible, and he hastened his preparations for his departure, reserving passage on the English ship *George Canning*, which was scheduled shortly to leave the Thames.

The favorite meeting place for these Argentines was a house, later demolished, called "Of the Venezuelan Deputation," which was in Grafton Street, near Fitzroy Square. There Miranda had lived, and there the "American Reunion" had its workshop. Young Simón Bolívar had also lived there, shortly before leaving with Miranda to start the Venezuelan insurrection. Now there remained in the house young Andrés Bello, also a Venezuelan, later to win great literary fame in his country and in all America. (Cf note 1 of this chapter.)

In that London "shop" there had been initiated in the task of liberation the adolescent Bernardo O'Higgins, of Chile; Mariño, of New Granada; Montúfar, from Quito; Caro, from Cuba, Servando Teresa Mier, of Mexico, and others of the same kind. San Martín attended with his countrymen the meetings held there by the "Rational Knights," new Templars like himself, who were planning, for the glory of God and the freedom of man, the New Temple of America. They spoke about Miranda, about his campaigns with Washington in the United States, and with Dumouriez in France; of his imprisonment with Madame Rolland; of his friendship with the Empress of Russia; and that flaming evocation lighted in the hearers the noble desire to emulate his heroism.

The Indian names of our countries were mixed in the conversation with the legendary names of Masonry: Memphis, Jerusalem, Delphi, Rome, and the initiating sanctuaries of the vanished Atlantis. . . . The London "shop" was not exactly a Masonic lodge, but it had taken from Masonry many names and symbols. The Algabil, the creator conceived of as an architect; the Pharaonic and Solomonic tradition; the Plan of the Work, the Pyramid, the Triangle, the Sun, the oaths of sacrifice unto death, the disciplinary secret promised for the good of the undertaking; all these gave to those Centers in which the patriots prepared the emancipation of the New World a mys tery which embellished with age-old reflections the modern feat.

San Martín was not a man for fantasies, but the discipline of abnegation and silence, as well as those geometric and military forms, was in keeping with his nature. The vision of America passed before his eyes: in the depths of his soul he heard then the voice of the inner inspiration that guides the heroes. . . .

In that state of grace, the future knight-errant of America embarked on the ship *George Canning* in January 1812, leaving London, capital of the world, wrapped in its fogs. He was accompanied by Alvear, Zapiola, Chilabert, Holmberg, Arellano, and Vera, all young, all in the gay age of adventure which knows how to mix gaiety with the hardest undertakings. San Martín was the eldest and he was the only taciturn one of the group of argonauts of liberty.

Alvear took with him his young wife, Doña Carmen Quintanilla, daughter of a Burgos accountant. They had married three years before, when she was only sixteen and he was hardly twenty. Before embarking in Cádiz, Carlos had received from his father, Don Diego, his share of his maternal inheritance. With those resources, his marital happiness, and the forthcoming triumphs he dreamed about in his ambition, Alvear overflowed with enthusiasm and transmitted his patriotism to his wife. Although a Spaniard, she embraced the American cause. When she arrived in Buenos Aires she figured among the patrician ladies of her day, and she was influential in having San Martín marry one of her friends. A woman full of Castilian beauty and youthful grace, her presence charmed the travelers on the long voyage.

When they left the English Channel and passed down the coasts of Spain, San Martín thought of the days of his childhood and of his arrival in Spain, and he thought of his mother, who was still there and whom he was to see no more. On February 25 he observed on board his thirty-fourth birthday, and he thought again of Yapeyú, his other mother, the American earth.

The crossing of the wide sea took fifty days. The progress of the sailing ships in those days was slow and the voyage hazardous. The crossings were made then for purposes of trade or of war, not of pleasure or the desire to know other countries. Manufactured goods were brought from England, and hides and dried meat were carried on the voyage back from the River Plate. Sometimes the merchants were the owners of the cargo, and they chartered the ships at their expense. The crew was limited to a captain, a mate, a lookout, a cook, and deck boy, and the few passengers used to help work the vessel, climbing up the shrouds to reef the sails, hauling on lines, trimming the sails, draining the decks, and even cleaning the cabins. The officers used to be as rough as the crew, and at table the conversation was of the sea, the weather, pirates, mixed with the age-old legends of sea life, recent anecdotes of past voyages, news of exotic countries, calculations of probable profits.

Fresh food lasted ten days, and as the voyage progressed it became necessary to resign oneself to soup made of hard peas, to moldly pork, tasteless dry fish, and bad biscuits reheated in the oven. Beds went unmade for several days; the cabins smelled of tar and dead rats; heat was lacking on cold nights; decks were greasy and walking was dangerous. When the Torrid Zone was reached, the sun was burning, and often there were no awnings and scanty cold water. Those days in the tropics were as a rule monotonous, and the ship seemed to be stationary, hanging between the leaden waters and the dense air. This was a kind of martyrdom hardly less torturing than seasickness and the anxiety of stormy nights. The captain, meanwhile, went around in his shirt sleeves, smoking endlessly or drinking his rum, when not his good Málaga or port, with which he was wont to entertain some of his favorite passengers. Perhaps San Martín, who appreciated good wine, deserved one of those exceptional treats from the master of the *Canning*.

Such was the painful voyage which the future hero of America had undertaken in order to fulfill his patriotic wish. Odysseus was returning to his Ithaca.

It may be said that for the first time San Martín was crossing the Atlantic, because on his former trip, when his parents took him from Buenos Aires to Spain, he was a seven-year-old child and probably he retained only childish memories of that adventure. But this time the case was different: he was past thirty years old; he had lived and suffered; he had cut his home bonds in order to dedicate himself to a transcendental mission, the nature of which only he himself knew. He had reached maturity, and the ocean was the immense background that best fitted the mystical feeling of his heart on the

eve of his magnificent undertaking. That immense ocean was the sea of the
vanished Atlantis, a bridge that perhaps connected Tartessos and Yucatán,
America and Iberia in past ages; bridges that were broken by geological
catastrophes but rebuilt in history by the epic of the Spanish conquerors,
Atlanteans themselves, and also by the American liberators who were Atlanteans, too.

San Martín felt, without telling it to himself in words, the universal significance of his undertaking, while he meditated in solitude, looking at the
immensity of the ocean. Two decades later, when the Liberator entered the
City of Kings (Lima) and captured the standard of Pizarro, the conqueror,
he was to decipher for himself the deep meaning of his mission. Meanwhile,
facing the ocean, he could only dream, and he dreamed as one who navigates
the inner ocean of a heroic conscience, where the memory of a message
becomes the premonition of a messenger. Mysterious voyagers coming from
the sea play a part in American legends, from Mexico to Patagonia; Tezalcoatl
and El-Lal—teachers, protectors, liberators. . . .

San Martín's instinct and his taste as a painter awakened him from time
to time from his absent-minded concentration to please his eye with the
shape and the color of the waves, which, in his old age, he took pleasure in
putting on canvas. Now they were steering to the west, bound for that America of their dreams, following the path of the sun. With the martial vision
of their secret plans were mixed, saddening him a little, the talismanlike
name of Yapeyú, the aboriginal cradle, and his memories of Buenos Aires,
the beloved city of his childhood, where nobody knew him now. The noise
made by his friends interrupted his meditations once in a while, when he
retired to read or when, leaning against the rail, he looked in enigmatic
silence at the horizon, far away. He had always loved the sea, and ever since
he had embarked with the Murcia Regiment in the Mediterranean squadron
he had said he would have liked to be a sailor.

Alvear used to tell how his mother and all his brothers had perished in a
shipwreck, going from America to Spain, only his father, the sailor Don
Diego, and himself being able to survive. Zapiola, a naval lieutenant, related
his experiences in the profession of the sea and how the governor of Montevideo had exiled him to Spain, along with Zufriategui and other patriots.
Holmberg told Germanic anecdotes, with Homeric guffaws, without foreseeing that he was destined to hold in his hands the new Argentine flag, at
Jujuy, as the flagbearer for Belgrano[3] a few months later, on the day of the
first oath of allegiance. Young Carlos de Alvear, time and again, would take
his turn in the conversation, full of optimistic loquacity. San Martín, meanwhile, listened to him in silence.

During those fifty days of traveling the chief topic of conversation was,
of course, their country. They discussed local conditions in Buenos Aires, the
situation in the continent as a whole, the United States, and world politics.

They spoke as soldiers and as statesmen. It was necessary to give cohesion to the Buenos Aires government, to re-establish the orientation set by the late Mariano Moreno, to give discipline to the army, to co-ordinate the continental campaign, to bear in mind sea action and European diplomacy. For all that it was necessary to establish a lodge in Buenos Aires. When alone, San Martín would unfold a map of America, and, looking at it, remain long in meditation.

At last, after a month and a half, the *Canning* entered the tawny waters of the River Plate, and in the morning of March 9, 1812, she anchored in the outer roads, in sight of Buenos Aires. At dawn everyone went up on deck to look at the river, broad as the sea, at their back; and ahead, at the harbor filled with the rowboats used in the daily labors. Closer to them was the fort of the period of the viceroys. Farther away was the shore of San Isidro and Quilmes. From among the houses emerged the spires of San Francisco and Santo Domingo, and of the cathedral, where Doña Gregoria had been married. San Martín thought again of his mother. . . .

After long preliminaries they were transshipped into boats, which took them to the beach, where some carts took them to the custom house. Fate was in the balance. San Martín was again on Argentine soil, after twenty-seven years of absence. And indeed he had not returned in vain.

IV. THE KNIGHT OF AMERICA

The arrival of San Martín and his companions on the *George Canning* was announced in Buenos Aires on March 14 through a laconic item in the *Gaceta Ministerial.* It named the seven pilgrims and said they had come to offer their weapons to their country. This news awakened popular curiosity, and conjectures about them began to circulate. The suspicion arose that they might be spies, inasmuch as they had served until recently in the Spanish Army. For Carlos de Alvear, who had come with his wife and had influential relatives in the revolutionary party, it was not difficult to ward off gossip. The case of San Martín was different, as he was a stranger in his own country, without family, fame, or fortune. Alvear, being a nephew of the respectable Don Gervasio Antonio de Posadas, who had connections with the Government, made himself responsible for the conduct of the whole group.

Some must have asked themselves, in reference to San Martín, how could it be explained that a young colonel, with such a brilliant career in Spain, had cut it short to undertake this adventure? The answer could be that he had come through love for his native land; but how, if he was not a son of Buenos Aires? The stranger said he had been born in Yapeyú, an uncertain and obscure birthplace. Perhaps there would be some who remembered his parents, Don Juan and Doña Gregoria, modest residents, once upon a time, of viceregal Buenos Aires, although that was thirty years before and the town had changed greatly since.

The marriage of his parents was recorded, however, in the archives of the cathedral. Those vague suspicions must have given San Martín his first bitter moments in his country, which was to give him later so many more. But he was not a man for sentimental discouragements. He knew who he was, and that sufficed him. He was the Knight of America, and with a secret fatalism he would tell himself, "One will be what one must, or he will be nothing." When his destiny materialized, he could have said, like Napoleon, "I am one of those men who owes everything to himself and nothing to his ancestors." But he never said it, because San Martín was devoid of all vanity.

As soon as they arrived the pilgrims went to the fort, former residence of the viceroys, on the Plaza Mayor, where at the time Pueyrredón, Rivadavia, and Chiclana, the triumvirs of the first councils, ruled. The guests were received, in the words of a contemporary chronicle, "in the manner deserved by the noble sentiments they expressed." News was exchanged about conditions in Europe and the progress of revolution in America. San Martín urged strengthening the Government, to maintain order among the civilian population, and organizing the Army to defeat the armed enemy. He submitted to the authorities his army record, which noted that he was "single, of noble class and a son of a captain"; that his ability and valor were excellent; that he had not had any furloughs in twenty years; that he had had rapid promotions won in war actions, among them the battle of Bailén, in which Napoleon was defeated.

The country needed a chief like that.

The dignified appearance of the soldier, his serene youthfulness, his clear ideas, his concise words, all made a favorable impression. He had taken part in the greatest military adventure of the times; he had seen the fabulous Corsican at close range; he had dealt blows of his sword to the French at Arjonilla and he had been wounded by a French saber. Cavalry, which had played a very important part in the Napoleonic wars, was his arm and the one best fitted to the needs of the country and to its intrepid horsemen. Thus he planned the creation of a unit, the Mounted Grenadiers, which he would train according to his system. This regiment would be used, for the time being, as a garrison for the city. His companions knew that his Grenadiers would be useful for something else, too, but he made his offer with cautious modesty, because such was his nature and because he wanted to avoid friction. However, both Rivadavia and another triumvir were a little suspicious of the newly arrived group; despite which, seven days after his arrival the Triumvirate recognized his rank as lieutenant colonel of cavalry, "in view of his merits, services, and military knowledge," in a decree sealed with the royal arms, which were still in use; only the following year were these replaced by the seal of the new nation.

Recognized in his rank, he was appointed commander of the squadron he was to organize, and as assistants he was given Alvear and Zapiola, his fellow adventurers, younger than he. Towards December 1812 San Martín had already recruited and trained a regiment, and he was appointed its chief. A half of the scanty salary he received he donated to the nation, inasmuch as he could not, like Alvear, give up all his salary; he needed a part of it for his living expenses. In this manner he began to acquire standing and to feel less of a stranger in his country.

In August 1812 the Triumvirate, in a decree signed by Rivadavia, commissioned Francisco Doblas to bring from Misiones "three hundred native young men, tall and strong, whom His Excellency details to the Regiment of Mounted Grenadiers commanded by Lieutenant Colonel Don José San Martín, born in that territory." The Misiones-born hero began his work with these three hundred Indians, his countrymen. . . . The Regiment of Mounted Grenadiers was quartered in the Retiro, a place which after 1702 had been a slave market and later a bull ring, and which after the English invasions was named the Field of Glory or Mars Field.

That section, lying today in the center of the city, was then a wild suburb, full of water in the rainy season and with ditches draining toward the river shore, which were crossed by rough little bridges. The aristocratic and bureaucratic section of Buenos Aires was composed at the time of the few blocks between the churches of La Merced, San Nicolás, and San Francisco. The shore of the river, near the fort, had as an improvement the Alameda, the only socially approved drive, and it offered as entertainment the scene of the landing of passengers on boats and carts, which went up and down the beach, where rocks and sand were visible on the days when the river was low. Behind the barracks the northern embankment fell sheer on the side of the Plate, being sufficiently high to give a full view of the river, down to the horizon. In that veritable "Retiro" (place of retirement), where his statue stands today, San Martín began his American career, and there he established a center for his austere labors. His original officers included Manuel Escalada, Hipólito Bouchard, Manuel Soler, Luis de Arellano, Ladislao Martínez, Rufino Guido, Carlos Bowness, Luis José Pereyra, Anselmo Vergara, José María Urdininea, Juan Manuel Blanco, José Hilario Basabilbaso, Angel Pacheco, Mariano Necohea; and almost all of them were later to carry out memorable exploits in the continental epic. This regiment created by San Martín gave America nineteen generals and more than two hundred officers, who were promoted, all, in war actions. Such was the school of such a teacher.

In those days of 1812 San Martín planned, knightlike, to create a patrician order of knighthood, and he succeeded. He wanted to unite all Americans under a common ideal: the independence of America; and he wanted his regiment to keep away, as much as possible, from the turbulent egoisms that were beginning to appear. He had a "mission," and to it he dedicated his life, to the end. He foresaw the dangers of military demagogy and Caesarian overlordship, curses of free America which were not long in appearing, as a sign of Roman and Visigothic atavism. From all that he drew away, from the beginning, and he sought a refuge to forge the weapons for his next undertaking, so different from the other extreme. He was, in the midst of the tumult of emancipation, something like an armed monk, a never-before-seen example of the holy paladin, a Cid of New Castile united with a Loyola, inspired by a laic mysticism.

His Retiro barracks were like a monastery for this man of action, for this new Templar Knight of future America. There he had, in his *criollo* comrades, the first militant community of the new ideal. For the officers he established a code which they themselves applied and which followed the best rules of knighthood. Severe penalties were the rule—

for cowardice in action, when even lowering the head is to be considered such; for not punishing insults, for not defending the honor of the regiment, for infamous dishonesty, for becoming shamefully familiar with subordinates, for lack of integrity in the handling of funds, for revealing decisions taken at secret meetings, for not helping a comrade in danger, for showing up in public with prostitutes, for gambling with indecent people, for laying hands on a woman, for drunkenness, for speaking ill of a comrade in front of strangers.

On the first Sunday of every month San Martín called a meeting of officers and cadets and entreated them to observe the knightly rules he had set. If a formal accusation was made against somebody, the accused withdrew and the others decided, over their signatures, whether the accused officer "is unworthy of acting with his honest companions and of belonging to the regiment." All this was done in secret, in defense of self-respect and "for the prosperity of the arms of the country." Military discipline was thus based upon moral discipline. He built the squadron and then the regiment, as he later built the Army of the Andes, upon the keystone of each individual. Rather than a chief who commanded, he seemed a teacher who illumined. He was the architect of a Pythagorean construction, this mysterious initiator.

San Martín himself chose the cadets and the soldiers; the former he picked from the best families, the latter from among the horsemen of the pampas. Thus there came to seek his teachings adolescents like Juan Lavalle, who arrived in his career at Pichincha and later at a generalship, when, in his fight against the tyranny of Rosas[1] he died for the civic liberty of his country. Thus there came to his ranks young *gauchos*, among whom he preferred the tallest, most valiant, and best-looking: they came uncouth and rough, and the master transfigured their appearance and their spirit. He infused into the troops the noble spirit of the officers. The chief wore a uniform without adornment, of blue cloth with red trimming, black leather boots, a curved sword, spurs, and a bicorned hat trimmed with oilcloth, on which, after 1813, he pinned the national cockade.

Thus dressed, he approached the soldiers paternally, and without losing any of his authority he instilled confidence in them. He joked with them when he thought it necessary; he taught with his own example; he felt that in those rough souls admiration and affection for him were born.

Heads of horsemen when mounted must be held high, eyes on the horizon, without ever turning the face back, the arm ready for the sword, "and if a Goth[2] resists," he said, "split his head as you would a pumpkin." Such is the elemental lesson he gave the troops. To each soldier, also, he gave a battle name, a name that magically evoked the best in him, as such names do.

In Mars Field was the old bull ring, and there the horsemen performed regularly in public exercises of horsemanship and swordsmanship. Real jousts were held, which awakened enthusiasm and applause.

Sometimes they practiced marches up to Olivos, at the sound of the bugles, which electrified the people. The ladies of the city, after Mass or following their walks through the Alameda, usually went as far as Retiro to see the handsome horsemen. Rumor had it that the chief himself was in love with a charming maiden who admired the grenadiers, and especially the creator of the new regiment. This maiden often went to watch the exercises, accompanied by Carmen Quintanilla, the wife of the second-in-command. Far from the enthusiastic and inquisitive public, inside the barracks, the school of strategy and the judicial lodge of the officers met. A certain mystery surrounded these meetings, and a legend began to take shape. The encampment was a shop, a school, a training ground, and a temple. When they got together to eat, San Martín and his men were like the Knights of the Round Table. They spoke with joviality, although without joking, which he did not tolerate; the colonel was a kind but dignified man. Sometimes he told anecdotes of the Napoleonic wars and of the Spanish uprising. They were all young and felt the impatience for something similar. San Martín understood that his work as a Templar was beginning to prosper. The iron instrument, the hammer of the Masonic symbol, the weapon for striking and building, would soon be ready to do its work. Ready also would be the spiritual eye which guided the work, the eye in the triangle, which was seen in the temples. This was neither Sparta nor Crotona; this was Mars Field in Buenos Aires, where San Martín worked in silence, with methodical precision. Some grumbled near by, without understanding him. No matter: he, enigmatic and tenacious, went on with his work.

Thus he instilled discipline into his regiment of grenadiers, and his weapon was ready when one day he received the order to go to the right bank of the Paraná River, because it was known that a Royalist squadron made up of eleven ships had left Montevideo, making its way up the river in the direction of Rosario. San Martín went immediately with 120 men of his troops and other auxiliary horsemen, following the course of the river. He left the city silently, dressed as a cowboy, with wide hat and poncho.

He left on January 28, 1813, galloping at night, in order not to be seen, rather than to avoid the summer sun. He passed through Zárate, San Nicolás, and Rosario, where there was a small garrison under the Uruguayan Don Celedonio Escalada, who reported on the movements of the enemy. The Spanish vessels were already facing the high cliffs of San Lorenzo, a small village located between Rosario and Santa Fe. In San Lorenzo there was a Franciscan monastery, whose church had a spire from which it was possible to watch the countryside and the river.

Order was given to withdraw all supplies and take all cattle from the coast to the interior. San Martín and his men had arrived at San Lorenzo at night, and they approached the post house to change horses. Suddenly two grenadiers stopped at the side of an unhitched carriage, inside which a man was sleeping.

"Who is there?" the grenadiers asked.

It turned out to be an English gentleman, William Parish Robertson, who was going to Paraguay on business, with food, wines, and merchandise in his vehicle. San Martín had known him in Buenos Aires, and when he learned who the man in the coach was he stopped the grenadiers in the dark, warning them aloud:

"Do not do anything to him, he is not an enemy."

Robertson, who had been informed on his arrival of the impending military developments by the postilion, recognized San Martín's voice and then said:

"Surely you are Colonel San Martín?"

"And if that were the case?" the latter replied.

"Then here is your friend, Mr. Robertson."

They shook hands; the traveler drank a toast, in his good wine, to victory, and both friends spoke about the imminent battle.

"The enemy has twice the number of men we have, but I doubt very much that they will get the better of it," affirmed San Martín.

Robertson asked the chief of the grenadiers to let him accompany him, and the latter answered, "All right, but your duty is not to fight. I shall give you a good horse, and if the battle goes against us, run to safety. You know that sailors are poor horsemen."

The Englishman knew it, and soon he was to witness it; years later he was to tell this dialogue and the action which he saw, in a book of his that was published in his country. This was the first British subject San Martín met in his South American career, and, like Lord Macduff in Spain, Haigh in Chile, and Mr. Hall in Peru, all of them were to sympathize with him and leave for posterity an impartial testimony of his feats or of his genius.

"To horse!" cried the hero, and with Robertson beside him and all the grenadiers following, they went to the neighboring convent, under the shadows of the night that covered the fields.

They entered the monastery through the back entrance; the gate was closed, and San Martín ascended to the tower to watch the enemy with his field glass. At dawn he saw the vessels. It was the morning of February 3. It was known that the enemy was endeavoring to sack the towns, to cut off trade with Paraguay, and to attempt a landing at that place in order to follow a road along the shore to Buenos Aires. San Martín saw that the invaders were beginning to land and that they were already climbing the steep bank of the river, some three hundred yards from the convent. He came down from the tower and distributed the troops, getting ready for the attack, and Robertson heard him say, "In two more minutes we'll be among them."

San Martín mounted a short-tailed bay horse, unsheathed his Moorish sword, and harangued the troops; he placed Captain Bermúdez at the head of the second squadron and personally started the attack, saying to Bermúdez, "On the center of the enemy columns we will meet, and there I will give you further orders."

The bugle of the grenadiers sounded, and from behind the convent the two divisions advanced at a gallop on the right and the left. The lancers were in front, with pistols in their saddle holsters, and behind them were the rest, armed with sword and carbine. They were only 120 men facing almost three hundred infantrymen and marines, who had already landed and were advancing, paced by fifes and drums, flag waving in the wind, amid a thousand shouts of encouragement and the fire of four cannon which they were bringing with them. At the head of the Spaniards there came Commander Zabala, and when San Martín with his men reached the line of combat the chiefs met face to face, like two combatants from the ancient days of chivalry. San Martín was met by shrapnel fire, which killed his horse; and the animal, in falling, pinned down the horseman's leg. In a fight with swords and bayonets which raged around the chief, he fell with a sword wound in his forehead. The bayonet of a Spanish infantryman who was coming in his direction would have killed him had not the San Luisian Baigorria stopped the thrust, piercing the Spaniard with his lance. Another grenadier, Juan Bautista Cabral, from Corrientes, ran to help San Martín, freeing him from the weight of the dead horse, at a moment when the Spaniards were going to finish him. Cabral saved San Martín's life but received two wounds and died a few hours later, saying, "I die happy. We have beaten the enemy!"

A brief moment after the combat had begun victory was already undoubtedly in the grasp of the patriots, but the battle continued to be fought hard and courageously. "Long live the King!" shouted Zabala to encourage his hosts. "Long live our country!" replied the Knights of America, in a confusion of horsemen, swords, and lances shining in the dust kicked up by the horses, under the summer sun of the cruel morning. The waters of the Paraná shone like brass polished by the sun, between the green of the shore and that of a neighboring island. Captain Bermúdez led a second charge, crushing the enemy. Second lieutenant Hipólito Bouchard had seized the Royalist flag. Lieutenant Manuel Díaz Vélez had rolled down the embankment, with two bayonet wounds in the chest and another wound in the forehead. Two volunteer officers, Vicente Mármol and Julián Corvera, faced their dangers with courage. Chaplain Julián Navarro, in his priestly robes, passed like a medieval specter in the midst of the confusion. The invaders, at last, succeeded in returning to their ships, leaving on the field forty dead, besides the wounded, some prisoners, the flag, two cannon, and other abandoned arms. The grenadiers, in turn, had fifteen dead and twenty-seven wounded, among them men from different provinces.

When the fight ended, the Englishman Robertson with his provisions and the chaplain with his benedictions helped the wounded, while an exchange of prisoners was made. San Martín, wounded, covered with dust, sweating, strong despite being tired, came serenely to sit in the shadow of a pine tree that still stands in the convent garden of San Lorenzo, and there he wrote the report of the victory, recommending all those who had distinguished themselves in the battle, without at all mentioning his own conduct.

After this, would those who thought him a spy continue doubting his American loyalty?

They went on doubting, as we shall see.

Olegario Andrade, the Argentine poet who best sang of him, said about that first combat of the hero's, half a century later:

> And a captive race
> Called upon the Savior with deep accent;
> And the Savior answered by giving
> The resounding cry of victory
> Among the ferocious tumult of the waves
> Of the Paraná, irritated
> At feeling itself oppressed by the keels
> Of the Spanish ships of war.

Thus the little battle of San Lorenzo became transcendental, according to what Torrente[3] himself, the historian of Spanish arms in America, declared in his book:

The Navy continued exerting a decided superiority, and it was the only force that could harass the rebels fruitfully. Making good use of this advantage, there was not a single place along the coast that could evade the Navy's power, and its triumphs were as many as its undertakings, without having had any other reverse than that of the landing at San Lorenzo, where it had had to clash with a leader as fortunate and valiant as San Martín, to whom it had to cede the honor of victory; and from that moment this leader acquired that military prestige which stimulated him to undertake new campaigns, and finally to win a fame not without its sadness.

The Buenos Aires government received the news of the action at San Lorenzo with great rejoicing. That brief combat was important for the country because it assured peace on the rivers and safety for the supplies for the army that was laying siege to Montevideo, which was not long in falling; it preserved the trade with Paraguay and scared off the invaders, who did not try again any adventures of this kind on the Argentine shore; it consolidated, in brief, the strategic situation of Buenos Aires, the center of the nascent revolution, in the region of the River Plate and its tributaries, on the banks of which three new nations were to be founded (Argentina, Uruguay, and Paraguay).

San Martín, the victor, although he has not left us any confidences about it, must have had a day of intense emotions. He had proved with his grenadiers the efficiency of his disciplinary system; he had fought his first battle in America, a duplicate of that at Arjonilla; he had announced himself to the New World with a victory; he could, then, look upon the distant field of greater feats.

A boatman of the Paraná River, the Paraguayan José Félix Bogado, fascinated by San Martín, joined the grenadiers at San Lorenzo; he later accompanied his chief in the campaigns of Chile and Peru; he went on serving under the orders of Bolívar, beyond the borders of Ecuador; and he returned to the Plate after Ayacucho, bearing the banner of his regiment after twelve years of struggles for liberty. This humble soldier, promoted eventually to colonel, returned almost naked and with the flag in tatters.

He came home in 1826 with only seven grenadiers out of all those who left with San Martín; they were the last remnants of the Army of the Andes —one hundred men, at the most. They were returning from their continental campaign after having fought from the River Plate to Quito, during twelve years. The arms they brought were deposited in the Retiro barracks and were kept in a cedar box with a bronze inscription which read: "Arms of the liberators of Chile, Peru, and Colombia." Colombia, too, because they had triumphed at Río Bamba, Pichincha, Junín, and Ayacucho, co-operating in the actions led by Bolívar.

The battle of San Lorenzo was the starting point of the triumphal career of San Martín.

V. THE SECRET OF THE LAUTARO LODGE

The idea of founding a patriotic lodge in Buenos Aires was one of the plans that San Martín had brought home with him, in accord with his companions in adventure. The Cádiz lodge, to which he belonged, together with Zapiola and Alvear, were now reunited in the command of the regiment of grenadiers, and to the influence which this gave them was added the prestige of their passage through the "Workshop of the Rational Knights" in the "American Reunion" of London. The three formed, effortlessly, the "triangle" which started the new "workshop," from which branches spread later to radiate inspiration in other countries of the continent. The "Lautarians" of Buenos Aires planned to organize public opinion, to strengthen the Government, to discipline the militia, to propagate the revolution, and to define the democratic aims of the American emancipation. The short life of the governments after 1810, the recent defeat of the patriot armies and the anarchy of the domestic parties persuaded San Martín of the convenience of having a secret association, perhaps not with Masonic rules nor following the methods of the Carbonari,[1] although inspired by such models.

When in the middle of 1812 the Lautaro Lodge was organized, there were in Buenos Aires the hidden and scattered traditions of similar societies. Already in 1795 a Lodge of the Blue Ritual had been formed, meeting in the parochial jurisdiction of San Telmo, with headquarters in Paris, and it is believed that Liniers and the agents of the plot known as "the French conspiracy" had something to do with it. In 1804 a Portuguese named Cordeiro founded the lodge called "St. John of Jerusalem," "for the happiness of this part of America." In 1806, after the British invasions, there were three lodges of British origin: "The Star of the South," opposite the San Juan church; "The Sons of Hiram," in the Montserrat section; and the "Order of the Sublime Knights Templar." All these Masonic centers sowed ideas of emancipation. Later there were other secret societies, like the "Independence Lodge," which met near the ruins of the San Miguel chapel, then a suburban place, and the "Society of the Seven," which had its headquarters in the farm of Rodríguez Peña and in the sessions of which the May Revolution was prepared. But with the downfall of the viceroys and the coming out into the open of the emancipation movement, those secret organizations relaxed their efforts, doubtlessly because the optimism aroused by the first victories considered that the aims of the conspiracy had been achieved.

Instead, the downfall of the viceroys had weakened the principle of authority, and the presence of the people in the debates of the council had brought about a demagogic pressure, and the coming of the provincial deputies into the council had caused a confusion of ideas and partisanship in passions. It was necessary to unify opinions and to safeguard the principle of rank in authority in order to make military action effective and to give organic form to the incipient democratic institutions. Such was the ideal of San Martín and his companions when they founded in Buenos Aires the Lautaro Lodge, although later, without any complicity from the founders, its original aims were distorted.

Lautaro is a personage in the conquest of Chile, idealized in *La Araucana*[2] as the native man who proclaims the freedom of his country, when he says to his compatriots:

> *Leave to the world an undying memory of yourselves*
> *By liberating your enslaved country.*

Although Ercilla's poem gives more vigor to the brave Caupolicán, an aboriginal Achilles, and to the wise Colocolo, a native Nestor, doubtless the founders of the lodge remembered that passage in Canto III, in which Lautaro incites to war against the oppressors of his land:

> *Drop your heavy yoke and servitude;*
> *To hard steel let us our breasts oppose.*

The adoption of the name of a Chilean leader for this lodge warrants the thought that already in 1812 San Martín harbored the intention of steering the war toward the Andes, although nothing existed there that might disclose such a plan. For the moment, in 1812, there was talk only of consolidating the democratic government of Buenos Aires, in order to direct from there the emancipation of the continent.

One day in 1812, when he had just arrived at a banquet given in the home of Señor Escalada, San Martín offered a toast to his country and mentioned the principles of the lodge. Señor Rivadavia,[3] who was present on this occasion, expressed his disapproval, and it is well known that he did not back the foundation of the lodge, doubtlessly because he feared that it might result in a lessening of his influence, as happened later. Alvear, instead, served the lodge with enthusiasm, although with the purpose of using it for the internal political struggles, which did not interest San Martín. Thus the Lautaro Lodge was born, harassed from outside by the solemn Rivadavia and animated from inside by the intrepid Alvear, who, with its backing, quickly reached the highest government positions.

For San Martín the constitutional problem was not the most urgent one. The most urgent thing for him was to go on with the war, with well-organized armies, and to declare the independence of the country, thereby giving a vigorous encouragement to the fight against Spain. He did not make it a question of unitarianism or federalism, centralized power or states' rights, nor of democracy or monarchy, if the latter were to find its inspiration in the liberalism of the British regime. In any event, that could be discussed later, according to the demands of social and international realities. The first thing was to break with Ferdinand VII, whose name the Triumvirate was still invoking, and to create an unimpersonal Executive Power to keep order internally and to control military movements; all of which did not prevent the calling of a Congress to reorganize the State. Personally, he was not interested in politics, except as a force at the service of that unpostponable military action, and he never felt the urge to power merely to exercise authority upon his fellow citizens. He would never use armed force to place himself in power, and he passed through all the nations through which he was to go later as a victor, always respecting popular sovereignty and their representative assemblies. These are facts which should not be forgotten when judging his conduct during the 1812 revolution, the only internal revolution in which he took a part.

The circumstances of Argentine politics in 1812 explain the action of the Lautaro Lodge in its beginnings. Selected as members were gentlemen of proved devotion to the country and of well-known liberal principles. The lodge was undertaken, above all, to give the emancipation of the colony from Spain a philosophical content.

Valuable adherents soon joined the secret organization which San Martín and Alvear had founded. From the first moment the other pilgrims of the *George Canning* joined the original group, besides Zapiola: Chilabert, Arellano, Vera, and also Holmberg, the Bavarian, despite the fact that only natives of America were supposed to join. Three impetuous Jacobins also joined: Castelli, Agrelo, and Monteagudo, doctors graduated in Chiquisaca, and several officers of the regiment of grenadiers: Terrada, Rodríguez, Necochea, Quintana, and Rojas. Some patriots of the first hour, such as Rodríguez Peña, Posadas, Passo, Guido, Rondeau, Balcarce, and Alvarez Jonte, also became members, and Pueyrredón and Belgrano joined later. Thus constituted, the Lautaro Lodge was not subordinated to Masonic centers or even to other purely political secret associations. It was autonomous, although it took from Masonry its discipline, its mystery, its hierarchy, and also some of its symbols.

Dr. Emilio Gouchón, who was grand master of Argentine Masonry, affirmed that the lodge had a Masonic character, which others deny. According to him, Miranda had been initiated into Masonry in the United States, where he had entered into lodge relationships with Washington, Franklin, Adams, Hamilton, and Lafayette; his membership in the Order, according to Dr. Gouchón, opened to Miranda in Europe the door of friendship with the men of the French Revolution, and in England with Pitt, Popham, Cochrane, and Lord Macduff, all of them Masons. The American Lodge of London is supposed to have been the parent association of the one founded in Buenos Aires by San Martín, after his escape from Spain, aided by

"Brother" Macduff, under the name of Logia Lautaro, adopting the symbolisms and the signs of the original institutions. The historian Mitre,[4] who also reached the highest rank in the Argentine Grand Orient, declares that in the Lautaro Lodge of Buenos Aires "neophytes were initiated according to the ritual of Masonic lodges": "Members gave themselves the title of 'brethren'; the chairman of the lodge had the title of 'Venerable.'" Its mystic legend was symbolized by these three letters, U.: F.: V.:, which stand for Unión, Fe (faith), Victoria.

All this is adduced by Gouchón in order to enunciate this thesis: "Had the Lautaro Lodge not been a Masonic institution it could not have been able to enjoy, as it did, the incalculable advantages derived from the universal Masonic recognition, through the solidarity that the Masonic bond imposed upon all the Masons of the world in the cause of American independence."

All this is logical, but there is no proof of it. Probably San Martín, like the great men above mentioned, was a Mason, initiated in Spain, where many personages in the Army and the Government were Masons. It is possible, too, that he gave the Lautaro Lodge the spirit and the standards of the Masonic lodges, without its being Masonic. Its local aims and its eventual disbanding make one think so. On the other hand, the secret that San Martín kept to the day of his death, and his very conduct, permit one to accept this hypothesis, in view of the purely political nature of the Lautaro Lodge and the more transcendental nature of San Martín's inspirations. The real "initiation" of San Martín was his experience with hard work and disappointment, until he reached the highest peaks of the spirit through the intuition of his genius. This is a mystery of which we shall speak with greater clarity when we come upon other revelations of his life.

No document is extant to prove that San Martín was a Mason, but many documents prove his friendship with Masons and his knowledge of Masonic ideas. The Order was fashionable in Europe when San Martín went through school; it had been restored in France by Napoleon, who joined it with the highest rank; in Germany, thinkers as influential as Fichte, Goethe, and Schiller belonged to it; and in Spain, statesmen like Floridablanca and the Count of Puñonrostro. Many high officers of the Spanish Army were Masons, and so were some of those who were fighting in America, who identified themselves as "brethren" with not a few of those who were fighting with the patriot armies, when they fell prisoners.

This happened in the case of General Primo de Rivera after Maipú, when, from Santa Rosa de Chile, he addressed to Balcarce, an Argentine general, a curious letter which is kept in the Archives of San Martín, in which the following is said: "General and Sir and M.: L.: H.: I cannot help but appeal to the protection of a h.: [brother] in circumstances as critical as mine." Primo de Rivera requests that he be sent to Mendoza or to Córdoba, and then says: "Excuse me, M.: L.: H.: [highly esteemed brother], and be sure that I am intimately acquainted with the duty which our F.: [faith] imposes upon you, to dispose of my uselessness as you see fit." Documents like this reveal the importance which, even in America and among enemy combatants, the Masonic vows had.

In 1816 there was a Masonic lodge in Buenos Aires, directed by Julián Alvarez, also a member of the Lautaro Lodge; but one should not be mistaken for the other, although they had common members and both had influence upon the Government.

From the Europe of the lodges, and of the Spanish Army they dominated, San Martín could bring suggestions of that kind. Cádiz was then one of the centers for initiation, as was London, and San Martín had been in both cities before coming to America. The official power of the Order in the Spain of Carlos III and in Pitt's England is a historically proven thing. The Scottish lodges of the Blue Ritual in Great Britain recognized their brotherhood with the freemasonry of the Continent. The traditions of both went back to the Templars, who were "the initiates of action, the messengers of the Sword," as they are defined by Maurice Magre in his book, *Magiciens et illuminés*. Besides that a lodge, called a lodge of the "Sublime Templar Knights," had existed in Buenos Aires before the revolution for independence, and the lodge was one of the workshops for the initiation of revolution.

Says M. Magre, referring to the medieval Order:

"The Order of the Temple endeavored to make the truths of the sages win by the sword. Its initiates followed the third of the roads open to man: after that of knowledge and that of love, the road to action." Its first undertakings were the Crusades for the reconquest of the Holy Sepulcher; but later, "they wanted to make the whole world a Holy Land."

During the twelfth and thirteenth centuries they tried to carry out that enormous dream. Had they won, they would have placed real "sages" over kings and warriors, to rule the world. Hugues des Payenes, in 1128, went to France and had St. Bernard approve the rules of the ascetic and warrior Order, which was ruled by a grand master and a council of seven secret brethren. Pope Clement V, in connivance with the King of France, suppressed it later, when it was ruled by Jacques de Molay, who was sentenced to death. The memory of this victim among some initiates dispersed by persecutions was kept as a symbol up to the days of the French Revolution:

At the moment when the head of Louis XVI had just fallen on the guillotine, a man who had marched in all the street parades after the fall of the Bastille rushed to the platform, lifted in his hands some of the king's blood, and, gesturing as if to sprinkle it on the multitude, shouted, "People! I baptize thee in the name of Jacques de Molay and of Freedom!"

In 1808 the Templar Order tried to restore itself with the consent of Napoleon, and it commemorated the anniversary of the death of Jacques de

Molay. The Templars had been the "mystic knights" of the First Crusade, those who received the message originally, but the truths of the ancient initiation became distorted in this Order of Christian knighthood, whose original power lay in disinterested courage and faith, until the sensuousness of power and riches brought it to failure. All these legends were known by the secret societies of the 1800s; and we have seen already that San Martín passed through Cádiz and London lodges before undertaking his American mission.

Although San Martín may not have been a Mason in the official sense, strictly disciplinary, there is something of the Templars in his military career, and of the Rosicrucians in his private conduct. In any event, it is not possible to deny the relationship of it all with the times, with his environment, and with his methods of action. The lack of documents bearing on this point and the absolute secret which San Martín kept about the lodges he founded in America make the figure of this exemplary soldier all the more mysterious.

When General Miller asked him, for his memoirs, for information about the Lautaro Lodge of Buenos Aires, San Martín, from Paris and twenty-five years after 1812, replied to his friend, who was in England:

I do not think it proper that you say anything about the Buenos Aires lodge; these are entirely private matters, and although they have had and still have great influence upon the events of the revolution in that part of America, *they could not be mentioned without my betraying the most sacred promises.*

I stress these words written by San Martín in 1837 because they reveal the religious seriousness with which he had created the lodge.

Nobody knows definitely what happened at the secret sessions of the Lautaro Lodge. Only incomplete surmises have been passed on to posterity. Some vague news given by Zapiola when he was an old man, some symbolic names for some of its members, some treatment of "brother" in a letter, some cryptogram like the triangle of dots ∴ or the ⋮ ⋮ in the abbreviations, or the two lines used as signature for certain phrases, or the symbol which refers to the Grand Council : o—o; these are the most concrete things we know of the lodge. The letters written by the members of the Lautaro Lodge at the time of the Andes campaign have permitted historians to establish that the phrase "Establishment of Mathematics" meant the lodge, and that the words "the friends" meant the brotherhood of its members.

In 1816 Pueyrredón sends this warning to San Martín: "In your letters please omit the letter H with which you close them. It suffices to place a ⊙, *pour éviter qu'une surprise donne lieu a des soupçons.*

We know that in 1812 San Martín and his brethren of the new Order had their workshop in the cellars of Thompson's house, not far from the fort. It is said that the oath of the neophytes was taken upon the Evangel pierced by a poniard, and that death was the punishment for the traitor; that they used a three-word motto, like that of European lodges, similar to the "Liberty,

Equality, Fraternity" of the French revolutionaries; that there were degrees of apprentice, master and select one, the latter forming a most secret council, which was the highest rank. But all this lacks documented proof, as is natural in view of the secret nature of the institution, and this mystery has enveloped the lodge and its chief founder in an atmosphere of legend.

The dogma of the Lautaro Lodge, according to certain more or less credible versions, was enunciated as an order to the members, with this formula:

Thou shalt never recognize as legitimate government of the country any other than that which is elected by the free and spontaneous will of the peoples, and the republican system being the most adaptable to the government of the Americas, thou shalt try by all means within thy power to have the peoples adopt it.

These words constituted the joining oath; and the neophyte was asked, "Will you use all your strength and power to uphold the independence of your most worshiped country, not only in the struggle it faces now but against any other power that may try to invade it?"

The initiated gentlemen then promised it under an oath carrying bloody penalties for non-observance.

"At the beginning of all the sessions of the Order, the members divided themselves into two groups. One of them," says Estrada, "represented South America and the other North America." But perhaps they rather represented the two "branches" of the London "Reunion": Caracas and Buenos Aires, Bolívar and San Martín, the North and the South of the continent.

According to Estrada's *Lecciones,* the following dialogue was held between the president or grand master of the Order and the secretary (I presume this was to initiate the neophyte):

"Whom must we imitate?"
"The valiant Lautaro."
"What did Lautaro do?"
"He died in defense of his country."
"Which was his country?"
"Ours."
"And do you know that all the gentlemen here present are willing to imitate him?"
"Not only those present but all those who cover the surface of the earth."
"How do you know it?"
"Because that is what they have sworn and promised."
"And if, through one of those rare occurrences that happen in this world, someone should break this promise, what shall we do with him?"
"Murder him; then burn him and throw his ashes in the air, that no memory may remain of such an infamous man."

Some of the revolutionary lodges of France and of the Carbonari associations of Italy extracted oaths as terrible as the above; but the penalty imposed by the Lautaro oath looks rather like the ones the Incas exacted on those who violated the *ayllahuasi,* or house of the Virgins of the Sun: to burn the culprit and throw his ashes away. Later we shall see how other Inca memories reappear in the Lautarian creation of that time.

One year after its organization, the Lautarians of Buenos Aires, like veritable Knights Templar of Liberty, had planned the Temple of America, the building of which was their aim. To bring this about they forged among themselves the link of the new knighthood, just like the "traveling architects" of the Middle Ages, who created Gothic Europe, and like the Knights Templar who undertook the reconquest of Christ's sepulcher. America was for these new Templars the Holy Land of their faith; the Colonies, a Holy Sepulcher of Liberty; and Democracy, the architect's plan for an emancipated America.

The Lautarian spirit was already in the mounted grenadiers for military action, and later it passed to the Sociedad Patriótica for civilian action. This society, founded in 1812, became a visible form of the lodge, with the purpose of agitating public opinion. The system of the ancient "masters" is here well in evidence: an esoteric center for creating "mental forms," and exoteric organs for the "realization" of them.

The members of the Sociedad Patriótica, almost all young men, met at the Café de Marcos, on the Plaza de Mayo, where Monteagudo[5] made spirited speeches. Its democratic ideas have been recorded on the pages of *Mártir o Libre* (Martyr or Free), its chronicle, in the memoirs of Ignacio Muñez, who was a member of the club. Alvear encouraged this movement, which was in a certain way demagogic; Rivadavia resisted it; San Martín, instead, looked upon it with hopes, although he was, too, carried away by the popular wave. The lodge inspired the revolution of October 1812, which overthrew the Triumvirate, and the Sociedad Patriótica was the instrument for democratic agitation. Says Mitre:

San Martín, had always two strings on his bow: one was visible and the other was not. Owing to a tendency of his complex nature—positive and of concentrated passion—while all his ideas became actions, he indulged in solitary meditations, *giving great importance to the mysterious.* His organization of the Lautaro Lodge, his plan for an underground war before crossing the Andes, his secret labors to prepare a revolution in Peru, his attempts to appease the Royalists through the influence of Masonry, and, finally, his dark plans for a monarchy are witnesses of this propensity. *It was, then, natural that his public labors should be accompanied by some underground work in the shadows of the mysterious.*

This serious assertion of the historian should be borne in mind in order to understand the mystic character of San Martín's actions.

The eclipse of San Martín in 1814 and the downfall of Alvear in 1815 were in part the result of the internal intrigues of the lodge. In spite of that, San Martín, owing to his silent and calculating nature, had faith in the system of secret societies with disinterested aims. As late as 1837, his mission fulfilled and living then in Europe, he wrote to his former comrade in arms, General Miller:

Speaking of lodges, I know, without any doubt, that these societies have multiplied in Peru in an extraordinary manner. This is an underground war which can hardly be stopped and which will compel a change in the best-laid plans.

It was a pity that the Lautarian lodges, as that of the Knights Templar, did not always keep the high spiritual standards their founder intended for them.

In the middle of 1812 the internal situation of the country suffered from a most serious crisis, owing to Alzaga's conspiracy and its repression. The energy with which the Triumvirate then acted had consolidated the American cause, but it helped to sow feelings of aversion against the Triumvirs, because of the executions they ordered and of the hanging of the bodies in the Plaza de la Victoria. But while these events had caused a commotion in the whole of society, the patricians were divided by the errors of the Triumvirate. This body was underhandedly heading towards a fearful or reactionary policy; it had reprimanded Belgrano when he hoisted the national flag in Jujuy; it had retarded the calling of a General Assembly; it had taken part in election frauds, which took away all its prestige. Such errors were already inflaming the democratic instincts of the masses, interpreted at that moment by the Lautaro Lodge—that is, by San Martín, Alvear, and Monteagudo, new actors who were to give a new impulse to the vacillating revolution.

On the morning of October 8 the Plaza de Mayo, between the Recova (arcade) and the Cabildo (City Hall), was filled with people—two or three thousand citizens in revolutionary attitude. Alongside the civilian multitude was the almost whole contingent of the military garrison of the city: Colonel Manuel Guillermo Pinto with the artillery; Colonel Ortiz de Ocampo with the infantry; San Martín and Alvear with their mounted grenadiers. Bernardo Monteagudo was the animator of the people, and he drew up a petition to the City Council, which had already met, his name being at the top of the list of signatures.

The "Popular Petition" addressed to the City Council enunciates the principles of the revolution and ends thus:

In view whereof, the healthiest-thinking part of the population requests of Your Excellencies, under the protection of the armed legions, that the Assembly be called off and the government terminate its functions, and that Your Excellencies resume the authority delegated by the congregated people on May 22, 1810; and that, immediately, an Executive Power be created, composed of the persons most deserving of the people's vote, and an Extraordinary General Assembly be called without delay, to decide in a worthy manner upon the great business of the community, it being understood that we are unswervingly resolved to offer the supreme sacrifice to the liberty of our country before permitting that tyranny be enthroned in this province.

The final sentence in the petition is even more threatening:

The people await the decision of Your Excellencies within the peremptory time of twenty minutes and make you responsible for any delay. The people promise, with dignity, but also swear before the Almighty not to abandon their position until their wishes are complied with.

Plaza de la Victoria, October 8, 1812.

Members of the Lautaro Lodge and other important men signed the document.

Under the central arch of the Recova two cannon had been placed, and other pieces at the corners, as if to ratify, in case of need, the voice of the people, which the Lautarian Monteagudo was articulating at that moment.

The troops showed a tranquil attitude; but the numbers and the restlessness of the civilian multitude were increasing as the hours passed. Faced with the threat and the show of force, the Council was in confusion, without deciding to orientate its deliberations, when it resolved to call in the military chiefs themselves, as a guarantee for the safety of all.

Colonel San Martín entered the Council chamber, accompanied by Alvear and Ocampo. The president of the Council asked them for their advice as to the appointment of the new authorities they were to name, and the chiefs answered that, despite the fact that they held as true the information given out by the representatives and as just the complaints of the people, they and the troops under their command could not take a part in the formation of the new government, and that the fact that they showed up in the square was only to *protect the freedom of the people,* in order that the people could thus freely explain their vote and their feelings, and so that they could be shown that the troops are not always, as some think, at the service of tyrannical governments; that the troops knew how to respect the sacred rights of the peoples and how to insure justice for them; that with this and no other purpose the troops had met in the square, placing themselves at the orders of the Most Excellent Council; and that if the latter so ordered them, they would withdraw immediately, only praying that the Council would labor for the good and happiness of the country, thwarting those factions and parties that are always the ruin of the State.

When the councilmen declared they wished to please the people and asked the military chiefs to participate in the election of new authorities, the chiefs replied that all intervention and the least influence of the troops should be avoided in an election that belonged to the people; because if the contrary was done, it would mean becoming exposed to the censure of the United Provinces; and, besides, their honor did not allow them even to mention the names of persons who could be elected.

The Council, calmed by the noble democratic declarations of San Martín and the chiefs who accompanied him, turned again to its deliberations, which were prolonged by the discussion of several opinions about the procedure to be followed. The ending of the Triumvirate was already agreed upon, especially the ousting of Pueyrredón and Rivadavia, as well as the acceptance of the promise of San Martín and his comrades that none of them would accept a position in the new government.

The crowd in the square, meanwhile, was beginning to become disorderly, owing to the delay, when San Martín, who had known ever since the murder of Solano in Cádiz what the blind fury of the populace is—the face of the Gorgon—returned to the Council chamber, very upset, and, with an energetic gesture, said to the Assembly:

"It is not possible to delay one more instant: the ferment is taking on larger proportions, and it is necessary to cut it off now."

This warning cut the debate short and precipitated the election. The votes were divided among several candidates, and those of the majority went to Nicolás Rodríguez Peña, Juan José Passo, and Antonio Alvarez Jonte, to form the new Triumvirate. Inasmuch as Rodríguez Peña was away, Carlos de Alvear was nominated to take his place *ad interim,* but the latter, being the vice-commander of the grenadiers, did not accept, following the obligation contracted with the lodge; and this resignation caused the appointment of Dr. Francisco Belgrano. The new Triumvirate thus elected was to carry out the functions of the Executive Power within the liberal tendencies which had inspired the revolution from which it sprang, and the oath which it took in the name of the country, when it was inaugurated that same day, excluded from the formula any obedience to Ferdinand VII. Independence, as an external purpose, and democracy as an internal plan were the two aims of the revolution of 1812, for the realization of which new vigor should be given to the war against Spain and an Assembly, representative of the people, should be called. The Lautaro Lodge triumphed with this act. The genius of San Martín, acting in consort with Alvear and Monteagudo, thus gave the May movement, which had been so beclouded in its beginnings, a clearer orientation.

The new Triumvirate immediately called an election for representatives; the Assembly met in January 1813, under the chairmanship of Alvear, and the liberal laws that were passed by this Congress were the immediate fruit of the 1812 revolution, which was a ratification of that of 1810. In all of this can be seen the work of Lautaro Lodge, and consequently of the San Martinian spirit in what concerns the emancipating course of the new policy. The new triumvirs of 1813 were Lautarians, and so were twenty-six members of the Assembly which made law the liberal principles of the inspiring lodge.

The ideals held by the Lautaro Lodge in the revolution of 1812 became clear in the legislative work of the Assembly: cleaning up of the popular suffrage, representative government, the legion of power, prerogatives of Congress, democratic constitution, American emancipation, creation of a nation, individual guarantees, political neutrality of the Army, freedom of the press, inviolability of the home, abolition of slavery, Inquisition, Indian peonage and torture, and consecration of the Argentine emblems—flag, anthem, and coat of arms. These institutions, which have passed into the 1853 Constitution, are the same which San Martín established in Peru when he was its Protector. There is in all of it the architecture of a pyramid, an esoteric symbol which the May revolution had adopted from its earliest days.

The May Government, when decreeing the building of the monument to the liberating revolution, ordered that it be a pyramid, the same one that still rises on the Plaza Mayor; the pyramid which had been before the emblem of Egyptian wisdom and of the most ancient American cults. I do not know whether this symbol came from the Masonic tradition, from the mysteries of Crotona and Éleusis, or if it was born in the Atlantean subconscious of the heroes of the liberation, as a reminiscence of Palenke and Tiahuanaco, unforgettable in the cosmic memory of the continent shaken by its epic.

But the sun was a true symbol of the Lautaro Lodge, and it was adopted by the Assembly for the coins it had made and for the coat of arms of the new nation. There is no legislative document concerning its adoption, nor is it known who could have suggested it to the authorities. It is significant, however, that San Martín should adopt it for his flag of the Andes four years later, and for the national flag which he gave to Peru, as well as for the arms of this latter country and for the insignia of the Order which he created in Lima during his protectorship and which was called, precisely, the Order of the Sun.

Such were, since the first days of San Martín's career, the aims which gave a moral content to his martial enterprises, and the glory of the ancient heroes —desirous of triumph and of power—never perturbed the austerity of his soul, leading it astray like Napoleon and several Americans. He was not even like Washington or Bolívar. He was different from all of them, and he founded the Lautaro Lodge to give a means of civilian action to his own genius, which had no predecessors in its virtuous originality. When he went away from Buenos Aires he founded new Lautaros in Cuyo, Chile, and Peru, leaving through them a symbol of the Argentine Revolution. To the principles of the lodge he was faithful up to the last years of his long life.

VI.   BUENOS AIRES, HIS EASTERN HOME

Shortly after arriving in Buenos Aires, where he was quickly confirmed in his rank, San Martín was introduced to some of the principal homes of the city, among them that of Don Antonio José de Escalada, whose family combined the patriarchal simplicity of the old colonial families with the courtly manners left by the viceroys. This house was located near the cathedral, and it was, as the Riglos home was later, the center of greatest distinction for the society of that time. Escalada, a rich *criollo*, had taken for his second wife Doña Tomasa de la Quintana, an elegant and beautiful woman, whose two daughters, Doña María de las Nieves and Doña María de los Remedios, inherited the beauty of their mother and the gentility of their father. María de las Nieves married Oromí;[1] María de los Remedios became San Martín's fiancée as soon as the colonel of grenadiers began to frequent the aristocratic salons of this family.

San Martín was a man of medium height, although his was an imposing figure because of his martial air. He was dark-skinned, and for this some envious people called him an Indian, encouraged by the fact that he had been born in Yapeyú, which gave plausibility to the rumor. His head was marked by harmonious strong lines; his nose was aquiline and his eyebrows gave an impression of energy. His black eyes, deep-set, moved as if they were ambushed in the shadow of his expressive eyebrows. His hands were bony and long and his gestures were eloquent; his step was at the same time agile and firm; his posture, cautious or elegant, according to the occasion; his gestures were sober, always submitting to his vigilant will; his voice was deep and masculine. He laughed little, but he had a gracious smile on his mouth, which was small, well outlined, and with good teeth. He shaved his mustache and he wore long sideburns which he combed forward, as he did his hair, which was black and straight and brought over the forehead. He listened with interest, trying to keep on the same plane as his interlocutors, giving more attention to learning from his companions than to dazzling them. With the ladies he was courteous and knew how to dance, as befitted a former pupil of the Nobles' Seminary, which was the school he attended in Madrid when he was a child.

Military life had hardened his manners somewhat, and sometimes he burst out in gestures of anger; but this happened in the barracks, never in the drawing room, where he always gave an impression of affability and spontaneity. He modestly kept his affections to himself, avoiding the sentimental and the sensual. He had not read much, although he knew what was necessary for his destiny, and he could talk about history, philosophy, and painting, besides his army subjects.

He believed in God, whom he always invoked, and his philosophy was that of a Stoic; on occasion he cited Epictetus, Seneca, and Diogenes. He thought for himself, with geometric clarity, and he spoke with Spartan precision in brief phrases, rather stony than lyrical. He showed assurance in his opinions, founding them on facts. He knew men and never asked them to do more than they could do. He never became presumptuous in success, nor did he complain in failure. He subjected his life from his young days to a severe discipline, and he made a religion of duty. In twenty years of service in the Spanish Army he never asked for a furlough. He died without leaving his heirs any personal debts. He was sober in his eating and in his dressing and fled from all kinds of theatricalities. In ten years of serving in American armies he suffered from cruel diseases, withstanding the attacks through sheer will power until completing his most arduous enterprises.

He was a good swordsman, a good horseman, and a good worker and he undertook his tasks with resignation. He was not a man of the pen and he did not like to write, although he left enough documents to fill several volumes.

Glory did not mean for him the pomp of the classical triumph but the peace of soul which is found in work well done and serene confidence in the judgment of posterity. In thirty years of exile he kept a noble silence, without answering his calumniators, who were numerous and active.

All this greatness of character, well balanced and firm like a pyramid, was felt in this thirty-four-year-old man when he arrived in Buenos Aires. His obscure origin, his absence from Spain, and his unexpected voyage surrounded him with a certain mystery, and to many he seemed enigmatic. Undoubtedly he was, because genius is always an enigma, the secret of which not even history succeeds in wholly deciphering

He knew for what great things he had been born and what hidden voice had brought him to his country in 1812; but the rest did not know it. Suspicion, emulation, and expectation instinctively crouched around this exceptional being, without a predecessor or a successor among the warriors. His comrades used to say that he thought for all of them. He was more than a capable warrior; he was an ascetic of patriotism, a Knight Templar of liberty.

Such was the man, in spirit as huge as a mountain, in whose shadow flourished the almost childish love of María de los Remedios, as a flower grows on the rugged slopes of the Andes.

She was fifteen years old when she met him, and she loved him with devotion, resigning her fate to his. Her almost childish being felt dazzled before the fire of those eyes, before the deep and magnetic look of the hero; before the seduction of his genius and the fascination of his strong will. Times were hazardous, and he had come to fight battles in distant and perilous lands; but even so, she wanted to link her destiny to that of this man, who certainly was not a person for romantic idylls. He had come from the sea, having arisen from tragedy, and he was going toward the mountain, along a predestined road to tragedy. In his old age he was to be an exiled, indigent, and blind old man; when that hour arrived, a daughter of his, like Antigone to her wandering, miserable, and blind father, accompanied him in his solitude. Such was the fatal sentence of the gods, which men still did not know. She, María de los Remedios, also did not know; but from her womb would be born later the hero's only child, his daughter. Destiny, which plotted its way through roads of blood and paths of glory, was also preparing by the path of love the consolations of agony. And María de los Remedios, who knew nothing of that, smiled at his side, still a child, as if she were the daughter, because she was only fifteen and he was thirty-four.

Pampered by her parents in their virtuous and aristocratic home, she danced and sang in a kind of naïve hypnotism, joining like a vine around an oak her gracefulness to his power. To be more beautiful she wore a diadem or a crown of jasmine and a pearl necklace, as she is shown in the portrait that has been kept of her: her face a fine oval, her skin rosy, the mouth delicious, eyes large, and looking as though filled with a faraway dream. The long curls reached her undraped shoulders; the slender figure was clad in tenuous veils that surrounded the Venuslike breasts and then fell from the high waist to the feet shod with short shoes according to the French Empire fashion.

Such was the figure, hardly entered upon womanhood, which San Martín saw and fell in love with at the Escalada salon.

While his tasks with the regiment and the meetings of the lodge were the object of his most serious attention, San Martín was making himself known in the best of Buenos Aires society, giving a few pleasant hours to feminine company, rather through political calculation than because of any gallant inclinations. Several distinguished families, like the Escaladas, opened their drawing rooms, either to hold civic celebrations or for more intimate gatherings. Some beauties were shining at the time, either because of their culture or their looks, among them Mariquita Sánchez (who married Thompson), a talented lady who was admired by her contemporaries and in whose home López and Esnaola rehearsed the national anthem in 1813; Melchora Sarratea (a sister of the patrician Don Manuel), also a woman of talent and good taste; Juana Pueyrredón (a sister of the Triumvir, Don Juan Martín), whose heart was aflame with patriotic fervor; and many others like them whom San Martín cultivated as a man of the world. Some historians have tried to depict San Martín as a rough soldier, but many Europeans who knew him give a different testimony about him: Captain Lafond, a French writer and seaman, says that San Martín spoke French very well, and Mrs. Graham, of the best English society, found him distinguished and courteous, thus confirming what had been heard about him: that no one could act more brilliantly in the drawing room.

The house which he frequented most, naturally, was that of the Escaladas, where he was attracted by the youthful charms of Remeditos,[2] as he called her, and because that house was a center of prestige in the city. Don Antonio José was in business which had brought him into contact with the principal French and English merchants who dealt in the Plate region; he also had some civilian posts, which gave him influence on the middle classes; and he had backed, although with his influence rather than his actions, the patriotic movements which took place from 1802 on, becoming an intimate friend of the military chiefs. Through his salon had passed Sobremonte, Liniers, Cisneros, the last viceroys, during the turbulent times which preceded the revolution; and also

Beresford and the British officers who fell prisoners during the English invasion. In 1812 Rivadavia and the other triumvirs visited the house frequently, along with Alvear and his wife, Segurola and other dignitaries of the church, as well as the principal figures of the Army and the Administration. The subjects for conversation there were politics, the Army, and business, besides European news and society affairs. To those gatherings also came the families of Riglos, Oromí, Lasala, Barquin, Balbastro, Casamayor, and many others, some of whom were related to the Escaladas. The feminine assemblage animated the parties in the rooms hung with blue silk, adorned with furniture in the Bourbon style, crystal chandeliers, and flower vases. The atmosphere was at the same time patriarchal and courtly. The ceremonious manners of the viceroyalty mixed with the new ideas and customs of the revolution. Some ladies played the clavichord, others sang accompanied by Andalusian guitars; and young couples danced the minuet or patriotic *cielitos*.

> *Beauteous Argentinas*
> *Of charming grace,*
> *For you crowns are woven*
> *Of roses and jasmine.*

In that atmosphere many engagements were made. The new generation of men sported their brand-new uniforms. There San Martín made a life-long friendship with the elder Escalada and his sons Mariano and Manuel, who joined the army and accompanied him on his campaigns in Chile. The spirit of the guest filled the house, and through the heart of his fiancée he communicated his patriotic ardor to Remedios' girl friends and to the men friends of her father, whom he slowly attracted to favor his hopes.

> *The whole of America*
> *Is throbbing at last,*
> *And her beloved sons*
> *She calls to the war.*

On June 26, 1812, there appeared in the *Gaceta Ministerial* the text of a note addressed to the Triumvirate by a group of Buenos Aires ladies, offering to help with their own funds to pay for the arms that the Government had just purchased for the armies of freedom; each one of them was going to pay for a musket. The first of the signatures was that of San Martín's fiancée, Remedios de Escalada. It was accompanied, among others, by that of her sister Nieves, those of her cousins the Quintana girls, and those of Señora Isabel Calvimonte, wife of Dr. Agrelo, that of Angela Castelli, daughter of the great speaker of May 1810, that of Mariquita Sánchez and, despite her being Spanish by birth, that of Doña Carmen Quintanilla de Alvear. Says the note:

The cause of humanity, with which the glory of our country and the happiness of future generations is so intimately intertwined, must necessarily interest with a passionate vehemence the mothers, daughters, and wives who are undersigned. Destined by nature and by the laws to live a retired and sedentary life, they cannot display their patriotism with the splendor of the heroes on the battlefield. They appreciate the honor of their sex, to which society entrusts the feeding and education of its chiefs and magistrates, home economy and order, eternal bases of public prosperity; but such sweet and sublime tasks hardly console them for their feeling of not being able to count their names among those of the defenders of the freedom of their country. In the activity of their wishes they have found a means which, being suited to their temperaments, in a measure gives an outlet for their patriotism.

The note expressed further the purpose of paying for the muskets with their savings:

They take the necessary sum, with pleasure, from that kept for the small but sensible needs of their sex, in order to destine it to a purpose which is the greatest that the country knows under the present circumstances. When public rejoicing carries to their families the news of a victory, they will be able to say with the exultation of their enthusiasm: "I armed the hand of that valiant man who assures his glory and our liberty." Dominated by this honorable ambition, the undersigned pray Your Excellency to order that their names be engraven on the muskets that they are paying for.

The Triumvirate accepted the donation. San Martín's fiancée was without doubt the inspiring genius of this Spartan gesture.

On July 8 the *Gaceta* carried an announcement saying that "from twelve o'clock noon until two in the afternoon and from the sounding of the call for prayer to that of the Angelus," Don Antonio José de Escalada, Remedios' father, would be at home to receive the donations that may be made to help in the purchase of arms, "with the understanding that the secret will be kept for those who for private reasons may wish that their names do not become known."

Five months after he had arrived in the country, San Martín requested the necessary military permission to marry Remedios de Escalada. The Triumvirate, composed of Pueyrredón, Rivadavia, and Chiclana, gave its authorization, after the expiration of the three proclamations, with no impediment resulting. The wedding took place on the twelfth of September of the same year, 1812, at the Cathedral of Buenos Aires, before the notary Don Gervasio Antonio de Posadas, who soon thereafter became Supreme Director of the United Provinces. The marriage ceremony was performed by Dr. Luis José de Chorroarín, delegated by the vicar, and the witnesses were the sergeant major of grenadiers, Don Carlos de Alvear, and his wife, Doña Carmen.

On the 19th the bride and bridegroom were given their benediction after Communion. There was a party at the Escalada residence on that day.

Although the fact that Alvear was a witness at San Martín's wedding is a good sign of the friendship that united them, as much as the brotherhood of both in the Lautaro Lodge and their comradeship at the head of the grenadiers, that friendship did not last for a long time with the same firmness. In 1815 the internal politics and professional jealousy would separate them somewhat, although without any real break, as it is revealed in some letters written by Alvear from Brazil after his downfall. What really estranged these men was the difference in their natures: one was impetuous in his dreams; the other was cautious in his plans.

Alvear said in the presence of Rivadavia, "Here there are no other men of action than San Martín and myself." And the triumvir, according to López, commented with a deprecating gesture, "You know, this little soldier is dangerous." And he was really dangerous: soon Alvear overthrew the Triumvirate, presided over the Assembly, took Montevideo, rose to be a general and Supreme Director of the United Provinces—all before he was twenty-five years old. San Martín's career moved more slowly, and during the first few years the newcomer acted as if he were groping his way through the dark.

In September an important subscription was opened to purchase horses for the regiment of grenadiers, to which all the men of the Government and the patricians contributed, and on October 9, a short while after San Martín's wedding, the *Gaceta* said: "The patriots who wish to contribute to the subscription for the purchase of horses for the Regiment of Mountain Grenadiers are advised that its colonel will receive the donations at the home of Don Antonio José Escalada." The colonel was San Martín and the home that of his father-in-law.

After organizing his regiment of grenadiers, San Martín had been appointed chief of all the forces in the capital and he had been put in charge of defense in case of an enemy invasion. The Spaniards of Montevideo, who had warships, were feared. In order to carry out his mission, San Martín asked the Government for a map of the city showing its divisions and sections and the names of their respective mayors; he advised the mobilization of the civilian militia to relieve the veterans in case of alarm. He urged the need for a surgeon, and he submitted a plan for the defense of the coast from beyond Ensenada up to the port of Zárate, with the combination in action of the three arms. He also requested one hundred recruits for his regiment, but the Government denied them to him. He then requested fifty to become sappers, but the Government replied with dilatory tactics. Afterward he expressed to the authorities his desire that he be relieved of the general command of the city, being left only with the command of the grenadiers, because he believed it better "to place myself at the head of my regiment, both because of my knowledge of this arm and for the opinion that I must deserve from a body that I myself have created and formed." He had said before that in view of the decision of the population to defend its rights, it was wise to expect a happy result, provided that the people were given an adequate direction for its defense and for the keeping of order, "which was liable to suffer in extraordinary cases." Did he remember then the fury of the Gorgon, the Cádiz mutiny in which he saw General Solano, his chief and friend, die at the hands of the mob? Was it that the Government, in not acceding to his requests, showed a lack of confidence in him? San Martín insisted on returning to his post of commander of the grenadiers, perhaps hurt.

"Having only my regiment in my charge, I shall be able to give a happy day to the country, and I hope that Your Excellency will not deny me this request, which has no other aim than the welfare of the inhabitants of these provinces." In these communications the hopes and the discouragements that were at work in the spirit of the unknown hero hardly show at all. We are back in the days of the Alzaga Mutiny, when it became necessary to shoot Spaniards and hang them in the Plaza de Mayo in order to punish a Royalist conspiracy: the plot had had its repercussions in all the homes of Buenos Aires and especially in those of the best society, to which the leaders of the conspiracy belonged: the Royalist Navy, with the base at Montevideo, was threatening our shores. Rivadavia and the triumvirs, meanwhile, had been going against the liberal opinion of the country. The moment was confused and grave. In the midst of such uncertainty, San Martín saw clearly the plans which were ripening in secret. But whom could he confide in, if they did not have confidence in him? He understood well that his military service in Spain made him a suspect in the eyes of some in that moment of hesitations and doubts. He was almost unknown in his country; he had neither relatives, a party, nor the command of armies. Many years later he was still to complain of those unjustified suspicions which hurt him so much. He did not say anything, however, about all this in the initial hour of his undertaking. With stoic firmness he went on waiting and working. Only his father-in-law could be his confidant at that moment, and the love of María de los Remedios was the balm which he applied to his wound.

When San Martín entered formally upon his engagement, he was training his regiment and organizing the lodge; when he married, the October Revolution, which took place three weeks after his marriage, was in preparation; when he left in February 1813 on the mission that ended with the Battle of San Lorenzo, he had been married for less than five months. Again he had to be separated from his wife in December of the same year to undertake an expedition to Tucumán. He did not see her again until 1815, and in circumstances that we shall see later.

Calumny, which respected nothing in San Martín, also tainted his home, when the hour of the hostile passions arrived. His love life was, however, very different from that of Napoleon and his Josephine, or that of Bolívar and his Manuela Sáenz.[8] The domestic virtues of San Martín were as clean as his soul and his sword.

The stranger who had arrived in March 1812 had succeeded at the beginning of the following year, in Buenos Aires, in having a lodge of "friends" which had influence upon the new government they had founded; an exemplary regiment which after the Battle of San Lorenzo had given him a certain prestige; and a home of his own, linked to the best society in Buenos Aires, with which he expected to cease being a stranger in his own land. The hazards of internal politics, however, did not permit him to conduct the lodge in accordance with the severe standards which he recommended: the Lautaro Lodge fell prey to anarchy in 1815, and it was necessary to rebuild it in 1816 for the Andean enterprise. The hazards of war, in turn, only permitted him very brief stays in his Buenos Aires home.

In any event, Buenos Aires remained after 1812 the center of San Martín's destiny: his regiment was the basis for the liberating armies; his lodge was the political spring of his American undertaking; his wife was to be the mother of the daughter who would accompany the exiled hero during his long, sad, old age.

The work of initiation was thus completed, and had prepared within itself the instruments of future triumphs and even the dramatic developments of the hero's life, so filled with strange harmonies and mysteries.

VII. FRONTIER OF THE TUCUMAN

With Belgrano defeated at Vilcapugio and his army dispersed at Ayohuma, the victories of Tucumán and Salta were thought to be futile. The governor then ordered that San Martín be transferred to the Army of the North; that he take command of a force composed of the 7th Infantry, 100 artillerymen and 250 grenadiers of the regiment under his command, and that he take all the steps necessary for this expedition to march promptly. The postmaster was instructed to co-operate in the preparation of the convoy. The artillerymen and the grenadiers would take with them the ammunition cars and their cannon, going in groups of fifty men and calling at the postal way stations, where they would find foodstuffs and fresh horses; the grenadiers would go on horseback, the infantrymen in wagons. In six days they began to move. San Martín left his wife at the home of her parents and then undertook the painful march, before the middle of December, passing through impoverished and deserted regions.

For the first time he would soon be in touch with the American hinterland after suffering the troubles of his long march in order to meet Belgrano, whose letters he was finding at the way stations as soon as he reached Santiago. On January 2, 1814, Belgrano, from Jujuy, addressed to him, "Wherever he may be," a letter in which he calls him "My friend and fellow soldier" which began thus: "I visualize you going through hardships of your journey, witnessing the misery of our countries and the difficulties which their distances make, together with their lack of population and the consequent lack of resources for operating with the celerity that is necessary." At that time the hardships of traveling were as great as those of fighting.

On January 11, 1814, thirty days after he left, Director Posadas wrote San Martín from Buenos Aires: "As I imagine that you are already resting from the fatigue of your trip, I have decided to write you to beg you earnestly to take command of the army which the Government must unavoidably entrust you with." San Martín was able to read this letter at Tucumán, the second paragraph of which said: "The unfortunate Belgrano may be an excellent person; he may be equally deserving of the eternal gratitude of his compatriots; but above all other considerations it is in our interest, and the good of the country demands it, that for the time being you should shoulder that cross." Belgrano was, then, to be replaced by San Martín; and later he was to be recalled to Buenos Aires to be judged for the disaster of Vilcapugio and Ayohuma, his former victories being forgotten. Such was the first moral annoyance which San Martín had on the thankless mission with which he had been entrusted. With this worry he went northward from Tucumán, and he stopped at the banks of the river Juramento, there to wait for Belgrano, who was already on his way down from his Jujuy headquarters, anxious to shake San Martín's hand warmly.

The two patriots did not yet know each other personally. They met at Yatasto, and there they greeted each other for the first time. They had written each other several letters expressing their mutual affection and confidence during the past month. When they met their friendship was born spontaneously, and it lasted a lifetime. Their personal dealings confirmed the reciprocal opinions which they had formed. In that wild spot, near the banks of the river where the oath of allegiance to the flag had first been taken in 1812 when Belgrano was going from Tucumán to Salta—the road between two victories—the two chiefs spoke of the country and of the terrible disaster which was the reason for their meeting there. He who had been defeated at Vilcapugio and Ayohuma must have repeated what he had already said in his recent letters:

Because God has so willed, I find myself being a general without knowing what I am about. This has not been my career, and now I must study in order to get through halfway. . . . I have felt very much the need of divisional chiefs, because a general cannot be everywhere. . . . I had not and I have not had anyone to help me, and I have made war like an explorer. . . . if we hadn't been Spaniards, the reinforcements which I was offered should have been with me before the action at Salta. . . . I haven't a single officer who can claim any professional knowledge. . . . I undertook this mission with eyes closed, and I shall die in the course of it rather than turn my back. . . .

San Martín must have been desolate when reading these confessions from the virtuous Belgrano, more so when that honest and strong man told him: "You must be not only my friend but my teacher, my companion, and my chief if you want to."

Belgrano made an excellent impression on San Martín. When it became necessary to seek a new commander for the Army of the North, after the failure of Rondeau at Sipe Sipe, the eyes were turned to him who had been defeated at Ayohuma. It was San Martín's advice in 1814 that the government should keep Belgrano at the head of that army in order to reorganize it. His advice was not heeded. The passions of others carried more weight than his wisdom. San Martín again spoke in favor of Belgrano in a letter written at Mendoza on March 12, 1816: "In case of having to appoint someone to replace Rondeau, I would decide for Belgrano. He is the most methodical man of all whom I know in America; he is full of integrity and of natural talent. He may not have the knowledge of a Moreau or a Bonaparte as far as the army is concerned, but believe me, he is the best we have in South America."

The Government of Buenos Aires decided in 1814 to start proceedings against Belgrano for his military failures, in the same manner as it had before proceeded against Castelli for his failure, and thus was carried out the fatal sentence that the revolution should owe its own children. After the removal of Belgrano, San Martín was to replace him on this prophetic frontier. Although against his wishes, the victor of San Lorenzo obeyed.

On January 30, 1814, San Martín, who had already taken command, addressed the following proclamation to the Army of the North:

Brave sons of the Fatherland:
The Government has just entrusted me with the chief command of the Army; it deigns to place upon my shoulders the august weight of its defense. Soldiers: confidence! I admire your efforts and I want to be at your side in your endeavors and to share in your glories. I shall do everything in my power that your sufferings may be lessened. Victors of Tupiza, Piedras, Tucumán, and Salta: let us renew those victorious days! The Fatherland is in imminent danger of succumbing. Let us then, soldiers, save her.

This was San Martín's first proclamation as a general in America to an army of the revolution. Its austere eloquence, which veiled his own misgivings, awakened the pride of the recently beaten troops with the mention of former victories. He was not unacquainted with the difficulties of the moment for any army whose condition he himself had described in a note to the Government:

I have found only the sad fragments of a beaten army. A hospital without medicine, without instruments, without clothing, which offers the spectacle of men lying on the ground who cannot be treated in the manner that humanity and their own merits demand. Naked troops, dressed like beggars. Officers who have not the means with which to show themselves in public. A thousand clamorings for overdue pay. Urgent expense for supplies, without which it is not possible to make our armament ready to hold the advance of the enemy.

San Martín did not exaggerate when he painted this picture, so different from that of the proud troops which posterity imagines today when evoking the days of the great epic. General Paz, in his memoirs, written many years later, paints an even darker picture of what he also saw then, being a lieutenant in the same army. It carried already the leaven of coming uprisings and the seeds of future civil war lords, the ferment of anarchy and sectionalism. San Martín, who from the day of his arrival had understood clearly the American reality in contrast with his ideals of discipline and strategic foresight, was disheartened by this spectacle, and he sought an effective way to remedy it. To accomplish this he had to disobey the Government for the first time. The Government had requested him to send the money taken from Potesí during the retreat of Belgrano, because Buenos Aires also owed four months' pay to the troops. San Martín, on his own responsibility, disposed in part of those sums to pay his officers and men, in order to muffle discontent, to bolster morale, and to improve discipline. His conduct was criticized in Buenos Aires, and it gave rise to calumnious gossip. His friend, Director Posadas, told him in a personal letter: "If you had obeyed, you would have exposed yourself to a critical situation; with your disobedience I have been placed here in the position of a swine." But he had done his duty honestly, spurred by a need that had to be met. From that moment he realized that no efficacious help could come to him from Buenos Aires. He should seek salvation from his own military experience, from his political ingenuity, and from his indomitable will. Where? How? That was his problem.

When he took over command, the army had only six hundred men. With the fugitives that were coming back and with the levies which he made in the neighboring provinces, he succeeded in getting more than two thousand; from Santiago he had three hundred recruits sent over. But all this was only a shapeless conglomeration of demoralized and unarmed men, facing the five thousand soldiers of Pezuela who later entered Jujuy, entrenched themselves in Salta, carried guerrilla warfare down to the river Pasaje and threatened with their better equipment, flushed with victory. It was out of the question to think of a full-fledged offensive or to plan even one pitched battle without first restoring civilian confidence and military capacity. For this purpose he concentrated all the forces on the outskirts of Tucumán; he built an entrenched camp which he called Ciudadela; he applied there the methods of training and discipline which he had already tried at Retiro when he was organizing his grenadiers; he presented these as a model for the cavalry; he

trained the infantry in accordance with the most modern European doctrines; he eliminated all the spectacular parades in order to concentrate on
training the soldiers; he established a school of mathematics to train engineers, and he worked with them on the ground to lay out the pentagon and
build the bastions of Ciudadela. One of his principles was that there cannot
be an army without mathematics; another that the soldier is formed in the
barracks, not in battle. All this was new there, as new as the authority of
the man who preached with his example, compelling decency and studious-
ness with iron will.

He had ordered, one day, that each unit at a specified hour should send over
twenty-five men to increase the effectives of the regiment of grenadiers. There
came Major Lamadrid, without the men, to make some objections. When
the loquacious Lamadrid began to talk, San Martín took out his watch,
looked at the time and interrupted him, saying severely: "Two minutes have
already gone by since the hour when the men were to be on the formation
I have ordered." Lamadrid withdrew in silence to carry out the order, and
this was a lesson for all the officers.

On another occasion the officers had met for instruction. San Martín, who
was explaining a lesson, had before him a table with a bronze candlestick
on it. Belgrano, who had not yet gone to Buenos Aires, was modestly in
attendance to learn, and among the present was also Colonel Dorrego, who
had a mocking disposition, and who had been warned several times by San
Martín because of his levity. It came Dorrego's turn to repeat a command,
and he did it imitating the thin voice of Belgrano. San Martín, annoyed,
seized the candlestick and, banging it ferociously on the table, pierced Dorrego
with his furious eyes and said just this: "Mr. Colonel, we came here to
standardize our commands." A few hours later he exiled him to Santiago, in
punishment for his levity.

Both Dorrego and Lamadrid later became heroes in the civil wars of the
period of anarchy, as was also Paz, who in his memoirs extols the teachings
of San Martín: "The new general," he says, "taught the army the rudiments
of modern tactics, which were unknown to us until then; we were most backward, in the darkest ignorance." General Luzuriaga, who was then a colonel
of infantry in the north, says in his memoirs that San Martín taught him
personally the theory and practice of his arm, and that he was "the first to
introduce the new tactics and to teach it in America, even before the Spaniards did it in the armies they had there." But officers like Luzuriaga and
Paz were not many. Types like Lamadrid, intrepid and talkative, and Dorrego, light-minded and ambitious, were the ones which most genuinely represented the kind of officers whom San Martín had to educate. The soldiers
were even worse. The gauche lack of discipline was traditional in that army
which had been defeated first under the terrible Castelli and then under the

good-natured Belgrano. Valor was not lacking, and thanks to it they were successful sometimes. But San Martín wanted to add honor and ability to the native courage. Thus he rebuilt the Army of the North.

With that experience in Tucumán and what he had already seen, he wrote to a friend in Congress in 1816, from Cuyo:

> You may trouble yourselves with supplying us the means to serve the country and you may fatigue yourselves in searching for the primary reasons for our misfortunes; well, let it be known to you that these misfortunes (I speak of the military) are due to the fact that we do not have a single man able to place himself at the head of an army. Seek six or eight generals in France (who nowadays haven't even got anything to eat), bring them here and you will see how all our operations and events change. Bear this in mind and you will realize that without this we shall not make any headway. Let us do justice to our ignorance and let us not allow our pride to push us into the abyss.

Of course, when he spoke thus, he wasn't forgetting the moral forces which he thought so much about throughout the whole of his enterprise. The regulations for the mounted grenadiers, which were a paradigm of the method which he used later to organize the Army of the Andes, were based on the individual conscience of the soldier; Negroes for the infantry, gauchos for the cavalry. The guiding thought of his campaign in Peru—a corollary of his mission—consisted in winning the war by means of public opinion. If his genius had not learned this by itself, he would not have forgotten the warnings of Belgrano, when taking leave of him in Tucumán, in this connection.

Belgrano, from Santiago del Estero, on April 6, 1814, on his way to Buenos Aires, where he was going to render an account of his double failure to the doctors of the Government, wrote San Martín a letter which is moving for the generosity of his advice and the accuracy of his remarks:

> The preoccupations of the peoples are very worthy of respect; much more so those which are based, even in small measure, in something that smells of religion.
>
> You will not have to make war there only with arms, but also with public opinion, with the latter being always buttressed by the natural virtues, Christian and religious; but our enemies have made war against us calling us heretics, and only by this means have they been able to attract the barbarians to arms, telling them that we were attacking religion.
>
> Perhaps someone will laugh at this thought of mine; but you should not be guided by the exotic opinions or by those of men who do not know the soil on which they tread, and I assure you that you would find yourself in much greater difficulty if they should see in the army under your command that you are opposed to religion and to the excommunications of the Popes. I will add only my request that you keep the flag which I left with you and that you raise it when all the whole army is in formation; that you do not cease to pray to Our Lady of Las Mercedes, naming her always as our patroness, and that you do not forget the

peculiarities of the troops. Let them laugh; the results will repay you for the laughter of the fools, who only see the outside of things. Remember that you are a Christian, apostolic, Roman general; be careful that in no wise, not even in the most trivial conversations, there be shown a lack of respect to our holy religion; bear in mind not only the generals of the people of Israel, but also those of the pagans and the great Julius Caesar who never neglected to invoke the immortal gods and for whose victories Rome decreed prayers.

Precisely because San Martín understood things like this very well, he could carry out so efficiently the plans he had made. To wage war, a technically organized army; but this army must have a soul, and as it has to move in a geographic theater to which it needs to adapt itself and in a social atmosphere in which it needs backing, it is not possible to do without other auxiliary instruments. Thus he understood that in the theater of the north there was no room for decisive battles, and that the way to Lima lay over the Andes and the Pacific Ocean. Thus he also understood that in the mountainous forests of the north the system of guerrillas could be efficacious.

The so-called war of partisans or of observation and surprise parties which had begun in 1810 was a genuine expression of the geographic medium on the northern frontier. When Castelli went through that year toward higher Perú, Güemes, with Gurruchaga and Moldes, had formed the "Squadron of Salta," which entered Potosí. They wore uniforms: red tunics, red busbys (with a white feather, white trousers, and high black boots with clinking spurs). They were all horsemen in those provinces, accustomed to ride for their work on the ranches. The bosses liked luxurious personal dress and saddles. But those luxuries were lost in the war, and years later there remained only the true figure of the gauchos, armed with whatever they had: blunderbusses, sticks, or improvised lances made with their knives tied to the end of a pole. Other times they armed themselves with the weapons taken from the enemy.

The Royalists' advance guard arrived on a Sunday at the little town of Chicoana, and after Mass a *criollo* said, "We should rise against this scum." With what weapons? he was asked. "With the same ones that we take away from them" . . . and the neighbors, led by Luís Burela, rushed the Royalist patrol.

Thus there came into being, as a spontaneous creation of the race and of the soil, what was called the Gaucho War. Güemes had been in Humahuaca in 1810 with a scouting party. After the disaster of Huaqui, with the patriot command demoralized and the troops of the King advancing to the south, the guerrillas multiplied, and to a much greater degree after Ayohuma, which brought about a new influx of Royalists to the Argentine provinces. When San Martín arrived at Tucumán in 1814, the Gaucho War was at its height, a natural phenomenon of the frontier. The advance of the Royalists, who had again occupied the cities of Salta and Jujuy, and the disorganization of

Belgrano's army after his defeat, made it advisable for the new chief to adopt a defensive plan in accordance with the circumstances. San Martín concentrated the army at Tucumán and withdrew the vanguard from the Pasaje River, leaving a line of hidden posts under the command of officers who knew the country well, and manned by horsemen whose mission was to scout and report, to cut the enemy's communications and to deprive him of resources. In reality this was something akin to the war of the Vendée and the struggle of the Spanish guerrillas against the Napoleonic invasion; but in that Argentine region this took on another aspect, when it became colored by the local atmosphere.

All the north arose against the enemy. The women of the cities acted as spies, and the children of the ranches as messengers; the forest shook with gaucho horsemen, as if nature itself were spewing them forth. "We shall never conquer this people," said a young Spanish commander after having seen that conflagration. General García Camba, who served under the Viceroy of Peru, refers in his *History* to the gauchos of the north in these fair words: "Extraordinary horsemen, skilled in the use of all arms, individually brave, able to disperse and return again to the attack, with a confidence, self-assurance, and cold-bloodedness that roused the admiration of Europeans; as good or better horsemen than the Cossacks and the Mamelukes; able to keep, both afoot and mounted, a fire similar to that of a good infantry, with excellent conditions for the war of guerrillas and surprise."

Castro, in the valley of Lerma; Rojas, Arias, and Alvarez Prado in the canyons of Jujuy; the two Saravias (Pedro José and Juan Apolinario), on the Pasaje River, as well as minor chiefs, directed those daily assaults.

The Royalists declared war to the death, and the patriots answered with the same cruelty.

It was clairvoyant of San Martín to have understood the importance of that kind of war. From Tucumán he advised the Buenos Aires Government in 1814: "The gauchos of Salta, alone, are conducting a war against the enemy with such terrible success that they have compelled him to detach a whole division with the sole purpose of getting mules and cattle." The Government replied praising San Martín's "prudent perspicacity" in having adopted the Gaucho War as part of his plan. This soldier who was an exponent of such a severe discipline was at the same time a practical warrior.

Captain Saravia, from Salta, with thirty men armed with sawed-off muskets, clubs, and hand-made spears, attacked the Spaniards at Sauce Redondo: "The tyrants will be amazed," he wrote in his report, "when they see that only thirty men with muskets, helped by unarmed horsemen, attacking against lively fire, will have defeated a force twice as strong; but if they notice that the men who have attacked them want in their hearts to be free, they will have no reason for wonder." That was the moral force which San Martín, with his leader's eyes, saw as soon as he arrived and profited by, taking advantage of the terrain and the nature of the inhabitants. But the new commander of the northern frontier had a greater merit, and it was that of having discovered the man needed to give spiritual unity to the Gaucho War. That man was Martín Güemes, a chieftain from Salta.

Don Martín Güemes was a son of a Spanish official of the Royal Treasury of Salta. He had studied at the San Carlos College in Buenos Aires, served during the British invasions, and joined the first Army of the Revolution, in 1810. With his squadron from Salta he accompanied Castelli to Tiahuanaco and Potosí, during the campaign in Upper Peru. He returned to Buenos Aires with prisoners and he had remained outside his own province when Belgrano was at the head of the Army of the North; because of this absence he had taken part in the victories of Tucumán and Salta. He was in Santiago del Estero when San Martín arrived in Tucumán and called him. San Martín was on a personal inspection tour of the Pasaje River line when Güemes, whose favorable record San Martín knew, reported to him. The two patriots met at Yatasto, and San Martín, after hearing him, entrusted him with the command at the frontier. Thus began the development of the personality of the chieftain from Salta, who was thereafter the servant of the Fatherland and the defense of the territory in the north. Güemes' Gaucho War, which continued until his tragic death in 1821, was a part of San Martín's plans, inasmuch as Güemes harassed the Royalists of Peru in Salta, while San Martín attacked them on the west.

Don Bernabé Araoz, an officer of the Army of the North and later a chieftain in Tucumán, wrote San Martín in 1820:

In the midst of the misery in which we live, nothing is kept back when we speak about Peru. Salta will do the same as Tucumán, and they will never expose themselves to being beaten, because we shall always make the kind of war that General San Martín taught us. For that we count on good horses and men who do not know fear.

Güemes, in turn, also speaks of the misery in which the gaucho epic carries on with spiritual strength:

The neighbors gathered in the house of the chief alderman, and among all of them they have only been able to give a couple of worthless rags, giving one shirt to a man, a cheap poncho to another, and a piece of old cloth to a third. What to say? Horses? Just a few, perhaps the worst they have been able to find, so that it will be difficult for them to reach Jujuy. In view of this, can I not praise the conduct and the virtue of the gauchos? They contribute their own personal efforts, not excepting even the only horse they have, whereas those who profit by the advantages of the revolution think only of ways and means to increase their fortunes.

Güemes was, in his own way, another Castilian and Christian chieftain. Having been born an *hidalgo*, he despised the bourgeois because of their selfishness, but he loved his gauchos and they loved him. Feverish in his task, he galloped across the fields like a legendary warrior. Salta was the feudal capital of his democratic kingdom, and all the frontier of Upper Peru was the objective of his enterprise. His influence reached up to Cuzco, where they conspired against the King, and his name was heard in Lima, where the Viceroy knew the price his troops must pay for the hostility of Güemes' guerrilla warfare. His communications to San Martín were assiduous, and he kept them up when the former withdrew from the Army of the North and went to Cuyo to prepare the crossing of the Andes: in 1820, from Chile, San Martín appointed Güemes commander of a division which was to invade Upper Peru, while Peru was being attacked on the coast. The lack of resources in the first place and the death of Güemes one year afterward were the reasons for the failure of that part of San Martín's plans. The close association between these two patriots is recorded in documents, but it has not been duly recorded by the historians. The death of the Salta chieftain during a Royalist invasion of Salta was marked with the transcendence of the moment in which it happened.

San Martín met Belgrano and Güemes at Yatasto, and from the moment he spoke to them he discovered the self-denial of both. His friendship for them he kept alive until the moment of his death, to the honor of the three of them. San Martín believed that Upper Peru was not the road to Lima, but nevertheless he gave to the war in Upper Peru the plan, the character, and the men which it called for. Such was the importance of his brief residence in Tucumán, whose gaucho defense became co-ordinated, in his continental plan, with the campaign on the Pacific.

From Tucumán San Martín wrote to his friend the triumvir Rodríguez Peña, in March 1814, this letter in which shines the subtle and deep view of genius:

Do not congratulate yourself beforehand, my dear friend, about what I may do here; I won't do anything and I don't like anything here. I do not know the men or the country, and everything is in a condition of anarchy; I know better than anybody else how little I can do. Laugh at gay hopes. Our country will not make any headway here on the north, outside of a permanent and purely defensive war; for this brave gauchos of Salta, with two good squadrons of veterans, are enough. To think anything else is to throw men and money down a bottomless pit. Therefore I shall not move or try any expedition.

When San Martín realized all this with clarity, he gave shape to his plan of attack against Lima through the Pacific—a plan made necessary by the geographic, historic, and ethnological conditions of the continent, and he found the way of withdrawing from the command of the north, which did not promise anything efficacious, and approaching the Cuyo frontier in order to find his way through Chile. That was the secret of his genius. His problem was to find a means of suggesting his wishes without wholly revealing his purposes.

Already in 1813, when they were going to appoint him major general of the Army of the North, San Martín had expressed his unwillingness to Rodríguez Peña, and in December the latter answered him: "We are most displeased because of your insistence in not accepting the command in chief, and please believe that we are much compromised by the continuance of Belgrano in that position." He accepted at last, but in 1814 he was looking for a transfer to Cuyo.

In his letter to Rodríguez Peña, mentioned before, San Martín added the following:

I have already told you my secret. A small and well-disciplined army in Mendoza to go over to Chile and finish the Goths there, giving support to a Government of solid friends, in order also to finish the anarchists who are in control; with the Allied Forces we shall go by sea to take Lima; that is the way and not this one, my friend. Be convinced that the war will not end until we are in Lima. I wish very much that you would appoint someone abler than myself for this post. Do all you can to see that my successor comes soon, and tell them that I will accept the governorship of Córdoba. I am ill and broken down; it is better that I withdraw to my corner and dedicate myself to training recruits whom the Government may use anywhere else.

What I should like that you give me when I recover is the governorship of Cuyo. There I could organize a small cavalry force to reinforce Balcarce in Chile, which I judge to be greatly necessary if we are to do anything profitable, and I confess to you that I should like to go over as the head of that force.

Astute fellow! He said he was "very ill" and that he wanted "to withdraw to my corner" in order to train recruits; but he asked for the governorship of Cuyo. He knew well what he wanted: an army in Mendoza to go over to Chile to finish the Goths, and from there by sea to Lima.

That is the whole plan of the Andean epic, clear and brief; but he spoke of it as of any ordinary thing, in order to get what he asked for.

In March 1814 San Martín had expressed, then, his idea born of his genius; this chronological priority proves the paternity of the Andean plan, which was carried out three years later by its author himself.

VIII. UNDER THE SOUTHERN CROSS

Victim of a sudden internal ailment, San Martín fell ill in Tucumán on April 25, 1814. He shut himself up in his house, where few people were allowed to visit him. The army band was ordered to play some distance away from his residence in order not to disturb him. After he had vomited blood, he delegated his command to Colonel Don Francisco Fernández de la Cruz, to whom he handed a confidential application for a furlough, addressed to the Government, to be sent to Buenos Aires. The brief note said "Most Excellent Sir: All the physicians of the army met yesterday to discuss the condition of my health, and they unanimously decided that I should leave promptly for the mountains of Córdoba, for which reason I beg Your Excellency to grant me a leave of absence to recover."

This request was dated at Tucumán on April 27; and while the Buenos Aires Government was considering it, San Martín left for La Ramada, the ranch of the Cossio family, located a few leagues from Tucumán, on the road to Burruyacu, a healthful and peaceful place. The house had several rooms opening onto a gallery supported by forked tree trunks, from which the mountains could be seen. Next to the house stood a giant carob tree which still stands, and in the shadow of which the sick man rested.

Despite being a strong man, San Martín was not a well man. With methodical sobriety San Martín protected his health, but his consciousness of duty led him to abuse his system in his never-ending work. Ever since the age of eleven he had discharged his duties in the army, taking part in a number of military campaigns on sea and on land. During twenty years of service in the Spanish Army, he had never requested a furlough. Since his arrival in Buenos Aires he had not rested a single day, having devoted his time to complicated tasks of war in the capital, in Santa Fe, in Tucumán itself. To all this there was added the mental and moral fatigue of one who had to adapt himself to an atmosphere that was new for him, and who had to know his men and to defend himself against underground intrigues. There was enough cause for his health to fail, and this was not the first time that he was ill.

In Spain, shortly before coming to America, he had suffered from rheumatism and asthma. These illnesses were entered on his army record, which he brought with him. This happened after Bailén and before he joined the Army of Catalonia. The Marquis of Coupigni wrote him at that time: "I regret very much that you are ill, and I shall be particularly pleased to hear of your recovery." From Seville, Carlos Gonzáles reported to José Moreno Daoiz, on May 18, 1809, that San Martín "has not yet entirely recovered, but he has told us that his breathing already allows him to travel." In spite of this, San Martín asked to be allowed to rejoin "in view of the fact that I am suffering much less now from the dangerous illness I have had"; and thus he resumed his services in Spain.

The hemorrhage he had in Tucumán was a new symptom, but one which was to be repeated in the course of his American campaigns. The physicians who attended him declared that "he suffered from an internal ailment of the chest," and therefore they advised him to go to Córdoba. It was believed that San Martín was tubercular (tuberculosis, nine years later, caused the death of his wife); but his long journeys, his titanic labor in Cuyo and in the Pacific, his rough crossings of the seas, the pampas, and the mountains of both worlds, the time he spent at the beach in damp climates during his old age in Europe, and his septuagenarian longevity seem to exclude that suspicion.

He suffered also from rheumatism and from sharp pains in the stomach, which compelled him to use opium; and after 1816 he abused this malevolent anodyne. To this was added an ailment which did not stop him from crossing the highest mountains of the globe with the army that he himself painstakingly created, and he also had a chronic dyspepsia which he never took proper care of, because he was an inveterate meat eater. These troubles and the insomnia from which he also suffered unbalanced his nervous system and broke the resistance of his vigorous fiber. Dr. William Colisberry, an American physician who took care of him in Tucumán, attended him for another attack in Mendoza four years later, and Dr. Isodoro Zapata, chief surgeon of the army, took care of him in Chile when he passed through another crisis, and both doctors expressed the opinion that unless he left his work to look after his health, he had only a few months to live. Pueyrredón (M.), Espejo, and Guido, of the Army of the Andes, were witnesses of the physical sufferings of San Martín during his campaigns. Several times he sought recovery in a water cure, but his usual treatment when the pains became too acute was to resort to opium.

It is not possible to deny that San Martín was a sick man, and only by dint of heroic will power was he able to face the task which he had imposed upon himself, that of serving the cause of freedom in America. In spite of this, when he had the attack in Tucumán, it was believed that it was only a deception, for the purpose of leaving the Army of the North. General Paz, who was then an officer of that army, recalls these suspicions in his memoirs, with these words:

> At the time, the fact of his illness was doubted; but later it became evident that it was simply a pretext to withdraw from a command in which he did not believe he should continue. The reason for this was the conviction he had that the faction which had enthroned itself in Buenos Aires was not favorable to him and that he would lack the resources with which to keep the army, while the young General Don Carlos de Alvear came to take his place when the moment arrived to undertake the offensive.

Perhaps San Martín had let his intimate friends understand something about his suspicions concerning Buenos Aires, his discouragement about Upper Peru, and his hopes about Chile; but this mental condition did not exclude the truth about his ailments, and the gossip was malicious.

One month before his illness in Tucumán, San Martín had written to Nicolás Rodríguez Peña, his good friend, a letter in which he uncovered his secret—the plan to cross the Andes and go to Lima by way of the Pacific —the text of which we have already seen in the last chapter. In that letter San Martín mentioned his illness and requested the governorship of Cuyo.

He knew, then, what he wanted; and if it was true that he wished to withdraw from the Army of the North in order to seek on the west another way for the victory of the arms of liberty, it was no less true that his health had broken down, that he was ill in body and mind, disappointed by a star which was taking too long to shine for him. So real was his illness that, in view of the medical certificates, the Government of Buenos Aires on May 7 appointed his successor. The decree began thus: "The general commanding the auxiliary army of Peru has, unfortunately, fallen mortally ill." He had not fallen "mortally ill," but the Government doubtlessly exaggerated in order to justify the removal. The very fact that influences adverse to San Martín had a part in the issuing of that decree could have demoralized the troops, which, on his retirement, saw the northern frontier open to the ambitions of others.

In those unpleasant hours San Martín found consolation in the words of Belgrano, sick like himself and also disheartened by the injustice of men. From Santiago del Estero, Belgrano wrote him in April: "You must know that you have enemies and that these, as well as other idle people, enjoy attacking you, no matter what you do, for even the most trivial things." The victor of Tucumán and Salta was on his way to Buenos Aires, where proceedings had been started against him for the defeats of Vilcapugio and Ayohuma; but he had stopped in Santiago owing to the illness which he also suffered: "I have not yet resumed my trip because of my complaints, which come again as a consequence of the damned fevers and of my work," says Belgrano. "If, however, I could be even a soldier under you, I would be glad; because I wish to fight against that indecent scum which only as a punishment from heaven was ever able to crush us." After their greeting at Yatasto, when the two great men met and recognized each other as brothers, they felt linked by a mysterious bond. In Santiago, Belgrano learned of San Martín's illness three days after the latter's hemorrhage, and he hastened to send him a brief note: "I have learned with the greatest regret about your illness. May God will that you feel better and that this letter will find you entirely recovered. I recall that you told me that you were over thirty-six and this relieves me, because I had heard famous physicians say that at that age it is not possible to spew blood unless because of a blow." Belgrano, as we see, believed in the sickness of San Martín. Others did not.

Also the second in command of the Army, Fernández de la Cruz, the patriot to whom San Martín had delegated command and who, because of his intimate connections with the chief, was able to see the truth and believe it, regretted it when he reported the retirement of the sick man to Buenos Aires, saying: "The high reputation which he enjoyed in the army, in all the towns, and even among his enemies, and which prevailed even among the lowest ranks, and the consternation and general disappointment which the news of his withdrawal would cause, led us to suppress it, without taking any new steps in order to keep the hope that all had in his resuming command." This was written by Colonel Fernández de la Cruz on June 8, 1814. A few days before, San Martín had secretly left La Ramada for Córdoba, on an official furlough, to look after his health in the mountains.

Colonel Fernández de la Cruz, a capable but not ambitious man, remained provisionally in command of the Army of the North. The rumor circulated then that Alvear, with his newly acquired laurels of Montevideo, was going to continue the war in Upper Peru. This did not come to pass, however. Rondeau, a general without energy, was appointed commander of that army. Alvear, who was already the most influential figure in La Plata, remained in Buenos Aires, and soon thereafter he was appointed Supreme Director of the United Provinces, succeeding Señor Posadas, his uncle. The young patriot was only twenty-five when he became a victorious general and President of the Assembly, in a breath-taking career of triumphs. His political and military career seemed to reach a climax at a time in life when others are just beginning. Crowned with glory, he chose his own post of victory, and it was not long before he ascended to the position of chief executive of his country, while his fellow traveler on the *George Canning* was going, in sickness and obscurity, through the highways of the interior, in search of a climate for his ailments and of hopes for his tenacious dreams. Many saw a rivalry between the two, and perhaps it existed, in spite of their dissimilar destinies. Young Alvear had taken possession of glory by force, as an adolescent who forcibly takes a woman; he had combined politics and the army, carried by a tumultuous passion which soon was going to devour him, as always happens in times of revolutionary agitation. San Martín, instead, had renounced politics to devote himself to the army as he understood it, using the arms as a mathematical instrument of methodical thought whose mystical sources of silent inspiration only he himself knew. But the hour of his destiny was late in coming. . . .

In the middle of May, San Martín was traveling across the miserable fields of inland Argentina, meditating in his carriage. With him was young Tomás Guido, whom he had known in London at the end of 1811 and whom he had seen again in Tucumán at the beginning of 1814. Guido was secretary of the Presidency of Charcas, when the defeats of Vilcapugio and Ayohuma compelled him to withdraw to Jujuy, whence Belgrano sent him with a mission to Salta. He was in Salta with Dorrego when San Martín, who was inspecting the frontier, had him come down to meet him. They met at the Puch ranch, resumed their friendship, and Guido accompanied his sick friend until he left him in an improved condition at the ranch of Saldán, in Córdoba.

San Martín, disillusioned and fatigued, left Tucumán like a fugitive, and, demoralized, rested in Santiago, where he was attended, on the recommendation of Belgrano, by two friends of his, Don Pedro Carol and the priest, Dr.

Uriarte, curate of the village, with exquisite deference. His pilgrimage continued afterwards, with precautions taken for the voyage, through the inhospitable forest, with stops at ranches where even water was sometimes lacking. He passed through Loreto, Atamisqui, Salavina, Ojo de Agua, and entered Córdoba at Río Seco, changing horses at the pitiful inns. He heard the countrymen speak Quechua, he saw them eat beans from the carob tree, and he thought that those men, so tough for soldiering, were going to be the citizens of the new republics. A shadow of skepticism fell upon his soul, and only the sweetness of the Santiago winter, with its golden suns, gentle in their warmth, made him love life, comforting his heart with waves of soft optimism. Tomás Guido entertained him with his admirable talk. In the nights of those slow days he saw the constellations of America shine in a dry and wonderfully blue sky. In his melancholy he remembered and he dreamt. He thought of Spain, of the career that he had cut short there, of all that he had left there, of his mother who had already died, perhaps of the pain of having seen him leave for America to fight against the King, while there his three brothers, *criollo* soldiers but Royalists all, were fighting in the armies of the King.

Mysteries of destiny! He thought of the center of ambitions which was Buenos Aires, where he had been looked at ever since his arrival with suspicion and malevolence. His wife, his only love, was there. He thought of that Army of the North which he had just left, demoralized by defeat and loose not only in discipline but also in its habits, an aggregation of badly armed, hungry, dirty, ragged men. From that mud of blood and tears the country was being molded. But suddenly, on the edge of his vision, he saw the Andes shining with snow, and the vision rose in his soul like a hope. If he could only go to Cuyo to prepare his enterprise! This was his secret, which only his good friend Rodríguez Peña knew, and which perhaps he let Guido guess during the confidences of their trip. And the inner self of his will murmured in the unfathomable abyss of his soul, "One will be what one must, or he will be nothing." Now came the Córdoba mountains, first shelf of the Andean pinnacles; and after passing through La Dormida and other inns, when the carriage reached the top of a hill the city of Córdoba, with its many spires, appeared in the valley. At last the end of his pilgrimage was in sight. Over the hills of the west the sun shone in a prodigious twilight, setting the clouds ablaze.

San Martín did not stop in Córdoba, for he wanted to be away from people. He sought refuge in a small ranch near the city. He would not lack either news or supplies there, but he would be far from the world.

From the peaks of La Punilla, the hills descend toward the plain of the city, and on the place where the Cosquín road traverses the Saldán creek, there is a height where stands the house of the estate where San Martín was a guest. The height rises sheerly from the creek, and this runs along red clay banks, which give the waters the color of blood. Looking from that tree in the shade of which the guest meditated about his destiny many times, the dark mountain is seen to one side and the endless blue horizon to the other. There is, near by, a cool and crystal-clear spring; vegetation abounds in the corners of the mountainside; the temperature is delightful in the summer. Tasty fruit and white goat-milk cheese are found everywhere. This estate, thickly populated by Indians at the time of the conquest, was given to the Miraval and the Tejeda families, the founders of Córdoba. The first Argentine poet, Don Luis de Tejeda, owned the property and he called it "my kindly Saldán" in an autobiographical ballad. Such was the place where San Martín spent the days of his illness in 1814, which passed between his withdrawal from Tucumán and his transfer to Mendoza.

Some people went to visit him there, and he also received printed matter which was sent to him by Director Posadas. The Supreme Director had received the news of his illness with consternation. He wrote him to Tucumán in March, saying: "I regret beyond words the condition of your health. It would be terrible not to find a remedy for an illness which would bring us many evils." He addressed to him several letters at his Córdoba residence, too, inquiring after his health. On July 18 he wrote:

Although you tell me that you are feeling better, all my friends assure me that you are in the worst condition in that desert; that you don't take good care of yourself; that your illness is serious and the treatment long and complicated. Why don't you want to come to your home? Why, I say, don't you go to Córdoba, which is so near, where at least you will have more help than in a country house, and will have company, which often turns out to be the chief element for recovery?

But San Martín did not want company now, he wanted solitude. He did not want even to take treatment at his home in Buenos Aires, where his wife awaited him. Like all the heroes whose mission has been sacrifice, he preferred the garden at Saldán, a Gethsemane in which he suffered, like a celibate monk, the trials of the flesh, in order to find himself and to reach the highest spiritual lights.

One day the foreman of the ranch, a Spaniard, punished a ranch hand who was American, striking him. The man complained, and San Martín told him that the Goth had done well in striking him if after three years of revolution there were still some criollos who would take such treatment.

"This is a revolution of sheep!" San Martín exclaimed with contempt.

The criollo learned his lesson and took vengeance, wounding the Spaniard with a knife. San Martín applauded the action.

On the evening of that same day he told the anecdote to some friends who came from the city to visit him. Among them was Lieutenant Paz, an officer of the Army of the North, who came from Tucumán to visit his family in Córdoba and wished to pay his respects to the sick general. Paz himself told of the strange occurrence and added that San Martín, irritated, as though he were alluding to something more than the domestic episode, repeated loudly his exclamation: "This does not seem to be a revolution of men, but one of sheep!"

What was the matter with poor San Martín in his solitude, that he was in such bad humor? The matter was simply that he thought of that Army of the North, defeated and in rags, unsheltered in the forests and in the deserted sands; and that he thought of the insurrection in Uruguay, unending; and of the defeats of American arms, from Buenos Aires to Caracas: briefly, the King had been winning since 1810. All that would end if he could organize an army like the one he wanted and cross the Andes, to crush the Royalist stronghold of Lima. But he had no health, no command, no resources: he could not even count on the faith of his countrymen.

The letters of Posadas, more friendly than official, took his mind off his worries. On July 4 he read: "Let your heart breathe: Montevideo is ours after capitulating! Carlos is there with his troops; the Navy has taken the harbor. French has brought the papers. I haven't the time to write more; you will receive the details by special mail. Recover soon and fight against the damned illness in order to be able to resist Pezuela, if, as you tell me, he is coming toward Tucumán." San Martín was happy, but then he was worried. "Carlos," who has taken Montevideo and its huge war booty, is Alvear, and he has prestige, an army, a navy. As for Pezuela . . . No! That was not the road to Peru. Peru must be reached by the west, over the Andes and over the sea. . . .

San Martín appreciated duly Alvear's feat, and in 1816 said of it: "I have seen throughout our revolution only partial efforts, except the one undertaken against Montevideo, the results of which showed what firm resolution can do." And then he added: "Let us make those efforts simultaneously, and we are free." That was his strategic theme: a continent-wide plan of simultaneous action, and enough resolution to carry it out.

On July 3 Posadas told him: "I have only the time to tell you that a few nights ago I had the honor to receive the visit of *La Gordita* [the little fat one], with Doña Tomasa, Doña María Eugenia, her father, and Don José Demaría, as well." . . . News of the family . . . Those were San Martín's father-in-law and the Escalada family, Remedios among them. San Martín was happy to hear it, but again he sank into meditation. It seemed to him, for a melancholy moment, that he was a man without love, without a home, and without a country. . . .

On July 18 Posadas wrote him: "The damned Napoleon put his foot in it at the worst possible moment: his Empire has died, and so the generations to come will not believe in history, and he has left us on the horns of the bull. I am of the opinion that our political situation has changed very much, and that consequently our future steps should also change."

Of course they had to change, but always provided that they appointed him governor of Cuyo and gave him the means to prepare the Army of the Andes in Mendoza!

From Montevideo, on July 11, 1814, Alvear, his former traveling companion on the *George Canning*, wrote him: "Fortune has favored me admirably in all my undertakings; may she be favorable to you in the same manner."

San Martín could not endure the life of inaction any more. His spirit demanded action as though it were lit by an inner fire. His black eyes shone with ardor. He walked in his room like a caged lion.

"The damned Napoleon put his foot in it at the worst possible moment."

That was the news of the abdication which reached Buenos Aires in the English periodicals. San Martín sought details in the *Gaceta Ministerial* and in the printed matter which was sent to him. The Corsican had fallen. The ephemeral work of his sword was broken down. But San Martín's would not crumble, because he gave it, for a foundation, the rock of the Andes and, for a soul, freedom, not conquest or despotism. He did not fight for his own power, but for the well-being of his America. He did not believe in glory, he believed only in sacrifice and duty. The fall of the Emperor relieved Spain: now Ferdinand VII would be able to send veteran troops to crush the American revolution. Now more than ever it was necessary to cross the Andes and go to Lima.

The old secret resounded now in his soul like a cry of obsession in a night of insomnia.

He remembered his charge at Arjonilla, Daoiz, and Solano, his action at Bailén, his march into Madrid, and the time when he found himself face to face with the Emperor, and the latter, holding the button of San Martín's tunic on which was written the name of his regiment, read out loud: *Murcia!* and looked him steadily in the eye.

The "damned Napoleon," said Posadas. Not "damned." Our war began with him. San Martín admired the military genius of Napoleon, but he did not love him, because their geniuses were different. His work was to be different.

In 1814, the year of the fall of Napoleon, a conqueror who crowned himself, San Martín had finished his initiation: he was already the master who knew what he needed to know about himself, about his liberating mission, about the American land, about the passions of men.

In September 1814 San Martín received his appointment to go to Mendoza and take charge of the governorship of Cuyo.

His feat was about to begin.

IX. MENDOZA, THE CUYAN REALM

After repeated entreaties, San Martín succeeded in having himself appointed governor of Cuyo, a post which he sought a long time. The Directory issued on August 10, 1814, a prized document, which, among other things, said:

> Whereas the authority of said province must be exercised by a chief having honesty, prudence, valor, and military ability, which qualities, together with the others that are necessary, are found in the person of Don José de San Martín . . . I have this day appointed him governor, at his request and on his application . . . with the double purpose of continuing the distinguished services which he has rendered his country and of attending to the improvement of his health in that delightful climate.

San Martín when requesting the post gave his health as the reason, but he was really impelled by the wish to be near the Chilean frontier, in order to study the Cordillera according to the plan he had secretly prepared.

Hardly had he been appointed when he went from Córdoba to Mendoza, which was the seat of the provincial government, and began to discharge his duties, as his father did when he was governor of Yapeyú, with a certain *gaucho*[1] good nature. He himself called the territory under his rule "my Cuyan realm," and for that reason his friend, Director Posadas, wrote him jovially in September of that same year, 1814: "I imagine you are resting in your Realm where you may have had a chance of eating fresh grapes." Later it will be seen how San Martín rested in Mendoza and what bitter grapes he had to swallow.

The Town Council of Mendoza had prepared lodgings for the new governor, but he, because of his unusual modesty and his wish to live near his soldiers, declined the offer at first; although later he accepted it in order not to be discourteous to the Council, which had insisted, and also because his wife was coming from Buenos Aires to live with him. The house where San Martín lived was located on the Alameda, and still stands. Close to the city, at Plumerillo, he established the army camp.

From the moment of his arrival San Martín felt like a new man in Mendoza. In order to grow deeper roots there he had Doña Remedios, his young wife, whom he still called "Remeditos," inasmuch as she was only eighteen years old, leave the Buenos Aires residence of her parents to go to him and help him win over the Mendoza society. "Remeditos' kindly disposition can be of very valuable assistance in gaining new friends," wrote old Posadas, who had known her from the time she was a child. Posadas gave the lady six hundred pesos for the voyage, a private loan which San Martín repaid later, out of his pay. She left Buenos Aires accompanied by the slave, Jesúsa, a Negro woman whom Señor Escalada had given her as a present. Also accompanying her in the same stage were her relative, Doña Encarnación Escalada de Lawson, and the Mendozans Doña Mercedes Alvarez de Segura and Don Manolito Corvalán with his wife, Doña Benita Merlo. The supplies which Doña Tomasa, her mother, had prepared, the letters of recommendation which her father got for the inns on the way, and the diligent company of those good friends made the voyage more agreeable.

The crossing from La Plata to the Andes was then a painful one: the highways could not have been worse, the plains were monotonous, and the desert really overwhelming, especially in San Luis. Once in a while a convoy of wagons, pulled by several pairs of oxen each and loaded to the top, was met on the way. Scared wild animals—hares, deer, ostriches—ran across the prairie, tempting the weapons of the travelers. At the bars in the inns men asked for or gave information on the condition of the roads. On the dangerous fords the postilion encouraged his charges with picturesque cries, and on the dusty stretches he intoned the allusive sing-song:

> A la huella, huella,
> Huella sin cesar,
> Abrase la tierra,
> Vuélvase a cerrar.
> (On the trail, on the trail,
> Always on the trail;
> Let the earth open,
> Let it close again.)

The lady from Buenos Aires was traveling across those deserts to join the paladin after a long absence. After their marriage they had enjoyed only a few months in their common home. Now Doña Remedios, close to her husband, was going to have her own house in Mendoza. It was the only long time she lived with her husband.

Señora de San Martín, once she had installed herself in her house on the Alameda, gave proof of the hospitable spirit of her paternal house. She made friends with the best ladies of Mendoza, among whom she organized a patriotic society. Her intimate friends were Doña Josefa Morales de Ruíz Huidobro, in whom San Martín placed his trust, and Doña Josefa Alvarez de Delgado, whose house adjoined San Martín's on the rear. Doña Remedios collaborated in the undertaking of her spouse, sweetening his disposition; she presided at entertainments and dances where marriages were arranged between officers of the army and young ladies of the city; she took an interest in the poor; she won the sympathies of all. She and her friends embroidered the flag of the Andes, which was carried triumphantly to Lima, and in this labor there took part, besides Doña Remedios, the Chilean Doña Dolores Prats de Huysi, and the Mendozans Laureana Ferrari, Mercedes Alvarez, and Margarita Corvalán. San Martín and his wife used to go, in the late afternoon, to a shop on the Alameda to have coffee in winter and ice cream in summer. Both were on friendly terms with all their neighbors, even with the dispossessed and the slaves. In the midst of this kindly life San Martín united all the wills for his political action.

The Cuyo jurisdiction then comprised the three present provinces of San Luis, San Juan, and Mendoza, linked to Chile since the times of their colonial origin. The post of governor carried with it military and civil duties. To both San Martín attended with equal zeal. For his administrative and political action he made use of the Town Council (Cabildo), which expressed its adherence to him from the moment of his arrival. For his military enterprise he extended his influence up to La Rioja on the north and the Neuquén frontier on the south, both being of strategical importance. His lieutenant governors were De la Rosa in San Juan and Dupuy in San Luis, both energetic patriots who co-operated loyally with San Martín. General Luzuriaga and Dr. Godoy Cruz were his right hand men in Mendoza. Governor San Martín felt happy in Mendoza despite his annoyances. He found the climate similar to that of Córdoba, and the sight of the Andes comforted him in his endeavors. Far from noisy Buenos Aires and troubled Tucumán, he felt happier in that region of simple people and magnificent fruit.

San Martín was then thirty-six; he had not yet arrived at the summit of his genius, but the figure of the peculiar and mysterious man, so misunderstood by his contemporaries, was already taking shape. Of him, the historian Gervinus was to say later:

He was a man surrounded by mystery and misunderstanding. Nobody had an accurate idea of his real talents or of his plans. The foreigners who approached him found a man of tall stature, animated—although serious—conversation, of a simple and clear language, free of coldness; of elegant, even winning, manners; with a pale face and live and penetrating eyes, which did not let one guess what was going on in his impenetrable soul. Some experienced in such degree the superiority of his intelligence that they were suspicious of him, and the truth is that with his sagacity and quickness to judge everything he knew how to show ably all the talents he possessed. On the other hand, others found that he had little education, that his notions of government were not healthy, and that he lacked the intelligence necessary for ruling men and winning their esteem.

As we progress in the tale of this life we will understand which of Gervinus' assertions were correct and which were erroneous, and we shall see lifted the mysterious veil which surrounded San Martín.

One secretary, Manuel José Amite Sarobe, and two clerks helped San Martín in his office; but he did everything himself, and theirs were only extra hands for his personal labor. Besides his military tasks he developed the city of Mendoza, whose irrigation works, streets, and habits he watched; he watched also, like a bishop, the conduct of the priests, to see that they did not deviate from their patriotic duty; as an educator, he stimulated public teaching, and to him was due the foundation of the College of Sciences and Humanities, which Don Lorenzo Guïraldes directed; he organized like a financier the public treasury, in order to increase its resources, using its income in the best manner; as a judge he passed sentence quickly on the most varied causes. His sentences in the Cuyan territory show how complex was his nature and how like the ancient patriarchs' was his rule.

A woman farmer was accused "of having spoken against her country"; San Martín sentenced her to deliver ten dozen pumpkins for the army kitchens.

A prisoner of war asked for mercy on the Feast of Our Lady of Mount Carmel; San Martín decided: "It has not been a small mercy that he has escaped with his life."

A certain recruit alleged he had sworn in Chile not to take up arms against the Spaniards. San Martín decreed: "The governor assumes the responsibility which the supplicant alleges; his hands are now free to attack the enemy; but if a ridiculous worry still binds them, they shall be unbound by the supreme penalty."

An officer gambled and lost a certain sum belonging to the army's treasury. He asked to speak with San Martín and said he was going to make a confidential report to him as a gentleman. San Martín listened to him with severity. When the confession was ended, and in view of the repentance and promises of amends made by the officer, San Martín gave him a sum to replace the loss, and added: "Deliver this money to the treasury, but keep the secret; because if *General* San Martín ever hears that you have revealed what happened, he will have you shot."

The same San Martín ordered that no officer might enter the powder factory with hobnailed boots and spurs. There was a sentry at the gate of the factory to enforce the order. One day San Martín tried to enter, violating the order, and the sentry stopped him. San Martín obeyed the sentry. He tried another time and the scene was re-enacted. San Martín withdrew humbly, put on a fatigue uniform and rope-soled canvas shoes, and returned to the factory; the sentry then let him pass, and San Martín rewarded him with an ounce of gold.

A spy for Osorio, named Mateo Alegría, was caught and sent to San Martín as a prisoner. He should have sentenced the man to death for this crime, but he relented for reasons of humanity, as he told Lieutenant Governor Dupuy when commuting the death penalty: "To Mateo Alegría, four years of forced labor, and let him be exposed to the public with a sign on his forehead reading, 'Traitor to the Fatherland and indecent friend of the tyrant Osorio.'" In this manner he wanted to warn "our ignorant peasants, who should hate such a foul crime against their own country." There was in this sentence a strange mixture of usefulness, severity, compassion, teaching, and sarcasm.

These sentences show the Cuyan Realm governed sometimes by a Sancho
Panza and at other times by a Don Quixote. Paladin and esquire are reunited
in him, as an extraordinary personage. But behind his Sancho side Don
Quixote always hid.

In 1814 the yearly revenues of Cuyo were 180,000 pesos; but after the
fall of Chile the trans-Andean trade diminished, and customs collections, an
important item of revenue, tumbled too. In the midst of this penury and of
increasing needs, San Martín had recourse to voluntary contributions and to
forced loans. He regulated social work, eliminating vagrancy, gambling, and
crime. He created the *"decuriones,"* who were precinct deputy mayors, with
ample powers to keep the order he had instituted. With the purpose of obtaining funds for the State he made a plan that was legalized by the Town
Council, which had become a sort of local legislature. He sold public lands at
auction. He appropriated abandoned assets. He sold the property of the temporal orders (monks). He sequestrated the patrimony of fugitives. He established a tax of 4 per thousand on capital, on the sworn declaration of each
individual. He confiscated the estates of Spaniards who died without leaving
any heirs. He allotted church tithes and the funds for the redemption of
captives to the service of the State. He levied taxes on wines and liquors,
applying these sums to war preparations. He organized donations in specie or
money and forced contributions, payable in installments. He used the taxes
on stamped paper[2] and barrooms, also fines. In short, he gave regularity to the
finances of the State, a greater sum to its coffers, and more certainty to its
financial calculations.

San Martín revealed himself as a real statesman in his small sphere, and an
ingenious administrator in his precarious realm. He reorganized the civil and
the military accounting, although everything depended on his will and he
handled funds for secret expenses. He made as much use of winning ways as
of coercion for getting what he needed from the people. Mumblings, resentments, and calumnies remained as a spurious offshoot of his crushing dyna-
mism, but he justified his actions by the disinterested ideal which inspired
him.

San Martín kept in his own handwriting some notebooks in which he
recorded his daily tasks. Day after day he set down his labors there, and on
reading those "memoirs" one is amazed by his capacity for details, as well as
by his prodigious mental organization. If any one of those days of 1815 is taken
—for instance, December 27—it will suffice as a sample of the rest of them.
The list is long and arid, but eloquent in its aridity.

The book says:

The 2nd class Grenadier of the 3rd, Clemente Ahumada, complains against Sublieutenant Arias, because the latter struck him when in formation.—Signs for the
laborers of the powder factory.—Call Don Clemente Godoy.—Ask San Luis whether

Don Lucas Durán has arrived there.—Tell Pescara that the 400 horses he is to send must be of the best.—Ask amount of cash in hand at the first of next month. —Tell the Town Council to advise the *decuriones* that a red flag is a danger signal, and the bicolor one of good luck.—Ask for the file on the Aldoy and Guerrero cases.—Tell the administrator to send two cases of candles to Uspallata.—The artillery proposals.—Muñoz to be set free.—See Plaza about what Cabot wants.—Ask Don Pedro Molina the price of his pistols.—His verbal communication received yesterday with date of the 22nd reports his arrival at Portillo with 100 men.— Fleytas' case.—Tell Lucas González to leave within three days for San Luis.— Letter to Hermida.—Tell the Customs to receive 10 dozen tongues from Don Domingo Torres.—Soto's papers.—Domingo Macias must pay a 50-peso fine within three days, for having stolen a poncho.—He lives in the house of Doña Petrona Cepeda, on the Plaza Nueva.—Remember the $25 given to Pizarro.—Tell P. to go to Sosa to inspect the belts and other things, and the lines.—Tell D. M. Corbalán to make an estimate of the value of the beds, camp beds, and mattresses and to report to the Government to be put in charge of this.—Tell the Customs that all the services of the Charity Hospital must be paid at the rate of 2 "reales," as per contract made by the Government with the Father Superintendent.—Note from L. González, of the Secretariat.—On Jan. 5 it was decreed that Don Manuel Sáenz be transferred to Buenos Aires, to report to the mayor, who will be notified by mail.—Tell Don Enrique Martínez that he has been ordered to the 8th.—Report it to the commander and to Buenos Aires.—Tell the colonel to have Martínez cited in the order of the day.—Call a meeting of blacksmiths and have the best horses shod.—Have Saro come here, sending a message through Major Lemos.—Send the Town Council six bags with pins and rings for padlocks for the Army Hospital.— Have a list made of all the Europeans living at Corocanto and their jurisdictions, in order to get information and act.—Tell Plaza to deliver an accounting of the ponchos given to Lemos, in order to send it to the Customs.—Alvarez C.'s commission to see the cloth factory.—Order 8 sprinklers for the camp.—Write the Town Council asking for a list of existing blocks and tackles, showing their owners, to be sent within four days.—Tell the commanders of all the units to send a list of the mules needed for carrying ammunition, 3 boxes with wine bottles and 2 with eau-de-vie. —Tell the commander of the cavalry to add 40 single men to his troops within 8 days.—Do., do. to the commander of colored, 15 men.—Tell San Luis to send 60 recruits.—Tell S. J. to increase the number of artillerymen to 30, besides increasing the effectives of the eleventh.—Tell San Luis there is one Gregorio Blanco at Río Quinto who is useful to catch deserters and vagrants. Commission him if useful. —Tell Vera to send the papers on the four bolts of cloth.—Tell Captain Vicente to come.—Write to the town council about saddle mules.—Call the Negro cook of Don Juan González tomorrow.—Ask the town council to give $20 to the police.— Also tell the council that everything gathered by the Supply Commission must be taken to the Custom House.—Send 400 goatskins to San Luis.—Ask the commercial judge to gather packing boxes from the business firms.—Tell Videla that he should deliver the saddle cloths to Plaza.—400 goatskins to San Luis, 200 white and 200 black.—Three kegs of eau-de-vie and one of wine to the commander at Chacayes.— Ask the Customs to look at the cloth in the stores and attach it, giving notice.— The jail guard to be decreased: 12 privates, 1 sergeant, 1 corporal. The hospital

guard to be one corporal and four men.—Eliminate the appropriations for Villota.
—The San Juan mules to be branded if they have not been returned to their owners, and the branding irons to be returned.—Tell Sosa to offer the Indians anything
he thinks suitable in exchange for producing Huici.—Regiments Nos. 8 and 11
to take turns in guarding the city.—Send Heras a book of the new tactics to be
delivered to O'Higgins.—Melián to be commander of Grenadiers.—Tell Mar-
celino Saavedra, of No. 11, to report.—Send Manuel Vial to No. 11 with a recommendation.—Make Heras chairman of the military commission.

This naked document is like a map which with its dots and abbreviated
lines evokes cities, mountains, and rivers. Through its stark lines we see men,
thoughts, acts, scenery, and innumerable things palpitating. Akin to that day
were seven hundred days spent by San Martín in Cuyo and as many in Chile
and Peru. The sight of those notes gives a thrill, like the footprints of the
puma which has left the imprint of its paws in the mud of the forest.

The hero carried out his task of inspiration and patience, doing the simple
chores of a major-domo, mayor, notary, artisan, inquisitor, yeoman, anything
that was necessary for his mission. Thus the breath of God is hidden in the
turf and in the ant. From these minute things he forged his greatness, in the
same way that grains of sand make a mountain. Other famous warriors have
used the materials accumulated by civilization; San Martín created in a
vacuum, and he did not let himself be carried away by brilliant but useless
dreams. In the midst of indifference, or in the midst of the desert, he obtained
everything by his own ingenuity or his creative will. A messenger spent one
month on a round trip from Mendoza to Buenos Aires. The Cuyo provinces
were poor and without any industry. Alfalfa fields, billets, money, clothing,
arms, and even men—San Martín had to produce all of this from the void.
Cuyo responded with self-denial to these claims, but he himself gave the
example. San Martín thought for everyone and provided for everything.

In the midst of so many fatigues and disappointments, San Martín inevitably weakened. He arose at dawn in order to work until noon; he lunched
standing, and his ration consisted of stew, homemade pastries, two glasses of
wine, and a cup of coffee. He smoked black cigars, to which he was very much
addicted. He took brief naps under the eaves of the roof, on a raw hide,
because this was so cool; then he arose again to continue working into the
night, and his supper was also frugal. During the day he talked and wrote,
he inspected men and animals, he examined arms, supplies, and utensils at the
encampment; sometimes he rode through the fields in order to know the land
and its people. After supper in his home he played a game of chess and at ten
o'clock he retired.

But sometimes he did not sleep. The nervous tension, the worries, the moral
disappointments, or the pains in his stomach did not let him sleep. In order to
fight insomnia, he took doses of opium, dissolving the anesthetic in a glass of
water. In January 1816 he again had a hemorrhage as he had had in Tucumán

two years before. But this misfortune did not turn him aside from his duty. And so he wrote to Godoy Cruz, a few days later:

A furious hemorrhage and the consequent extreme weakness have kept me nineteen days in bed; the bad condition of my health after that compelled me to stay more and more in my office. The attentions of the enemy and the preparations to receive him in case of invasion were the cause of my forgetting my friends. For all these circumstances I beg your indulgence.

In 1816 he wrote in several letters to Tomás Guido:

I lack time for everything; money, ditto; my health, bad; but this is the way we are pulling ahead. . . . I do not know how my head is; I am surrounded with misery; next month I cannot have a single penny to give to the Army. . . . I am in an awful confusion with so many mules, supplies, hospitals, horses, and countless other things which torment me. . . . If I succeed this time as I hope, I shall go to some corner to take care of my poor health, because this is unbearable for a sick man.

Thus the laborious days of his stay in Cuyo passed for San Martín, in the midst of physical and moral suffering. The flesh weakened, confronted by so many trials, although the spirit of the hero, tenacious and watchful, continued alive in him. Its fuel seemed to be consuming itself in that fire, but the light of it was every time more intense and his love for Mendoza ever more profound.

At the beginning of 1815 the Directory appointed him brigadier general, through a decree signed by Alvear. San Martín declined this promotion, saying he would refuse new promotions and adding: "After Spain is beaten I shall resign my rank in order to spend my sick days in retirement." His enemies pretended to see in this incomprehensible renunciation an act of astuteness or of pride; but if there was any calculation hidden in it, it is only that of suggesting that he was not impelled in his services to America by any feelings of personal ambition. Similar gestures confirmed this attitude, up to the last years of his life.

In 1816 the Town Council requested his promotion; but he protested: "The ill-intentioned will believe that I am instigating this." Consistently with what he did in Buenos Aires when he renounced one half of his salary as a colonel, in Mendoza he had given up one half of his salary as governor. As he could not keep his household with such meager resources, he decided to give it up and send his wife again to the home of her parents. The news of the trip of Doña Remedios to Buenos Aires produced great consternation among her friends, because of the love they felt for her, and among the whole neighborhood, because it was suspected that the action was taken in order to send her away from a possible Royalist invasion, which, since 1816, had threatened from Chile. The Town Council met and expressed its fears to San Martín, offering to pay him the other half of his salary, if such was the cause for his decision. San Martín rejected the offer and, in order to reassure the people in the face of the Royalist threat, decided that his wife should remain in Mendoza to run with him, and with all the Cuyans, the risks of war.

On the second year of his stay in Cuyo Doña Remedios gave birth to a girl, the first and only child of San Martín, born in Mendoza, August 24, 1816. Seven days later she was baptized with the name of Mercedes Tomasa by the army vicar Don Lorenzo Güiraldes, the same who blessed the flag of the Andes and who was later principal of a school. The godparents at the baptism were Colonel José Alvarez Condarco and Doña Josefa Álvarez. Mercedes was entered on the parochial register as "Spanish," a word which then applied to race rather than to nationality. It is significant that San Martín, son of a Spanish mother, should have his first child, born like himself on American soil, registered as a Spaniard. His daughter, as the years passed, was to play a moving role in the destiny of her father.

The birth of his daughter made him think of old age and the future of his family. Then he dreamed of owning a farm. He wanted to become a farmer, as if Don Quixote, accepting the advice of Sancho, should have decided to become a shepherd in a fictitious Arcadia. And then he sent to the Government of Mendoza an interesting document, hardly known today, which said:

It is very natural that a man should think of the condition in which he plans to spend the tired years of his old age. The condition of farmer is one that I feel to be most analogous to my nature, as a resource and a refuge against the worries and labors of my whole life, which I have devoted to the service of the Army. My scant resources have never given me the wherewithal to acquire a rural property on which to count for that old age to which I look forward; moreover, I cannot establish myself in any territory or province that enjoys peace. The Province of Cuyo is the one which has finally decided me, because of the good character of its inhabitants, to choose a corner where I could devote myself to breaking the soil, cultivating it and enjoying it. And because I myself have encouraged the development, population, and cultivation of the immense lands that stand to the north of Retamo, I am deeply attracted to them. The small space of fifty squares would fulfill my aspirations and wishes, but I cannot have them unless Your Lordship grants that they be given me as a gift.

The highest value attained by a square of land is four pesos, and that, one half cash, and one half on time, in order to find buyers, and in order that the owners may have land to cultivate, and the land an owner to take care of it. That is to say that fifty squares, which I ask as a gift, are worth only two hundred pesos. I have not got this amount, and if I had it, I would buy the land. The voluntary cession of one half of my salary has compelled me to live a frugal life, without being able to save anything, adjusting my existence to an economy which is as critical as my position with the salary which I receive.

If Your Lordship believes that said land could be given me as a gift, the deed of ownership could be made out in my name, and possession given immediately to Don José Herrera, domiciled at Los Barriales, who is entrusted, because of his ability, with the management of the lands acquired from the Government by individual purchasers.

At that time the Government of Mendoza was in the hands of Luzuriaga, who succeeded San Martín, so that the latter could devote all his attention to the military command.

The Government decided to give him the fifty squares which he asked for at El Retamo, and, besides, two hundred squares at Los Barriales to Mercedes, the infant daughter of the hero. San Martín declined this gift in the name of his daughter and suggested that those lands be kept to be given as a reward to officers of the Army of the Andes who distinguished themselves in the service of the country. The Government referred this to the provincial attorney, Ortiz, and he decided that the parents could not make use of their right of *Patria Potestas* to the detriment of their minor children, and the Government maintained its donation to Mercedes, although reserving another two hundred squares for the military rewards suggested by San Martín.

The Government resolved also to build a monument to San Martín in the rising town of Los Barriales, because he was its founder and the developer of its population and agriculture, having given the town water. The monument would consist of a pyramid built in the public square, with the following inscription engraved on the side looking toward the west: "To the virtuous hero, the most excellent Captain General of the Province, José de San Martín, First Commander in Chief of the Army of the Andes." And on the other side looking to the east, this motto: *"Multa Meruit Fecerat Ille Magis."*

Such was the origin of the Mendoza farm which San Martín spoke of so nostalgically in the last years of his exile.

In spite of the many trials, the days of his Cuyan realm were the happiest of his life. In the middle of 1816 he wrote confidentially to a friend: "The most tranquil peace reigns in this province, thanks to its good and peaceful inhabitants." He never stopped loving Mendoza, and he always remembered it in his exile, as if it were the whole of his country or something necessary in his life.

General Don Gerónimo Espejo, who had served in the Army of the Andes since 1815, records some observations on San Martín in his memoirs: He called the officers "my boys," with the affection of a father or a teacher, and he was proud of them; "never a word escaped him which could wound anyone's sensibilities"; he possessed the difficult gift of being able to speak to each man in his own language, without losing authority, even if his interlocutor were a gaucho. All believed blindly in him. To these virtues were added his physical qualities: "His eagle-like look," his handsomeness. "As good-looking on horseback as afoot," he sometimes rode the streets astride a beautiful chestnut. "His extraordinary genius for dominating men," says Espejo, "seemed to have hypnotized the people of Mendoza."

Thus was forged his earthly link with Mendoza, the anvil of the Army of the Andes, which was his glory, and the cradle of his daughter, who was his consolation. For all that, San Martín loved his Cuyan realm deeply. There, in the sufferings heroically withstood by him, ripened the enterprise which his genius had conceived. In Mendoza there began for him the second epoch of his life, and from there he undertook the heroic deed.

X. THE HERO CURSES HIS STAR

"Accursed be my star!" wrote San Martín in Mendoza, one year after his arrival.

The hero knew he had a star; but why did he curse it?

Several times, in hours of decision, he alluded to his destiny as a stellar curse. His destiny was to be his triumph in Lima or his failure in his own country. That was why he went to Cuyo, because there began the trail of his mission; but as he became more and more immersed in his enterprise enemy forces plotted against him.

When his inner self told him, "One will be what one must, or he will be nothing," it was alluding to that mission; but a cruel fate seemed to accompany him ever since he had arrived in America, and it was there, in Cuyo, that the most terrible adversities followed one another as if in concert, darkly striking at his heart, as if to break the titanic designs of the hero.

The optimism of the first days darkened suddenly, because there came bad news from Chile: The patriot revolution had just been defeated by the Spaniards.

The Chilean revolution had begun in 1810, as a repercussion of the events of Buenos Aires, and had suffered four years of external blows and internal strife. Finally the defeat of Rancagua had overthrown the patriot government; the Royalist army had resumed control, and the defeated Chileans were fleeing across the Andes to seek refuge in Cuyo. San Martín went to meet them in the mountains and offered them hospitality: O'Higgins and Carrera[1] were among them.

This was a terrible reverse for the American cause; but San Martín was not discouraged, although his plan of going to Lima by way of the Pacific had become more difficult of accomplishment with this defeat. San Martín had called Chile "America's Citadel," and it held that position in the strategical combinations of his still secret plan. With a friendly government in Chile and the country free of Royalists, the passage to Peru was greatly facilitated. Now it would be necessary, as a first step, to reconquer Chile. For this he must prepare.

For these circumstances, San Martín, who, on arriving at Mendoza, believed himself to be near a materialization of his dream, saw again the evil fate that had crossed his path ever since he returned from Spain. His plan, touched with genius, of going to Lima by the Pacific became, however, more imperative in his mind. This was his personal mission. He could not give up his enterprise. And in the midst of those adversities he called upon his will power and went on working. He was going to prepare for defense until he could undertake the offensive.

Among the refugees from Rancagua came the chieftain, Carrera, member of a stormy family composed of three brothers and Javiera, a sister with a man's will. Carrera was at the head of the government overthrown by Osorio in Chile, and he presumed to continue exercising his authority in Argentine territory. He camped with his followers on the outskirts of Mendoza, having quarreled with O'Higgins, who had also come with the refugees and who had his own followers. Both had been educated in Europe and been members of the lodges of Cádiz and London. They were sincere patriots, but of different make-up: Carrera was ambitious and arbitrary; O'Higgins, unselfish and prudent. San Martín had to choose one of the two, and he chose O'Higgins, who was to be his loyal companion on his Andean adventure.

This wise choice awakened the rancor of the Carreras, who ever afterward were ruthless enemies of San Martín. The Chileans, already split into factions, were demoralized by defeat. San Martín decided to stop this evil, and for that purpose he gave the upper hand to O'Higgins in his plans for the reconquest of Chile and the restoration of its liberty; for this purpose he disarmed Carrera and sent him a prisoner to Buenos Aires. Thereafter the Carreras lived a hazardous and evil life until they began to perish one by one, tragically. There have been calumniators who accused San Martín of being responsible for the death of those turbulent men. The truth is that Luis and Juan José Carrera were executed in Mendoza when they tried to cross into their country after the disaster of Cancha Rayada, without San Martín, who was busy with the defense of Chile, having had anything to do with the process. When José Miguel was also sacrificed, later, as a result of the political struggles in Chile, San Martín was away in Peru. These circumstances, and historical documents, clear San Martín of those calumnies; but the Carreras were his constant detractors from the time they found themselves in Cuyo with him.

This incident, the trouble with the Carreras, which happened in 1814 and was disagreeable in itself, made San Martín's life miserable and sowed the seeds of discord in Argentine-Chilean relations; but the gravest factor at the moment was the reconquest of Chile by the Royalists.

Things were going very badly for San Martín across the Andes, but the American cause was not faring any better elsewhere in the world.

In Europe the Holy Alliance's reaction, which backed Ferdinand VII, was advancing. In America the Spanish armies were crushing the revolution from

Mexico to Colombia, while reinforcements arrived in Peru, commanded by veteran generals, some of whom San Martín knew because he had been their comrade or subordinate in the Peninsular wars. In spite of the fact that the prospects were so unfavorable, it was not this that made San Martín so pessimistic that he cursed his star. He was not crushed by the obstacles inherent in war, because he knew that war consists in fighting one's enemies; therefore he countered the loss of Chile with his plan of restoration, and the Carreras' anarchy he fought by jailing the troublemaker, and the new monarchical aggressions he countered with his unbreakable resolution.

The news that General Morillo was leaving Spain at the head of a powerful expedition against the River Plate aroused in him the spirit of sacrifice, and he promoted subscriptions for defense. He signed a decree in which he said, "Let us stop being selfish. . . . To the idea of the common good and of our existence, everything must be sacrificed. . . . The lack of funds does not even allow us to take care of the most elementary things. . . . As from today our salaries are cut in half. . . . I shall measure patriotism by generosity. . . . From this moment on, luxury and comforts must make us ashamed."

In the face of those admonitions the ladies of Mendoza offered their jewels to their country. The Town Council received them in solemn session, and the ladies divested themselves of their ornaments. "Diamonds and pearls would ill fit the critical situation of our country, and before dragging the chains of a new captivity we offer our jewels on its altar." Doña María de los Remedios, the wife of San Martín, headed that donation made by the Cuyan ladies.

In November 1815 Pezuela's Royalist army defeated the Army of the North, commanded by Rondeau, at Sipe Sipe. Consternation was general. There was talk of reinforcing the border of Upper Peru with the Army of Cuyo, the only force still in being. It was believed that the cause of the Fatherland was lost, after the other defeats on the continent. San Martín gathered his officers at a banquet and gave this toast: "To the first bullet fired against the oppressors of Chile on the other side of the Andes." His words and his gesture reassured everyone.

In the spring of 1816 the danger of a Royalist invasion seemed imminent, and San Martín, who was preparing his ineluctable undertaking for the forthcoming summer, addressed the following proclamation to the people of Cuyo:

The moment is near when, the snows of the Cordillera that separates us from Chile having melted, the danger of an invasion will be present, from the side where a triumph is promised by your patriotism. Prepare yourselves for new sacrifices to avoid that risk. I have spared no fatigue, even in my hours of leisure, for your protection. It is for you to win the struggle and gain a permanent peace, in which agriculture and trade may play a part sufficient to repair the unavoidable losses of war. Neither the country nor you have anything to fear if the co-operation of the people is preceded by a great effort of unselfishness and intimate union, the foremost condition the undertaking must fulfill to be victorious. I make bold to predict it, counting on your help, under the protection of Heaven, which looks with horror upon the unjust cause of America's oppressors.

This was the word of a clever leader. The moral work of obtaining the Cuyan adhesion was already concluded, but it needed to strain the generous fiber of Cuyo in order to inspire it to give more. This was, also, the word of an inspired ascetic.

Thus could react his strong heart in the face of adversity; neither small ambitions nor selfish meditations gnawed his soul: in his life there was only one goal, and to it he went with the unconcern of a sleepwalker.

The picture could not have been any more sinister. From 1814 to 1816 everything seemed to conspire against the dreams that San Martín had when he sought the governorship of Cuyo. Dark prospects on all the horizons: in Chile, Rancagua; in Upper Peru, Sipe Sipe; in Colombia, General Morillo triumphant in the name of the King. But this was not the worst for San Martín, because it was war and he had been born for war. The worst for San Martín was the internal anarchy of the Argentine provinces and the envy of men. If his own country failed him, what would he rest his heart against? Therefore the hero cursed his star. . . .

On January 10, 1815, Alvear was elected Supreme Director of the United Provinces, replacing his uncle, Señor Posadas, who shortly before had appointed San Martín governor of Cuyo. Despite their old comradeship, relations between San Martín and Alvear were now a little strained, because of political intrigues and professional jealousy. San Martín then resigned as governor of Cuyo. Alvear appointed Colonel Don Gregorio Perdriel governor of Cuyo, and the latter immediately started for Mendoza to assume his post.

When this became known in the Cuyan capital there was something like a peaceful revolution, favorable to San Martín. More than five hundred citizens gathered in the main square on January 16; as many unarmed militiamen came to back the movement; and the prominent citizens met in Open Council (Cabildo Abierto) to express the municipal opinion, which was that San Martín continue in his position "for the tranquillity of the State and the safety of the country." San Martín attended the assembly in person in order to pacify the people and explain that he had not been dismissed and that the appointment of Perdriel had its origin in the resignation which he himself had submitted and which he read. No explanation seemed to satisfy the Council. It was in vain that San Martín counseled prudence and promised to stay in Mendoza until the winter, to defend the city if the Spanish invasion that was feared came from Chile. The Council invited San Martín to withdraw from the room because there was going to be a debate concerning him, and San Martín withdrew from the assembly. It was then resolved to appoint a representative to go to Buenos Aires and present the point of view of the province. As a result of this *démarche* the central authorities reconsidered their step; Perdriel had to go back and San Martín remained governor of Cuyo by popular demand.

Three months later, on April 3, the government presided over by Alvear fell, together with a part of the lodge and of the assembly that were his followers. The Town Council of Buenos Aires, headed by San Martín's father-in-law, expressed itself against the Director, with the backing of Colonel Alvarez Tomás and several military units. This was a revolution similar to the one in 1812 against the Triumvirate, in which Alvear and San Martín had taken a part, and, as had happened before, there was a demand for a new Congress and a new Executive freely elected by the people. The uprising of Alvarez Tomás in Buenos Aires had been backed by Rondeau in the Army of the North. When the case was submitted to the Cuyo garrisons, San Martín called his officers for consultation, and they decided to sever all links of obedience to the central government and to demand the appointment of new officials elected by the nation's will. The Town Councils of Mendoza, San Juan, and San Luis, in turn, expressed themselves in the same way and acclaimed San Martín governor of Cuyo; thus his influence on the province and on the new national order that was about to be established was consolidated.

San Martín's personal attitude in the Cuyan revolution of 1815 was conciliatory and prudent. So were his words to the Town Council, his relations with Perdriel, and his notes to the Buenos Aires government; but it is evident that his resignation was an astute move and that so were his later acts, in order to save his popular prestige in Mendoza and his official position in Cuyo, not out of thirst for power but in order to keep his plans for an expedition into Chile from being frustrated. The events of the country in general favored him; but these episodes left two bitter marks upon him: his estrangement from Alvear and the spectacle of the anarchy that was beginning to show itself and to place the revolution in danger.

Alvear, fallen from the Government, wrote from abroad in order to vindicate himself from the charges inspired by political passions, and, recalling his arrival in Buenos Aires in 1812, set forth, among other things, this obvious truth: "My first request had for an object to recommend Don José de San Martín, who had come in my company; which recommendation opened to him the door of command in his military career, notwithstanding the fact that he was a man without any acquaintances or relations in the country."

The stormy currents of the revolution, which had brought these two men together, were now separating them. The neophytes of Cádiz, the friends of London, the pilgrims of the *George Canning*, the brethren in the Lautaro Lodge, the comrades in the regiment of mounted grenadiers, and the companions in the revolution of 1812 against the Triumvirate were now in opposite camps, and doubtlessly to the sorrow of all. Alvear and his wife Doña Carmen had been, besides, best man and maid of honor at the marriage of San Martín and Doña Remedios. The services which Alvear had rendered San Martín could not be forgotten through military jealousies, and San Martín did not forget them.

From Río de Janeiro, on February 2, 1816, Alvear wrote San Martín:

I do not know the degree of resentment that you may harbor against me, because our common friends have tried incessantly to compose our differences; but, inasmuch as my conscience has nothing to reproach me with in respect to you, and I am aware of your virtues, I am impelled to write to you, my fellow countryman, and request that if you have any influence with the Buenos Aires government you try to obtain from it the return of my properties; otherwise it will be impossible to go on living and I shall have to spend the rest of my days in the most horrible misery, with an innocent family which has had the misfortune to have a father who has lost everything because of his fanaticism in making all kinds of sacrifices for a country that has repaid him with so much ingratitude. . . . It can never be an honorable thought for those provinces that foreign nations may see one of their provinces' generals, who has served them with the most ardent patriotism, at the point of dying of hunger in alien lands. Oh, my fellow countryman, what a contrast between the condition of misery in which I find myself and the condition of public thief in which my enemies pretend to believe I am!

San Martín did what Alvear asked him to do, and the latter thanked him in another letter; he thus repaid his old friend for the services rendered in 1812; but it is sure that San Martín could only measure the sufferings of his companion many years later, when the time came for him, also, to suffer similar adversities and injustices.

All these things left a wound in the soul of San Martín, when he cursed his star, because the stellar fate of heroes is that of going inevitably toward suffering. This man who did not love power or demagogic agitation or acts of force saw himself involved by fate in these distasteful things. For these reasons he was worried by the symptoms of anarchy, the consequences of which he foresaw. He said to a friend in 1815:

I die every time I hear people talk of federation.[2] Would it not be better to transfer the capital elsewhere, thus putting an end to the justified complaints of the provinces? But—federation! Can it be? If an established government and a cultured nation, well peopled by artists, farmers, and traders (I speak of the North Americans), have found difficulties during their last war with the English [War of 1812] because of a federation, what cannot happen here, where we lack those advantages? My friend, if with all our provinces and their resources we are weak, what cannot happen with each province separated and isolated? Add to this local jealousies and the conflicting interests of all of them, and you will see that this will become a den of fighting lions, and that the only one to profit thereby will be the enemy.

A den of fighting lions! Certainly: one of its beginnings was the revolution of 1815, and he was there. Perhaps that is why he suffered all the more. This seer "knew" what was going to happen, but he "knew" also what he would have to do: the epic feat in the midst of the civic tragedy. Therefore he cursed his star. He knew his sacrificial destiny; his suffering was anticipatory and clear-sighted.

In that same year 1815, beclouded by anarchy, he celebrated the reconciliation of Güemes and Rondeau, and he ordered a great ringing of church bells in Mendoza, because the internal peace among chieftains and leaders was "worth a hundred victories."

To prevent those evils San Martín had been one of the moving spirits behind the Congress that met at Tucumán. "From the Congress we expect the improvements we need," he said, "and if it does not do it, we shall resolve to carry on the Gaucho War." He expected from the Congress a declaration of independence and the consolidation of central authority, which were necessary for his Andean undertaking. Although a republican by principle, as he declared, he let himself be carried by the shifting monarchical plans then in fashion. With his acute sense of reality, he understood that those disagreements were idle because they were premature, inasmuch as the only urgent and real thing was the expedition to Chile, the only way of obtaining independence. The Cuyo deputies were his agents for presenting these ideas: Maza, Oro, Laprida, and Godoy Cruz: especially the latter, who was his correspondent in Tucumán when the Congress opened.

San Martín knew that inside his country there were many influential Argentines who did not wish him well. About these people he was kept informed by loyal correspondents. The post office brought to him with every mail printed matter and letters bearing bad news. The governor of Cuyo read everything with calm, and answered his friends thus:

To Godoy Cruz, in December 1815:

So the Cordobese are very angry with me? Patience! I had already seen this in several letters where they showed their displeasure. It is peculiar that they should have been written by men of sound judgment and knowledge, but in terms that could have made any conscience less tranquil than mine lose control of itself. Oh, my friend, how much does the liberty of this country cost to honest men! Suffice it to tell you that not in one letter, but three or four letters, the following is said: "You have there a chief whom you do not know; he is ambitious, cruel, a thief, and little to be trusted, because there are sound suspicions that he has been sent by the Spaniards; the force which he is raising so fast has no other purpose than to oppress that province and then do the same to the others." You might think that this made me angry. Well, my friend, yes, just a little. But then I called cold reflection to my help and did what Diogenes did: dived into a philosophic tub and said: "All this is necessary for the public man to suffer, so that the ship may arrive in port."

In 1816 he spoke with the tone of a stoic:

I received your two letters of January 29 and February 11 by the same mail: they tell me about the cordial hate with which I am favored by the deputies from Buenos Aires. Repetition makes masters; my heart is hardening before the shots of malevolence, and in order to become inured to them I have taken refuge behind Epictetus' maxim: *"Si l'on dit mal de toi, et qu'il soit véritable, corrige-toi: si ce sont des mensonges, ris-en."* In fine, my friend, I do not feel the shots fired against me at all, but their repetition bores the most stoic of men.

The copious correspondence exchanged between San Martín and Godoy Cruz discloses the influence the former exerted upon the calling of the Congress of Tucumán and the declaration of independence, because the bitterness of knowing that he was being harassed did not stop his political labors; he wanted the country to be organized, but this was only a preliminary condition for his plan of continental war, the only idea that kept him on foot in the midst of his illness, fatigue, and disappointments. It is significant that one of his Cuyans, Oro, from San Juan, opposed the monarchical plans at the Congress; and that another of his Cuyans, Laprida, from San Luis, presided at the session of July 9, 1816. For a long time he had been asking Congress for a declaration of independence.

He asked Godoy Cruz:

How long must we wait to declare our independence? Don't you think it is ridiculous to mint coins, have a flag and coat of arms, and make war against the very government that is supposed to rule over us? What is there to do but to say it? Besides, what international relations can we have when we act as minors under a guardian and the enemy (with perfect reason) calls us insurgents, inasmuch as we still call ourselves vassals? Be sure that nobody will help us under these conditions. Besides, the system would gain fifty per cent with this step. Courage! Great undertakings are for men of courage. Let us see clearly, my friend: if this is not done, the Congress will be invalid in all it does, inasmuch as if it assumes sovereignty, this would be an usurpation against him who believes himself the true sovereign, that is, little Ferdinand. [*Fernandito.*]

"Little Ferdinand!" That is what he called the King, as if making fun of his crown—he, the man charged with having monarchical aspirations. He knew, besides, who was that man who had been the Prince of the Asturias, because he (San Martín) was in Spain when Godoy humiliated the prince before his mother and Napoleon repeated the humiliation before Ferdinand's father.

It is interesting, in this dark period of the life of San Martín, to follow the course of the adverse events and watch the fervor with which he struggled in the shadow. We see him laboring in his Cuyan realm to recruit his army; but the mental labor with which he steered politics was not less admirable. The temper of his nature was that of a soldier, but the clarity of his vision was that of a statesman. Being an astute politician, he did make use of the latter quality for his own benefit; he counseled what was necessary so that the nation might be organized, but he knew that there would not be any established nationality so long as there were Royalists in the rest of America. This was his unchanging idea, and from it emanated his clarity and his strength. His inspired mind succeeded in bringing the unity of a system into this chaos of regions and passions. His solar spirit illumined the disorder of this earth. With justification Mitre called him "Hermes Trismegistus."[3] He is the demiurge, the orderer.

As in 1812, he fathered the Congress of 1816; he counseled a declaration of independence, which implied the obligation of going to Lima; but the work of internal building he had not yet finished. A friendly government was needed at Buenos Aires; a government to back his plans, because there was still talk in Buenos Aires of making war in Upper Peru, of campaigns in Uruguay and of the threat of a maritime expedition that might come from Cádiz against Buenos Aires. All the while the Chilean border was forgotten or neglected.

At the beginning of 1816 he wrote to Guido:

When the expedition to Chile is undertaken, it will be too late. I was convinced that it would not be done, only because I was at the head of it. A curse be on my star, which only awakens suspicions! That is why I have never expressed an opinion about it. Oh, my friend, what miserable creatures are we, bipeds without feathers!

Such an explosion of pessimism springs from the unpleasant events recorded here, and from the intrigues with which his enemies were covertly trying to hamstring him in Buenos Aires:

I knew well that as long as I was at the head of these troops not only would there be no expedition to Chile, but I would not be helped. My resignations have been repeated not so much because of my ill health but because of those reasons. *San Martín will always be a suspected man in his country.*

"Our dissensions are dragging us to our grave," he said. "At the first misunderstanding I am going to any foreign country to beg."

These are not sickly complaints. He had friends, but he also had enemies. He knew it well.

Thus arrived the moment—climactic in his life—for the election of the new Supreme Director by the Congress of Tucumán, after independence had been declared. The deputies of the north spoke about the candidacy of Belgrano, and the deputies from Buenos Aires about that of Gazcón; the candidacy of San Martín was advocated by the deputies from Cuyo, his loyal friends. In these negotiations the presence of an able politician was felt: he did not want the post, but his candidacy brought about a compromise with the men from Buenos Aires, resulting in the nomination of Pueyrredón, deputy from San

Luis. With the backing from Cuyo, Pueyrredón displaced Gazcón. As to Belgrano, he was in a fitting position at the head of the Army of the North, where he should stay. Thus Pueyrredón was elected unanimously, carrying the votes of San Martín's friends, with Godoy Cruz at their head.

Pueyrredón had been overthrown by the revolution of 1812, in which San Martín had taken part, and this fact had estranged them, naturally, but without ending their friendship.

From Tucumán, on March 4, 1816, before their interview in Córdoba, Pueyrredón wrote to San Martín, calling him "my dear friend." Later the Director called him sometimes "mon frère cheri" (my beloved brother); and this affectionate name will last forever.

Godoy Cruz, chief factor in the nomination of Pueyrredón, acting in all respects in accord with San Martín, who did not seek power for himself but for someone who would back his plans, later served to attract Pueyrredón's help for San Martín's plans. Elsewhere, Balcarce, Director *ad interim* in Buenos Aires, backed those plans, as did his minister, Guido, who wrote a report about crossing the Andes—a document considered by some as a source of inspiration for San Martín, which is inadmissible, because the document dates from 1816 and San Martín had told his plan to Rodríguez Peña in 1814. The great merit of Tomás Guido, confidant, friend, admirer, and collaborator of San Martín, was that of having contributed to the triumph of that idea in the ranks of the government, thanks to the persuasive clearness and eloquence of his presentation.

When Guido's report was sent to Director Pueyrredón the latter decided wholly in favor of the idea. He thus desisted from reorganizing the Army of the North, and he continued the war in Upper Peru only as a defensive measure, as San Martín suggested in 1814, when Pueyrredón entrusted hostilities to Güemes and agreed that it was better to create the Army of the Andes, under San Martín, in order to attack Peru by way of the sea. When the Director had agreed to all this, San Martín requested an interview through Godoy Cruz, who arranged it for the moment when Pueyrredón went from Tucumán to Buenos Aires to take charge of the Government.

"With this letter," said San Martín in one sent to Godoy Cruz on May 19, 1816, "I am sending a special note for Pueyrredón. Its only purpose is to secure an interview with him in order to arrange the plan that we must follow. Time is short. There is a lot to do and distances are great. Three mails and winter is gone, and all of a sudden summer is here." And winter is a bad season, because the mountain passes are clogged with snow.

The meeting of San Martín, the Captain of the Andes, and Pueyrredón, just elected Supreme Director of the United Provinces, took place in Córdoba on July 16, 1816, the year of Independence. San Martín explained his plan to the Director and won his approval of the undertaking, obtaining his promise of backing it up officially in order better to equip the Army of the Andes and get authorization for the crossing of the Cordillera. San Martín left for Mendoza with his heart comforted by a new hope. At last he could bless his star, after two years of hostilities and anxieties.

Thus ended the first stage of his life and began the second one. The itinerary which began with the voyage from Cádiz to Buenos Aires, by way of London, showed the following stops in Argentine territory: Retiro, San Lorenzo, Yatasto, Saldán, and Plumerillo. The man from Yapeyú had made contact with his native soil; his country knew who he was, what he was after, and how he must act. The apprenticeship of San Martín ended in Cuyo. Meanwhile he meditated in his solitude about this American land that he was beginning to know and which would be the theater of his feats. He knew now the rivers of his native place, and the pampas of Buenos Aires, and the forests of Tucumán, and the mountains of Córdoba, with their soft feminine curves; and in Cuyo he had the Andes before his eyes. He was touching the body of his homeland, not with the passion of a lover, but with the magic of a conjurer. His soul, ancient and firm as the Plutonian rock of the Andes, sought that rock, America's spine, as a foundation for his dream of glory.

PART II

(1816–1822)

𝔄𝔠𝔥𝔦𝔢𝔟𝔢𝔪𝔢𝔫𝔱

"I must follow the destiny that calls me."

—SAN MARTIN

I. THE ARMY OF THE ANDES

"THE ARMY CALLED of the Andes had for a foundation only 180 men of Battalion No. 11, without the least training and very badly disciplined. Eight months before undertaking the expedition to Chile the Government sent Battalion No. 7, with 450 men and 220 mounted grenadiers; the rest of the army was recruited in Mendoza, the patriotism and sacrifices of which are beyond all praise." This was written by San Martín in Europe, in his old age, recalling his Andean undertaking.

For a period of six months Pueyrredón fulfilled his promises made at Córdoba, sending to San Martín from Buenos Aires all the help he could muster, in spite of Argentina's poverty. In November 1816 the Supreme Director sent San Martín the last contributions, and in the midst of the good humor with which he tells him about it one senses the exhausting effects of an effort that has lasted half a year:

Besides the 4,000 blankets sent from Córdoba there go now 500 ponchos, the only ones I have been able to find. . . . The order has been given to send you the

1,000 *arrobas* of jerked beef which you request for the middle of December: it will be done. The notes of thanks to the Town Councils of yours and the other cities of Cuyo are being sent. Here go the clothes ordered, and many shirts. If by chance there should be a shortage of blankets in Córdoba, have recourse to asking for donations of blankets, ponchos or old blankets from the citizens of your city or San Juan; there is not a house that cannot deprive itself of an old blanket: it is better to beg when there is no other choice. Here go 40 saddle blankets. By separate post there go, in a small box, the only two bugles I have been able to find. In January of this year there shall be sent to you 1,387 arrobas [35,000 lbs.] of jerked beef. . . . Here go the 2,000 spare sabers you request. Here go 200 tents, and there are no more. Here goes the World. Here goes the Devil. Here goes the Flesh. I don't know how I shall ever extricate myself from the debts I have incurred for this. One of these days I shall just go bankrupt, thus canceling everybody's bills, and go over to you, so you can feed me the jerked beef I am sending you. H——! Don't ask me for anything else, if you don't want to hear that I have been found hanging from a rafter in the fort.

The Government at Buenos Aires was in a state of utmost poverty, without being able to send to the north the supplies that Belgrano requested for his soldiers in Tucumán and that Güemes asked for his men in Salta, so all of them went around half naked. There was a shortage of arms and ammunition, inasmuch as attention had to be paid to the war in Uruguay against the Spaniards and Portuguese, besides the internal quarrels. The diplomatic agents that the Government maintained in Brazil, England, and France also demanded expense money. The Treasury did not have enough to take care of all this; but a way was found to satisfy San Martín, or at least a half way, inasmuch as his plan had the approval of the Lautaro Lodge and had been accepted by the Government, on which the lodge exerted a decisive influence. Not in vain was it said that this undertaking was going to be carried out "to seal the independence of America and for the glory of the United Provinces." The sacrifice was theirs, although the feat was San Martín's.

San Martín wrote Guido something of his plan in 1816, and he himself commented: "I can hear 'my lancer' [Guido] saying, 'What a plan! Like a sergeant's!' " But he knew his plan was not like a sergeant's.

At the beginning of 1817, when the moment came for the expedition into Chile, the army which San Martín had formed in Cuyo exceeded 5,000 men, a number a little less than the effectives of the Royalist army against which he proposed to fight. The patriot army was composed of 3,000 infantrymen, 700 mounted grenadiers, 250 artillerymen, 120 engineers, and 1,200 horsemen for the transportation of supplies, besides a few for the services of nursing, technical corps, supplies, and communications. An army as complete as this for its discipline and equipment had never been seen in America, nor a more numerous one for mountain fighting.

All this recruiting was the product of San Martín's initiative, ingenuity, ability, and patience. He had to mobilize the inhabitants of a sparsely inhabited region in the midst of the disasters that struck at the revolutionary cause from abroad and at its paladin through the intrigues of internal politics. His heroic call had to instill faith in his cause among the Cuyan people and to arouse in them the will to fight in remote countries. Thus he succeeded in making a soldier of every man, instructing him personally, according to his system, in technical and moral rules, for an orderly military action. The *criollo* horsemen answered his call, and for two years he constantly increased his troops with new conscripts.

For this he used the most varied methods, and when private persuasion was of no avail he appealed to public emulation, as he did in that proclamation issued in Mendoza, in which is revealed his intuition as a leader: "I have one hundred and thirty swords in a corner of the mounted grenadiers' barracks, for lack of courageous hands to lift them." The one hundred and thirty volunteers that were needed presented themselves to take their places, leaving in their Argentine huts their families and their interests in order to follow the great paladin with whom they crossed the Andes and went, by way of the Pacific, beyond Ecuador, where some of them died fighting.

The well-born young men of Spanish descent he made officers; the gauchos, more or less cross-bred, he made mounted grenadiers; the slaves he had freed he preferred for the infantry. To the latter, at the camp of Plumerillo, in order to reach their soft spot, he used to show some papers he pretended to have received from Chile and say:

"Here I am told that if the Goths beat us they are going to sell our free Negroes in the markets of Lima. But they will not be able to sell those who know how to fight. . . ."

And in truth they fought like men, dying by the thousands at Chacabuco, at Maipú, and on the Peruvian coast, as he admitted in a letter to Miller[1] ten years later.

The Chilean refugees he sent to the ranks of the Army of the Andes, organizing them in units that were going to be the foundation for the new army of Chile, once the country had been reconquered. With them he formed the skeletons of two regiments of infantry, one of cavalry, and a battalion of artillery, and he created, besides, a flying detachment of dragoons named the "Patriotic Legion of the South." He appointed a committee of prominent Chileans, with authority to issue temporary commissions; he made O'Higgins his chief collaborator in this part of his task, thus training the future Supreme Director of the sister nation. He discovered Don José Ignacio Zenteno, a tavernkeeper who had taken refuge in Mendoza and who was called "The Philosopher" by his countrymen, and he made him his secretary, with such good judgment that Zenteno later held important public positions in his country. He made Freyre and Portus commanders of flying detachments which had for their purpose to draw the enemy to the south.

To all the Chilean émigrés he addressed a proclamation in 1816, couched in terms which moved them:

Chile, enriched with the treasures of nature, arbiter of the Pacific Ocean because of its location, well peopled and endowed with industries and easy means of communication with the bordering provinces, is almost the center of this region of America, and its restoration is going to establish the bases of our political being. Peru will fall under its influence and the continent will become unified. . . . Nothing must occupy our minds but the larger objective of universal freedom. . . . The foundation of the Chilean army will carry this task to completion.

Thus San Martín aroused the feelings of the Chilean soldiers in favor of his American plans.

There were in Cuyo some foreigners born in neutral nations, among them a hundred Englishmen, most of them refugees from Chile. He was especially interested in them, and he tried to win them over, not through proclamations but through private conversations, which was his most efficient method. San Martín admired British institutions, he knew London, he spoke English passably, and he knew how important was the commercial and naval influence of the English in Valparaiso and along the whole coast of the Pacific, where he planned to go if he won in Chile.

The names of the British residents of Cuyo have reached posterity: they were Ruch, Tuckerman, Lynch, MacGregor, Ferguson, Row, Herring, Forbes, Humphrey, Brownson, MacEachan, Wise, Smith, Martins, Holmes, Knowles, and many more. All of them saw San Martín and declared that, "being under obligation for the hospitality received and full of enthusiasm for the rights of man, they could not look with indifference upon the risks that threatened the country, and they were ready to take up arms and shed their last drop of blood, if necessary, in its defense." San Martín accepted this valiant offer and authorized the creation of a company of chasseurs, to be financed by those who enlisted in it, and he allowed the Britishers to elect their own officers.

These met on January 24, 1815, and elected John Young captain, James Lindsay second in command, and John Jefferson sublieutenant. Of course, the importance of this small unit was moral rather than military. But San Martín followed in this the opinion of Belgrano: "War must be waged not only with arms but also with public opinion." It was proposed that there should not be any foreigners in Cuyo and that the American cause should show its universality. Some of these good Englishmen left criollo descendants in our countries.

Among the Chilean émigrés there were some ebullient followers of Carrera, O'Higgins' rival. These San Martín tried to send away or keep under check.

The same he did with some Spaniards and Portuguese of whose loyalty he was not certain, either taxing or confining them. Already at the end of 1815 he had written Godoy Cruz: "About the *maturrangos*,[2] do you know that all of them have left this place and that tomorrow the bad Americans and some Portuguese will do the same? This means a clean shirt." Thus San Martín was able to cleanse public opinion in Cuyo and unify the spirit of all the inhabitants, without neglecting even the Indians of the south, melting them all in the pot of a single ideal, which was his own, until he recruited the five thousand men he needed for his army. From the plains of La Rioja on the north to the banks of the Diamante on the south, along the Cordillera, the prodigious will of the great leader disciplined the minds, distributed the forces, and prepared the invasion.

While in this work San Martín accomplished amazing feats as a politician when gathering his hosts, and as a tactician when instructing his army he was no less admirable as an honest and exacting administrator when he prepared the ammunition and the means of transportation.

The army supplies were manufactured partly in Buenos Aires and mostly in Mendoza, where San Martín established a factory which he put in charge of Padre Luis Beltrán. This curious personage was discovered by San Martín in a cell in Mendoza. He was born in Mendoza of a French father and had been a chaplain in the Army of Chile. He had taught himself mathematics, physics, and chemistry, he was a man of ingenuity, he knew the country, and he showed at the factory an inventiveness and energy that can only be compared with his patriotism. In 1816 he took off his habit, put on his uniform of colonel, and crossed the Andes with the army. He melted church bells to make guns and bullets; because there were no canteens he made water carriers from the horns of cows; he made caissons, knapsacks, shoes, saddles, horseshoes, bayonets, swords. In his shop he listened for months on end to the sound of hammers and saws, in the light of the forge. San Martín wanted the guns to go across rivers and ravines. "He wants wings for the cannon," said Beltrán, "and he shall have them." And he manufactured portable suspension bridges and invented portable sets of block and tackle which were later put to good use.

San Martín found other immediate collaborators in Mendoza. He entrusted Major José Antonio Alvarez Condarco, a Tucumanian who knew something about engineering, with the manufacture of gunpowder, taking advantage for this purpose of the waterfalls and nitrate fields of that region. He charged Major Plaza and Captain Picarte, Chileans, with the care of the arms depot, and he established a severe watch over the cleaning and custody of arms. He had the miller Tejeda, a Mendozan, install a water-powered textile mill in order to use the yarn sent from San Luis, and in this way he obtained rough cloth for army uniforms; the cloth was dyed blue and the women sewed the uniforms gratis. He placed Dr. Vera y Pintado, from

Santa Fe, in charge of military justice, with adequate ordinances. He placed medical services under Doctors Diego Parossien, an Englishman, and Zapata, a Peruvian. He put José Gregorio Lemos in charge of the scrupulous accounting of the army. In the fever of his dream San Martín squeezed all the abilities and all the resources which he found within the reach of his hand. Nobody remained inactive in Cuyo under the spur of that powerful will. Nothing was useless to his ingenuity. Were there no money and no shoes? Well, sandals and rough shoes would be made for the soldiers from the hides, that were formerly thrown away, of the cattle that were killed for the city's meat supply.

Cuyo responded generously to the appeal of San Martín, and this justifies the words with which, in 1816, he praised to the Government the sacrifices of those provinces, once the preparations for the expedition had been finished. He says:

It is admirable that a country with a small population, with no public treasury, with no trade or great capital, lacking timber and raw materials, has created an army of 3,000 men, divesting itself of even its slaves, which were the only agricultural labor; that it could meet pay rolls and supply bills, besides the expense of the émigrés; that it could establish manufacturing shops, nitrate and powder manufactories, arms shops and depots, a textile mill, barracks, and an encampment; pay for more than 3,000 horses, 7,000 mules, and innumerable heads of cattle; guard the Cordillera with these troops; and use the services of its artisans. . . . America is free! Its enemies will feel themselves defeated in the face of such solid virtues.

The virtues of poverty-stricken Cuyo were sublime; but San Martín was the animator of Cuyo. The Army of the Andes was the creation of his genius, because of the source of its origin and the watchfulness over its materialization. Teacher of the souls and artist of the wills, he labored for years on this creation of genius, and finally the sun of America illumined him with its glory.

To Alvarez Condarco he entrusted also the making of maps of the Andes. San Martín said to Alvarez Condarco, "Major, I am going to entrust you with a very delicate diplomatic mission in Chile—to President Marcó."

"I, sir?" he replied, surprised.

"Yes; but your true mission will be to inspect the roads of Los Patos and Uspallata, and make a mental map of both, without writing anything, but without forgetting a single stone."

Alvarez Condarco had an excellent topographic memory, and this explains the choice.

"I will send you through the Los Patos road, which is the longest and the most distant, and inasmuch as it is sure that as soon as you deliver the sealed envelope that you are carrying you will be unceremoniously sent back by the shortest route, which is that of Uspallata (if they do not hang you), you will then have made a round trip, and upon your return you will be able to draw me a map on paper."

Alvarez Condarco stood looking at his general in an attitude of resigned obedience.

"Go and prepare yourself, and above all keep this a secret."

The courier was ostensibly to present himself to Marcó in Santiago de Chile with the pretext of delivering to him a note from San Martín himself, in which the latter, in his capacity as governor of Cuyo, informed him that the Provinces of the Plata had just proclaimed their independence. Marcó received the note, had it burned in the public square, replied with haughtiness, and it is said that when about to sign his answer he exclaimed: "I sign with a white hand, not like San Martín, whose hand is black"—making an allusion thereby to the sunburned skin of the insurgent Argentine general.

In view of the diplomatic nature of Alvarez Condarco's mission, he was not taken prisoner but was ordered to leave Chile immediately, and with this he returned to Mendoza and there drew the maps which San Martín needed, because, as he said, "We could not go on making war like the Hottentots."

In connection with President Marcó's white hand, let the phrase not be forgotten, because San Martín, he of the dark hands, remembered it after Chacabuco.

In his files there has remained a copious documentation, which points out what was to be done every day, point by point, and gives the minutest instructions about the handling of animals and equipment, even indicating the precautions to be taken with the arms in bad weather and the cold of the Cordillera.

San Martín was not satisfied with accumulating all his material resources in the ingenious way that we already know; he also had recourse to similar methods to disconcert Marcó by the use of false information which the patriot agents supplied to the Royalists and through false letters he let fall into the hands of the Spaniards.

He told a friend not to sign his name, but to use instead the sign OOO; and he signed the same way when he did not say simply, "You know who."

When the expedition started he instructed the post-office way stations to watch the army mail, which would bear on the reverse side this sign: =O=, with the purpose of taking better care of it.

He utilized all the moral forces, without excluding the religious feeling, so efficacious among the Spanish-American peoples and so difficult to handle in politics when one does not act with accurate psychological intuition.

San Martín was born in a Catholic family and educated in the army of Christian Spain, he had lived among naïvely superstitious peoples, but at the same time he was a man of that age which was called "enlightened."

The Royalist influence of Charles III's ministers and the liberal contagion of the French Encyclopedists reached him.

In a prepared answer to José Miguel Carrera, San Martín said, "I swear before God and America," when testifying on the death of the Carreras. He swore before God and America, his two deities.

He believed in God, whom he continually invoked, and he respected the religion of his parents, but in his astute action as leader he knew how to use the Church for political purposes. He was neither clerical nor anti-clerical. His genius prevented his touching either extreme. In order to tell how far his spiritual freedom reached, let us recall two episodes.

On May 13, 1815, in Mendoza, he issued a kind of pastoral addressed "To the curates and all the other prelates," in which he ordered that the curates and priests should underline in their talks and sermons the justice with which America had adopted its liberal system; that they should "enlarge upon this matter," explaining "the legitimacy of the Government established by the general will of the people and the penalties which await the subjects who disobey it," including the clerics, who will be punished "if they do not fulfill so sacred a duty."

On another occasion, on July 5 of the same year 1815, he addressed himself to the Father Superior of San Francisco in Mendoza, advising him that the friars Agustin Muñoz, Miguel del Sar, Francisco Yares and Joaquín Corao "are opposed to the sacred cause of our political regeneration" and therefore they are "forbidden to confess and preach," besides which they must "stay in reclusion in their cloisters until further orders." The note to the prior, signed by San Martín, added: "This Government, convinced of your intense patriotism, does not doubt that this order will be faithfully complied with."

He knew that in Chile the priests preached against him. There the Royalist clergy, at the service of Marcó, called the patriots of Cuyo "detestable heretics, abortions of hell, envoys of Satan, fellows thirsty for blood and for robbery." A friar named Zapata said that he should not be called *San Martín*, because he was not a saint, but just *Martín*, like his namesake Luther, because one was as much a heretic as the other.

To regulate the doctrine of preaching and to deprive one of the right of hearing confession are acts of ecclesiastical authority. San Martín exerted that episcopal authority without any scruples. Someone then said that free America would triumph, "unless God is a Spaniard." But God was not a Spaniard, therefore San Martín believed in God.

In his urge to take advantage of all the forces which might be useful to his plan for freedom, he did not disdain the collaboration of the Indians. There were Araucanian tribes south of Mendoza, living on strategic points in the mountains. Through those southern passes he might come into contact with the Araucanians of Chile and distract the attention of the Royalist authorities.

The uprising of the Indians in order to attract them to the cause of emancipation was from the beginning one of the purposes of the Argentine Revolution. In 1810 it had already been proclaimed by Moreno at the Council and by their representative, Castelli, when he proclaimed the freedom of the aboriginal peoples, on the pre-Inca ruins of Tiahuanaco, when entering Upper Peru. Argentine proclamations, written in Quechua and Aymará, were then circulated among the peoples of the north. Belgrano addressed himself in Guaraní to the peoples of the littoral (by littoral is meant the Argentine provinces between the rivers Paraná and Uruguay and Paraguay). San Martín spoke in Araucanian to the Pampas, Pehuenches, and Mapuches who lived in the mountains south of Mendoza.

Beyond the Diamante River, at Fort San Carlos, these aborigines had been called in the name of the Government of Buenos Aires for the purpose of requesting their solidarity. The paymaster-officer Don Alexo Navarro distributed some presents to them and harangued them as follows: "Your happy posterity will not see arbitrariness and despotism reigning in our America. We and you, who have been born upon this soil where the blood of our forefathers has so many times been shed, let us be the rulers. Let us reestablish the mercy and the justice which distinguished the throne of our Incas." That feeling of historical continuity gave the War of Emancipation the character of a vindication, and in 1816 gave rise to the plan of restoring the Incas of Cuzco.

San Martín availed himself of these purposes, we do not know whether through conviction or for political reasons. Be that as it may, in September 1816 he made a trip to the banks of the Diamante and at Fort San Carlos he called the chiefs of the region with the object of holding a conference with them. More than fifty of those Indian chiefs were the lords of southern Andean valleys. Their names were, among others, Calimilla, Millatur, Antepan, Jamin, Huanguenecul, Manquepi, Peñalef, Goyco, Marilinco, Epiman, Ancai, Neyancari, Necuñan. The latter is the one who served as spokesman. He spoke Araucanian and he was, like Colocolo, an elderly man with long gray hair. The friar Ynalicán, chaplain of the converts, was San Martín's interpreter.

What San Martín had planned was an alliance with the Indians, so that they could watch the southern passes into Chile for him, and at the same time make the Royalists believe that he intended to invade Chile through that section. San Martín took from Mendoza to San Carlos several packs of mules loaded with aguardiente, wine, cloth, sweets, saddles, and glass beads to give to his new friends. The Indians celebrated his visit with bacchic festivities which lasted six days, at the end of which San Martín returned to Mendoza with the treaty of alliance he wanted. The chiefs paid special homage to San Martín, and each one of them embraced him when taking leave, amid great libations and dances, ceremonies to which San Martín lent himself resignedly.

At the end of 1816 several chieftains came to Mendoza, bringing information for San Martín, and he received them at the encampment of Plumerillo. Once the general and the chiefs sat in a circle on the ground, he told them through the interpreter Guajardo: "I have called you to tell you that the Spaniards are going to cross over from Chile with their army to kill off all the Indians and to steal their wives and children. In view of that *and as I myself am also an Indian,* I am going to finish up the Spaniards who have robbed you of the lands of your forefathers, and for that I shall cross the Andes with my army and with these cannon."

"The army maneuvered at that time with a great show and the artillery boomed constantly, which excited the Indians," says Manuel Olazábal in his memoirs. He was an eyewitness and he heard that significant phrase, "I am also an Indian."

"I must cross the Andes on the south," San Martín added; "but for that I need your permission, you are the owners of that country." He was not going by the south, but he said it to deceive Marcó, and the latter weakened his front when he divided his troops. The Araucanian plenipotentiaries, strong and naked and "smelling like horses," burst out in shouts and acclamations for the "Indian" San Martín, whom they embraced, promising to die for him.

With ingenuity and patience San Martín labored for two years in Cuyo, until, at the end of 1816, the Army of the Andes was ready with all its men and equipment. There remained then outside the barracks only the indispensable farmers, shepherds, and artisans; but the whole country was a great arms factory and encampment. Even women, children, and friars co-operated in the task of the last feverish days, on the eve of the expedition.

The Andes expedition had, at the start, more than 10,000 saddle and pack mules, 1,600 cavalry horses, and 600 live cattle, the latter to be killed on the way. All these animals walked single file through the narrow and winding paths of the mountains. San Martín and the 5,200 men who accompanied him on the crossing of the Andes went on muleback. There were other mules for replacements or loaded with war ammunition: 9,000 rounds for muskets and carbines, 2,000 rounds of cannon shot, 2,000 rounds of shrapnel, 600 shells.

The cannon had been removed from their carriages and placed on special barrows, and special implements were carried, which had been invented in Mendoza, to hoist them over the cliffs. The mules brought also the food: toasted corn flour, jerked beef both in pieces and ground with grease and red peppers, biscuits, cheese, wine, aguardiente, all of it calculated for the frugal feeding of 5,200 men for the two weeks which were estimated it would take to cross the mountains and reach the plains of Chacabuco. Food was left at the way stations in case of a retreat. Besides that, corn and oats were carried for the animals and even logs for fires, owing to the lack of vegetation on the arid Andean heights. Finally there were medical supplies and enough onions and garlic to combat the cold, the dizziness and the hemorrhages caused by the altitude. All the horses and mules had been previously sent to graze on the alfalfa fields of Cuyo for the winter and had been shod in the shops of Plumerillo. The army also had guides and runners.

When marching time came all that enormous aggregation of men, animals, and things started moving, guided by the genius San Martín and moved by his formidable will. How different that was from war on the River Plate and the littoral, where the provinces were fighting each other in a struggle for power, or from the war on the north and Upper Peru, weakened by shortsightedness and defeat! This war of Cuyo and the Andes was going to be carried out with mathematical precision, as coherent in its disciplinary spirit as in its martial instruments. For that San Martín had had maps made of the mountains; he had learned from the horsemen and the guides the smallest details of the terrain; he had adapted his historical plan to geographic conditions; he had undermined civilian morale in Chile by means of secret agents; he had thrown the enemy front out of joint by false reports about the possible points of attack, carrying out an ingenious underground war against the Royalist chief, Marcó, who became morally and materially disorganized.

Everything was ready for the "let's go," as San Martín said, when he gave the last touch to the preliminaries of his undertaking: an appeal to esthetic and religious feelings, which are as many parts of patriotism, being a collective emotion. For this he ranged the Army of the Andes at the encampment of Plumerillo; the army in dress uniform entered through the canyon of the city of Mendoza, with its general at the head; it marched up to the church through streets adorned with flowers, banners, hangings, and national flags; it proclaimed the Virgin patroness of the army, as Belgrano had done in Tucumán; and then in the main square, before the soldiers and the people, San Martín raised the flag of the Andes to invite an oath of allegiance.

The flag, which had been embroidered by San Martín's wife and the ladies of Mendoza, was white and light blue with a coat of arms between a branch of laurel and an olive branch and with two hands lifting the Phrygian cap above the Andean crest, with a rising sun above the emblem. When the multitude saw the flag raised by the paladin, it fell into a deep silence. San Martín, from a platform and bareheaded, raising in his hand the flag that he proposed to carry to Lima, exclaimed in his powerful voice: "Soldiers: This is the first independent flag to be blessed in America."

San Martín waved the flag three times, as it was caressed by the breeze of the near-by Andes.

The people and the troops then cried, "Long live our country!" And San Martín added laconically, "Soldiers: Swear to die in the defense of this flag as I swear it!"

"We swear it!" answered a chorus of ten thousand voices.

The blasts from the cannon, the cries of the multitude, the pealing of all the bells filled the air from the city to the mountains with a clamor that had not been heard since the Andes were created by the fire and the water of primeval cataclysms.

In the afternoon of that same day there was a festivity with a bull fight and sports, and in the evening there was a dance. Both events took place in the main square. In the bull fight groups of Indians, gauchos, "Moors," and Negroes took part, duly made up and costumed and on horseback. San Martín attended both events with his wife; and when he saw them taking part so enthusiastically in that bull fight he said of his officers, "Our country needs these madmen."

A young officer threw a bull in the arena; he castrated it with his knife and offered the "prize" to Doña Remedios. She, with justifiable modesty, was embarrassed; but San Martín, who was with her in the box, asked her to accept the present. The lady received it blushingly.

The laborious year of 1816 had come to an end. The following year, an afternoon in January, there arrived at the house of Soler, in Santiago de Chile, an itinerant vendor who entered the courtyard and called out loudly, "I have fat chickens, landlord!"

The owner of the house came to the courtyard immediately, leaving his wife and later returning to her, saying he had bought some chickens.

A year later Soler's son, who tells the anecdote, learned that the itinerant vendor was a disguised spy of San Martín's, sent by the latter from Mendoza on the eve of the march to the Andes. Together with the chickens, the messenger had delivered to Soler a little note from San Martín, saying, "January 15. Brother S.: I am sending through Los Patos 4,000 pesos; within one month brother José will be with you."

This was one of "brother José's" frequent tricks; and you know already that those 4,000 were not pesos but soldiers.

A few days later the Army of the Andes began its march from Mendoza, bound for the Cordillera.

II.   WHAT THE ACONCAGUA SAW

The first days of 1817 found Mendoza in the midst of feverish agitation, as it did all the towns and highways of the Cuyo region. With the thaws there came the propitious season, although no one knew the hour or the direction of the march. San Martín, with his usual reserve, jealously kept even this last phase of his old "secret."

In front of the Cordillera, which can be seen from Mendoza, the never-sleeping hero had written Guido the year before: "What does not let me sleep is not the opposition of the enemy, but the crossing of these immense mountains." The moment had now come to cross the Andes, and San Martín could not and would not sleep. The whole population seemed to be possessed of his own watchful spirit.

Troops and arms were ready, and the mule packs and oxcarts now went through the streets with supplies. Wine, aguardiente, jerked beef, toasted corn, wood, maté made up the principal part of the loads. Children went from door to door collecting blankets, clean rags, and whatever could be useful for bandages or for the cold of the mountains. Families went to Plumerillo to talk with their relatives and share the emotions of those last hours before the parting. Mules and horses were brought from near-by pastures. A nondescript confusion of all the people, friars, children, and women, boiled in the homes and in the streets.

San Martín had worked for two years to build his war machine, and now the moment had come to move it. His indefatigable thought, his painstaking will, controlled the popular excitement. The Andes, to the west, were waiting for him, with either victory or defeat. His destiny and that of America were, at last, to be decided.

The passes known to be usable along a front of 140 leagues were: Los Patos in the valley of Putaendo; Uspallata, in the valley of Aconcagua; Portillo, in San Gabriel; Las Damas, in Colchagua; and Planchón, in Talca. San Martín studied all of them minutely, and he knew that "each one of them has such narrow passages that fifty men, in a defective fortification, are enough to defend them." San Martín went with O'Higgins, the general staff, and the vanguard through Los Patos, while Las Heras followed, with his division by way of Uspallata, and Cabot went through the San Juan passes to Coquimbo, in the north. The Indians of the south, toward Malargüe, deceived the enemy with false news, and the latter knew nothing definite about the strategic plans of the invader.

When San Martín left Mendoza to go into the Andes he was dressed in his blue grenadier uniform, with a curved sword at his left and a bicorned hat with an Argentine rosette. He had lined his tunic with beaver skins, and he carried a large cloak for protection against the cold of the mountains. A peon carried medicines and other supplies in his saddlebags for the chief, who was almost always ill.

Thus prepared, the leader of the Andes said farewell to his wife and his little daughter. The farewell of the Cid, in San Pedro de Cardeña, when he left his wife and his daughters, was not any more sober.

Both heroes suffered from the separation "as when a nail is torn from the flesh," as the ancient song says. San Martín's wife and daughter left for Buenos Aires shortly afterward. Mercedes, San Martín's daughter, was not yet six months old when the hero left her in the arms of her mother.

San Martín mounted his mule, which was saddled, according to Chilean custom, with wooden stirrups called "trunks." He was wearing black boots with bronze spurs, and he spurred the mount that was to take him to the mountain of his dream.

He went through farms, vineyards, and alfalfa fields until he entered a rocky country, and finally he made for Uspallata along the undulating trail, having dropped the reins of his mount. The mule, watchful-eyed and cautious of step, went on towards the west, while the horseman, with the eye of a strategist and an artist, looked around at the great cliffs and snow-covered peaks far away. He was thoughtful, pensive. There was something in that flag of the distant landscape of white snows and blue skies. The summer sun gave the air a comforting warmth. His aides and some servants rode in a file behind him. Ahead of them went the *criollo* Estay, his faithful guide.

Says San Martín in some notes which he wrote in exile, at the request of Miller (cf. supra):

The difficulty that had to be overcome in the crossing of the mountains can only be imagined by those who have actually gone through it. The chief difficulties were the lack of population and roads, the lack of game, and especially of pastures. The army had 10,600 saddle and pack mules, 1,600 horses, and 700 head of cattle, and despite the most scrupulous care there arrived in Chile only 4,300 mules and 511 horses in very bad condition. The rest either died or were rendered useless during the crossing of the mountains. Two six-inch howitzers and ten four-inch field pieces, which went through Uspallata, were transported by 500 wheeled carriages, although a great part of the way they had to be carried by hand, with the help of block and tackle, when reaching the higher peaks. Food supplies for the twenty days the march was to last were taken on muleback, inasmuch as there was no house or town between Mendoza and Chile by way of Uspallata, and five mountain ranges had to be crossed. The greater part of the army suffered from lack of oxygen, as a result of which several soldiers died, besides others who succumbed to the intense cold. Everyone was convinced that the obstacles which had been overcome did not leave the slightest hope for a retreat but, on the other hand, there reigned a great confidence among the ranks, which carried out their tasks heroically, in the midst of keen rivalry among the different units.

This was the mountain (Aconcagua) which did not let him sleep for two years, and into the bosom of which he was now penetrating like a sleepwalker. Thorny brush and yellowish herbs were the only vegetation of that desolate region. Mountain upon mountain, a river of broken rocks and volcanic ashes, and the 21,000-feet-high Aconcagua, with its snow-covered top shining above the heights, such was the spectacle that the eye beheld. Snow-covered mountainsides and glaciers shone at a great distance from each other, and impetuous torrents ran among the rocks. A prodigious transparency was in the air; in the distance, the earth of a thousand hues, molded by fire and water, simulated gigantic cathedrals and legendary monsters. The paladin could have imagined that he was going to the Sacred Mountain through a land of prophetic dragons.

"I have hardly started and already it seems to me that I am far away," could have said San Martín, as Parsifal says when he goes through the Sacred Mountain.

"So you see, my son, here time becomes space," his inner self would have answered, as Gurnamanz says to Parsifal, in the dark heart of the rock.

And if the pilgrim asked for the Grail, the veiled inner self would answer: "This is not said; but if thou art also one of the elect thou shalt know who it is. There is no material road that leads to Him, and those whom He does not guide shall not be able to recognize Him."

So San Martín went dipping into his own inner illumination as he penetrated into the mountain, identifying himself with it.

Beyond Uspallata, on the north, nature becomes ever more desolate. The hero's path crossed the Los Patos River near Carrizal, and from Manantiales, next to the mountain of La Ramada, it turned toward the southwest alongside the Volcán River, going toward the high peaks of the frontier. When reaching this point, in the hollow of Valle Hermoso, a hailstorm stopped the daring traveler, who sought refuge in a cave.

There San Martín dismounted from his mule; he untied the knot of the handkerchief with which he had improvised a head covering to protect himself from the bitter wind of the mountains; he took off his sword, and without removing either his cape or his boots, he threw himself on the ground to sleep, using the Andean rocks as a pillow. Tired by the march and by so many hours of sleeplessness, he fell into a deep sleep. He had been dreaming for a long time, but now he was sleeping in the bosom of his mountain as he had slept on his mother's lap when he was a child.

The Andes are the spine of America, a geological backbone of the two continents, from Alaska to the Straits of Magellan, passing through Panama. The hero of America slept on the millenary rock, and he himself seemed like a rock. The mystery of the mountain penetrated his spirit, filling it with a great telluric silence. In his dream the body of San Martín became one with that of all the continental land, and one might say that it had become stone. His dream was like a mystic passage to the land of the Grail, whence he came to serve men. That was the peak of his itinerary and the eve of his feat. Time and space fused forever in his will.

On awakening from his dream, San Martín called his assistant, Quintana, to have a drink of Mendoza aguardiente, because the cold was increasing, being six degrees below zero (centigrade), and he needed to warm his frozen flesh. He then lighted a cigar and remained pensive, looking at the formidable panorama of the mountains, among which the snow-capped Aconcagua stood out. After a brief silence he ordered the band of the vanguard to play the Argentine national anthem, whose solemn notes resounded for the first time in those heights. The hailstorm had already passed. The sky was limpid. A few condors then appeared, flying majestically above the border peaks. And the paladin resumed his march toward Chile, weighted with his own greatness, as if he already foresaw what the poet was to sing to him later:

> *Thy name shall not perish,*
> *Nor shall one day Thy cry*
> *Of battle cease to resound,*
> *While a single rock remains in the Andes*
> *And a single condor on its forbidding peaks.*

Meanwhile, through various breaks in the Andes, San Martín's legions were descending toward Chacabuco, a pre-established point of concentration. They had ascended from Mendoza to the heights, as the condors do, and now they had come down from the peaks to the plain, as the torrents do. Those who swarmed through a canyon, led by Las Heras, had arrived at Santa Rosa; those who surged from another with Soler and from still another with O'Higgins, were converging, alert-eyed, upon the theater of the forthcoming feat. The Chileans of the legion wept at the sight of their beautiful homeland.

From a gulch San Martín saw the rocky landscape; he pored over the maps that Alvarez Condarco, his Tucumanian cartographer, had drawn for him; he listened to the advice of his guide, the Chilean Estay; he heard the news brought to him by an able spy, disguised as a *roto* (poverty-stricken peasant of Chile), who came from Santiago with information about the enemy. The Spaniard, Marcó, was in Santiago, in utter confusion; he knew that guerrilla warfare had broken out in the mountains and that the invaders were pouring through the valleys. "Run to the field," said President Marcó to his troops, in a proclamation. "If my presence is necessary, I shall be there." But at the same time he was preparing to flee to Valparaiso. On the other hand, General Rafael Maroto, commander of the ferocious Talavera Regiment, famous in Spain, had come to Chacabuco to cut the insurgents off, accompanied by the intrepid Elorreaga and the cruel San Bruno. With them were also, besides the Talavera Regiment, the volunteers of Chiloé, the carabineers of Abascal, the dragoons of Penco, the cavalry of Colonel Altero; two thousand veterans in all. The Spanish plan was to occupy the mountainside which runs from the Andes to the Pacific coast and then to launch an assault upon the invader.

San Martín listened to the reports, consulted the maps, looked at the landscape, recounted his troops, gave his orders. In the ranch house on the plain was the enemy's general headquarters: the house would have to be attacked. San Martín had dismounted from his Mendozan mule and now rode his battle horse, and, in the words of the old Spanish ballad,

> *He has abandoned a mule*
> *And now he rides on a horse.*

Near him were the flag of the Andes and his staff. Besides O'Higgins and Soler there had already arrived his brother-in-law, Manuel Escalada; Alvarado, Zapiola, Necochea Melián, Ramallo, Guido, Suárez, Martínez, Mansilla, and other officers.

The General of the Andes called a war council.

At the moment the young officer, Manuel Olazábal, approached the chief, and the latter, in a paternal accent, asked him:

"How do we feel about tomorrow?"

"Perfectly well, as always, sir."

"Well, bear down on the tinware [meaning the swords] until the *matuchos* [Spaniards] are crushed."

It was February 11, and he had made his calculations for giving battle on the 14th; but thought it better to do it sooner, before the enemy concentrated more troops. The patriots were two thousand men, ready to die; the rest of the artillery had not arrived yet, and some cannons were needed. It did not matter. At dawn on the twelfth day they came down on the plain. Two roads led to the Chacabuco ranch: one, at the left, through which Soler descended, preceded by the battalion of chasseurs; and another on the right formerly called the Cuesta Vieja (Old Hillside) and thenceforward "Of the Cuyans," through which went O'Higgins, the great Chilean and good friend of the Cuyans.

The whole field is a labyrinth of hillocks cut by torrents and forests of soapbark trees (quillai), which impeded or hid the marches. The enemy forces were camped on the plain, expecting a battle. San Martín's plan was to threaten them frontally and to attack them on the flanks, at the same time surrounding their rear guard in order to cut their retreat. Each man received seventy cartridges; the combatants had got rid of their knapsacks; the units were cleverly articulated, according to the plan of attack, which was adapted to the terrain. At midnight they began to come down the mountainside; cavalry patrols explored the forest and prepared ambushes. It was a moonlit night: toward the Argentine east the Andes shone in their whiteness like specters. In the darkness of the plain a few yellow lights glowed in the enemy camp. The whole mountainside was alive with warriors marching to the points of attack with careful step. San Martín watched from the eminence with his condorlike eyes. He was suffering from his old ailments;

he had pains and he was tired out and feverish; he was soon to be forty years old: he was not any more the young swordsman of Arjonilla, but a wise chief who directed the action of everyone. He had to fight now with his intelligence, not with his hands.

At dawn on February 12 the battle began. Drums, bugle calls, and the galloping of horses resounded in the mountains. The sun lighted the whole scene. There were many partial encounters. Along the hillside infantrymen and horsemen poured down, amidst the crackling of musketry and the flashing of swords. The fight spread flaming to the whole valley. Who was that man who commanded more than a thousand men and who in disregard of the plans attacked the enemy with complete temerity? The Chilean O'Higgins, who had been defeated at Rancagua and who during the twenty-six hours of that fatal battle had sworn to reconquer his homeland, and who now saw it "after three years of prayers addressed to heaven for the mercy of seeing it again." San Martín, realizing O'Higgins' danger, gave an order to Condarco, nervously shouting to him: "Run and tell Soler to charge immediately against the enemy flank!"

The right wing, under Soler, debouched upon the valley. The fight continued without quarter. The afternoon now began. Cannon were silenced at one point. Escalada and Zapiola rolled back the enemy cavalry on the right and on the left. The grenadiers hacked down artillerymen and captured cannon. The infantrymen charged with their bayonets and assaulted enemy positions. The Royalists formed a square on the plains for a desperate final resistance, but the enveloping attack of the patriots crushed them. The greater part of the Spaniards tried to retreat, but Soler, on the rear, closed the road to Santiago to them. At the height of the struggle San Martín himself, although he was ill, charged in person and joined the fight sword in hand.

In the midst of the confusion, the last squads, who had taken refuge in the ranch house, fought hand to hand in the vineyards and olive groves.

Night began to fall. The courageous Elorreaga had been killed in the morning, and in the afternoon, near the end of the fight, Marquelli, another Spanish chief, also died. The Spaniards had lost five hundred dead, and among the bodies there were some with their heads split by the swords of the grenadiers: "If any Spaniard resists, split his head like a pumpkin," San Martín had taught them at Retiro, five years before. This they did, as they had learned the lesson. The patriots had lost only twelve dead and 120 wounded. At the end of the action, with the Royalists defeated, there remained six hundred prisoners, the artillery, the ammunition, the armament, one standard, and two flags. Victory was complete and in accordance with the plan which San Martín had prepared in Cuyo. Nothing failed in his calculations.

On the night of the triumph San Martín slept in the ranch house of

Chacabuco, and the next day he sent his brother-in-law, Manuel Escalada, colonel of the grenadiers, to take the report on the battle to the Government in Buenos Aires. Escalada recrossed the Andes and arrived at the Argentine capital on February 26, bringing, besides the good tidings, a flag taken from the Royalists. The emissary entered the city at three o'clock in the afternoon and delivered the trophy to Director Pueyrredón, who was waiting for him at the fort, accompanied by many prominent personages. At six o'clock on the same day the Royalist flag was taken from the fort to the bishopric, escorted by battalions, patricians and people, amid the firing of guns, pealing of bells, and acclamations of the multitude. The flag was then publicly exhibited at the Cabildo. A portrait of San Martín, crowned by a Winged Victory, was illuminated at night in the Plaza de la Revolución. In these festivities homage was paid to "Worthy Cuyo" and to the "Hero of the Andes." The name of the latter was continually acclaimed in the streets. Such was the public enthusiasm in Buenos Aires after Chacabuco that nothing seemed to remain of the suspicions of those who thought San Martín a secret agent of the Spanish Government.

"Yesterday was a day of madness for these people," Pueyrredón told San Martín, speaking about the impression caused in Buenos Aires by the news from Chacabuco.

The poets of Buenos Aires celebrated the victory then, as they would do later with others of the San Martinian epic.

On being attacked by the forces of Cuyo, Marcó had asked Pezuela to exert pressure on the front of Upper Peru, to compensate for the pressure of the patriots on the front of Chile. La Serna did something along these lines, and when this became known in Buenos Aires the Supreme Director wrote to San Martín: "La Serna has advanced on Salta. I wish he would come down to Tucumán. His purpose, in my opinion, is only that of diverting the attention of the gauchos, sacking that town and then withdrawing to the interior of Peru." San Martín had not been wrong in his conception of a continental plan, because his movements in Chile, as in Peru later, were going to have repercussions on the southern Peruvian border, where Güemes and his gauchos were fighting, and on the northern borders, where Bolívar was fighting at the head of his legions.

Meanwhile, at Chacabuco, after the battle, the bodies were burned on the field, and a great pyre rose toward the sky. Once this Vedic rite was performed, San Martín galloped to Santiago, only a few hours away, and entered the Chilean capital incognito.

General Marcó, when hearing about the defeat, had tried to flee to Valparaiso, but he was arrested by the patriots, brought to the capital and into the presence of San Martín, who was waiting for the prisoner at the palace. San Martín offered him his hand, saying: "Señor General, let me shake that white hand."

This phrase was a sarcasm, because San Martín knew that Marcó, when signing a note addressed to him, had said the year before, "I sign with a white hand, not like San Martín, whose hand is black." We know that he was alluding to the color of the hero born in Yapeyú, and to the legend that he was either Indian or half-breed.

After that greeting, San Martín entered with Marcó into an adjacent room, where they conferred at length.

The legend tells that the defeated one offered his sword to the victor, but that the latter refused to take it, saying with ironical courtesy, "Let that foil remain on the belt of Your Excellency, Señor General, because that is the place where it could least hurt me." After the conference San Martín took leave from Marcó with due courtesy, and not with the contemptuous gestures which the gossip of the times invented; finally he ordered that Marcó be sent to Mendoza and from there to San Luis, with other prisoners of war.

"Marcó escaped several times when he was a prisoner of the French," said Pueyrredón, and he advised that the former be held at San Luis, where in 1819 he took part in an attempt at escape which failed tragically.

As to the independence of Chile, due to the genius of San Martín, it would be better to repeat the words of O'Higgins when he was elected Supreme Director after Chacabúco and said to his people: "Our friends, the sons of the provinces of the River Plate, have just regained for us the freedom that had been taken from us by the tyrants." And in a communication to the foreign nations, he spoke thus:

The Kingdom of Chile has been restored by the arms of the United Provinces of the River Plate, under the orders of General San Martín. . . . Chile announces a new refuge in these countries for the industry, the friendship, and all the citizens of the globe. . . . The wisdom and the resources of the neighboring Argentine nation, which has decided our emancipation, warrant the hope of a prosperous and happy future for these regions.

It was in vain, in the face of such testimony, that selfish regional passions tried to belittle the merit, the generosity, and the transcendence of the magnificent effort. It was in San Martín's destiny to suffer injustices which even to this day live in the school texts of the nations which he served with his sword.

San Martín had instructions from the Argentine Government to respect Chilean sovereignty; his was not a new war of conquest, but a fraternal campaign of liberation.

Speaking about the reconquest of Chile, begun at Chacabuco, Viceroy Pezuela of Peru said, when explaining his withdrawal from command, that San Martín's campaign "changed entirely the state of things, gave the dissidents comfortable places to control the Pacific, and changed the theater of war for attacking Spanish power at its foundation."

About the crossing of the Andes, which had its ending at Chacabuco, Francisco Manrique wrote in the *Memorial de Artillería,* of Madrid, in 1853:

In this march, as well as in those of Napoleon and Suvarof through the Alps and that of Perosylki through the deserts of Touraine, there is ratified once again the idea that an army may face all kinds of sufferings if a solid and true military discipline is rooted in its ranks, as it should be. It is not possible to carry out any great undertaking without order, a great love for the service, and a blind confidence in the leader. San Martín showed himself worthy of being at the head of such a daring enterprise.

He could have conducted his campaign like a madman, on the Bolivarian model that others prefer, letting men die like dice which fall from the cup; but that was not his style. Courage was not in him a Dionysian intoxication; nor was his soul insensible to the death of his soldiers. His Pythagorean genius prepared his machinery intelligently, and he used his troops as a weapon of precision.

This was what the Aconcagua saw, and this was the importance of Chacabuco, the outcome of the crossing of the Andes; a victory which gave back freedom to Chile and was also the beginning of a more vast continental undertaking.

San Martín, when reporting his victory, summed it up with classical brevity: "To the Army of the Andes belongs the glory of saying: In twenty-four days we have carried out the campaign; we have crossed the highest mountains in the world, put an end to the tyrants, and given freedom to Chile."

III.   AFTER CHACABUCO

One of Marcó's most bloodthirsty lieutenants was the Spaniard San Bruno, who was taken prisoner at Chacabuco. This man had acquired a sinister fame for his cruelty in the persecution of the patriots after Rancagua. It was said of him that, among other insults and tortures, he had mutilated defenseless prisoners. When the patriots took him prisoner they sent him from Chacabuco to Santiago, with his hands bound, riding a mule backwards. When he reached the city "the populace threw rocks, mud, and filth at him," according to the chronicler, Haigh, an Englishman who witnessed the events. He was first thrown into a dungeon and a few days later "sentenced to death for murder and taken to the gallows in a large basket tied on the back of a horse, for the transportation of coal or similar things.

San Bruno cried like a baby, revealing "that imbecility peculiar to people of his ilk, comparable only to their cowardice." When on his way to the gallows the crowd attacked him again. "His face was a horrible mask, because the populace had gouged one of his eyes out, and it was blood-covered. . . . When the executioner tore off his bandage he let out a cry of agony, which only awakened the contempt of the multitude. . . . He was hanged in the morning and taken down at sunset."

This episode of collective vengeance must have impressed San Martín. He had seen the face of the Gorgon in Cádiz, when his chief, General Solano, was murdered, and he saw it again in Santiago, when the populace wreaked vengeance upon San Bruno. Whatever there is of the infernal in human passions was repugnant to San Martín's harmonious spirit.

After the cruel impressions of the war, the patriots engaged in celebrating the victory.

The sons of the Chilean gentleman Don José Enrique Rosales (exiled by Marcó to the Island of Juan Fernández as a punishment for his patriotism), decided to make a celebration in the home of the exile, in honor of San Martín and his victors of Chacabuco. Awnings for the courtyards and hangings for the dance were improvised from ships' sails brought from Valparaiso; chandeliers were made with bunches of bayonets, their tips down, and holding tallow candles in their rings. Transparent drawings alluding to the occasion and painted by the artist, Dueñas, were placed on the doors and windows opening on the two great courtyards. Flower arches were placed at the entrance, where two cannon fired salutes during the festivities. An improvised table, covered with a cloth with frayed edges, held heavy silver tableware and porcelains from China, which British merchants brought sometimes across the Pacific.

When dinnertime came there was a parade of "roast turkeys with gilded heads and with flags in their beaks, suckling pigs, stuffed, with oranges in their snouts, hams from Chiloé, almonds prepared by the nuns, custards and other sweets. Sliced cold roast pork, pickled onions, and olives stuffed with red pepper stimulated the thirst for Santiago's *chacolí*. Concepción's *asoleado,* and some Spanish wines."

The Chilean ladies attended the ball with flowers in their hair, all of them wearing Phrygian caps and the Argentine colors. Among the gentlemen the officers were outstanding, and the Chileans—O'Higgins, Zenteno, Calderón, Freyre—talked fraternally with their "Cuyan" friends Guido, Soler, Quintana, Las Heras, Plaza, Alvarado, Lavalle, Conde, Zapiola, Necochea, Melián, and so many more, some of whom married in Chile.

In that atmosphere of soldiers and ladies San Martín was the object of the general admiration and enthusiasm. At the beginning of the dance there was a 21-gun salute, which shook the building. Then, in the midst of a religious silence, the Argentine national anthem was sung in chorus (there was not a Chilean anthem yet), and the hero of the Andes joined his martial voice to the feminine ones of the chorus. Dancing then began and minuets, *contredanses,* and other tunes were followed with enthusiasm. The youthful élan of the couples contrasted with the melancholy gaiety of a few elder people, who remembered the cruelties of San Bruno in the midst of the celebrations.

The noise was all-pervading, and San Martín was thinking about the silence of the recent Andean nights, about the vision of the Aconcagua, about the eve of the battle that was now being celebrated. Toasts were drunk and San Martín, standing near the table, proposed a toast that electrified everyone. When he was about to raise his glass to his lips he asked, addressing himself to Señor Soler, the son-in-law of the absent landlord, "May I, Soler?" The latter, who understood the question, replied, "That glass and everything there is on the table is to be broken."

And San Martín, after drinking his toast, smashed his glass on the floor so that no one could later desecrate it with a vow different from the one that had been drunk to the freedom of America.

After Chacabuco, the victor had said in a proclamation, "We should not expect anything from what has been done; the United Army must proceed with its undertaking." Words which recall those of Napoleon's, after his crossing the Alps and his victory over Italy: "You have not done anything, inasmuch as you still have something to do."

After the crossing of the Andes and the restoration of Chile's freedom, San Martín did not lie down to sleep on his laurels; on the contrary, he redoubled his efforts to continue his liberating campaign across the Pacific. As in Cuyo he prepared the first phase of his plan, in Santiago he devoted himself to preparing the second phase, not less audacious and difficult.

The victor of Chacabuco having been elected ruler of Chile, he declined, faithful to his spirit of political self-denial. O'Higgins was then elected Director of his homeland, and San Martín retained the military command, in order to organize a united army with Argentinians and Chileans, which he proposed to take to Peru by sea. With this purpose he established an arsenal, shops, and a camp for the training of new recruits, while at the same time he set the basis for a future navy; and he created, finally, in agreement with O'Higgins, a Lautaro Lodge as a secret instrument for local politics and for his forthcoming maritime undertaking.

He had before created a Lautaro Lodge (cf. Chapter V, Part I) in Mendoza. In 1816 that center was already working, organized by San Martín, with O'Higgins, Zenteno, Godoy Cruz, and others. When the Army of the Andes crossed over into Chile the Santiago lodge called a meeting of the principal leaders of both countries. San Martín's correspondence of those years with Pueyrredón, Guido, and O'Higgins is full of symbolic signs and veiled allusions to the secret society ("Mathematical Establishment" or "Our Friends"), telling about the development of his military and political tasks, within the framework of the San Martinian plan for the liberation of the continent.

A few days after Chacabuco, while the victory celebration was still going on in Santiago and hostilities against the remainder of the Royalist Army continued in the south of Chile, San Martín was eating his lunch, standing, as was his custom, in the kitchen of his Chilean residence, when he suddenly said to his aide, O'Brien: "O'Brien, we are leaving tomorrow for Buenos Aires; with just what we have on, of course."

That is to say, they were going on a military mission and would return immediately; and this they did, accompanied by the guide, Estay.

Before leaving Chile for Buenos Aires, San Martín learned that the city of Santiago had voted him 10,000 pesos for the expenses of his trip. San Martín refused the present and gave the money "for the creation of a public library, which should perpetuate the memory of the municipality." Thus he showed himself doubly generous, because he did not do it as a memorial to himself. "Education and the encouragement of learning," he says in his note announcing the donation, "is the master key which opens the doors of abundance and makes peoples happy: I wish that everyone should learn the sacred rights which make up the conscience of free men." This master knew well that the sword is not enough to liberate peoples.

San Martín left Santiago, leaving the Chileans well impressed with his refusal of the ruling place that was offered him and with the donation of the money that was voted him. His disinterest, his achievement, and his friendship with O'Higgins insured popular sympathy for him. Prospects were good in that respect at the moment of undertaking his trip.

He stopped at Mendoza a few days, to accept congratulations for the victory that had been prepared there, and in turn congratulating Cuyo, which had been the forge of his victorious arms. After a brief rest he resumed the hard and long journey through the pampas to the east. That voyage was in itself a sacrifice.

After leaving Mendoza, and stopping at Alto de Coria, he halted at the village of El Retamo, where the customs guards used to inspect travelers' baggage. The way stations of Arroyo de Chacón, Las Catitas, La Dormida, Corocorte, and Corral de Cuero were located some ten leagues from each other, and some of them were miserable huts. The worst part was "the crossing," before reaching San Luis, and on that part of the voyage many horses were used, which were brought along for the purpose of changing mounts frequently. Beyond San Luis, on the way to Buenos Aires, the new stations of Río Quinto, El Morro, El Portezuelo, Achiras, Barranquita, and Alto del Molle were aggregations of huts where horses were changed; somebody played the guitar, and people ate, danced, or slept, according to the hour of arrival. The stages of the trip were estimated beforehand, and in order to take advantage of daylight, travelers were on their way before dawn. The places had picturesque names: the Corral of the Cliffs, Lucas' Canyon, Medrano's Corner, Three Crosses, and so on up to Dead Friar. In these half-savage regions the alarm was often given that Indians and raiders were about.

In the zone near Buenos Aires one had to pass through Arroyo de Pavón, Arroyo del Medio, Ramallo, Fontezuela, Arrecifes, Chacras de Ayala, and Arroyo de López before arriving at the garrison town of Luján and crossing Puente de Márquez, near Buenos Aires.

Through this painful route San Martín came from the Andes to the Plata —long and hard days of travel across a land without trees or towns. On those deserts was to be built later the imaginary republic for which San Martín, the knight-errant, was fighting.

The traveler entered Buenos Aires incognito; but after his arrival and against his will homage was paid him for his recent victory.

A few days before his brother-in-law, Escalada, had arrived with a report and the trophies from Chacabuco, so that the Government, as well as the people and the poets, paid tribute to the victor.

The Government of Buenos Aires notified him that he had been promoted to brigadier general; but San Martín declined the promotion twice:

I consider myself more than enough rewarded with having deserved approval for the service that I have rendered; it is the only reward which can satisfy the heart of a man who does not aspire to anything else. Long ago I gave my word solemnly that I would not accept any rank or military or political position; for this reason I hope that Your Excellency will not compromise my honor before the people, and that you will not attribute my returning this appointment to excessive pride, and you may be certain that in the discharge of the duties with which I have been entrusted I will gladly sacrifice my life in the service of my country.

The hero of the resignations was beginning to disconcert his contemporaries, because this was not the first one nor was it going to be the last.

As it was necessary, in order to fulfill a public wish, to reward him in some way, a life pension of six hundred pesos a year was decreed for his daughter, little Mercedes, and this was done because the father had not the right to decline it. With this pension he was to defray, years later, the education of the girl, in the painful circumstances which will be eventually described. For himself, on the other hand, he accepted only a special coat of arms which the Government granted him, with this legend: "The country, at Chacabuco, to the victor of the Andes and liberator of Chile." This praise was enough for the heart of the man who was not after official rewards and did not accept bureaucratic promotions.

Of course, despite his modesty, San Martín could not entirely avoid other demonstrations: a dance, a banquet, and a popular parade.

The unpublished memoirs of Beruti contain a brief impression of those triumphal days and record a typical and peculiar gesture of our hero:

The municipality and the people took pains to express their gratitude to their liberator. . . . Exterior lighting of buildings, distribution of refreshments, parties, *vivas*, pyramids, triumphal arches, and the purest enthusiasm have been the nature of the demonstrations which General San Martín has received of the love and veneration which we all have for him. The streets through which he was to pass were hung with decorations by the neighbors, and in the main street was erected a magnificent triumphal arch with four sides, under which, when San Martín passed, four girls dressed as Fame placed upon his head a crown of flowers, as a symbol of the homage with which he was being received; and San Martìn instantly removed it from his head and kept on going.

That was the severe and almost discourteous gesture which repeated in diverse forms all along his triumphal career: "He removed the crown forthwith and he kept on going." Thus Beruti, the naïve chronicler, relates the incident.

On April 9, 1817, the Town Council entertained San Martín in the salon of the Consulate. "It was one of the most brilliant entertainments that have ever taken place in Buenos Aires," according to *El Censor*. Besides the Supreme Director, the most distinguished persons, both native and foreign, attended. The festivities lasted from three-thirty in the afternoon until ten o'clock at night. According to the report, "Magnificence and good taste competed with each other at the table." Toasts were drunk to the country and to the advancement of liberal principles.

After the official part of the festivities, the promotions and the honors were concluded, in which San Martín was very little interested, he devoted himself in his conversations with the Supreme Director, the congressmen, and the members of the Lautaro Lodge, to obtain the resources he had come to seek. His plan for a united army and maritime co-operation made it necessary to consider the need for the Peruvian undertaking and to study the danger of the Spanish expedition still threatening from Cádiz. In turn, Director Pueyrredón pointed out the dangers of Argentine anarchy and of war in Uruguay and suggested that Chile should also make an effort, because the sacrifices made by Buenos Aires had been many, and the Government was extremely poor.

San Martín wrote O'Higgins in those days:

The future is clear and the circumstances favorable; the country demands it [the Peruvian undertaking] for its freedom, and fortune is smiling upon us. It is necessary, then, to take advantage of it, carrying our arms to the heart of Peru. . . . The first thing to do is to move the army with safety, and this cannot be done without a naval force of five corvettes, no less, well equipped and armed; but money is needed for this. See whether 300,000 pesos can be obtained in Chile. We have estimated that this will be sufficient for the armament and crews. The expedition should be at those ports in October or November, and there is no time to lose. If this plan does not succeed I shall never expose the army to be annihilated by two or three warships which Lima will send out in order to prevent this evil, which is the greatest that may threaten its existence.

At last, after numerous letters and lengthy conversations, San Martín succeeded in convincing everyone, both in Chile and in Buenos Aires. The

Chilean-Argentine Alliance was concluded: the Chilean Zañartu came from Santiago to Buenos Aires as a special ambassador, and the Argentine Guido went with San Martín to Santiago in a similar position; a united army for both countries was created, and the needed navy was co-operatively formed. Once this had been obtained, San Martín returned to Chile, satisfied with his success, although saddened because he had had to leave his wife, Doña Remedios, ill at the home of her parents.

San Martín, who after Chacabuco had entered Santiago incognito, could not avoid popular demonstrations on his return from Buenos Aires in 1817. A great crowd, both on horseback and afoot, went to meet him at the outskirts of the city. Thus he crossed the stone bridge over the Mapocho River, and he was compelled to go to his lodgings in a coach, passing under triumphal arches made of palms, with Argentine flags decorating the way.

In those days the Government of Chile made him the object of new demonstrations.

Inasmuch as he had refused the 10,000 pesos which Santiago had presented him, this body insisted in showing its gratitude, "in view of the labors and sacrifices with which General José de San Martín had recovered the freedom of Chile," and it gave him a farm near Santiago, "which he made use of as a place for rest in the midst of his tasks." This time he had accepted the present, not for those purposes but for others which were quite different: that one part of its produce be given to the women's hospital and the other be used for defraying expenses of a vaccinator, to combat smallpox. Thus the hero maintained his line of disinterest and charity.

The Chilean State made him a present of a set of silver tableware and voted him a salary of 6,000 pesos per year: San Martín returned the present and declined the salary. The Government insisted on its decision and San Martín insisted on his renunciation. The Government said that it was "a supreme order" and that he must submit to it "because of his personal needs and for the decorum of his position," because "his frugality will appear to the foreigners not as Spartan virtue but as censurable poverty." San Martín answered, as a Spartan, about the silverware, "These are not times for such luxuries," and about the salary, "The State is in a condition of need, and it is necessary that we all contribute to remedying it." He asked the Government to keep his attitude confidential and not to make it known to the public; a request which excluded any intention of seeking popularity on the part of this sincerely virtuous man.

San Martín lived austerely in Chile. Lodging in the old Episcopal Palace, his furniture was scarce and his table was frugal; with an excessive modesty he saved even on his own dress. At the beginning he had the oilcloth changed on his bicorned hat and he had the lining of his campaign cloak changed by the same tailor who turned his long-worn tunic.

A Royalist, wishing to flatter the victor, presented to the latter's tailor a length of cloth for a new tunic for San Martín; but San Martín became indignant and ordered the tailor to make eight frock coats for the sycophantic Royalist, and ordered the latter "to put on a new coat every day and show up in front of the palace and bow deeply at his window."

Save on exceptional occasions or on evenings when there was a game of cards or chess, San Martín went to bed at ten, at the end of a day that began very early in the morning. He started work at five; he received his secretary, arranged his notes, looked after the army administration, inspected even the seams of uniforms, and granted audience to women and soldiers. In the early evening he took a walk through the Alameda and along the waterworks. A monk would not have lived differently.

At his residence he kept a state dining room for his officers and visitors, but he ate standing in the kitchen, at his own time, frugally. Table expense was generally very light, and Friar Juan Antonio Bauzán, his chaplain, kept a detailed account of the household bills, in revealing documents that history has examined with amazement, in view of the little that Chile had to pay for entertaining the hero:

At four o'clock in the morning he used to rise from his portable campaign bed, and he himself prepared his military coffee. His breakfast was very light. At one o'clock in the afternoon he had his only heavy meal, in the kitchen, in soldierly conversation with his Negro cook, choosing two dishes which he washed down with a couple of glasses of the wine of his beloved Mendoza. His favorite dish was roast beef. . . .

At four in the afternoon the state dinner was served, at his expense, on which he spent ten pesos a day and at which Don Tomás Guido, his intimate friend and roommate, presided. He used to appear at the end of the meal to have his coffee, and on these occasions he behaved in a comradely manner, telling jokes and anecdotes, which he seasoned with the Andalusian spice of his days spent at Cádiz.

Such was the man whom his enemies were to describe as a sybarite, a glutton, and a drunkard. "He did not love pleasures, nor wine, nor the delights of mysterious passions," says the witness, "although he liked to see other people enjoy themselves, and understood that gaiety, and the social cordiality of banquets and dances, are simple means for ruling men." Therefore he sometimes gave parties in his own residence, where there was dancing, although for reasons related to the war.

In October 1817 San Martín wrote to Viceroy Pezuela, of Lima, suggesting an exchange of prisoners:

I am sure that Your Excellency's humanity will lighten the horrors of the present war as much as it is in your power to do. I offer Your Excellency to do so myself, and we both shall have the pleasure of having done some good to our fellow men. . . . Our personal affections have nothing to do with our public position, and a fatal destiny makes us enemies without knowing each other. I shall only be a foe in battle.

Commodore Bowles, a friend and admirer of San Martín's, took from Valparaiso, on the British Navy's frigate *Amphion,* the Argentine commissioner Domingo Torres, an army major, who was the bearer of the letter in which the victor of Chacabuco proposed such humanitarian measures to the viceroy.

This commander of a British ship, who served him on this occasion, was entertained by San Martín at a party, about which Haigh, the English traveler, related the following:

That night General San Martín gave a great dance in honor of Commodore Bowles, British Commander in the Pacific, whose frigate *Amphion* was at anchor in the Bay of Valparaiso. All the Englishmen residing in Santiago attended the ball. The courtyard of the Cabildo had been decorated for this purpose with intertwined flags of Argentina and Chile. Multicolored lamps and crystal chandeliers lighted the awning-covered courtyard and the ballrooms. That evening I was introduced to General San Martín by Mr. Richard Price, and I was deeply impressed by the appearance of this Hannibal of the Andes.

He is tall and well built and has an extremely military appearance; his face is very expressive, of a dark olive color; his hair is black and he wears long sideburns, but no mustache; his large and black eyes have a fire and liveliness that would make them remarkable under any circumstance. He is very gentlemanly in his demeanor, and although I saw him talking with the greatest ease and affability with those around him, he received me with much cordiality, as he is very friendly to the English nation.

The gathering was most brilliant, composed of all the first-rank people in Santiago, as well as of all the higher officers of the Army; hundreds gave themselves to the pleasure of the waltz, and general contentment was visible on all the faces. To be so suddenly removed from the lonesome mountain that I had just crossed in a horrible voyage to this gathering of gentlemen and beauties of the capital, in the midst of civilization and elegance, seemed to me a thing of magic.

Frank, easy-mannered, and charming, San Martín, in the flower of his years, reigned in the salons and was the most notable figure, present everywhere, as he was in the army encampments.

Those parties of San Martín's were inexpensive, according to the record of the costs: "two pesos, which were given to the man who played the guitar an evening when there was a gay dance." At those gatherings, toward 1819, the beautiful Lady Cochrane, wife of the newly arrived Admiral,[1] triumphed with her beauty and her dress; but the ladies, in general, dressed modestly. When a Chilean lady once showed up more expensively dressed than ordinarily, San Martín made a reference to this wastefulness, although without being discourteous, and she answered: "You are surprised at luxury because you have become accustomed to the poverty of the women of Mendoza."

Although San Martín was in Chile without his wife (she was ill in Buenos Aires, at the home of her parents), no gossip has remained in Chile about any love affairs of the hero; if he did have any, he hid them in a dignified manner. The Argentine officers who lived nearest him married Chilean ladies, as did Las Heras and Guido. No erotic legends are known even of Monteagudo, and not because Chilean women were not charming. Monteagudo, a recalcitrant bachelor, was introduced by San Martín to a Chilean lady to whom the former paid special attention during the evening, and when San Martín asked her what she thought of him she smilingly replied, "He is very charming, but he has the eyes of a highwayman." The anecdotes that have remained concerning those parties are never any more spicy than that.

Dances like the one given in honor of Bowles were not frequent, nor was San Martín's life a continuous festivity. In three years he crossed the Andes seven times and went to Buenos Aires twice, going 5,000 kilometers across the pampas each time. To this were added the illness of his wife and the worries about his daughter. Under such conditions he fought battles, organized armies, ruled peoples, and suffered calumnies, but the light of his ideal never darkened in the face of poverty and anarchy.

The last months of 1817, on his return from Buenos Aires, and the first few months of 1818 he dedicated to organizing the United Army and to continuing his negotiations for the creation of a navy.

It was indispensable, so as not to lose the advantage of the new victory, to undertake an offensive against the coasts of Peru. The eyes of the hero were still looking at the sea. The sea, and not the mountain, was what did not let him sleep now.

Before San Martín's victories in Chile, the Buenos Aires Government had given Admiral William Brown letters of marque. Brown's flotilla left the River Plate and harassed the Pacific coast from Mocha Island to Colombia, disturbing the Spaniards, who until then had been masters of these seas.

After Chacabuco a start was made toward the creation of the first Chilean navy, under the command of the Argentinian Blanco Encalada, who was a naval officer. That fleet, gathered with many sacrifices, was composed of the brigantine *Aguila,* which was renamed *Pueyrredón;* the frigate *Lautaro,* formerly *Windham;* the corvette *Chacabuco,* formerly *Coquimbo;* and the brigantine *Columbus,* bought from the United States and renamed *Araucano.* Valparaiso was the base of operations, and an academy for midshipmen was established there, in order to train personnel. It was difficult to obtain crews, because the Pacific corsairs offered better pay, with the added prospect of rich prizes. In spite of the fact that his fleet was weak, Blanco Encalada left for the south with 1,220 men to fight the Spanish ships anchored there. Off Talcahuano he boarded and took the *María Isabel,* and at Valdivia he took two transports. He returned with his booty to the port of Valparaiso, where he was enthusiastically received. The Chilean Senate ratified this reception and granted him several honors. The *María Isabel* was renamed *O'Higgins,* and it became one of the important ships of the infant navy.

Meanwhile, San Martín, during his stay in Buenos Aires in 1817, had arranged with the Argentine Government for the purchase of other ships for the expedition which was being prepared in the Pacific. Alvarez Condarco was sent to London to buy some vessels, and a similar mission was entrusted to Don Manuel Hermenegildo Aguirre, who was to contract for ships and crews in the United States. As a result of these negotiations the *Cumberland* came from England. "Possession of the *Cumberland* is interesting, but where shall we find sailors for her crew?" asks Pueyrredón of San Martín on the arrival of this ship. The *Cumberland* joined the navy with the name of *San Martín,* and sailors were found to man her. On board this vessel the general of the same name was to go from Valparaiso on his liberating expedition.

At last there arrived in Buenos Aires from the United States the corvette *Curiatius,* which joined the fleet with the name of *Independencia.* A second corvette, the *Horatius,* sent by Aguirre, could not be paid for according to the terms of the contract, and her owner, Skinner, who had brought her to Buenos Aires, sold her to Brazil.

Alvarez Condarco's mission gave rise to calumnies against San Martín. It was said that San Martín had appropriated 100,000 pesos, which his friend was to deposit in London at Condarco's order. It has been made clear that San Martín did not give him 100,000 pesos, but 29,500, of which 25,000 belonged to the Government of Chile, and only 3,000 to San Martín and 1,500 to Alvarez Condarco himself, who, when drawing his contracts in England, had spread the rumor in London that he had 100,000 pesos, in order to interest shipowners.

This infamous calumny was one of the first to be circulated against San Martín in reference to his private honesty. Worse ones still were to bring him bitterness later.

About 1815 José Miguel Carrera (exiled from Mendoza to Buenos Aires by San Martín) had gone to the United States with the purpose of chartering, for his own account, some ships, in order to go to the coast of Chile and reconquer the Government which he had lost at Rancagua. With the help of the American consul Poinsett[2] and Commodore Porter,[3] he was introduced to President Madison, from whom he got nothing, and later to the shipowners, Davey and Didier, with whom he contracted for four ships to be paid for in Chile. The Spanish consul then sued him criminally, and Carrera fled to the River Plate on the *Grifton,* which was one of the vessels he had contracted for. In Buenos Aires, where he arrived in February 1817, he learned of the reconquest of Chile by San Martín, and heard that O'Higgins, his rival in 1814, was now governing his country. In spite of this, he talked of going to Chile and landing in the south to harass O'Higgins. It became necessary to arrest him. José Miguel was in jail when San Martín arrived in Buenos Aires. He still resented the incident of 1814 in Mendoza, when, after Rancagua, San Martín found himself compelled to send him prisoner to Buenos Aires. In 1817 fortune was still against the Chilean leader, favoring instead the Argentine victor.

When San Martín left Buenos Aires to return to Chile, José Miguel Carrera escaped from jail and took refuge in Montevideo, where he continued conspiring under the protection of the Portuguese Lecor. There he published, in *El Hurón* and other sheets, bitter attacks against San Martín, Pueyrredón, and O'Higgins. As Carrera could not pay for the *Grifton,* the Buenos Aires Government bought her and sent her to Valparaiso, for the Chilean Navy. This new failure of José Miguel's, and of his brothers who helped him in the undertaking (with Javiera, his sister, who was as restless as they), was a new reason for his hate of San Martín and an incentive for new anarchical adventures, until 1821, when José Miguel died tragically, as his brothers had died in 1818.

While the lowest passions were libeling him and general poverty impeded his maritime plans, San Martín was handling from Chile a subtle underground work in Peru, through secret agents and propaganda leaflets; a master work of patience and ingenuity, in preparation for his forthcoming undertaking.

Already in 1817, soon after his victory at Chacabuco, he had commissioned Major Domingo Torres, an Argentine, to go to Lima as an envoy, but really with a secret mission of gathering information about the forces of the viceroy and to promote the revolutionary plotting. Several revolutionary attempts had failed in Peru, some of them, like the one at Cuzco in 1814, promoted from the northern part of Argentina. Torres entered into negotiations with Peruvian patriots, among them Riva Agüero, Quirós, López Aldana, and others; he gathered his information; he arranged for liaison work and for the secret code for the correspondence along the coast. A woman, Doña Brígida Silva, was a romantic intermediary in those intrigues. Later new characters played a part: José García and Francisco Fernández Paredes (Peruvians), who used the pseudonyms of Cario and Mario in their letters to San Martín. Alvarez Jonte silently kept this machine working, from off the coast, on board a navy schooner.

From Chile, San Martín managed this complicated plot; he furnished resources, instructions, and plans, and he handled men with the dexterity of a genius. He explained to Cario and Mario in order to instruct them in their roles:

> Every popular conspiracy has three difficult moments: that of preparation, which may suffer from imprudence; that of execution, which may suffer from weakness; and that of the aftermath, which may suffer from an unwise overconfidence. Consequently only the wisest and most courageous people, operating secretly, should ever direct a plan of revolution.

His instructions often show this psychological understanding and verbal precision. The control over his own agents and over the means of communication to escape the enemy's watchfulness was no less able; and in 1819 the

Peruvian conscience, thus awakened and organized, was anxiously awaiting a liberating expedition.

More exhausting were the personal labors to which San Martín devoted himself in Chile for the preparation of the United Army whose fate shall be seen later on.

This life of work and worries continued to undermine San Martín's health. He wrote to Godoy Cruz:

My health continues in a very bad condition. I know the remedy for it: it is tranquillity. But my extraordinary situation makes me an unfortunate victim of circumstances. There is no philosophy when one sees oneself on the way to the grave, with the discouragement of knowing it and not being able to remedy it.

This was written by the man who won battles and danced in salons. Hemorrhages and gastric pains (as in Tucumán, Córdoba, and Mendoza) still tortured him. "The pressure of business," said Guido, "which burdens the general, doubles his work, and with his physical strength diminished by violent attacks, the dangers which threaten such a valuable life are increasing every moment." And so it was, because San Martín's body had had to resist for two years the fatigues of the march and the sufferings of the altitude in his crossings of the mountains, his emotions and labors of war, his worries about Chilean-Argentine politics, and his anxiety to march into Peru as soon as possible. Inasmuch as he had not the means which he needed, he traveled and labored to have them; and in the midst of these sufferings the surgeon Zapata prescribed for him a double dose of opium in order to alleviate his pains.

Young Manuel A. Pueyrredón, who lived with him in Chile at the time of Maipú, related the following:

In the days when I was lodging at his house, I had taken it upon myself to go to his room every day at seven o'clock to say good morning. As soon as I had complied with this duty, he would give me the key of a chest which he had in the room and ask me to fetch him a small glass containing medicine, which was thick and greenish and which he drank in one gulp.

Guido, a witness of this suffering and heroic life during the years of the Chilean epic, gave new data about illnesses and remedies:

Besides an almost chronic ailment which tortured him every day, he suffered once in a while from very acute attacks of arthritis, which, by impeding the movement of his right wrist, made it impossible for him to write. His physician, Dr. Zapata, took painstaking care of him, but unfortunately induced him to make an excessive use of opium. This was carried to the point that, this drug having become, in the judgment of the patient, indispensable for his life, he closed his ears to the urgings of his friends, who endeavored to make him abandon this narcotic (many times I myself took away the little tubes containing it), and he did not pay any heed to the noxious effect of the drug, which slowly but steadily undermined his physique and threatened his morale.

A letter from Director Pueyrredón to Guido in 1817, when the victor of Chacabuco came to Buenos Aires to organize his expedition to Peru, said:

We have spent a few good days with San Martín and other friends at my farm. I have tried insistently to persuade San Martín to cease using opium, but to no avail, because he tells me that he is sure to die if he abandons it; however, he promises me that he will only take it when he feels fatigued.

Thus he took the drug to stave off death, and he promised not to take it except when fatigue overcame him; and as if this misfortune of the ill man were not enough, his enemies invented the version that what he took was alcohol, and they called him a drunkard, publicly, as they also called him a murderer and a thief.

In the midst of so much suffering, pessimism invaded his soul at last. He wrote to Godoy Cruz, his good Cuyan friend:

I force myself to continue living in this country. In the midst of its beauties, everything in it is repulsive to me. The men, especially, are of a nature which does not agree with my principles, and here I live in a continuous ill-humor, which corrodes my sad existence.

The Chilean revolution was undermined by the "Carrerista" (the reference is to the Carrera family; cf. supra) passions; local rivalries gave rise to small disputes; O'Higgins had fought with Soler and Guido; some Chileans looked with misgivings upon Monteagudo and Quintana. San Martín had to solve these quarrels with patience, and he always solved them properly, but with much private distaste, all the more bitter because he must hide it.

Above all he had to seek funds to organize the United Army and to create a navy to go to Peru; but he felt weak, and at that hour of disgust he exclaimed, "Two months of tranquillity among the virtuous people of Mendoza would give my life back to me." Just an illusion of despair! Undoubtedly he forgot how much he had suffered in Mendoza, and he did not know how much he was going to suffer in Peru, where his destiny was leading him.

IV. THE EPIC OF CHILE, CANCHA RAYADA

The expansion of San Martín's genius continued in 1817, ostensibly widening toward the rest of America, which it reached in its entirety, following his old plans. The whole continent was now, from one sea to the other, under his strategical eye.

The vision which in 1817 animated the acts of the hero is the one that San

Martín had announced confidentially to Rodríguez Peña in 1814, three years before Chacabuco. In 1816 he had communicated it with the same secrecy to the Supreme Director, Pueyrredón, at their meeting in Córdoba. Through his private correspondence with Godoy Cruz and Tomás Guido we can ascertain that these friends also had known it for some time, at least in its general outlines, if not in its strategical details. The San Martinian plan consisted in going to Lima by the seacoast, in order to attack Spanish power at its center. The conquest had begun in Peru; there the colonial system should end (meaning, of course, the Spanish rule in South America). Since 1810 other peripheric regions had been fighting against Spain, while Peru continued being her stronghold. But in the plan of going to Peru, the crossing of the Andes and the reconquest of Chile were only one stage of the journey.

That initial stage, which seemed chimeric at the beginning, had just been consummated. The second was now to come, and San Martín was assiduously planning for it. Such a plan required many resources; but both the provinces of the River Plate and Chile had been impoverished by eight years of war. San Martín won over O'Higgins, Chile's Supreme Director, as he had won over Pueyrredón, Supreme Director of Argentina, so that both peoples, allied, could carry out the final effort. Therefore, the astuteness and tenacity of the hero were to tie in a single unit, for the common sacrifice, these sister nations.

This vision of genius encompassed the Pacific and the Atlantic, swept across the Andes, connecting the harbor population of Buenos Aires with the harbor population of Valparaiso, and linked in a common brotherhood, under the Lautaro Lodge, the Government of Buenos Aires and that of Santiago, making of the whole a single unit brought together by the will of the visionary paladin. Concord was needed to transform the Argentine Army of the Andes into the United Army of Chileans and Argentinians, and money was needed to arm a navy capable of defending the coasts against the expedition with which Spain was threatening from Cádiz in the Atlantic, and also to overthrow the viceroy of Peru, by fighting him from the Pacific. In the framework of the geographical unity of the continent and of the colonial system, San Martín's conception was inspired, because it fitted in with the historical and territorial reality of America. San Martín was great in conceiving this idea, but he was greater in carrying it out.

It has been said with justice that he Americanized the Argentine revolution, and it would be equally just to say that his patriotism was American. He looked with pain upon the regional jealousies of the new states, because he conceived America as a whole, harmonious in its differences. What to him was easy was, in the selfish eyes of others, a great obstacle. That is why his undertaking compelled him to use so many means of ingenuity and patience in order to harmonize the wills of others and place them in the service of his sweeping plan.

Bolívar had a similar vision, but after San Martín: the former had not yet

left Colombia, when San Martín, who was going from Buenos Aires, arrived
in Peru after having crossed the Andes before any other American warrior,
and after having restored liberty to Chile. The American vision of Bolívar
was, besides, of an imperialistic type, while the San Martinian undertaking
respected the autonomy of each people: he went to Chile with an Argentine
flag and with democratic instructions from his Government; to Peru he went
with a Chilean flag and instructions from the Government of Chile; in Peru
he founded a new nation, giving it its own flag. To arrive at those results, an
inspired vision was not enough: a strategic plan, political ability, and financial
resources were necessary. For that, after Chacabuco, San Martín had to recross
the Andes in order personally to remove the obstacles which were delaying
the execution of his plan between both seas.

The victory of Chacabuco and the restoration of Chile by San Martín had
repercussions in Lima emotionally in proportion to the magnitude of the
Spanish disaster. The fugitives who succeeded in saving themselves at the time
of Marcó's downfall brought to Peru the first news of the Royalist debacle.
The fear that the liberating invasion would continue its march to the Pacific,
transferring the theater of war to the Peruvian coasts, gave birth, as a desperate effort of reaction, to a plan for the reconquest of the Chilean territory.
The viceroy of Lima, Don Joaquín de la Pezuela, raised for this purpose a
powerful army of five thousand men, which he placed under the command of
his son-in-law, General Mariano Osorio, who, in case of victory, was to take
over the Government of Chile and apply a severe punishment to the revolutionaries.

At the end of 1817, the year of Chacabuco, the reconquering expedition
left Callao, and at the beginning of the following January it landed at Talcahuano, the last stronghold of the Spaniards in Chile. Director O'Higgins had
just attempted without success to take Talcahuano when the news came of
the enemy expedition, and on his return to the north he learned that Osorio's
army was landing at that port. The moment was dangerous for Chile, because
to the foreign peril there were added the internal dissensions; the quarrelsome
brothers Carrera continued plotting from their exile, and the restless chieftain
Manuel Rodríguez was agitating public opinion from Santiago, taking advantage of the bad news that was arriving in the capital, from which Director
O'Higgins was absent on military missions.

San Martín has been criticized because after Chacabuco he did not personally pursue the remains of the beaten Spanish army toward the south;
but it is necessary to underline that that sector did not then have the importance it had later, when the auxiliary army arrived from Peru. Besides, Las
Heras was charged with that pursuit, and O'Higgins took the command of the
patriot army, because San Martín had left for Buenos Aires, to arrange for
the expedition to Lima. If fate did not favor the patriot arms on the south of
Chile, San Martín cannot be blamed for it, because he took the necessary

steps to prosecute the campaign and because he left for Buenos Aires for such serious reasons and he returned a few months later.

It is known that as soon as San Martín entered Chile he sent a strong division to the south, commanded by Colonel Las Heras; but the latter's defeat at Talca enormously jeopardized the operations, with great chagrin for O'Higgins, who had remained at the head of the army because San Martín had left for Buenos Aires to arrange the expedition to Peru. The Spaniards defeated at Chacabuco concentrated themselves on the south, where they had a formidable position at Talcahuano. An assault against this fortress was attempted, but it failed, in spite of the bravery which Las Heras and his troops showed in the action.

San Martín attributed this failure to the fact it had followed adoption of the plan proposed by the French general Brayer, "as a result of which the attack was directed against the strongest point and without the necessary coordination of other attacks, which should have been simulated in order to distract the attention or divide the enemy."

San Martín's method called for war not only with arms but also with moral forces. When he learned the news of the Royalist invasion, he arranged with O'Higgins to proclaim Chilean independence. With that he sought to strengthen morale, placing an unsurmountable barrier between Spain and its old colony of Chile. It was the same irretraceable step which he had urged the Congress of Tucumán to take for the United Provinces, until he obtained it in 1816, shortly before undertaking the crossing of the Andes. Now he was doing the same in Chile, before casting the dice for his expedition to Peru. Thus the independence of Chile was proclaimed on February 12, 1818, and the proclamation was dated retroactively January 1, in order to give an older status to the irreparable fact, at the time when Osorio was landing in Talcahuano.

While Argentine independence was declared at a time of universal defeats for the American cause, the independence of Chile was proclaimed at the moment of greatest danger for the local cause. Those audacious actions, which contrast so much with other evasive or dilatory acts in San Martín's career, show the complexity of his mind, the flexibility of his soul, the temper of his spirit, his serene boldness at the decisive moments, his deep faith in moral forces, to which he always entrusted his destiny. Therefore on his return from Buenos Aires, when he learned that the Royalists from Peru were landing on the coast of Chile, he prepared public opinion for the decisive encounter, which was not going to take long to materialize.

The date of February 12 was set apart for the oath of independence, celebrating thereby the first anniversary of Chacabuco. In those days of 1818, O'Higgins was between Talcahuano and Talca, as an advance force of defense, and therefore he was not present at the ceremony in Santiago. This was presided over, however, by the Deputy Director, Don Luis de la Cruz, and by San Martín, who accompanied him on the stage set on the Plaza Mayor. At this act were present the civilian and ecclesiastical corporations, the Army and the people, and souvenir medals were distributed. The Chilean flag was displayed before the crowd; the proclamation was read; brief speeches were made; all swore to defend national independence with their lives.

The Archbishop of Santiago, who was receiving the oath, asked San Martín if he also was swearing fealty to Chile's independence, and the hero answered smilingly, "Yes, very much, very much."

To ask this of him, who had been born for the purpose!

O'Higgins made the proclamation in Talca. Similar oaths were taken by all the towns, from the Maule River to Copiapó, during the month of February. The decision to take such an extreme step was born, as it is possible to imagine, in the Lautaro Lodge, founded in Chile after Chacabuco by San Martín and O'Higgins, in eternal solidarity, in the brotherhood of this heroic adventure. The friendship between the two great men survived unaltered until the end of their days.

Under such bitter circumstances San Martín prepared military defense in a few weeks, taking minute precautions. He ordered that every county seat should organize reserve infantry, that the Santiago arsenals should have ready 14,000 lances for the peasants, and that foodstuffs and ammunition should be kept ready on the road to Coquimbo in case of a defeat. Meanwhile, O'Higgins recrossed the Maule with his troops from Talcahuano, taking with him all the resources he was able to carry. San Martín felt happy at the news of the Spanish invasion, because he preferred to beat the last forces of the viceroy on Chilean territory, thus facilitating the carrying out of his undertaking, that is, the eventual expedition to Lima, which he was planning then. That was the reason for the strategic retreat of the patriots, in order to draw Osorio away from Talcahuano and make him cross the Maule in the direction of Talca, as he did, with the results that we shall see.

On January 2, 1818, San Martín wrote O'Higgins, who was retreating and abandoning the lands of the Maule to the invader: "We do not mind losing a few leagues of land, as long as we feel sure to reoccupy them later solidly. Let us concentrate our forces and we shall be invincible. For this purpose I hope that Your Excellency will tell me whether his troops will be able to establish themselves at San Fernando, leaving on the Maule a small flying detachment of infantry and all our cavalry with good horses, so that they may check any attempt from the right bank of that river."

The army of San Martín, which was camping at Las Tablas, four leagues from Valparaiso, had 6,000 men and was divided into three corps, one under San Martín himself, as commander in chief, the second under the Chilean, O'Higgins, and the third under the Argentine, Quintana. With Osorio there had come General Ordóñez and General Primo de Rivera, whose troops, always advancing to the north, were arriving at the banks of the Teno. An advance force of 1,700 horsemen was sent by San Martín, under Balcarce, to attack the Royalists; but when this force entered the zone of Cancha Rayada, the natural ditches which give it its name (Cancha Rayada means Furrowed Field) impeded the movements of the cavalry.

It was March 19 and, as it was beginning to get dark and this made movements impossible, San Martín ordered them to camp at the northwest until the following day. That night, however, the Royalist chiefs, gathered in Talca, decided to surprise the patriots; and thus they fell upon the latter, helped by darkness, dispersed the divisions of San Martín and O'Higgins, and brought confusion to the whole army of liberation. This is what the history of America calls the "Surprise of Cancha Rayada," an episode which was worse than a defeat because of its effects on morale immediately afterward. Darkness, panic, and dispersion gave rise to sinister news which brought about discouragement in the capital of Chile, as if the whole work of San Martín had crumbled the night of the surprise.

The fatal news reached Santiago as if brought by the mysterious wind which broadcasts the rumors of disasters: fugitive soldiers and peasants entered into the city showing the surprised expression of defeat.

Monteagudo, general judge advocate of the Army, passed through Santiago, fleeing toward the mountains to seek refuge in Mendoza, and he confirmed the debacle. If Monteagudo was running away, surely everything was lost. This was thought then, although later it became known that Monteagudo was going to Mendoza to forestall a Carrerista reaction and to assure a refuge to patriot arms. A few days later Monteagudo took part in the execution of the brothers Carrera, tried in Mendoza for common crimes and for plotting against the Chilean Government.

The people crowded the plaza in front of the palace of the Government, asking for news, amidst voices of tribulation and protest, as often happens on unfortunate days. More refugees arrived on Saturday of that sad week, bearing worse news. Nothing was known about San Martín, O'Higgins, or the principal chiefs. The shadows which enveloped the surprise magnified the horror and favored the naïve inventions of the fearful or the pessimistic talk of the reactionaries who thought the moment had come to make friends with the presumed Spanish victor. "Some said that San Martín and O'Higgins had gone to sea from Valparaiso; others, that both had crossed the Andes. . . . The streets filled with pack mules taking the refugees from the city," going to Cuyo with their silver and their valuables. The Government's money was packed in bags to be transported by mule, with the same destination. Government officials also made ready to leave. Women wrung their hands and tore their hair, requesting information about their relatives in the army and uttering cries of despair. Nobody knew anything definite, except the bitter truth of the night surprise and of the dispersion in the darkness. It was said that the Royalist victor was coming in forced marches to punish the rebellious city.

And as if all this confused horror were not enough, someone came and said he had seen San Martín commit suicide in Cancha Rayada, in the midst of the disaster to his troops. . . .

This news, brought by an alleged eyewitness, brought anxiety to a paroxysm, while the Royalists who had hidden themselves after Chacabuco, and the opportunists who are always present, believed that the moment for getting even or profiting had arrived, and as in 1814, after the disaster of Rancagua, following the hazardous fate of the Chilean epic, the cry was heard again on the streets of Santiago (because San Martín was thought to be dead) that had been heard before 1810: "Long live the King!"

After so much suffering, other news came. The surprise of Cancha Rayada had been a terrible clash in the dark, with horses and men that ran one way and the other, some of them having been taken by surprise in their sleep and thrown into flight by an instinctive terror. But the right wing, composed of thirty-five hundred soldiers, had not been affected by the surprise, and it was intact in San Fernando, under the command of the Argentine Las Heras, whom it had recognized as commander. San Fernando was a meeting point for the dispersed men, and the army could be remade. San Martín was alive, and a letter from him arrived "which it was necesary to show to the people to convince them." O'Higgins, on the other hand, "had been wounded in an arm by a musket shot"; but he also was alive and would not delay his return to Santiago to resume his exercise of the Government.

With this news the hopes of the patriots were reawakened, although doubts remained in many hearts. The last days had been bitter. Many homes had been abandoned by their fugitive owners. The populace had sacked the stores. The English businessmen had decided to form a unit called Death's Hussars, to defend their interests. Houses remained closed. The temporary Director, Cruz, and the chieftain Manuel Rodríguez were meanwhile doing everything possible to keep order and rekindle hope. The closing of the Andean passes was ordered, to stop the flight of people who were taking their valuables with them, thus impoverishing the country at that moment. Lives and fortunes were needed now more than ever to fight the Royalists, who had again taken possession of the south of Chile with six thousand men and who were getting ready for a new attack.

On Wednesday of the following week O'Higgins, with an arm bandaged and in a sling, entered the capital on horseback, accompanied by the Argentines Quintana, Zapiola, Necochea, Melián, and Martínez. None of them had changed clothes since the fatal night. They all went to the house of the widow Mackenna, and there they held a meeting, where it was resolved to establish a Council of Public Safety. These facts were announced with salvos from guns, but the spirits were deeply dismayed.

And San Martín, meanwhile, where was he? Was it true that he was dead? This question was asked by some timid voice in the gathering.

"No. San Martín is not dead. He has been in San Fernando with Las

Heras, organizing the reunion of the dispersed troops and taking precautionary measures; but he is already on his way to Santiago, where he is expected with anxiety."

He was on his way to Santiago, when, nearing Paine's ranch, the owner of the property, Doña Paula de Jara Quemada, with her children and peons, came out to meet him, and after listening to the hero's tale of the disaster and of the hopes of salvation that he still had, said to him, "My property, my family, and myself are at your disposal. I have brought here fifty of my servants and my sons, too, to join your army."

"The disaster which we have suffered must not cause discouragement or alarm. The army will soon be reorganized and the enemy will be discouraged forever," San Martín replied to the lady.

Her estate served as a camp for the men, and from there the commander continued his trip to the capital.

San Martín entered Santiago one day after O'Higgins, on March 25, in the afternoon. He was accompanied by Colonel Paroissiens, his physician, and Captain O'Brien, his aide, both Britishers.

When San Martín entered the city church bells were loudly rung and the artillery roared a salute in the Plaza Mayor, the same square where fifty days before the people had sworn Chilean independence.

Samuel Haigh, mentioned a number of times previously, a British gentleman who conducted business between London, Buenos Aires, and Chile, was at the government palace when San Martín came in. There is always a British gentleman to give testimony before history about the decisive moments in San Martín's life: Lord Macduff, when he left Spain; Robertson, at San Lorenzo; others later. Now it is Samuel Haigh, who tells us:

"I was at the palace when the commanding general arrived. He seemed very tired and was covered with dust. He had not changed his clothes, or even removed his boots, in several days. However, despite his fatigue, he was in good humor."

Where did this ill and defeated man draw his energy from? He entered the palace among the clamors of the people, and the house was full of citizens who questioned him.

"Do not despair," San Martín told everyone, with amazing aplomb. "Do not despair. The country is still standing, and it shall triumph."

The clamorings of the crowd compelled him to show himself at the balcony. But the people, who were applauding in the Plaza Mayor, did not want to go away. They were waiting for San Martín to leave the palace.

San Martín mounted his horse and, surrounded by the crowd who wanted to hear his words, he made this extempore address:

"Chileans: One of those hazards that man does not know how to avoid made our army suffer a defeat. It was natural that this unexpected blow and the consequent uncertainty should make you hesitate. But it is now time to take stock of yourselves and to realize that our country's army is holding with glory in the face of the enemy; that your companions at arms are gathering fast and that the resources of patriotism are inexhaustible. The tyrants have not advanced a single step in their entrenchment. I have put in motion a force of over four thousand men, without counting the militia. The Fatherland exists and shall triumph, and I give my word of honor that I shall shortly give a day of glory to South America."

"General, let me embrace you!" cried a *roto* in the crowd.

O'Brien tried to push him away, but San Martín, obeying a characteristic impulse, dismounted and put his arms around the *roto* while the crowd cheered.

With San Martín there came into Santiago Captain Miller, a Britisher like Haigh, and they dined at the house of their compatriot, the merchant, Mr. Begg, with whom they commented upon the defeat of Cancha Rayada.

"The disaster was due to the panic that overtook the soldiers," said Miller, "but they will re-form their ranks and fight even better, to recover their glory."

"The Spaniards have not obtained any great advantage from this blow," Samuel Haigh commented, "because the Negro regiment Number 8 stopped the first two attacking columns; and because, when the Negroes retired, the two Royalist divisions, which were trying to flank them, clashed in the dark, without recognizing themselves on account of the darkness; and finally, because the Royalists devoted themselves to sacking, giving Las Heras time to withdraw his division intact."

The patriots lost only 120 men and some arms, besides a few prisoners and wounded.

San Martín later requested, in a manifesto addressed to the population, four thousand mules and food.

"The general stakes his head on not leaving any on the enemy, if the citizens believe his word. But he asks, as a condition, that he be helped in the measure of everyone's possibilities. The Government will pay religiously for everything."

This proclamation lifted the morale, and preparations for evening the score were begun.

Colonel Las Heras, who was coming from San Fernando with the men who had been saved from the disaster, entered the Molino encampment at the head of 3,200 men, on March 29. His attitude on the 19th had prevented the disaster of Cancha Rayada from being complete. San Martín, in recognition of his presence of mind and courage, appointed him commander of one of the divisions for the forthcoming battle. Men who had been dispersed joined again, and with this the number of effectives rose to over four thousand combatants.

San Martín, the swordsman of Arjonilla, San Lorenzo, and Chacabuco, had proved his own courage amply; but after Cancha Rayada he proved to have another and rarer virtue: that of moral courage. In spite of this, there have been those among his enemies who taxed him with being a coward.

A biographer of Napoleon mentions this phrase of his hero: "Rarely did I unsheath my sword. I won my battles with my eyes and my hands." It is known, besides, that this warrior appreciated men who displayed presence of mind in the face of the unforeseen, more than he did mere courage—the former quality he called "the courage of two o'clock in the morning."

We should not be surprised that someone should deny that San Martín had courage, because the same fault of cowardice has been attributed to Napoleon. Besides, we do not know precisely what is courage when the subject is, not the soldier who obeys, but the general who plans and directs a whole action. The legendary feats of courage in war, such as that of the soldier who dies to take a trench or defend his own position, are often manifestations of drunkenness, of neurosis, of despair, and even paradoxical expressions of fear. What is interesting in the case of men like Napoleon or San Martín is not that they could carry out the assaults of Arcola or San Lorenzo, because many of their anonymous soldiers were capable of the same thing, but that they knew how to keep their lucidity of mind in the midst of danger. The courage of the great warriors is not in those cases anything but a manifestation of intelligence, of conscious self-control; in a word, what we call civilian courage. San Martín had it in a high degree and also possessed the magnificent quality of infusing courage into the legions which, as in the crossing of the Andes or in the fatal discouragement of Cancha Rayada, he led to victory.

At the beginning of 1816, when it seemed that his plan of the Andes was going to be frustrated for lack of official backing and of means to equip an army, he exclaimed, "I wish we had a Cromwell to give us liberty and the splendor that is not so easy to get in our land!" Were soldiers lacking? Then let every slave be declared a soldier and we shall have 10,000 men in arms. Were means lacking? Then let all public employees and officers have their salaries cut by one half and let the working of silver be forbidden, to be used only for coining money. "I would rather that we use spoons made of bone and wear crude sandals than that the enemy hanged us."

This was said by the man of steel at a moment of misfortune, and such was the temper of his indomitable will.

V. THE BATTLE OF MAIPU

Ten days after Cancha Rayada the Army of Liberty which had been dispersed there had regained its numbers and its strength. The enemy continued his march toward the north in the direction of the capital. An encounter became necessary, and on April 3, 1818, at dawn, San Martín left Santiago, at the head of his troops, ready for battle.

San Martín, helped by Las Heras and O'Higgins, paid special attention to readjusting discipline and strengthening morale, which had been broken by the recent surprise. Faith in victory had disappeared from many hearts. Therefore San Martín had to prevent any new contagion of panic. For the forthcoming battle he did not prepare a rhetorical harangue, but, instead, minute instructions, worthy of a warrior and of a master who knows the human soul:

Each soldier will have for this battle one hundred cartridges and ten rocks, half of which he will carry with him and the other half will be kept behind with his respective unit. Before the beginning of the battle he will be given a ration of wine or aguardiente, the former to be preferred. Commanders will address words of encouragement to the troops before joining battle, and shall impose the penalty of death on anyone who separates himself from his rank, either when advancing or when withdrawing. Commanders will tell their soldiers in a clear and energetic way that if any unit withdraws it is because the commander in chief has ordered it for strategical reasons. If any unit of infantry or cavalry is attacked with side arms, it shall not wait standing still for the attack, but instead it shall advance fifty paces to meet the attack, with bayonet or sword. The wounded who cannot walk unaided shall not be saved while the battle lasts, because four men are needed for every one wounded, and this would weaken the line in a moment. In the place where the commander in chief will be a tricolor flag will fly and a red flag will show the location of the reserve ammunition. When at the place where the commander in chief finds himself three flags are raised at the same time, that is, the tricolor of Chile, the bicolor of Buenos Aires, and a red one, all the troops will shout, "Long Live Our Country!" and forthwith each unit shall charge with bayonet or sword on the enemy facing it. As soon as the enemy line is broken he shall be pursued hotly, and at the bugle call of assembly, everyone shall be in line. The chiefs of staff must be persuaded this battle is going to decide the fate of all America and that it is preferable to die honorably on the field of honor than die at the hands of our executioners. I am sure of victory with the help of the army chiefs, to whom I recommend to keep these remarks in mind. I advise the cavalry chiefs to keep behind a squad of twenty-five to thirty men, to strike with their swords the soldiers who turn their backs to the enemy, as well as to pursue the enemy while the rest of the squadron is gathered. Inasmuch as the nature of our soldiers lends itself better to offense than to defense, the chiefs shall not forget that in case of emergency they should take the offensive.

Osorio's army, meanwhile, had continued its march toward the capital, convinced of the total defeat of San Martín in Cancha Rayada. Halfway along the route he understood his mistake and diverted his troops toward the coast. Three patriot divisions, the right wing commanded by Las Heras, the left by Alvarado, and the reserve by Quintana, were distributed strategically to stop the enemy. On April 4 both armies came into sight of each other on the plain of Maipú.

The plain of Maipú is bound on the east by the Mapocho River, which separates it from Santiago; on the south by another river, which gives its name to the place; and on the north by the mountains which separate it from the valley of Aconcagua. A height named Loma Blanca (White Hill), on the north, was the position occupied by the patriot army; and another height, on the opposite extreme, on the ranch of Espejo, was the position occupied by the Spanish army. A hillock to the east stands at the side of a triangle of hills, which mark the boundary of the plain. Farther away, especially to the east, greater heights bind the mountain panorama, which is characteristic of this region. The nearness of Santiago, which is hardly two leagues away, and the terrain itself gave the battle a more dramatic setting.

General Balcarce and almost all the chiefs favored the defense of the fords of the Maipú River, and in case this plan was accepted, to withdraw to Santiago in order to defend the city from the suburbs. "Neither one nor the other of these plans suited the ideas of San Martín, because his own plan was better," San Martín himself wrote to Miller many years later. His plan consisted in giving battle upon the field where the two armies were; a field which is alternately rocky and covered with bushes.

On the evening of the 3d, when San Martín was preoccupied with the enemy advance and with the steps to be taken, General Brayer, who for the last two weeks had been sulking, presented himself, and with the tone of self-importance which he used, talked to O'Higgins about the difficult fight that was in the offing, trying to spread discouragement: "My knowledge makes me realize, without any doubt, that everything is lost. Our army, composed of defeated and dispersed groups, is not capable of fighting a triumphant and proud enemy."

There were present the aides to the commander in chief and several officers of the Secretariat. O'Higgins made an effort to repress his annoyance at listening to the gloomy forecast of a man nobody esteemed. And Brayer ended his perverse speech with this hypocritical advice: "Your own person is very important. Place yourself in a situation of being able to save yourself from a disaster which I believe inevitable."

This conversation gave rise to criticisms when Brayer had withdrawn, and it spread among the people. This French general had arrived a year before in Buenos Aires, brought by Carrera, who had found him in the United States, where the Frenchman had emigrated after the downfall of Napoleon. His military record in Europe was rather honorable, and its memory filled him with pride and made him look upon the American officers with undisguised contempt. He had fought ably at Hohenlinden and Austerlitz; he had taken part in the campaigns of Prussia, Spain, and Silesia, winning his high promotions by his own merit. He commanded a division of 20,000 men at Waterloo, and he was one of those who advised the Emperor to resume the war after that disaster. In the Spanish battle of Albuera he was wounded, fighting against the cause that was then served by San Martín, who was also wounded in the same battle. It could not be the memory of that past antagonism in Europe that now engendered antipathy between him and the man who commanded the Army of the Andes, but rather his links with the Carreras, or his presumptuous and quarrelsome disposition. On the attack on Talcahuano, Las Heras had followed Brayer's plan and failed. In Talca, Brayer had withdrawn from the action in a manner that was not very clear. These local occurrences cast a shadow over the prestige of his European campaigns.

Two days after this conversation Brayer presented himself, nervously, to speak with San Martín at the encampment of Maipú. In spite of his advice the battle was going to be fought, and he had not been assigned any position for the action, which was already imminent. It was April 5, and the patriot columns, with San Martín at their head, were moving upon the hill of Loma Blanca, with the enemy facing them. Feeling himself excluded and his self-respect wounded, Brayer approached San Martín and told him: "I need a furlough to go to the baths of Colina, because I am ill."

Brayer walked lamely because of a recrudescence of the rheumatism from which he suffered, and this untimely request, which looked rather like an excuse for justifying his absence from battle, made San Martín indignant. He was very nervous because of his exertions; so much so that he could not repress his annoyance:

"With the same permission with which you withdrew from Talca, you could go to the baths. Within a half-hour we are going to decide the fate of Chile. You could remain, if your illness allows you to."

"I am not in a condition to stay, because my old wound in my leg prevents me from doing it."

San Martín's indignation exploded at that answer. His first impulse was to have Brayer shot, as he himself declared later. But an insult burst from his lips:

"The last drummer in the army has more honor than Your Lordship, General."

The Englishman Haigh, who was present, tells in his memoirs that the insult was worse than that:

"You, General, are a c———"

Brayer looked at San Martín with impotent fury, and San Martín turned back with his horse and said to Balcarce:

"Make it known to the army that this general of twenty years of battles is relieved of his post because he is not worthy of it."

Brayer walked off ashamed and returned to Santiago, whence he departed amid public comments the same day that San Martín fought the battle he had forecast as a defeat. From Chile he went, full of hate, to Montevideo, where he met Carrera again, and under the patronage of the latter, he published calumnious pamphlets against San Martín, which compelled the chiefs of the patriot army to answer him publicly.

The anecdotes of those days reveal the military temper of San Martín and the quality of his enemies. Carrera before, Brayer later, and Cochrane and others still later, attacked him for similar personal motives. But in those conflicts San Martín acted with justice.

The army officer Luis S. Merino published in Chile, in 1909, a technical study of the battle of Maipú, with maps of the action, and said: "General San Martín was a real army commander in the most complete sense of the word; his ability as an organizer, his energy for discipline, and his most complete knowledge of the military art placed him high above his adversaries."

The night of April 4 San Martín, covered with his cape, had slept at the mill of Loma Blanca, after a very tiring day. Fires lighted the encampment, while the sentries watched. He was awakened before dawn, because the enemy seemed to be moving. He left the mill with his head covered with a peasant hat and wearing a Chilean poncho; he mounted his horse, accompanied by the engineer D'Albe, a Frenchman, who had the maps of the field, and by the Irishman O'Brien, his aide. After the incident with Brayer, he cantered a moment toward the south, under the first beams of dawn, and he stopped at a height, while he watched through his field glasses. "How stupid are these Spaniards!" he exclaimed, as if talking to himself.

He had just seen that the Spanish army was moving on its flank, with flags flying and drums rolling, going toward the road to Valparaiso.

"Osorio is a bigger fool than I thought," he added, smiling. The sun was then coming over the Andes, in a limpid sky. "Victory is ours today!" His companions, D'Albe and O'Brien, who tell it, looked with expectant emotion to the paladin, who then exclaimed, "The sun is my witness!"

And he spurred his horse, after giving the order for the battle that was going to be joined.

Maipú (or Maipo) means "The Native Soil" in the language of Lautaro, and the sun of Maipú, on that beautiful day, was really the sun of America, the sun of the homeland. San Martín, son of the sun, well knew it when he invoked his solar parent as a witness of the victory which was going to save the cause of emancipation, not of Chile alone, but of the whole continent. Says a witness:

In the morning of Sunday, April 5, the most delicious time of the year in Chile, not a single cloud darkened the brilliant and eternal blue of the firmament; birds sang and orange blossoms gave off a delicious perfume, which was carried away by the breeze. There was a balmlike softness in the air, characteristic of that climate. Church bells were summoning the faithful, and a religious feeling permeated the senses with the sanctity of the day. It seemed sacrilegious that such a holy quiet should be interrupted by the noise of battle.

Osorio's intention, when moving his forces from Espejo's farm toward the road to Santiago, was doubtlessly to drive a wedge between the city and the patriot army. San Martín then moved his forces in close columns and with a rapid march frustrated that maneuver. Osorio halted on the wide hill of Espejo. He placed the Burgos Regiment to the right, the Infante Don Carlos Regiment to the left, and he placed in the center the troops from Concepción and Peru. At their sides were a squadron of dragoons and a regiment of lancers.

On a side hillock four pieces of artillery were placed. The Spanish army numbered more than six thousand men. The infantry's uniforms were made of drilling with white belting; the cavalry's uniform was blue; and the King's Dragoons wore red tunics, light-colored trousers, and high boots. The day was so clear that from the top of Loma Blanca one could see the glitter of the arms and belting.

The battle took place under really spectacular conditions, because of the position of both forces, because of the terrain, and because of the high visibility, which allowed the whole field to be seen at one glance. San Martín ordered that a red flag, showing the position of the general staff, be hoisted alongside the flags of the two allied countries, following the instructions given beforehand. The Royalist forces continued silent. The republican commander ordered a salvo of artillery to see how the enemy answered, and the latter replied with artillery fire, without moving his troops. An Argentine shot killed the horse of the Royalist general. San Martín saw that the Spanish plan was only defensive, and he ordered an attack against the right flank of the adversary, because it was the weakest. The columns forming the patriot left threw themselves with enthusiasm against the enemy for the first attack. The battle had started.

San Martín kept for himself the command of the reserves, of which the cavalry, under Quintana, was a part; he entrusted the infantry to Balcarce, and divided the rest of his forces into two corps, the right one under the command of Las Heras, and the left one under Alvarado. All the commanders, as one sees, were Argentine, although there were Chileans at the head of minor units: Freyre, Cáceres, and Borgoño. Blanco Encalada, also an Argentine, took charge of eight field guns. The troops in general were formed by natives of both countries, and there were entire regiments composed of Negroes from Cuyo, who fought heroically and died in great numbers.

The patriot army wore a blue uniform, with white belting and red piping, and some battalions wore light-colored trousers. All these troops occupied Loma Blanca, divided into three principal sections, the center and the wings, besides the artillery, which was to protect the advances. The noble O'Higgins had been forced to stay in the capital, because of the wound which he received at Cancha Rayada. He took charge of the defense of Santiago in case of disaster, and for this purpose trenches were dug in the streets. The black memory of Rancagua gave a mute terror to the feverish population. The April nights which preceded the battle of Maipú were pathetic. Everyone knew that the powerful Spanish army was in the neighborhood and that it could attack the city if San Martín did not stop it.

Upon the hill of Espejo, naturally divided into three sections, and on a lateral hillock, the enemy, commanded by General Osorio, awaited the attack. On a hillock to the east, to protect the road to Valparaiso, the initial objective of the Spanish advance, or to harass the patriot right wing if it advanced upon Espejo, four field pieces were placed, under Primo de Rivera. The right was entrusted to Ordóñez, with the soldiers of the Infante Don Carlos and the Arequipa regiments. The left was under Morla, with the Burgos and the Concepción regiments, plus several pieces of artillery. The incline between the hillock and the triangle was covered by the Dragoons of the Border, commanded by Morgado, and the extreme right was covered by the King's Lancers and a regiment of dragoons.

The combat was to be a frontal attack; but later, because of the movements of the enemy, it became an oblique attack, reinforced by a timely and efficacious maneuver of the reserves under Quintana. "The battle of Maipú was won by his courage," says San Martín in justice to Quintana; but this adaptation to the circumstances was San Martín's own inspiration in the field. There have been arguments about whether Maipú was really an oblique-attack battle, following the classic type which military history associates to the name of Epaminondas. Some technicians have denied it, and we shall see later what San Martín thought of it; but Mitre, with his authority as a soldier and an historian, solved the question technically in the manner just mentioned.

The Englishman Haigh, who was near San Martín on Loma Blanca, describes the panorama of battle as follows:

The action was begun at about eleven by the patriot artillery of the right; it fired at intervals upon the Royalist left, which was advancing, and before twelve o'clock the action became general. When the Infante Don Carlos Regiment descended the hillside it was met by a very destructive fire from the artillery of Colonel Blanco, whose effects were visible at each shot, carrying destruction and discouragement to its columns. The battle was well fought out here, and it remained indecisive for a long time. Colonel Manuel Escalada, at the head of his squadron of mounted grenadiers, charged upon the hillock where the four pieces of artillery were placed, and he took them. The guns were immediately aimed against their original owners. . . . On the right the Royalists gained an advantage; the heavy and well-aimed fire of the Burgos Regiment caused confusion in the patriot left wing, composed chiefly of Negroes, who were finally completely dispersed, leaving four hundred dead on the battlefield. At this critical moment the reserves commanded by Quintana were ordered to attack. The Burgos Regiment advanced so rapidly that it became partly disorganized, and it had withdrawn somewhat in order to re-form its ranks when the patriot reserves threw themselves upon it, suffering a deadly fire aimed with admirable precision and effect and with such regularity as if this were only a maneuver. This was, without doubt, the most doubtful moment of the action; and so it was considered by Quintana, who, having been reinforced by a squadron of mounted grenadiers, gave the order to charge. . . . The clash was tremendous. The fire ceased suddenly and both sides crossed bayonets. The repeated cries of, "Long Live the King!" and "Long Live Our Country!" were proof that every inch of terrain was being desperately fought for; but, because of the dust and smoke, we could hardly tell which side was being favored by victory. Finally, the Royalist cry was muted, and the patriots, advancing at the cry of, "Long Live Liberty!" proclaimed that victory was theirs. When the Burgos Regiment realized that its ranks were broken it abandoned all idea of further resistance and fled in all directions, although chiefly toward Espejo's mill. They were pursued by the cavalry and pitilessly cut to pieces. The virtue of pity had disappeared from both sides. The butchery was very great, and some officers who had served in Europe told me that they had never seen anything bloodier than what happened on this part of the battlefield.

In the instructions which San Martín had given his army he said, "Special attention shall be paid to the Burgos Regiment, because it is the hope of the enemy." It was called "The Sun," because it had in its flag a golden sun on a field of azure, with this legend, *"Civitas Solis Vocabitur Una,"* a quotation from Isaiah which means, "Only one shall be named the City of the Sun." And as if these heraldic emblems were a mysterious coincidence for San Martín, who dreamt of going to Peru, that flag had been decorated at Bailén, the battle where also San Martín was decorated before he came to America seeking the real City of the Sun.

The soldiers of the Burgos Regiment were so proud of its traditions that when they joined the battle they shouted, "Here is the Burgos! Eighteen battles won! None lost!" But at Maipú that war cry ceased to be true.

This happened in the early afternoon. The battle was already decided in favor of the patriot arms. San Martín, who was still at the post with the three flags with the general staff, sent for Colonel Paroissien, chief surgeon of the army, to arrange for the care of the many wounded that covered the field. The surgeon was at the mill, converted into a hospital, amputating the leg of an officer that had been shattered by a shot from a musket. San Martín came to this place and on a piece of paper which he picked up from the floor—a blood-stained piece of paper—he wrote for O'Higgins the laconic report of the victory:

"We have just obtained a complete victory. Our cavalry pursues them to finish them. The country is free."

The report is dated at the battlefield: "General Headquarters, Lo Espejo, April 5, 1818," and signed, "San Martín."

In the face of this laconic report, adverse commentators will say that San Martín was drunk when he wrote his dispatch; but the Chilean historian Vicuña Mackenna is indignant: "Imbeciles! Drunk with glory, not with wine!" he says.

San Martín delivered the report to Haigh, whom he ordered to take it to Santiago. The Englishman galloped to the city, and soon the report of victory spread among the anxious populace. Everywhere the cry was heard, "Long Live Our Country! Long Live San Martín! Long Live Liberty!"

But O'Higgins was not in Santiago. He had not been able to endure the effects of doubt and inaction; while the battle which had begun in the morning continued into the afternoon, he mounted his horse and started toward the field of Maipú. San Martín had already left Loma Blanca and the mill and was in a lowland near the farm of Espejo, where the fight still continued against the enemy, at his last stronghold. O'Higgins, with his arm in a sling, saw San Martín and cried generously, "Glory to the Savior of Chile!"

San Martín, covered by the dust of battle, left the group of officers of his general staff, and approaching his friend, he embraced him without dismounting, saying, "General, Chile will not forget your sacrifice when presenting yourself at the battlefield with your glorious wound still open."

This scene has been recorded on canvas by the painter Subercasseaux, as others have painted San Martín in the hour of other great battles, and at meetings such as the one at Guayaquil, equally glorious in his life.

While O'Higgins and San Martín talked, their voices were drowned by the clamor and the musket fire at the near-by farm of Espejo, where the last attack was being carried out.

The courageous Royalists, when they saw the Burgos Regiment defeated, realized that both wings had been destroyed, and then they retreated, seeking a refuge at the farmhouse. Before the house there were three corrals bound by walls, and a narrow path led up to the building. This stronghold could contain a thousand men, but those who had taken refuge there had fallen prey to panic, while the rest of the troops fled to the south through the fields. General Osorio himself had disappeared, and nothing was known of him. Later it became known that he had escaped with a few men and taken refuge in Talcahuano.

The soldiers under Las Heras invaded the corrals of Espejo, the path and the house, the doors of which had just been closed. The Royalists had raised a white flag; but a shot from a cannon blew open the doors. From the roof and the windows an intense gunfire answered. The assailants, enraged, entered like a torrent, massacring the enemies they found. In the midst of the confusion some fled to hide in the adjacent vineyard; but more than five hundred Spaniards were killed in the house and the vineyards. This epilogue of the battle turned out to be bloodier than the battle itself. Only the presence of Las Heras could, at length, control the unleashed soldiery, and this is admitted by the Spanish chronicler Torrente, who points out the nobility and pity with which that commander treated the defeated. It was there, in the house of Espejo, that General Ordóñez was then taken into the presence of San Martín. They had known each other at Cádiz when they were young.

The emotions of the two men, when they recognized each other, were impressive. San Martín, when he saw his old comrade, offered his hand to him and embraced him fraternally.

Ordóñez and other Royalist chiefs were taken to San Luis, and there they died, soon afterward, when an attempted uprising failed.

When the men who had taken refuge in Espejo's farm gave themselves up, the house had a macabre appearance. Doors and windows had been shattered by bullets. Courtyards and rooms were spattered with brains and blood. The vineyards were covered with dead and wounded, as was the plain where the main part of the battle took place. The sun still lighted that tremendous day when the work was started of gathering in the equipment of the beaten army, in order to restrain the brutal sacking of the unruly soldiery.

The victory had been complete. As trophies of it there were: The Spanish general, four colonels, seven lieutenant colonels, 150 officers, and 2,200 soldiers prisoners; there were, besides, four flags, twelve cannon, 3,850 muskets, 1,200 blunderbusses, the military funds, the equipment and the ammunition of the defeated. A thousand Royalists lay dead upon the field of battle, and the patriots had suffered a thousand casualties. Says Mitre:

This victory, the hardest-fought of the battles of the war for South American independence, was bought by the independents at the price of a loss of over 1,000 men between dead and wounded, most of the tribute being paid by the Negroes from Cuyo, of whom more than a half perished on the field. Rather than for its trophies, Maipú is noteworthy because it was the first great American battle, from a historic and scientific viewpoint, because of the accurate strategic marches that preceded it and because of the able tactical maneuvers upon the field, as well as by the able co-ordination and timely use of the arms. Militarily it is a notable model, almost perfect, of a parallel attack which becomes an oblique attack; it is outstanding for the convenient use of the reserves upon the weakest flank of the enemy, an inspiration which decided the victory. It is to be noted that San Martín, like Epaminondas, won only two great battles, and both were won by the use of the same oblique attack invented by the immortal Greek genius. The battle of Maipú can only be matched by those of Boyacá, which was its immediate consequence, and that of Ayacucho, which was its final consequence; but without Maipú, there would not have been either a Boyacá or an Ayacucho.

Bolívar, at Angostura, learned of the victory of San Martín, and he attributed to Maipú, as it will be proved further on, a decisive continental importance; on learning of this victory, he wrote, "The day of America has arrived."

Enemies of San Martín, like Cochrane's friend Stevenson in his memoirs, repeating hearsay reports about all this, do not deny the importance of this battle, but they suggest that San Martín, drunken, cowardly, and inept, did not direct the action; but we have seen already whether or not Maipú was the exclusive creation of the warring genius and the moral temper of our hero.

When the day was over it became necessary to write, for the Government of Buenos Aires, a detailed report of the action. San Martín read it to Las Heras before sending it, and the latter remarked, "General, this that you say here, that our line was at an angle on the right of the enemy, showing an oblique formation upon that flank, was, you know, the whole merit of the victory; but nobody is going to understand it the way you say it."

"That is more than enough," answered San Martín, smiling. "If I say anything else, they are going to shout that I want to compare myself with Epaminondas or Bonaparte. Down to brass tacks, Las Heras, down to brass tacks! We have destroyed the Spaniards and we are going to Peru! Did the oblique maneuver turn out well? Fine, even though nobody may know what it was."

Las Heras looked at him in amazement, and San Martín, rubbing his hands, added: "I would rather that they do not know it, because even so there will be many who will never forgive us for having won. . . ."

VI. FROM ONE SEA TO THE OTHER

Five days after Maipú, San Martín deemed it necessary to make another trip to Buenos Aires. Despite the fatigues of Cancha Rayada, of his failing health, and of the troubles of crossing the Andes again, and then the pampas, the anxious paladin undertook his voyage from the Pacific to the River Plate. At the beginning of May it became known in Buenos Aires, through messengers sent by the voyager, that San Martín was approaching the Argentine capital.

By special mail San Martín had written to Director Pueyrredón on April 9, announcing his trip to Buenos Aires, with the purpose of "resting a bit in the midst of his family" and "making the necessary arrangements for giving the final blow to the enemy." San Martín added, "I do not want any noise or fandangos," that is, any receptions or dances, or victor's honors. To which the Director, his friend, replied on May 1: "It is necessary that you reconcile yourself to receive from this thankful people the demonstrations of friendship and tenderness it is preparing."

While the reply was on its way San Martín was coming to Buenos Aires, and on the way he was able to read again other thoughts of the Supreme Director about the demonstrations that were being prepared in honor of the traveler:

If I tried to avoid them, I would be insulting the noblest sentiments; and you cannot resist them without offending the whole city, which is setting up triumphal arches along the streets as a tribute to the hero of the Andes and Maipú. It is, therefore, absolutely necessary that you measure your daily traveling so that you enter the city in the daytime; and that from your last stop you let me know one hour beforehand the time of your arrival, so that the General Staff, etc., may go to meet you at San José de Flores, where an artillery division is already encamped. A committee of three friends (of the Lautaro Lodge) must also go to congratulate you. Finally, there are certain sacrifices that are necessary and must be suffered in favor of the society wherein one lives and of the position that one occupies. If you want to enter on horseback, let me know and I shall send you one of my horses.

So they were preparing for him a Roman hero's procession, with arches, cannon salutes, reception committees, acclaim, flowers, and crowds around the victor on horseback, from outside the walls to the Forum? Ah, no! San Martín was not the man for these masquerades of martial glory. His conduct in those cases was not for him a matter of dialectics but of conscience, of deep mystic conscience. It was useless that his friend Pueyrredón try to convince him with political arguments. It is an enormous sacrifice to make war to found liberty; but the victories must not, by themselves, be an occasion for revelry, thought San Martín.

He came from a distant place not to gather ephemeral laurels but to seek the means of crowning his undertaking still farther away. The paladin of the Mountain was about to become the paladin of the Sea. Now he sought the means for cutting off any Spanish expedition on the Atlantic and for harassing Spain along the coast of the Pacific. He sought, above all, a fleet to take him and six thousand men from Valparaiso to Lima, in order to put an end to monarchy in America. This was the mission of his life. For this he was born at Yapeyú. For this he came from Cádiz in 1812. For this he cut short his Peninsular career. For this he crossed the Andes.

They asked him whether he wanted to enter the city on horseback. Well, neither on horseback nor afoot nor in a state coach did he wish to enter. He wanted only to talk confidentially with Pueyrredón and with the friends at the lodge and with the men of the Congress, to obtain equipment. The rest was just vanity. He was not interested in it.

The poets of Buenos Aires had celebrated with enthusiastic odes the epic victories of San Martín in Chile; but one among them, Esteban de Luca, poet and soldier, had pointed out, in a poem about Chacabuco, with a poet's intuition, the geographical transcendence of the epic, which already embraced the whole continent, from one sea to the other:

> *Oh, homeland, thy warriors*
> *The mountains and the plains have occupied;*
> *And the flag of Castile from them they, fiery,*
> *Pulled down to the ground.*
> *Honor to thee, homeland, a thousand times! Proudly*
> *Wave in all of Chile thy flags.*

From the hard and lofty seat
Of the snow-covered Andes, today fame,
Touching the starred pavement
Of the worlds, acclaims
Thy heroes; their resounding echo
Goes from the southern sea to the Atlantic.

After leaving Arroyo del Medio, following the route of the mails, San Martín arrived in the village of Luján, from where he went on to Puente de Márquez, in the neighborhood of the capital. Paying no heed to the advice of Pueyrredón, the traveler did not announce his arrival in Buenos Aires and instead of "measuring his journeys," in order to arrive on Tuesday, May 12, he hastened his pace, and on Monday, the 11th, at dawn, he entered the city incognito. Thus he arrived at his home, and after embracing his wife and daughter, he presented himself suddenly to Pueyrredón, spoiling the triumphal reception which was being prepared for him.

On Wednesday, the 13th, the *Gaceta* commented upon that peculiarity in an editorial which began with a thought of Tacitus, after the French version of Robinet: "Most generals seem to come from the same mold. To paint them is to multiply the copies. Only superior genius offers its own traits, worthy of passing on to posterity."

Which is, in San Martín, his own trait? His ability to defeat his enemies and to defeat himself, in order not to make victory a source of selfish power or a theatrical spectacle. Says the *Gaceta*:

Last Sunday the news came that General San Martín was, on Saturday night, sixty-two leagues from this capital; thus it was, in truth, and it was not expected that he would enter until Tuesday afternoon. Señor San Martín does not usually do things as one expects: Monday at six o'clock in the morning he was in his home, having succeeded in escaping the gay demonstrations which, with extraordinary impatience, were being prepared, for a long time, by the gratitude of the public. This sobriety is not less admirable than his victories, and it is very opportune that no one should be kept in ignorance of the fact that he who has had the glory of deserving it cannot be so small as to request the honors of victory. But while the illustrious victor of Maipú refuses the applause, it is for public gratitude to compel him to accept it. Our poets have already sung, as never before, the glories of the general and his heroes in works worthy of their lofty subject and of posterity. Already our supreme Government and the august National Congress have duly accorded the honors due to the valor and other military and civic virtues to the hero of Chacabuco and Maipú and to his illustrious companions.

The *Gaceta* inserted thereunder a law enacted by Congress, ordering a monument to the victories of San Martín, and another law which presented San Martín's daughter with property in Buenos Aires.

The Congress resolved to give to "the heirs and descendants of the said general a valuable property from among those owned by the State, for the purpose that hereafter it may be a source of revenue which may contribute to their livelihood, endangered by the virtues and heroic selflessness of their father." The house which in virtue of this law was deeded to Mercedes was the one that bore the number 11 on Bolívar Street, in front of the Plaza de Mayo, a building which has disappeared. The rent from this house helped San Martín during his exile to take care of the support of his daughter.

At a session held on April 27, 1818, the Congress, which had decided before to thank San Martín for the services given in Chile to the cause of America, resolved that thanks should be given him personally. On May 8, 1817, the Director opened the session of this body in Buenos Aires, after its removal from Tucumán.

The solemn reception of San Martín at the legislative hall took place on Sunday, May 17, in a special session.

On May 25, 1818, San Martín attended the national festivities in which the people and the Government participated. Having come to the country in 1812, he saw in the capital the celebrations of 1813 in which his grenadiers took a part; but since the year 1814 he had been away from the capital on the anniversary date. The recent victory of Maipú gave the eighth anniversary an exceptional emotion. The Plaza was decorated with arches in Doric style around the Pyramid, and at night 3,560 lights were lit. During the day there were parades, songs, and speeches. In the evening there was a solemn show at the Coliseum theater, with the authorities in attendance; the act was opened with the singing of the national anthem; the tenor Tritto sang an overture; a salutation in verse to the people of Buenos Aires was recited; and *The Death of Caesar* was performed before an enthusiastic audience.

San Martín, who had arrived in Buenos Aires on May 11, 1818, held numerous talks with the Supreme Director; one of them, at a solemn meeting of the Lautaro Lodge, took place on June 13 of the same year. Besides Director Pueyrredón and San Martín, the following personages attended this conference: Tagle, Azcuénaga, Saavedra, Balcarce, Viamont, Grela, Gazcón, Chorroarín, Sáenz (Antonio), Gómez (José Valentín), Pinto (Guillermo), Rivadavia (Santiago), Irigoyen (Matías), Gallo (Pedro León), all of them prominent in Congress or the Army. Also present at the meeting was Don López, who told his son, the historian, the details of the debate.

The point in question was whether the Army of the Andes, once the independence of Chile was restored after Maipú, should come to serve in the River Plate, as some wanted it, or continue across the Pacific on an expedition against Peru, as planned by San Martín. The Director argued that the Argentine Provinces had already made enough sacrifices in favor of Chile and that it was the latter country that should fight the enemies in Lima, because it was necessary for the Government of Buenos Aires to quell the anarchy of the River Plate littoral and to take precautions against an invasion of 20,000 men that were going to leave from Cádiz against Argentina. San Martín replied that this expedition with which Spain was threatening was only a phantom to scare them, because that army was undermined by liberal ideas, and that as far as the chieftains and the Portuguese of the littoral were concerned, Buenos Aires could fight them without annulling the sacrifices made in Chile with a view to a vaster and more efficacious plan for the American cause.

The exchange of ideas reached at times a most heated stage, and more than once the quieter men had to calm the more excited. The minister, Tagle, watched the conversation silently and quietly, perhaps because he did not have any too favorable ideas about San Martín, whom he considered as a man who was not overfriendly to Buenos Aires. At a certain point in the debate, San Martín, annoyed by the lack of backing, said, affecting a ceremoniously official air, "Your Excellency knows, Mr. Director, that I am a man without any other ambition than that of throwing out of the American soil the tyrants who oppress it under the banner of the Spaniards. As Your Excellency, badly informed," he added, looking at Tagle with annoyance, "tells me that this is not any more the cause of the Army of the Andes, Your Excellency will have to accept the resignation that I will make of the command that had been entrusted to me."

This threat awakened in everyone the sensation which the able San Martín was looking for; but the Supreme Director, recovering his familiar tone, replied, "General and dear friend, you know how bitter that pain will be in my heart. My duties are heavier than yours; and as I do not know how to triumph, I have to conserve for the country the soldiers that are its only safeguard against the trials that await us."

The conference ended without adoption of the opinion contrary to San Martín, that is, of the necessity of the recrossing of the Andes. Everyone left worried; San Martín because of the possible failure of his plans, and the others owing to the announcement of his resignation.

Another meeting was held at Pueyrredón's farm in San Isidro, overlooking the River Plate. In the shadow of an ombú tree which is still alive, the Supreme Director and the Captain of the Andes talked. Pueyrredón was of the opinion that the expedition should not go as far as Lima, but only to the intermediate ports, to cause an uprising among the peoples of the coast; his reason was the lack of resources for a larger undertaking. In May 1819 he still wrote:

I look with more confidence upon the intermediate-ports undertaking than upon that of Lima, and it would remedy immediately the penuries in which we are sunk because of the lack of cash. Five thousand men and the armament for another five thousand are irresistible, except in Lima. That was my opinion when we met at my farm.

Against these opinions and without the necessary forces, San Martín, on his sole inspiration and will, carried out the campaign later and entered Lima. This foresight and these accomplishments give him his pre-eminent position among the contemporary great.

At last, after many discussions, an agreement was reached: The Government at Buenos Aires would help San Martín with 500,000 pesos, to complete the equipment of a fleet on the Pacific and of the United Army, in order that the latter might undertake an action against Lima. On June 16, at noon, he left the Plata for the Andes, happy with his success and in the company of his wife and daughter.

Instead of going on to Chile he stopped at Mendoza, to wait for the outcome and in order to maneuver from there on Chile and Argentina simultaneously.

In spite of the agreements, Director Pueyrredón wrote San Martín on August 22, 1818, officially, under the joint signature of the minister Gazcón, a "confidential" note, praising the plans, but telling him that it would not be possible to send him the 500,000 pesos which had been promised:

The great scope of the plans that Your Excellency has conceived in the good of the common cause, and so worthy of the auspices of this Government, led me, for lack of other means, to base my calculations on the money that is in circulation in the markets of this capital, so that these commercial enterprises should contribute toward the sum of 500,000 pesos with which Your Excellency, according to the agreement, should be helped. I regret to have to announce that, when trying to collect the entire sum, the steps taken have turned out to be inefficacious; so we have been forced to reduce the quota, and it can well be said that the 500,000-pesos loan will hardly be available in one third of that amount. These and the former causes of the conflict in which the present circumstances place me should persuade Your Excellency that there is enough reason to eliminate any calculation having as a basis the existence of these funds. Therefore I have decided to warn Your Excellency, before making any engagement, against making absolutely any drafts on the Treasury.

The official note ended with vague and consoling hopes, and a private letter from Pueyrredón confirmed the impossibility of negotiating the loan, "even if the jails are filled with capitalists."

This communication fell upon San Martín as a bolt of lightning. What had happened in Buenos Aires after his return? Had the influence of the minister Tagle been at work behind his back in his absence? Were there already in circulation the calumnies according to which San Martín, the bad Argentinian, was sold to the gold of Chile? Was it simply that there was no money, nor means of getting it?

The latest assumption was true, and even if other selfish passions had interposed themselves against him, it was also true that his plans crumbled suddenly, like a house of cards: the undertaking in Peru could not be carried out.

We can imagine what San Martín suffered after reading the note from the Argentine Government. On September 2 he had written urging help for the army, if its imminent dissolution was to be avoided; but on September 4, two days later, having read that crushing communication, San Martín sent in his resignation:

Having resolved to make the sacrifice of my life, I was on my way to take charge of the United Army, despite the fact that the physician, Don Guillermo Calisbury, who attended me when I was ill in Tucumán, assures me that I have not six months left to live; however, I was risking everything under the supposition that said army would have to operate outside Chile; but the circumstances having changed, I beg you to accept my resignation of said command.

And perhaps to prevent any thoughts of a desertion, he added this paragraph: "My weak services shall at all times be at the disposal of my country, in any danger that may threaten it."

San Martín's resignation, although "confidential," had a dramatic effect upon the governments of Chile and Argentina. The Lautaro Lodge intervened in both countries in order to smooth out the difficulties. It was realized that the withdrawal of San Martín was a catastrophe for the American Revolution. O'Higgins wrote him: "When I was preparing to receive you with open arms, I learned the bitter news of your resignation. San Martín is the hero destined to save South America, and he cannot renounce the preference with which Providence points at him."

Pueyrredón wrote him also, explaining the matter of the loan: "I don't know why I haven't gone crazy," he says, and adds, in a familiar tone, "Let us forget now about resignations; if circumstances made yours excusable, it is not so now, and I swear to you on my life that if you persist in it, I will forthwith resign myself. We have to come out of this honorably, helping each other."

Other friends intervened with the same purpose, and the conflict was solved with a new promise to furnish the needed aid.

San Martín, judging himself to be in a strong position, then stopped a courier in Mendoza who was taking funds from businessmen in Chile to Buenos Aires, and gave him drafts against the Government in exchange for the funds. He justified this abuse by alleging the lack of safety on the highways; but the Director nearly had a stroke when he had to pay the drafts to the individuals who presented them for payment: "If another draft comes, I declare the Government bankrupt and we all sink." That was true; but they did not dare stop that man possessed of the devil that was San Martín at the time, and from Buenos Aires they sent him in a short time and by several remittances almost 200,000 pesos, with which his hopes and activities were rekindled.

The horizon on the River Plate having cleared, San Martín left his family in Mendoza and crossed over to Chile in order to take care personally of the preparation of the expeditionary army.

The victor of Maipú entered Santiago incognito, and on October 31 the *Gaceta de Chile* said:

Last Thursday there came into this city His Excellency the Commander in Chief, General Don José de San Martín. He knew that the whole population of this city was waiting for him impatiently and was looking forward to giving him a triumphal reception on Friday, and for this reason his modesty and moderation made him make haste. Nevertheless persons of all classes, sex, and age have called at the palace since his arrival, in order to congratulate him and have the opportunity of seeing him again among ourselves; and those persons who did not have the honor of knowing him expressed silently their admiration when they saw the victor of Chacabuco and Maipú. His Excellency received everybody with his usual affability and courtesy, which win for him the people's hearts just as much as his heroic efforts and his victories.

After these Chilean compliments San Martín had to suffer new travails, worries, and illnesses at the end of 1818 and during the following year.

In November 1818 Lord Cochrane had arrived from England, and his arrival posed a delicate question, because he demanded for himself the admiralship, and Blanco Encalada, whose patriotic abnegation smoothed out all the difficulties, had to be put aside. He remained as second in command and subordinate to the Englishman. San Martín, who had already returned, helped in that emergency to put an end to the conflict, backing the demands of Cochrane, who repaid him so unfairly later.

It can be said that the liberating fleet of the Pacific was ready at the beginning of 1819, when Lord Cochrane took command. As a secretary he was given Alvarez Jonte, who had met him in England, and from Buenos Aires and across the Andes were brought English, American, French, and Portuguese seamen, who were easier to engage in the Argentine port than in Valparaiso, and with them were completed the crews, quite cosmopolitan indeed for such an undertaking.

In January 1819 the Chilean fleet set sail from Valparaiso bound for Callao, a Spanish fortress called the Gibraltar of America because of the strong castles that defended it. Cochrane tried to attack Callao but failed, owing to the fog. In view of this he declared a blockade of the Peruvian coast, from Atacama to Guayaquil; an inefficient blockade. He brought unrest to the ports, alarmed the populations, distributed proclamations and landed spies, following San Martín's instructions; he landed in Paita to take on supplies; at Huanchaco he captured the *Gazelle*, bound for the Philippines with 60,000 pesos on board.

Having obtained these results, he returned to Valparaiso in April of the same year, and he sailed again in September, with Blanco Encalada, taking with him the *O'Higgins* and the *San Martín*. He again threatened Callao; he tried to set fire to the Spanish ships with some Congreve rockets, the power of which turned out to be far less than the admiral had anticipated; from the bay he sent a theatrical challenge to Viceroy Pezuela; he attacked Pisco, where Guise, Miller, and Charles were put ashore, and later he carried out other acts of hostility against the Spaniards at Valdivia and in the south of Chile.

One of the reasons for San Martín's worry was the Spanish expedition that had been announced so many times. San Martín had proposed that if the expedition left Cádiz the American fleet should come out and stop it in the Atlantic. These threats kept Chile and the River Plate under alarm, and the gaucho singers dedicated to them several boastful *cielitos* (a kind of poetical composition for singing), which were written in Buenos Aires and circulated among the patriot camps, sung with the *criollo* guitars:

> *He who in battle at Maipú*
> *Knew how to sing a cielito,*
> *Now that the fleet is coming*
> *Again takes up his guitar.*

The singers had celebrated the victory of Maipú with a very picturesque cielito, and this other one about the expedition was similar:

> *To take from us our homeland*
> *A Spanish expedition is coming.*
> *Whenever you please, Don Fernando,*
> *Go ahead and take it, by the tail.*

> *The Count of I-don't-know-what*
> *Is said to command the armada,*
> *A man of evil intentions,*
> *With an embroidered tunic.*

> *Spaniards, throw from his throne*
> *A king so dumb and so lazy,*
> *And so that he may be amused,*
> *Let him come and plant thornbrush.*

> *Cielito, heavens, yea,*
> *The king is a man like any other,*
> *And to die that he may live,*
> *Hell, that's a foolish thing.*

This song, which is abbreviated here, ended with a friendly invitation to the Spaniards:

> If you want to come in peace,
> Friends you will find here,
> And eating good, rich meat,
> You'll live here with us.

The feelings of aversion to the King and of love for Spain which the gaucho muse so expressed were the same that San Martín himself expressed more than once, in that letter of 1816, where he spoke derisively of "Fernandito," or in that toast of 1821, at Punchauca, when he lifted his glass with Viceroy La Serna, as we shall see later, to the friendship of Spain and America, reconciled through liberty.

Despite the optimism of the gaucho singers, the possibility of an expedition sent from Cádiz became a cause for justified alarm in Chile and Argentina, even though later this danger vanished.

In 1819 the expedition, commanded by Brigadier Porlier, sailed from Cádiz with three ships of the line and numerous landing troops; but one of the vessels turned back, another was lost with Porlier off Cape Horn, and the third one, the *Prueba,* with forty-four guns, was captured by Cochrane at Guayaquil.

Another and more serious threat of a Spanish expedition was announced in 1820. According to the news from Cádiz this new expedition was to have 20,000 men under the command of O'Donnell, Count de la Bisbal; but this army mutinied before embarking, and this rebellion coincided with Riego's uprising at Cabezas de San Juan, a kind of liberating revolution inside Spain, aimed at placing upon the throne the king of the liberal constitution. The Spanish revolution of 1820 and the mutiny of the army destined for Buenos Aires are partly the work of secret agents sent by the Buenos Aires Government, as is proved by several documents. I believe that if San Martín had had a powerful fleet and greater resources he would have been willing to take a liberating revolution to Spain.

In October 1816 he had written to Guido: "I am very pleased with the progress of our corsairs. What will they say in Spain when they see the American forces on the great district of Cádiz?"

While a maritime attack was threatening from Spain, civil war was breaking out in the Argentine provinces. In the face of both dangers the Government of Buenos Aires ordered the Army of the Andes to return from Chile, and with this San Martín felt that his plans for an expedition to Peru had fallen through. The withdrawal of Argentine troops weakened at the same time the O'Higgins government and broke, in effect, the Chilean-Argentine alliance.

The mixed troops of the United Army were composed of two parts: the

Army of the Andes, which had come from Cuyo, and the Army of Chile, which was organized after Chacabuco. The former had at one time 468 men in the artillery, 866 mounted grenadiers, 342 horse engineers, and the rest, made up of various battalions, numbered a total of 4,791 soldiers. The Army of Chile reached a maximum of 4,413, including Battalion No. 3 from Arauco, No. 1 of chasseurs, No. 2 of militiamen from the south, the Homeland's Infantry, Military Academy, Artillery, Lancers, Supreme Director's Escort, artillery, and others. As will be seen, Argentina and Chile together had in 1820 more than 9,000 soldiers; but at the beginning of 1819 this number was vastly inferior.

A separation of these forces meant manifold dangers: stripping the garrisons of Chile on the Peruvian border, and exposing the troops to the contagion of civil war. Tortured by this conflict, San Martín fell acutely ill.

Such a point did San Martín's condition reach in Chile that he had to resign the command of the army: "The good of my homeland shall be the last wish that will go with me to my grave; for this reason I must warn that the condition of my health exposes me to an early demise, and that in this case there could arise evils of incalculable import for our cause, if they are not met beforehand and my successor is not appointed."

In the face of this clamor the Government appointed General Antonio Gonzáles Balcarce to be second in command. This Cireneus helped San Martín for some time to bear the cross of his mission, which he did not want to throw off, and the vision that haunted the great missionary gave him renewed strength to continue his painful and patient labors.

That was the condition of physical suffering and moral pains in which he was when the events of Argentine anarchy took place in 1819. The chieftains of the interior had coalesced for civil war; Buenos Aires felt its authority imperiled; the vision of America had been darkened by the shadow of each local church spire. It was then that the Government of Buenos Aires ordered him to recross the Andes and return to Mendoza with the forces that had been prepared for the expedition to Peru, to crush the forces of regionalism. Almost two thousand men returned to Cuyo then, and the rest of the Army of the Andes waited for orders on the western side of the mountains.

The division which crossed over to Mendoza after the battle of Maipú had been ordered by the Buenos Aires Government to open a campaign against the provinces of Santa Fe and Entre Ríos; in those circumstances General San Martín called a meeting of officers, and there it was unanimously decided not to comply with that order, since it surely meant the dissolution of the division and consequently the total renunciation of the expedition to Peru.

Thus San Martín explained, in notes written in France, the gravity of that moment, the reason for the recrossing of the Andes and the cause of his disobedience, which began there. He avoided being dragged into an internal war, thus saving the army for a greater undertaking. If he had not acted thus, perhaps everything would not have been lost; but his conduct was judged at the time as a hypocritical maneuver or an act of selfishness. From that moment date the rancors which were to hound him in his country.

In this conflict San Martín reflected upon what he must do, and he told O'Higgins, in a confidential letter, "A terrible responsibility is going to fall upon me; but if the expedition to Peru is not undertaken, the Devil will take everything."

For a brief period he was in Mendoza with a part of the army in 1819, hesitating between two duties: that which he owed to his Argentine birthplace, and that which he owed to the American homeland of his mission— between the military and the heroic duty. His meditations in those days bit at his conscience in the deepest part of his being. He sharpened his ingenuity and thought up excuses, writing one thing to O'Higgins and another to Pueyrredón, to see whether fortune and time would take him out of his slavery.

With patience and caution San Martín negotiated some measures of compromise, such as the return of a part of the army in order to frighten the chieftains of the littoral, but without abandoning totally the maritime undertaking aimed at Peru, which was his obsession, prompted by his knowledge of his destiny.

He then wrote O'Higgins, Director of Chile:

The eyes of America, or rather those of the world, are set on the decision of the present struggle against the Spaniards, in respect to the expedition to Peru. All await its outcome and know that General San Martín is the man to decide it. . . . I have to speak to you as to a gentleman, because I know you are one from every viewpoint, as I write to the Government of the United Provinces under the same date. My honor is pledged to the cause of America: I shall not have a homeland without it, and I cannot sacrifice such a precious gift for anything in the world.

Such was the desperate clamor that came from the breast of San Martín at this dramatic moment, when he avoided being involved in the Argentine struggle and sought from O'Higgins the last help necessary for his continental enterprise.

In those uncertain moments San Martín decided to send his wife and daughter to Buenos Aires. Both were on the point of being seized by the Indians and the *montoneros* (civil war bands) when passing the way station of El Desmochado in Santa Fe. They were saved from the danger by a detachment of Belgrano's army which was going through that section, according to Paz in his memoirs.

San Martín himself, in order to carry out orders from the Government, tried to go from San Luis to Buenos Aires, but he turned back at the Posta del Sauce because the men from Santa Fe had started hostilities against the capital. He thus tells O'Higgins, in October 1819: "A happy coincidence has prevented me from falling into their hands." Such already was the state of anarchy in the country.

At the end of 1819 San Martín, who was ill in Mendoza, became much worse when he learned of the uprising of the Army of the North and the imprisonment of Belgrano at Tucumán. Broken in health and in the presence of a nation in anarchy, he sent his resignation to Buenos Aires:

For three years I have been demanding my separation from the command of the army. A new demand is not necessary any more: my absolute prostration makes me separate myself from my post. If Your Excellency does not appoint another general, the army will be exposed to dissolution. The day after tomorrow I am going to the baths of Canquenes, and even if this brings some relief to my rheumatic pains, my chest ailment will not let me, for a long time, undertake any work.

The Buenos Aires Government replied authorizing him to take the cure at Canquenes, keeping the rank of brigadier general.

In those days there came from Chile, going to Buenos Aires, the Englishman Haigh, who visited him in Mendoza in order to deliver some letters to him.

"I found the hero of Maipú sick in bed," says Haigh, "looking so pale and thin that if it had not been for the brilliance of his eyes I would hardly have recognized him. He received me with a languid smile and put out his hand to welcome me." He took from Haigh two letters from Chile. Pleased at their contents, he showed them to Quintana, who was present. The news brought to him was that O'Higgins—Chile—would back the expedition to Peru, with San Martín at its head and however it could be done. The moment had come for the decisive act.

San Martín, who was really very ill, was placed in a stretcher, and gangs of peons took him over the Andes on their shoulders. Thus he crossed the Andes, from Mendoza to Chile, in January 1820, he who three years before had crossed them at the head of his army. Lying on his back, his eyes directed at the mountain sky, he looked upon the darkened land, as in a feverish hallucination—the last vision of his Peruvian chimera, not yet entirely vanished from the will of the fighter.

VII. THE VOYAGE OF DESTINY

In 1820 San Martín arose from his sick bed in Mendoza, crossed the Andes, resumed the command of the United Army, and installed himself at the encampment of Rancagua, near Valparaiso, where the Navy was preparing to take him to Peru. At that moment the news came to Chile that the Government at Buenos Aires had fallen.

When the general government of the provinces of the Union was dissolved, General San Martín sent from Santiago to the chief of the General Staff, Las Heras, who was with the army at Rancagua, a sealed note, with a warning not to open it except in the presence of all the chiefs and officers of the army. In this note the commanding general remarked that, the Government from which his authority emanated having been dissolved, he believed it his duty to resign his command, as he was doing, so that immediately thereafter the officers should elect, by secret ballot, a commander who would take charge of the army: this meeting voted for the re-election of General San Martín, according to the record of the proceedings which was drawn up on this day.

This résumé is that of San Martín himself. He wrote it in exile in France, in his old age, and in his customary brevity. But this event, so easy to relate, was the blow of his sword upon the Gordian knot. It seemed the maneuver of an astute politician: the Government which had appointed him had fallen, he resigned his command before the chiefs, and allowed these to choose their new general.

A great clamor arose in Buenos Aires and other cities, and San Martín was accused of being a traitor to his country. There was talk of court-martialing him if he returned to Argentine territory. He was accused of being indifferent to the misfortunes which afflicted his country. He was considered an adventurer, because he had appropriated an army which was not his, and he was called a common seeker for power, because it was believed that his reason for going to Lima was to acquire power for himself.

Much more serious than all this was the calumny, spread at the time, that San Martín had received 500,000 pesos from Chile in payment for his attitude, or that he had stolen this sum from the Chilean Treasury, helped by his uncontrolled handling of the undertaking. Wounded by such infamies, he sent a note to O'Higgins:

It seems that revolutions open an immense field to calumny, and that the main shots are aimed chiefly against those who have the misfortune of being in command. . . . In the Province of Cuyo, especially, the rumor had spread that the Government of Chile had delivered to me 500,000 pesos as a compensation for the expense met by said Province for the liberation of Chile, which amount I had hidden and kept in my possession. Your Excellency will tell me, with justification, that this untruth is of the grossest kind: that I know. In spite of that I beg Your Excellency to answer me on this point, and also about the fact that you were in possession of all the reports from the Ministers of the Treasury who had existed and exist in this state, and I beg Your Excellency to declare whether or not there is any order of mine for the delivery of a single peso anywhere in this state, and also whether I have had the least participation in anything that has any relation with its interest; which documents I expect Your Excellency to send me as soon as possible.

O'Higgins replied, when he sent the information requested: "The voice of responsible men, that of deserving patriots, and that of the Government itself, would arise immediately to vindicate Your Excellency after such gross attacks, were it not that public opinion is so centered upon the justice that is due to the merits of Your Excellency."

In spite of these declarations of his innocence which he received from the Government of Chile through its Supreme Director, San Martín suffered in his innermost feelings because he knew that in his own country he was being accused of venality and treason. In these physical and moral conditions he prepared to undertake the expedition to Lima. One would say that it was not he who undertook it, but his inner self. Perhaps he knew it, because he said: "I must follow the destiny that calls me"; and this was the source of the energy with which an ill man, who a short time before was dying in Mendoza, now rose proudly against calumny and danger. With fewer troops than those called for in his plan, he was ready to throw himself, for his own account, into this great adventure.

The three years which San Martín spent in Chile correspond to the time of his maturity: there he observed his fortieth birthday, a few days before the battle of Maipú. It was then that he accomplished his greatest feats as a warrior, and it was then that he planned his greatest undertakings as a liberator. At the end of his mission in Chile he performed an extraordinary act: he disobeyed the Argentine Government—an act which aroused vituperation at the time and which posterity still misunderstands. That rupture with his homeland is, however, a proof of the energy derived from his genius. What there was of fatalism in his undertaking was uncovered by this action. The terrible step which he took in 1820 was like a jump into the abyss.

He had reckoned for his Peruvian plan upon the basis of 6,000 men and he had only a little over 4,000, which diminished the probability of success. Under those conditions he took the terrible step, in bad health, without resources, and with his Argentine homeland a prey to anarchy and calling him a traitor and a thief. Watching him leave for Peru under such adverse circumstances, one feels in him the presence of a superhuman spirit which drove him to the fatal consummation of his destiny.

San Martín was in Valparaiso, ready to embark with his legions, when, on July 22, 1820, he addressed from his general headquarters a proclamation to the people of the provinces of the River Plate, with the purpose of justifying his disobedience, and to entreat them to meditate. He made prophecies about Argentine anarchy, in which he did not want to mix, and about American freedom, the exclusive mission of his life.

The hour had come for the hero, but a cloud cast a shadow on the midday sun. Never did San Martín speak with more spiritual depth than when he wrote his 1820 Proclamation. It was his inner self, the angel of his message, who then spoke. In the hours of crisis, his internal vision of things be-

came more lucid, and his will power more firm. But never did he act or
see with so much clarity as he did in 1820. His "Proclamation of Disobedience" is not an outlet for his pain; it is an expression of his virtue.

Let us hear and interpret, in order to measure the depth of his soul, the
heroic words of that message:

> Fellow countrymen: The moment approaches when I must follow the destiny
> that calls me: I am going to undertake the great work of giving liberty to Peru.
> But before I leave I want to tell you some truths, which I would regret that you
> came to know in the long run through your own experience. I shall also tell you
> the complaints I have, not from impartial and well-intentioned men, whose opinion
> has always been a consolation for me, but from some who know very little of their
> own interests and of those of their country, because in the long run, like all
> crimes, calumny is only the work of a perverted discernment.

Thus began the epistle, the virtue of which recalls those letters of St. Paul
when he addressed himself to the primitive churches of Asia. The hour had
come when the genius was going to triumph or to fail forever, and, gathering
all his strength, he came out, fortified by the strength of God, to challenge the
world. It was not any longer simply a man who speaks through his own
mouth, but a messenger of the Eternal.

> Your situation does not permit any concealment of the facts; ten years of constant
> sacrifices are now used as a trophy by anarchy; the glory of having made those
> sacrifices becomes a suffering now, in view of the poor fruits of it. You have dug
> a precipice with your own hands, and having accustomed yourselves to look at it,
> no sensation of horror is enough to stop you. The genius of evil has inspired in
> you the delirium of a federation. this word is full of death, and it does not mean
> anything but ruin and devastation. I appeal to your own experience and I beg you
> to listen with frankness to the opinion of the general who loves you and expects
> nothing from you. I have reasons for knowing your condition, because in the two
> armies which I have commanded I have had to investigate the political conditions
> of the provinces over which I ruled. To think of establishing a federal[1] government
> in a country which is almost deserted, full of jealousies and local antipathies, with
> scant knowledge and experience of public affairs, without the income necessary to
> meet the expenses of the general government, without mentioning the demands of
> the civil lists of each state, is a plan whose dangers do not permit any delusions,
> not even with the ephemeral pleasure which is always caused by the delights of
> novelty.

When San Martín said "federation" he referred to civil war between half-
literate chieftains and gaucho multitudes, because that was the picture of
Argentine federation at its beginning in that terrible year. Hatreds and pover-
ties of miserable villages lost in the desert began to burn before the frightened
eyes of the hero, and he believed, with a mystic terror, that "the genius of
evil" blew upon this fire. In the armies which he had commanded on the
littoral, in Tucumán and in Cuyo, he met many sergeants and officers who

now appeared as leaders; chief among them were Francisco Ramírez, Felipe Ibarra, and Facundo Quiroga, who, later, were to exclaim "Federation or Death"; and for all those reasons he felt that that word was full of death. And he turned his back upon the peoples of the River Plate, leaving his country, under the flag of Chile, to liberate Peru, because his country was the whole of America, and because the emancipation of America was his mission. Therefore, he did not wish to be involved in the premature struggles of the chieftains.

Fellow countrymen: I speak to you with the frankness of a soldier: if, obeying the experience of ten years of conflicts, you do not give your wishes a more prudent direction, I fear that, tired of anarchy, you may hope at the end for a return of oppression and that you may welcome the yoke of the first fortunate adventurer who shows up, who, far from consolidating your destiny, will only prolong your servitude.

And now it was the Spirit of Time who spoke through the mouth of San Martín, the prophet. It was the year 1820; Juan Manuel de Rosas, who played no part in the first decade of the revolution, was only an obscure rancher on the pampas of Buenos Aires[2]; but San Martín knew that from that inferno of civil war would emerge a devil with blue eyes who would take a seat upon the bloody throne of tyranny "to prolong our servitude." When Argentina, prey to anarchy and darkness, sought a new master, Juan Lavalle and other unfortunates offered San Martín the dictatorship, but the latter rejected it, because never were his arms used for usurping power. And then Rosas came from the ends of the pampas with his red-clad horsemen "to prolong our servitude" under the terror. These praetorian guards wearing *chipirás*[3] and these myrmidons with the red ribbons were still concealed in the shadows of time; but San Martín, the prophet, foresaw the event and announced the tragedy, because he was the messenger of our American destiny. He was the man who knew, but nobody would listen to him. . . .

Now I will express to you the complaints I have, not because silence may be a difficult trial for my feelings, but because I must not leave honest men in perplexity, nor can I abandon the judgment of my conduct, libeled by men whom someday gratitude may possess again.

After outlining the bitter panorama of the Argentine homeland, he spoke of himself, something he usually avoids: "Silence is not a difficult trial for his feelings." But the moment was exceptional and he broke his silence, because he must justify his conduct before honest men. The strength of his prestige was not his only, but of all his countrymen. These calumniated him, and he, full of pride, spoke at last in order to reveal the sense of his mysterious life.

I was serving in the Spanish Army in 1811; twenty years of honest service had won for me some recognition, in spite of my being an American; I learned of the revolution in my country, and when I abandoned my fortune and my hopes I only regretted not to have something more to sacrifice for the liberty of my land: I arrived in Buenos Aires at the beginning of 1812, and since then I have devoted myself to the cause of America; its enemies can say whether my services have been useful.

When he said this, San Martín was not boasting. A Spanish colonel at thirty, promoted on the battlefield, his ability and his courage were appreciated by illustrious chiefs in the Peninsula. He had won decorations at Bailén, fighting against Napoleon. Spain was in a crisis; a field for fresh triumphs was open to him in Europe. But on learning of the May Revolution, he remembered he had been born at Yapeyú, and a new man arose in him. He renounced his European hopes; he left Spain and his Spanish mother; and poor as he was, he came to his country, where nobody knew him and where many looked upon him with suspicion, "to devote himself to the cause of America." Hardly had he arrived in Buenos Aires when he formed his family, established the Lautaro Lodge, promoted the calling of the Assembly, organized the mounted grenadiers, and beat the Spanish flotilla at San Lorenzo, insuring the hegemony of Buenos Aires over the River Plate. All this he did in only one year. Then he restored the morale of the Army of Upper Peru, and seeing that the road to Lima did not lie on the north, he returned to seek it on the west.

In 1814 I was governor of Mendoza; the loss of this country endangered the province which I governed: I placed it then in a condition to defend itself until the time should come to undertake the offensive. My resources were scarce, and I had only the embryo of an army; but I knew the good will of the Cuyans, and I undertook to form it under a plan which would make it clear how much can be accomplished by economy when carrying out great undertakings.

In 1817 the Army of the Andes was already organized; I opened the campaign in Chile, and on February 12 my soldiers received the reward for their constancy. I knew that from that moment my success would excite jealousies, and I made an effort, although a fruitless one, to calm them with moderation and disinterest.

In spite of this, calumny was working against me with perverse activity; but it sought the shadows, because it cannot exist before light. Up until the month of January, I deserved public appreciation in the provinces which formed the Union, and only after the triumph of anarchy has there entered into the calculations of my enemies the purpose of calumniating me undisguisedly and of piling upon my name the most exaggerated insults.

But I have a right to ask them, What mystery of iniquity has there been in waiting for the time of disorder to sully my reputation? How can their suppositions be reconciled with the conduct of the Government of Chile and of the Army of the Andes? The former, with the concurrence of the Senate and the vote of the people, appointed me commander of the expeditionary forces; and the latter re-elected me as its general, in the month of March, when, the central authority having been overthrown in the United Provinces, I resigned the command which I had received from it, in order that the army then encamped at Rancagua could appoint a chief whom it would willingly obey.

If such has been the conduct of those who have observed closely my actions, it is not possible to explain the conduct of those who calumniate me from a distance without lifting the veil which conceals their feelings and their purposes. I swear that I am pained at the thought of them, not because of what may concern my own person, but because of the evils which threaten the people who are under their influence.

There was in all this part of the proclamation an echo of pain, but so light that it could hardly be noticed. More than a lamentation, it was a reproach. San Martín, the stoic, was not a man to make unnecessary complaints; but when speaking of himself he was defending himself before history. Since his arrival in 1812 a sordid hostility had enveloped him, born in part of his conduct, somewhat secretive, because he was reserving his effort for his plan of the Andean campaign, which until 1816 he kept in the greatest secrecy. At the beginning he was thought to be an agent for Spain, and later there were added to the first absurd suspicions the reactions of the parties he drew away from in the internal struggles. His emulators, his rivals, or his victims later exaggerated the cry of vengeance to the point of calumny. In 1820, with his loyal friends Belgrano, Pueyrredón, and Rondeau fallen from power, he was thought defenseless, and the pack attacked him with the worst insults.

The oligarchy, beaten by democratic federalism, felt offended because he denied it the help of his troops, with the purpose of saving them from a civil war to be used in a nobler war; and the federalists also mistrusted him. San Martín's attitude toward the Argentine provinces seemed selfish to some, if not cowardly or traitorous, and still more blameworthy when the paladin enlisted under the flag of Chile, which was for him also a part of the great continental homeland.

The charges of cruelty, for old military executions, such as those of the Carreras, in which he took no part; those of venality, for his alleged appropriation of moneys in Chile; and finally his alleged indifference before the struggles in Buenos Aires, were the topics of his detractors. Against all this protested the saddened soul of him who in 1816 had said, "San Martín will always be a suspected man in his country." He knew well that that injustice was an unavoidable burden imposed by his genius, in the mission of sacrifice which, on his return from Spain, he had undertaken as a religious vow for his selfless will.

Fellow countrymen: I leave you with a deep regret that I experience at the prospect of your misfortunes; you have accused me of not having contributed to increase them, for such would have been the result if I had taken an active part in the war against the federalists: my army was the only one that kept its morale, and I would have exposed it to the danger of losing it if I had opened a campaign in which the example of licentiousness should have armed my troops against order. In such case it was necessary to renounce the undertaking of liberating Peru, and supposing that fate had favored my arms in the civil war, I would have had to deplore the victory along with the beaten themselves. No, General San Martín will never shed the blood of his compatriots, and he will unsheath his sword only against the enemies of the independence of South America.

No. General San Martín did not want to be the founder of a demagogic Caesarism, nor did he want to dip his sword in Argentine blood. He was born for cleaner feats and not for wearing the laurels of South American praetorianism, which others founded. The only revolution in which he took a part, that of 1812, was aimed at defending the liberty of the people.

Lastly, in the name of your own interest, I beg you to learn to distinguish between those who labor for your health and those who plot your ruin; do not expose yourself to the risk that well-meaning men may abandon you to the counsel of the ambitious; the firmness of virtuous souls does not reach the point of suffering that evildoers may be placed on the same level with them; unfortunate is the people among whom such a scandalous parallel may be established and go unpunished.

From the shores of the Pacific, across the Andes at 21,000 feet, through eighteen days of travel through the pampas, the cry of outraged virtue arrived in Buenos Aires. San Martín was getting ready to undertake his voyage to Peru, not as a homeless mercenary, but as the Cid, when he left Castile among insults in order to defeat Moorish kings and win trophies for Christianity: "You shall see so many lances held aloft. . . . Ringing goes the news of him to the other shore of the sea. . . ."

Provinces of the River Plate! The most joyous day of our revolution is about to dawn; I am going to give the last answer to my calumniators; I cannot do anything but compromise my life and my honor for the cause of my country; be the fate of my campaign in Peru what it may, I shall prove that ever since I returned to my country its independence has been the only thought in my mind; and that I have not had any other ambition than that of deserving the hate of the ingrate and the appreciation of the virtuous.

Here again was the sure accent of prophecy: the eyes of the genius encompassed all his America, and his ear heard the orders which came to him from the invisible. The voice of destiny was calling him. Divine visions lighted his word, and reflections of superhuman light illumined the whole continent, whose destiny was his. San Martín drew away from the corner where he had been born in order to undertake the mission of the continent on which he was to survive. His cradle of Yapeyú was the cosmic navel of his being, but all of America was his maternal womb. Therefore, he went to consummate his sacrifice in Lima, because his homeland extended beyond Lima; a land too large for the pigmies who insulted him because they did not understand him.

Having sent this proclamation to the Argentine people in the month of July, he hastened the latest steps for the voyage. The hour of destiny had come to San Martín.

The crisis in the Argentine Government had changed the basis of the United Army and placed San Martín in an anomalous situation. To this was due the reorganization of the Lautaro Lodge in Chile, with an amply American vision of the forthcoming enterprise. The preamble of the Lautarian Constitution, adopted in 1820, said:

America was crying under the most shameful and humiliating servitude, ruled with an iron scepter by Spain and its kings, as the whole world knows, and as all nations have watched with just indignation for three centuries. At last came the favorable moment in which, the Spanish Government having been dissolved through the imprisonment of its monarch, justice, reason, and necessity, because of their repeated experiences, because of the occupation of Spain and because of other innumerable causes, imperiously demand shaking off this yoke.

The Provinces of the River Plate gave the signal for liberty; they revolted; they have sustained for ten years their enterprise, with heroic constancy, but unfortunately without method, without co-ordination, and without any other design than that which was suggested by circumstances, events, and accidents.

The result has been to give rise to guerrillas among the peoples, to the straying of opinion, to partisan fury, and to the interest of ambition, without the true friends of the country being able to face these most grave ills with any remedy other than their suffering and confusion.

This has been the reason for the establishment of this society, which must be composed of American gentlemen outstanding for the liberalism of their ideas and for the fervor of their patriotic zeal, who should work with method and plan for the independence of America and for its happiness, dedicating to this most noble purpose all their strength, their influence, their faculties and talents, sustaining themselves with faithfulness, acting with honor, and proceeding with justice, under the guidance of the following provisions.

The provisions to which this preamble referred were the organic rules of the lodge, its exoteric phase, so to speak, because the esoteric one has remained in a mystery similar to that of the Buenos Aires Lodge, which was the subject of a former chapter[4]; but it was the chief continental orientation of 1820, the one that inspired the Peruvian undertaking, and was also the key to San Martín's thoughts at the time. The government of the lodge having been dissolved in Buenos Aires, San Martín readjusted the Chilean lodge in the light of the new circumstances of his mission. This preamble and the proclamation offer us, in all its American amplitude, the thought of the hero, and both allude to Argentine anarchy.

In May 1819 Director Pueyrredón wrote nobly to San Martín: "You know that your opinions have always been the guiding rule for my deliberations in everything relative to the Army of the Andes"; but later Pueyrredón left the Directorate and his place was taken by Rondeau. He recalled the

Army of the North in order to defend his authority against the provincial bosses, but this army mutinied at Arequito, on January 7, 1820, and Belgrano, its commander, was imprisoned in Tucumán. Rondeau had also recalled the Army of the Andes, and the delays of San Martín prevented it from being inoculated with anarchy, although not entirely, because the first regiment of chausseurs, stationed in San Juan, mutinied two days after Arequito, when San Martín had returned to Chile.

This mutiny was led by the officers Mendizábal, Morillo, and Corro, who deposed Governor La Rosa, and the soldiery committed excesses. Soon also fell the governors Luzuriaga in Mendoza, Dupuy in San Luis, and those of other provinces, where local bosses or mutinous officers enthroned themselves. Director Rondeau also fell, and then the hordes of Ramírez arrived in Buenos Aires, bringing about a headless national government and being responsible for the process against the congressmen who had taken part in secret monarchist undertakings. Mendizábal and some of his accomplices were arrested in 1821 and sent to Peru, where they were shot. One thousand men from the garrison of Mendoza, commanded by Alvarado, returned to Chile, thus avoiding general chaos.

So that those who could understand would understand, San Martín, on the eve of his embarkation, on August 19, addressed himself to the council of Buenos Aires, the only authority which represented the tradition of May in the midst of anarchy:

Tomorrow the expedition for the liberation of Peru sets sail. As its commander I have the honor to inform Your Excellency that it represents the heroic people, the virtuous people most worthy of the history of South America and of the gratitude of its sons, and I declare that my most ardent wishes are for its happiness; and that from the moment in which the Central Government of the Provinces is constituted, the Army of the Andes shall place itself at its superior orders, with the most complete and respectful obedience.

After his victory in Peru, he corroborated this message with other acts of love toward his Argentine homeland.

At the beginning of August the port of Valparaiso was ordered closed, for greater safety in the task of loading. All the ships of the expedition anchored in the beautiful bay. It was necessary to place on board twenty-five land cannon, 15,000 muskets, and 2,000 swords for the new troops which would be recruited in Peru; ammunition, saddles, ironware, and other equipment; food for 5,000 men: biscuits, flour, beans, jerked beef; 800 horses with their fodder; and a printing press for propaganda.

The task began on August 10 and ended nine days later, under the supervision of Las Heras, chief of the general staff.

On the 19th, San Martín and O'Higgins attended a secret meeting of the Lautaro Lodge in Santiago, and at night they attended a meeting of the

Senate, in order to agree on instructions. According to these, San Martín was entrusted with the direction of the war, and his undertaking was given these two goals: to liberate Peru and to establish a democratic government once the country was in a condition to elect its popular representatives.

On the 20th, on his return to Valparaiso, Admiral Cochrane was notified that he was to be under the orders of San Martín, the generalissimo of the expedition.

A last farewell, almost confidential, was then addressed by San Martín to his old friend Godoy Cruz, who had just taken over the governorship of Mendoza: "I am going to make," he says, "the last effort in favor of America. If this cannot be done because of the continuation of the disorders and of anarchy, I shall leave the country, because my soul is not made to watch the country's ruin."

The troops had already embarked when San Martín, on board the ship that bore his name, reviewed the fleet, which was ready to sail. The harbor and the hills which overlook the bay were alive with people, men and women, who had come from Santiago and from the neighborhood of Valparaiso to watch the departure.

The clear atmosphere, vibrant with martial noise, and the green sea, speckled with white sails, offered a superb spectacle. The heroic feeling fused itself with the emotion of nature, and when the ships began to move a clamor of ovations and good wishes arose from anxious breasts, mixing itself with the Argentine anthem which was being played by the ships' bands.

San Martín, on the flagship, heard his name cheered together with those of the country and liberty, and he thrilled at the sight of the beginning of the materialization of his last heroic dream. The mountain and the sea offered themselves together to him, as they had been for so many years in his thoughts. On the shore of the bay gray hills arose sheerly, as the last western shape of the Andes: he had crossed them coming from the east, like the sun, and now he was going toward the setting sun. He knew very well his destiny, which he had invoked on his departure in the proclamation of his disobedience. He thought, perhaps, that Buenos Aires would forgive him someday for his heroic evasion. Still as a bronze statue, he kept looking at the mountains while the fleet got under way. From the shore many tear-filled eyes looked at the ships, until the numberless white sails, swollen by the wind of the ocean, slowly lost themselves beyond the horizon.

VIII. THE MAGIC WAR OF PERU

The expedition which had left Valparaiso on August 20, 1820, was carrying on board 4,700 soldiers and enough equipment for 15,000 men which could be recruited after the expedition's landing. On the *San Martín,* the flagship, was the general of the same name, commander of the army, with his General Staff; the *O'Higgins,* commanded by Lord Cochrane, was the flagship of the vanguard; the rear guard was made up of other vessels.

The fleet for the liberation of Peru was composed of the following warships: square-rigger *San Martín,* 1,300 tons, 64 guns; frigate *O'Higgins,* 1,220 tons, 44 guns; frigate *Lautaro,* 850 tons, 46 guns; frigate *Independencia,* 380 tons, 28 guns; brigantine *Galvarino,* 398 tons, 18 guns; brigantine *Araucano,* 270 tons, 16 guns; brigantine *Pueyrredón,* 220 tons, 16 guns; schooner *Moctezuma,* 200 tons, 7 guns. Besides these units the following transports were enlisted: *Dolores, Gaditana, Consecuencia, Emprendedor, Santa Rosa, Aguila, Mackenna, Perla, Jerezana, Peruana, Golondrina, Minerva, Libertad, Argentina, Hércules,* and *Potrillo,* 7,178 tons in all.

These names, combining those of aborigines with those of the rulers of Buenos Aires and Chile, themselves reveal the American spirit which inspired the expedition. Among the seamen, besides Cochrane, there were many Europeans, almost all English, as material agents of that spirit.

The navigation, not far from the coast, lasted more than two weeks, and when stopping at Coquimbo a new contingent of Chilean troops was taken on board. On September 7 the squadron arrived at the bay of Paracas and the landing began, while San Martín, who had gone on board the schooner *Moctezuma,* with two hundred men under the Count of Montemar, explored the coast. Three thousand soldiers, divided into three battalions under the command of Las Heras, camped at Pisco. From Pisco San Martín gave his first proclamation to the Peruvians:

"I have made known the purpose of my mission among you; I come to satisfy the expectations of all those who wish the freedom of the country which gave them life and who wish to be ruled by their own laws."

The news of this landing was not long in reaching Lima, where the new Constitution, under Ferdinand VII, had been sworn. Viceroy Pezuela, on learning of this, exclaimed sarcastically, "Each brown pig gets its San Martín."[1]

On the 12th, after noon, the viceregal emissaries coming from Callao arrived at Pisco. The delegates of both sides met at Miraflores, and they began by arranging an eight-day armistice. The Royalists proposed recognition of the constitutional government which had just been established, and the evacuation of the territory; San Martín demanded recognition of American independence. The conferences ended on October 14 without any agreement having been reached, and on the 15th hostilities were resumed. San Martín himself writes in his old age:

General San Martín's plan upon his landing in Pisco had as its principal aims, first, to seize the slaves in order to increase the numbers of the army, which could not be done, except on a very small scale, because the lateness of the ship which was bringing the horses gave the landowners time to withdraw the slaves; second, to send, as was done, a division with the purpose of creating an insurrection in the country, and of going over the mountain in order to link its operations north of Lima with those of the main body of the army, and under these conditions to operate according to the success of the campaign and of the insurrection of the population. . . . There never entered into General San Martín's calculations a frontal attack on the capital of Peru, in view of the lack of discipline in the army, which had been undermined by the revolutions in the United Provinces and by the partisan struggles in Chile.

These words of San Martín explain the necessity for his plan and the cautiousness of his operations.

After Miraflores, San Martín wrote the viceroy deploring to see himself forced to open hostilities and consoling himself with the idea of having as an adversary a gentleman "who will do what is in his power to diminish the misfortunes of this fatality, assuring you that on my part I will do everything toward the same end." The viceroy replied, "I shall make war with all the consideration which humanity demands."

General Arenales says in his memoirs: "General San Martín possessed the most original resources to arouse among his enemies as many worries as he wanted, and it is difficult to explain how far his extraordinary ability in this connection went." Such remarks on the part of an agent of San Martín's point to the purely spiritual recourse which the hero had to use in the war in Peru, either in response to conditions in the environment, or out of the maturity of his genius. There he triumphed more with his intelligence then with his weapons.

This is what many of San Martín's critics have not understood, and which, if it is understood, places San Martín, the master liberator of Peru, at a higher rank than the warrior of Maipú, admirable as the latter was. Neither his military forces nor the social atmosphere of Peru counseled him to rush into open battle, which in 1821 could have been adverse to him. However, he carried out a plan of hostilities the efficacy of which cannot be denied.

On October 24, 1820, San Martín gave, in Pisco, his decree about the flag and the coat of arms of Peru, symbols of the new nation. The flag was to be in white and red, and the coat of arms was to have at the center a crown of laurel within which could be seen the sun coming up from behind sheer mountains arising from a tranquil sea. The decree had as its foundation the fact that independence was incompatible with the emblems which reminded one of the long years of oppression, and it was prescribed that the new symbols would be maintained until such a time as a government, elected by the popular will, should be established. This decree was printed on the press which San Martín brought with his army; the same one which printed numerous proclamations destined to sow the spirit of revolution in the inte-

rior of the country. One of these proclamations prohibited his soldiers from
engaging in any useless cruelty, reminding them that "their duty is to console Americans."

He sent General Arenales to the interior of the country, in order to arouse
the mountain people, and he won, on December 6, the victory of Cerro de
Pasco, a battle in which the Royalists lost 58 dead, 18 wounded, 343 prisoners, 2 cannon, 300 muskets, and all the flags, equipment, ammunition,
and band instruments. The enemy commander, Brigadier General O'Reilly,
was taken prisoner. This victory was celebrated in Buenos Aires with a
drama entitled, *The Battle of Pasco,* and San Martín conferred upon his
soldiers an emblem bearing this legend, "I am one of the victors of Pasco."

Meanwhile, the Numancia Battalion, craftily undermined by San Martín's
agents, mutinied against the King and went over to the patriot forces, a happy
event, which, without any bloodshed, was as important as a victory. The
Numancia, a battalion composed almost entirely of Americans (natives of
South America) and commanded by Heres, went over to the patriots on
December 3, 1821, abandoning at Changai the Royalist chief, Valdez, who
had planned to cut off Arenales, while San Martín was advancing toward
Changai to protect Arenales, who was returning from the mountains.

These defeats and the underground war demoralized Viceroy Pezuela's
troops to the extent that there was an uprising against him, which compelled
him to resign, and he handed over his position to General La Serna, the
chief of the discontented, who took over the viceroyalty. This event was in
itself a revolutionary act, and it must be remembered, in order better to understand it, that Pezuela represented the absolutist tendencies while La Serna
was an exponent of the liberal ones which had been reborn in Spain with
the revolution of 1820 and the restoration of the constitution of 1812. Such
were, when San Martín had hardly landed, the triumphs of San Martinian
action; a battle won, a battalion in mutiny, a viceroy overthrown, and popular
opinion in full unrest.

San Martín transferred his encampment from Pisco to Huaura. In this
town the commander occupied a two-story house (which still stands) with a
typical balcony on the corner. The fleet anchored at Huacho, and San Martín
continued, ashore or on board, directing the astute movements his plan called
for. Discontent was ever increasing among the Royalists, while the revolutionary ideas penetrated as if by art of magic among the Indians of the mountains, the Negroes of the plantations, the natives of the villages, and even
among the white *criollos* of the capital.

The situation of the patriots was not, however, very promising, because a
malignant fever began to weaken the troops at the Huaura encampment, and
even the commander himself fell sick. To this was added the fact that no help
was coming from Chile; that on the frontier of Upper Peru the Argentine
civil war had brought about the failure of Güemes' movements; that in Quito

the revolution was still in an embarrassing position; and that a certain discontent was beginning to be noticed in the fleet under the command of Cochrane, because of the delay in the payment of salaries. In these circumstances an interview took place between the new viceroy and the Argentine commander.

San Martín and Viceroy La Serna met at Punchauca on June 2, 1821, to talk about the possible understanding. The viceroy arrived carrying the red band of his office across his chest, while San Martín was dressed in his simple blue uniform of the grenadiers. Both were accompanied by the principal chiefs of their respective armies: Las Heras and Guido among the Argentines, and among the Spaniards, Canterac, Valdez, La Mar, and the royal commissioner, Abreu, who shortly before had come from Madrid to propose peace on the basis of the recognition of the King and of the new constitution recently sworn to by Ferdinand VII.

San Martín and the viceroy embraced when they met and then began to talk in the presence of the other chiefs.

"General," said San Martín to Viceroy La Serna, beginning the dialogue, "I consider this one of the happiest days of my life. I have come to Peru from the shores of the River Plate, not to shed blood but to establish the freedom and the rights which the motherland itself established when she proclaimed the constitution of 1812, which Your Excellency and your generals defended. The liberals of the world are brothers everywhere."

This pleasant introduction characterized the war not as a racial antagonism between Spain and America, but as a struggle between two philosophical systems, absolutism and liberalism. The ideal which San Martín and the Americans defended was the same that Riego and his followers in the Peninsula had defended in the motherland. The democratic revolution, then defeated in Spain, had taken a century to emerge victorious there.

"If in Spain that constitution was once abjured, with a return to the old regime," San Martín went on, "it is not to be thought that its first protagonists in America, who accepted the undertaking of upholding it, may ever abandon their convictions, renouncing the noble aspirations of preparing in this hemisphere a safe haven for their fellow believers."

Speaking like this, San Martín sought the adhesion of the Spanish chiefs, whose liberal leanings he knew, and thus he could, without difficulty, pass on, astutely, to his real subject:

"The delegates of Your Excellency, reaching a loyal understanding with mine, have arrived at the agreement that the independence of Peru is not irreconcilable with the interest of Spain, and that in giving way to the opinion declared by the peoples of America, they would perform a signal service if they avoid war and open the doors to decorous reconciliation. The time is past when the colonial system can be upheld by Spain. The Spanish armies will fight with the traditional bravery of their brilliant military history; but even if the struggle could be prolonged, its successful outcome cannot be doubtful for millions of men who have resolved to be independent, and who will serve mankind and their country better if, instead of ephemeral advantages, they are in a position to offer large centers to trade, and fruitful and friendly and permanent relations among men of the same race, who speak the same language and who feel in the same degree the wish to be free. If Your Excellency will co-operate in putting a stop to a sterile fight and join your flags to ours in order to proclaim the independence of Peru, the two armies will embrace each other on the field."

These words impressed all those who heard them. History has not paid sufficient attention to them, and we must underline them. The picture which San Martín draws with them is that of Spanish America reconciled with the motherland at the beginning of the twentieth century: a prophetic vision, without a shadow of hate, which the anachronistic obstinacy of the monarchy could not understand at the time. Those words, besides, reveal that San Martín was then in full lucidity and maturity. The man of arms, a Christian paladin, wanted to avoid war, and the politician sought to trap the adversary in his plan for Peruvian independence.

The Spanish generals felt touched by those words and showed their sympathy for the superior man who uttered them and for his generous ideals. The viceroy, meanwhile, kept his reserve, and he asked about the concrete basis for a possible accord, to which San Martín answered:

"Let there be appointed a regency, designated by the viceroy, which would rule an independent Peru, until an agreement is reached in Spain about a prince of the reigning house who would take the throne of the new nation."

The Royalists did not expect so much, and this proposition was tempting to them. The viceroy, who accepted this in principle, said that the proposition should be discussed with the corporations and the army. Moved by these promising prospects, the guests took their places at the banquet which San Martín had prepared for them. The liberator-hero and the viceroy sat at the head of the table. At the end of the banquet, La Serna, raising his glass, proposed this toast, "To the success of the meeting of Punchauca."

And San Martín replied, "To the prosperity of Spain and America; to the fraternity between Europeans and Americans."

When the viceroy and his companions returned to Lima and consulted with the Royalist army, the proposition was rejected; the independence should not be recognized without previously consulting the Spanish Government.

The conference of Punchauca had failed, then, as that of Miraflores had failed a year before. The second armistice was broken and hostilities were to be resumed. When Valdez and Camba, the Royalist envoys, reported to San Martín, he told them frankly, "I regret such obstinacy, because I see with sorrow that within a short time the Spaniards will not have other recourse than shooting themselves."

The Royal commissioner, Abreu, who had arrived from Madrid a short time before, had brought some conciliating suggestions upon the basis that the insurgents should swear to uphold the constitution of 1812; the Holy Alliance and the House of Bourbon were then in full restoration; in Mexico Iturbide had just founded an empire. Those circumstances justified the monarchist propositions of San Martín's; but this was only a trick of war, as he himself explained in Europe to Miller, when, his work at an end, he had no interest in hiding the truth:

The propositions made at Punchauca by General San Martín to the viceroy of Peru were:

First, and as a preliminary basis for negotiation, the recognition of the independence of Peru, as a sovereign nation; second, that a governing council be formed, composed of three individuals, who would be elected, one by the viceroy, another by General San Martín, and a third by the capital, which council, working together with one deputy for each province, would be charged with the drawing of a provisional constitution, to be observed until the time of the meeting of a general congress; third, that two commissioners should be appointed, one of them chosen by the viceroy and the other by General San Martín, to go to Spain to report the independence of Peru and to invite the King to name a prince of his dynasty to be crowned in Peru, after having sworn to uphold the constitution that would be presented to him. The other proposals were simply related to the positions that both armies were to occupy. Viceroy La Serna agreed to all these proposals at the meeting; but two days later he wrote to General San Martín saying that, having consulted with the chiefs of his army, they had refused to admit them.

And following this San Martín himself added on this document:

General San Martín, who had a deep knowledge of the policies of the Madrid Cabinet, was well persuaded that the Cabinet would never approve this treaty; but inasmuch as its main object was that of compromising the Spanish chiefs, as in fact they were compromised if they recognized the independence, they had no other way to choose than that of joining their own destiny to the American cause.

This is, then, all there is about the "monarchist" proposals made by San Martín in Punchauca, and in the presence of this almost posthumous confession, we cannot but praise its political astuteness. The manner in which he outlined the question at the meeting and the aims which he harbored exonerate him from the charges which his conduct has merited in the eyes of some American historians who judged him severely. Nor was he in a state of intellectual decadence when he acted in Peru; nor was he abjuring his liberal principles. Rather, he showed himself to be a humanitarian warrior, a well-informed diplomat, and a politician with safe ideas. Let one not forget, besides, how precarious was the situation of America in the region occupied by Bolívar; nor let it be forgotten that at the time the monarchical reaction was victorious in Mexico, and that anarchy was weakening the Argentine provinces.

Add to this the inferiority of the liberating army of Peru in the matter of military results and the passiveness of the Peruvian public opinion. Only through the work of his genius and his ingenuity could San Martín carry on a successful fight in that moment of ingratitude.

In spite of the failure of Punchauca, the dilatory conversations continued for some days with subtle astuteness. In a discreet letter dated June 26, 1821, San Martín wrote O'Higgins: "Negotiations have continued, delayed on my part, first, in order that the men and horses of the division of Arenales may be strengthened; secondly, in order to replace my sick soldiers, who number not less than 1,200."

The astuteness with which he planned the conference of Punchauca inspired these delays, for the reasons which this letter reveals. Since his army had disembarked on the Peruvian coast, San Martín had found himself placed in an inferior position as to numbers, health, arms, terrain, and popular cooperation. From Chile he was receiving some resources: drugs, cattle, lumber, clothing, canvas, fruits, and everything that could be distributed immediately among the demoralized troops. Money was lacking with which to pay the soldiers. He writes O'Higgins:

I am going mad. Believe me truly when I say that at times I find myself desperate and I have been on the point of attacking the enemy and trying my luck in a decisive action in order to leave this hell as soon as I can and to rest for once; but the thought that on the success of this campaign rests the good of so many generations makes me go on suffering.

In the midst of these penuries Callao is blockaded and Lima is besieged.

The enemy has been re-enforced by four battalions and three squadrons from Upper Peru; in spite of this I do not believe that they will leave the mousehole in Lima to look for me, partly because of the quality of the troops and also because, if they do move, half of the troops will desert.

The fever epidemic which decimated the patriot army in the Huaura encampment produced by itself 50 per cent of the casualties, including dead and wounded; worse than a battle. "There was one day in which one hundred soldiers died." San Martín himself was sick in bed: "If I continue like this, I will soon be dead," he wrote to Chile on March 3, 1821. In this fatal condition, he was able to overcome his own physical sufferings in order to replace the casualties and to restore the morale of the troops decimated by the pestilence. He asked Chile for men and arms, inasmuch as he was going to prepare aid for Sucre in Quito and for Olmedo in Guayaquil. He freed the slaves on the coast who came to his ranks, and he armed the mountain Indians even though it was only with stones and sticks. He also fomented desertion in the Royalist ranks, in order to compensate for the enormous difference in both armies. Under these conditions he was able to rouse the

various valleys on the coast, threaten Callao, start an uprising in the mountains, and encircle Lima until it surrendered, as it finally did.

I have Lima half blockaded; I am proceeding to inundate it with patriot followers who are harassing it so that they have arrived to within one league of the
Peruvian capital. Each soldier, in order to eat, and badly, too, costs the viceroy
four *reales* daily. From this you can ascertain whether the city can hold out much
longer, especially with all the northern provinces in a state of insurrection, with
no entry and Callao in a rigorous blockade. . . . You cannot imagine how well
I could use even a thousand carbines, muskets, old shotguns, indeed, any firearms
at all which you are not using, in order to arm the guerrilla factions.

So clamored San Martín, begging for help in his letter to the Chilean
Government. Notwithstanding his need, he sent a thousand rifles to
Guayaquil "on account of the need of them."

General Alvarado, who was residing in Peru, said in 1823:

Never had San Martín shown himself to be more of a genius than at that time:
now undermining Lima and its outskirts with warriors; now hiding our definite
weakness from the enemy; now undertaking a campaign against the mountains,
with skeletons instead of men; now making an expedition against the coast; now,
finally, negotiating and intriguing to gain sufficient time to overcome that fearful
condition. Never, on any occasion, did I find him greater.

The army which he brought from Chile was made up of 4,872 men: half
of them fell sick or died, but at the end of a year he still had 6,700 men whom
he succeeded in reuniting by the force of his will power, even though they
were badly disciplined and worse armed.

The viceroy was able to mobilize an army of 12,000 men, of whom 7,000
garrisoned the city of Lima.

The lack of foodstuffs, because of the blockade of Callao and the siege of
Lima, was increasing the popular discontent in the Royalist camp immeasur-
ably. The soldiers believed themselves privileged and appropriated foodstuffs
and looted stores. San Martín's secret agents undermined opinion until finally
the Cabildo, representing the neighborhood, addressed itself to the viceroy in
these plaintive terms: "If this town continues like this, what will be our fate
within a short time? Peace is the general vote of the people. The public is
gathering perfidiously under the banner of San Martín. The public has force-
fully increased our silence and already has begun to fear evils worse than the
war itself." This capitulation displeased the army and created a very difficult
situation for the viceroy.

Meanwhile San Martín from the coast continued manipulating the threads
of his political intrigue in Lima, adding thus to the magic of his ideas. Some
Peruvians, already converted to his side, were serving his plans from the
capital. He then proposed that permission for the entry of foodstuffs be requested of the besieging chief, and the magnanimous warrior consented. Some

of his circle criticized him; but he said, by granting permission, that food-stuffs could enter as long as they were destined for the people and the sick soldiers, "for the soldiers are my enemies only on the battlefield." This gesture gained for him the sympathy of the people and even of the soldiers.

In this way Royalist resistance slackened in that country where revolutionary conspiracies had failed several times in ten years. Public opinion was being transformed under the San Martinian pattern, which was made up of intelligence and patience.

In June 1821 San Martín found himself on board the schooner *Moctezuma*, anchored in the harbor of Callao. He had used his ship during this time for carrying on conversations with his agents in Lima. He wished to work on public opinion before having recourse to arms. Thus he remained in apparent military inaction while manipulating moral forces in the secret pattern that was his preferred system. At the same time he maintained contact with the squadron of Cochrane and the coastal troops who were penetrating the interior of Peru. Lima was under siege; but he didn't want to enter it forcibly. Some, impatient, criticized him for his inertia, or they labeled him a coward. San Martín, nevertheless, continued weaving his plan silently, attentive to his "internal vision" of things and to the quiet prosecution of his ends.

At this point, on June 25, the English captain, Basil Hall, a seaman detached from the Pacific Fleet by order of the British Government, went to visit him on board the schooner. Captain Hall had traveled along the coasts of Asia and North America; he had previously been in Buenos Aires, from where he brought news of Escalada and a letter from Doña Remedios; he had written about those countries, and now he was keeping a diary of his observations in the Spanish-American cities since 1820, which he published in London toward 1824. In this diary are found the chronicles of his first interview with San Martín on board ship, and in it is given a faithful portrait of the hero in those days. He says of San Martín:

At first sight there was little that was striking about his appearance; but when he stood up and began to speak, his superiority was evident. He received us on deck very simply, dressed in a loose coat and a large fur cap. He was seated close to a table made from several board planks and placed over some empty barrels. He is a handsome man, tall, erect, well proportioned, with a large aquiline nose, abundant black hair, and long black whiskers which extend from one ear to the other and below his chin; his eyes are large and penetrating, as black as ebony, and his whole appearance is completely military. He is highly courteous and simple, unaffected in his mannerisms, excessively cordial and unassuming, and possessed of a kindly nature; in short, *I have never seen a person whose enchanting manner was more irresistible.* In a conversation touching important topics, he disliked wasting time with details; he listened attentively and answered with clarity and brilliance of language, showing admirable resources of argumentation and a ready abundance of knowledge, the effect of which was to make those people with whom he talked feel that they were understood as they desired to be. Nevertheless, there was nothing ostentatious in his words, and he appeared at all times perfectly serious and deeply possessed of his subject. At times he became highly animated, and then one could observe the brilliance of his look and the liveliness of his expression, as if to clinch the attention of his listeners, in order to make it impossible for them to be mistaken concerning his arguments. This was more noticeable when he talked about politics, a subject on which I consider myself fortunate to have heard him express himself frequently. But his calm manner was no less surprising and revealing of an unusual intelligence, for he could also be jovial and informal, according to the occasion, and whatever effect the acquisition of great political power may have had upon his mind, I am certain, nevertheless, that his natural disposition is good and benevolent.

This picture of San Martín on the eve of the surrender of Lima coincides with other testimonials; but this one is the most pleasing because of the impartiality and the acuteness of the author, who knew many men and many peoples.

During the visit the English captain heard San Martín speak on military and political events of that time, on the apparent inactive front at Lima, on his aims in the continental campaign which he was then carrying out. Said San Martín:

The people are asking why I do not march on Lima immediately. I could do it and I would do it right now if it were convenient to my plans; but it is not convenient. *I do not seek military glory, nor am I ambitious for the title of conqueror of Peru: I only wish to free it from oppression.* What good would Lima do me if its inhabitants were hostile politically? How could I further the cause of independence if I should take Lima militaristically, or even the entire country? My views are very different. I want all people to think as I do and not to take one single step ahead of the progressive march of public opinion; since the capital is ready now to show its feelings, I shall give it the opportunity without danger. In the certain expectation of this moment, I have delayed my advance until now; and for those who understand the variety of methods at my disposal, sufficient explanation for all these delays which have taken place will be apparent.

I have certainly been gaining new allies in the hearts of the people day by day. As to the second point of military strength, I have been for the same reasons equally fortunate, augmenting and improving the Army of Liberty while the Royalist side has been weakened by scarcity and desertion. Now the country has given an account of its own interest, and it is reasonable to expect that the inhabitants have the means of expressing what they think. Public opinion is a recent machine introduced into this country; the Spaniards, incapable of directing it, have prohibited its use; but now they are experiencing its force and importance.

These words of San Martín, listened to and reported by Hall, give a complete clue to his conduct in Peru and reveal the soul of an unusual man. He was not a Caesar, nor was he a conqueror, nor did he wish the glory of arms; he repudiated bloody praetorianism and serenely sought to reign in the kingdom of the spirit. He believed in the mysterious forces of the individual soul, and he respected the opinion of the people. He was not an impassioned chief, vain or theatrical, but rather a teacher, an enlightened, a true liberator. Thus he formed his grenadiers in Buenos Aires, thus he organized his army in Cuyo, thus he conducted himself in Chile, thus he was conducting himself in Peru, thus he would conduct himself in Guayaquil, to the amazement of history. His Lautaro Lodges, his army printing presses, his underground war, the libraries he founded, were all, just as much as his sword, the tools of a moral principle.

Later San Martín discussed the backwardness of liberal thought in Lima, compared with other regions of America. Peru had been the first stronghold of the Spanish Empire, and would be, logically, the last to fall. Colonial and aristocratic tradition had secular roots in the City of Kings. He had come to uproot them, and he would uproot them, but with fraternal hands, rather than with the sword. Hall heard him say:

In the last ten years I have busied myself constantly against the Spaniards, or, better say, in favor of this country; because I am hostile only to those who are hostile to the cause of independence. My whole desire is that this country should be ruled by itself, and only by itself. As to the manner in which it governs itself, it does not concern me in the least. I propose only to give to the people the means of declaring themselves independent, establishing an adequate form of government. And when this is done, I shall consider my task done and I shall withdraw.

It would be well not to forget these words when the hour arrives for Guayaquil, as it arrived the following year.

The man who spoke thus had been for months undermining the enemy in his own fortress, with the patience of a saint and the astuteness of a wizard. The independent fleet was blockading the coast; an army of Indians was besieging the city; their advance guards were inciting the mountaineers in the interior to insurrection; secret agents were operating in the homes of Lima, until, finally, the viceroy, choking, announced by proclamation his intention to abandon the capital, indicating the Castle of Callao as a refuge for those who wished to follow him. The bulwark of Lima was beginning to fall without any bloodshed. It was what San Martín had sought.

With the action of the viceroy, equivalent to a lost battle, panic spread in Lima. People in confusion discussed and prepared themselves for escape. Homes were filled with weeping and supplications. Through the streets ran wagons and mules loaded with the household goods of the fugitives. In the midst of terror, it was said that the slaves were going to rise and massacre the whites; that the Indian besiegers were going to penetrate into the city in order to set fire to it and loot it. San Martín appeared in the imagination of the Royalist families as a demon bent on extermination.

When the viceroy fled from Lima he delegated his command to the Marquis of Montemira, an old *criollo* and a man highly esteemed. Public confusion increased with this change. Meetings were held in the Cabildo and in the government house, to work out a plan best suited to the dramatic danger in which all saw themselves. Some proposed that a deputation invite San Martín to enter Lima and protect it. This was approved. The deputies departed with the message to the governor. They boarded San Martín's schooner, and he answered them laconically, "I do not wish to enter as a conqueror. I will not go unless the people invite me to."

The besieging army was feared, and San Martín arranged that it should withdraw to a point named by the provisional authority appointed by the residents. With this, confidence was restored.

Some days later San Martín entered Lima, not as a victor but as a man invited by the people.

In a learned book from Moorish Spain, titled the *Sirach de Tortuxi* (The Lamp of the Princes), by Abubéquer de Tortosa, this sentence is found: "The soul of war is valor; its body, strategy; its eyes, foresight; its wings, discipline; its tongue, cunning; its guide, comradeship; and its leader, divine help."

And in this same book is related that when the warrior intended to besiege the city, he ordered a wide rug spread on the ground and had a coin placed in the center of it. Then he said to the leader of his troops, "If any of you can reach that coin without stepping on the rug, I shall consider him wise enough to give orders." They all stopped at the edge of the rug, and none could reach the coin. When they confessed themselves incapable of reaching it, the king ordered the rug to be folded along the borders in front of him and told each man to fold the part that was on his side. The whole rug was folded, and by simply stretching out his hand the chief could reach the coin.

San Martín had not read the *Sirach*, which had not yet been translated, nor did he learn these things in books, but from the sources where those who write books learn them. His genius consisted in possessing, like the perfect warrior, valor, strategy, foresight, discipline, cunning, comradeship, and divine help; and in knowing how to use these virtues in each case—one time rashness, another time patience. For this reason he was a master of war, and for this reason his war in Peru, which has been so badly judged by many historians, has some features of magic. He took Lima without shedding blood, folding the rug until he could reach the coin, as the warrior in the story.

In this way the City of Kings fell on July 9, the day of Argentine independence and the anniversary of the beginning of San Martín's career—he had entered the army on July 9, 1789, the month and year of the Bastille.

On that fateful day, according to Torrente, there was a severe earthquake in Lima, which the Royalists attributed to a sign of divine anger, but which the patriots attributed to a commotion of the Incas in their tombs, as the Argentine anthem says, which the liberating armies had been singing since 1813.

IX. THE CITY OF KINGS

Silently San Martín entered Lima, which had surrendered without blood-shed, and he secluded himself in order to rest, or perhaps secretly to enjoy the possession of the beloved and romantic city which was already reclining sweetly in his arms.

Some patriotic friars discovered his retreat and hastened to pay their re-spects. He received them with gentleness: one of them compared him with Caesar, the other with Lucullus. The speech could not have been worse, and when the visitors left he exclaimed with pain:

"Good heavens! What are we going to do? This is not promising."

His aide informed him that more friars were waiting in the anteroom, and San Martín answered:

"Is it possible? Then let us again saddle the horses and escape, quickly."

They again mounted and went to the home of the Marquis of Montemira, to whom the viceroy had entrusted the Government when he retired from the capital. From there they went to the palace, and when San Martín entered it, the news of his presence had already spread throughout the city, and the people began to gather. Many ladies gathered in the salon in which he was, and moving scenes took place. The great nervous tension which Lima had lately experienced, with alternating terror and hope, the courtly customs, the dreamy temperament, caused those women around San Martín to burst into tears of joy. One of them fell on her knees before the hero and, embracing his legs, offered him her three sons for the cause of America. After this, the other two placed their arms around his neck, fighting over him in friendly rivalry. The room, meanwhile, had become crowded: military men, clerics, citizens.

With the atmosphere now electrified, a beautiful young lady worked her way through the multitude and, standing in front of San Martín, who looked at her, dazzled by her beauty, strongly embraced him and reclined her head, as if asleep, on the breast of the hero, muttering between sobs of emotion:

"Oh, General, my General!"

San Martín kissed her tenderly.

She raised her eyes, as if recovering herself with his action.

"Now are you happy?" he asked her.

"Oh yes; happy indeed, sir!" and after withdrawing her arms, like a sleep-walker she became lost in the crowd.

A friar got through the crowd and related his story, which ended with a

"Long live our General San Martín!"; but San Martín, in an affable tone, corrected him:

"No. Don't say that. Say with me, 'Long live the independence of Peru!' "

The emotion of the people was increasing between sobs, laughter, and confused cries, when San Martín, seeing a ten-year-old girl before him, raised her to his arms and kissed her on the forehead like a father. Perhaps at that moment he thought of the little child he had left in Buenos Aires, when he departed to give a fatherland to the Peruvian children.

People anxious to greet him and congratulate him were detaching themselves from the crowd. For hours he was in this cordial atmosphere, shaking hands and comforting hearts, without losing his dignified and magnificent bearing. At last he left the palace, in the midst of popular ovations; he mounted his horse and went to Mirones, on the outskirts of the city, to withdraw from all homage.

On the following day, in his new residence, he received delegations, petitions, information of many kinds. He took several military measures; heard from his spies about the movements of the enemy army; read and wrote many letters; attended to the most varied matters with his customary thoroughness.

He felt himself in the midst of a society quite different from that of Cuyo, the River Plate, and Chile: Lima was a courtly city, seasoned with Spanish spirit and romantic voluptuousness. In this atmosphere, foreign to his nature, his task was even more difficult. Now that he had taken Lima, he would have to defend himself so that the city would not take possession of him. He proposed to remodel it according to his ideal; but directing opinion in the coastal capital would be more arduous than the military struggle in the mountains. As the first fruit of such observations, he gave the Peruvians a manifesto in which he spoke of the social reforms which should be undertaken.

As a beginning he decreed the oath of allegiance to independence, which took place July 28 of the same year, 1821. In the Plaza Mayor of Lima a platform was raised for the authorities and outstanding citizens. Among them appeared San Martín with the flag of Peru created by him in Pisco, and before the troops and the multitude gathered there, he proclaimed in his powerful voice:

"From this moment Peru is free and independent by the will of the people and for the justice of their cause which God defends."

Then he waved the flag before the multitude and exclaimed with emotion:

"Long live the Fatherland! Long live independence! Long live liberty!"

Each of these shouts was echoed by the populace. Then souvenir medals were distributed with this inscription on the obverse side: "Free Lima swore its independence on July 28, 1821," and on the reverse side, "Under the protection of the Liberating Army of Peru commanded by San Martín."

After this ceremony the assembly marched from the square to the palace, headed by San Martín and made up of the Army, the University of San

Marcos, the oldest university in the Western Hemisphere, the civil and religious bodies, the populace. From the balconies women threw flowers, and vibrations of unanimous merriment made the air gay. San Martín must have experienced a profound emotion on that day that was the goal of his life and, notwithstanding, says an eyewitness—the Englishman Basil Hall—"a fleeting expression of impatience or disgust of himself could be seen in his face, for lending himself to this masquerade, but if it were so, he soon recovered his customary aspect of attention and good will toward those who surrounded him."

In a letter to O'Higgins, Director of Chile, San Martín told of his entrance into Lima in simple words:

Finally, with patience and aided by revolts, we have compelled the enemy to abandon the capital of the Pizarros. . . . Our labors have been rewarded with the holy end of being assured of the independence of South America. Peru is free. . . . I foresee the end of my public life, and I am going to try to entrust this heavy charge to safer hands, and retire to a refuge where I can live like a man.

In several public and private documents, he reiterated his intention to retire, and he fulfilled his promise. When he fulfilled it after Guayaquil he did nothing but carry out a vow taken, as is seen, at the moment of his arrival in Peru, and renewed several times during the year as a faithful intention and as a genuine expression of his temperament.

San Martín, after his entrance into Lima, assumed the governorship with the title of "Protector of Peru." At the time there were those who muttered their criticisms of this action, which some historians also censured later. It is said that in this San Martín disobeyed the instructions of the Chilean Government, which ordered the creation of a democratic government; but it is forgotten that he himself called the Congress and handed the power over to it. It is also said that with it the paladin besmirched his otherwise ambitionless conduct; but it is forgotten that he then acted through necessity rather than through ambition, since the viceroy and the Royalist army were still occupying the interior of the country and revolutionary opinion was not very strong in Lima, as was afterward proved.

The Protector began his work of governing by appointing as his ministers José Hipólito Unanue, a Peruvian patriot; Juan García del Río, a friend he had met in Cádiz, and Bernardo Monteagudo, whose dramatic personality found power, adversity, and death in Lima. From the first days the revolutionary government knew that it moved in an atmosphere of conspiracy, intrigue, and danger. The Royalist troops comprised 12,000 men, and still occupied Upper Peru, in the mountains, and Callao on the coast. The enormous power of the aristocratic families was entrenched in the capital and in the country estates, ready for espionage and treason.

Among the patriots themselves, there were some like Riva Agüero, who were not happy with everything, although they concealed it: Riva Agüero would have preferred, in 1820, that the army of San Martín come as an auxiliary; and his ulterior attitude disclosed his resentment and ambitions. Such was the situation for San Martín in 1821, and if he assumed the protectorate it was only because a representative government could not be quickly established, and because in its initial stage, the protectorate was in reality a necessity of war.

One of the first and most significant decrees of the revolutionary regime instituted by San Martín was that ordering the destruction of the busts of the King and of the Royal insignia, replacing them by the arms of Peru, with the legend: "Independent Lima." Something similar had been done in Buenos Aires by the Assembly of the Year XIII, which the Lautaro Lodge had inspired.

The City Council of Lima, which had taken over the representation of the people when San Martín entered the city and had placed itself under his protection, tendered a dance to the victor on the evening of July 28, to celebrate the oath of fealty to Peruvian independence. San Martín, in turn, gave another ball on the following evening, at the Palace of the Viceroys, which victory had transformed into his residence. There was enthusiastic dancing until dawn, and the famous *tapadas* (masked women) added their piquant grace to the noise of the feast—a genuinely Liman spectacle, which was new to San Martín and to many of the Argentine officers. Later on the Protector attended bullfights and theatrical performances.

The taste for bullfights had taken as much root in Lima as in Madrid. The traditional spectacle had occasionally been prohibited in Spain, but it survived in Mexico and Peru. In Lima there was a magnificent bull ring, which the viceroy honored with his presence once in a while. The pretty women of the country were no less charming than those of Spain; they wore the same flowery shawls and they had the same bewitching eyes. Fine fighting bulls were bred in Peru; the sport tempted the people of the aristocracy; the crowds felt the tragic sensuousness of the arenas. San Martín, who had been educated in Spain and who permitted some bullfights in Mendoza, attended the Lima performances with pleasure. The whole town had come to the bull ring that Sunday.

The beasts which came out into the arena bore picturesque names. Some indicated the place the bull came from: Gargantilla de Bujana, Cano de Guata, and Tornasol de Cuyo, because the latter had been born in Mendoza. Others bore a name related to the owner through their nature or their color: Porfiado, Hosco, Buscapié, Overo, Muy Sabroso, Va de Fuerza, Gran Guachambe Gateado; but there were two whose names should have meant something to San Martín's heart—Yaraví, which is the name of the native song of America, and San Lorenzo, his first American victory.

When the Protector came into the square, the crowd, made up of enthusiastic patriots and pretty women, burst into an ovation, thus expressing with the eloquence of the masses the same feelings which the poster announcing the holiday had expressed in courtly verse:

> *Thou who art the object*
> *Of such solemn pomp,*
> *San Martín, who art the delight*
> *Of all America,*
> *Accept the grateful worship*
> *Which Lima, faithful and heroic,*
> *Joyfully tenders thee*
> *And earnestly offers thee.*

The theater was another of the Madrid tastes which the viceroys had established in the capital of Peru. Lima society enjoyed the spectacles, which were pseudoclassical arrangements of the works of Lope de Vega, Tirso de Molina, and Calderón de la Barca, pieces like Moratín's *The Young Ladies' "Yes"*, and some translations from the French repertory. The building was oval-shaped inside, and across its shorter diameter were placed, on one side, the stage, and on the other, the official box. The orchestra seats were reserved for men, and the ladies used separate seats, following the Spanish custom.

Between the acts men and women smoked, lighting their cigars (smoked by both sexes) with flint lighters, a habit which the Protector soon banned. The quality of the audiences changed somewhat after 1821, because the titled nobility, which was numerous in Peru, had fallen upon evil days, was in exile, or kept away from public functions. But the new society created by independence filled the openings with new ranks, inasmuch as the aristocratic spirit was firmly rooted.

On the first gala performance attended by San Martín after taking over the protectorate new decorations, won on the battlefield, were seen, and also bearers of ancient titles, among which it would suffice to mention the Marquis of Torre Tagle, who had joined San Martín's cause, and new beauties, like Rosa Campusano, whose friendship with the Protector opened her to the admiration and the gossip of the people.

Lima had witnessed, a few years before, the ostentatious career of the heroine of Thornton Wilder's novel *The Bridge of San Luis Rey*, La Perichole, Viceroy Amat's paramour, and the popular imagination seemed to enjoy itself at the chance of a new and analogous adventure, although this was against the nature of San Martín and against the circumstances of his life.

On September 4, 1821, San Martín attended a theater performance. He took his place in the official box, and after a good part of the show had been performed an aide arrived to bring him news about the Royalists: the viceroy's army was on its way from the mountains to the city, with the intention of attacking Lima. The rumor leaked out, and the audience became panicky.

In order to stop the alarm San Martín arose and addressed the people from his box, entreating them to be calm and to have confidence. He was going out to stop the enemy, and nothing serious should be feared in the city as long as calm and love for the sworn liberty were preserved. This he later repeated in a proclamation:

The courageous men who liberated Lima will know how to save it from the fury of the Spanish army. My troops will not abandon you. We shall triumph over that army which comes thirsty for blood and loot, or we shall perish honorably. We shall never be witnesses of your misfortune. Unity, tranquillity, and efficient co-operation is what I need to make Peru safe for its happiness and splendor.

When the news came that the enemy was approaching, the populace ran to arms, and the multitude shouted in the square, "Liberty or Death!" A document from those days compares the spectacle of Lima to that of Greece under the Persian threat and that of Rome when the Gallic invasion was near.

The Royalist army, which had its headquarters in Jauja, had moved on August 25, 1821, under General Canterac, in the direction of Callao, but with the intention of recapturing Lima. When he learned of this possible aggression, on the night of September 4, San Martín left the theater in order to take the most urgent steps—he ordered barricades to be erected, he stationed the Negroes on the walls, and he himself went out to place himself at the head of the army, stop the enemy, and defend the city.

The armies sighted each other soon thereafter, between Callao and Lima, and then took place one of the most discussed and mysterious episodes of San Martín's strategy.

San Martín, who was watching Canterac's movements, said to Las Heras: "They are lost! Callao is ours! They haven't got enough food for fifteen days. The auxiliaries from the mountains are going to smash them. Within eight days they will have to surrender or be stuck on our bayonets."

Nobody knew what was San Martín's plan. But it was readily seen that ever since his entrance into Peru he preferred not to give battle. With his magic inaction or with his strategic tricks he had taken Lima without any bloodshed. He preferred to take Callao the same way. Besides, his army did not even number seven thousand men, and this was vastly inferior to the enemy's forces. The patriot chiefs, on the other hand, inflamed at the sight of the enemy, wanted to fight and grumbled against that silent inaction, which they attributed either to fear or to decadence of the undefeated warrior.

While the chiefs grumbled and boasted, Cochrane arrived at the camp, and approaching San Martín began to urge him to fight and to give him advice.

"My decisions have been taken."

Such was the evasive answer from San Martín, who drew away from Cochrane and went to listen to a peasant bringing information. Cochrane, his pride hurt and being unable to come face to face with San Martín, took it out on the peasant: "The general's time is too precious for you to waste it with foolishness!"

San Martín turned his horse away disdainfully and went to his lodgings, thinking perhaps that Cochrane's advice was also foolishness.

Urged by the other chiefs, the admiral followed San Martín in order to give him advice, "and even offered to place himself at the head of the troops"; but San Martín, tired of that talk, cut it short with one of his laconic phrases: "I am alone responsible for the fate of Peru."

Of course, battle could have been joined there; but if it had been lost, everything would also have been lost. This explains San Martín's prudence on this occasion, and the immediate results justified his attitude. Canterac, disconcerted and fearful, withdrew from his camp without attacking either Lima or San Martín; he went back to the mountains, and Callao surrendered a few days later.

Paz Soldán, the Peruvian historian, says about this: "Extraordinary phenomenon of war: to beat a powerful army with only the force of opinion and tactics, backed by well-conceived tricks." This is what San Martín's contemporaries did not understand, nor even his comrades; this is what his detractors called the "decadence" of the warrior. The Saint of the Sword[1] won then, systematically, with the spirit and for the spirit.

The Royalist troops withdrew, completely demoralized, and the demoralization spread later inside Callao, which was considered by the Spaniards as their most powerful arsenal in America and the strongest base on the Pacific. When Colonel La Mar, commander of the fortress, was informed that Canterac had withdrawn and that he was warned to surrender, he did not believe it. To which San Martín replied, "Both as a public man and as an individual, I have always had the right to be believed. The chiefs of the Spanish army made a mistake in their calculations and they have had to withdraw to the mountains, with their forces disorganized and pursued. If this statement requires still more confirmation, an officer from the Callao garrison may come out and verify it."

After this answer, the surrender of the stronghold was negotiated. La Mar resigned his rank. Thousands of muskets and much ammunition were taken, besides cannon and prisoners. Two thousand men of the garrison, and a thousand auxiliaries who had come from the mountains to help them, surrendered unconditionally.

The patriots who lay like specters, chained or ill in the dungeons, recovered their freedom. The castles remained in the possession of San Martín without the firing of a single shot. This bloodless victory was worth as much as the best of his battles, judging by its results.

Thus, by magic art, the stoutest colonial strongholds crumbled in front of him, after ten years of war. What occult force had this master of war acquired, that he was able to win without sacrificing the lives of his soldiers?

His enemies called it cowardice; but we must confess that such things belong to the realm of the extraordinary.

San Martín returned to Lima as a victor, bringing the liberated prisoners from Callao, as a warrior crowned by laurels untainted by blood. This was new in history. The tradition of classical triumph demanded the beaten foe to be tied to the chariot of the victor, the chariot reddened by massacre. This other man was, in truth, the Saint of the Sword.

Lima had made itself ready to resist with firmness if Canterac tried to attack it. San Martín, moved by this spectacle, said later in a proclamation to the Peruvians: "My gratitude will have as a model your heroism." In this same proclamation he promised once more to retire later: "Once the enemies of this country are done away with, I shall step down and become just a citizen, depositing the destiny of Peru in the hands of the sovereign Congress." This he said in August 1821, one year before Guayaquil, as he had repeated formerly several times, even in private letters.

Between the adulation of courtly life and the dangers of latent war, the Protector tried to keep his balance, in accordance with republican ideals. He created a Peruvian Legion in order to give the country an army of its own, which he placed under the Englishman Miller and the Frenchman Brandsen. He reorganized the finances. He opened the country to free trade. He eliminated the servitude of the Indians, "because it is against nature and the principles of liberty." He emancipated the slaves. He established freedom of the press. He abolished the Inquisition, censorship, corporal punishment in the schools, and torture in the jails. He decreed the inviolability of the home, habeas corpus, and individual guarantees. He opened a public library, to which he donated his own books. He established the division of governmental functions, giving special security to the judiciary. He recognized the public debts arising from acts of war of the Royalist government. He consecrated, in one word, the principles of popular sovereignty and democratic government. All this constructive and liberal work was complemented by the statute which he himself promulgated in order to regulate his own authority. When this statute was put into effect in 1821—the first constitution of the new Peru—he said in a proclamation: "If after liberating Peru from its oppressors I can leave it in possession of its own destiny, I shall dedicate my remaining years to a contemplation of the work of the Great Maker of the Universe and to renewing my supplications for a continuation of His prosperous influence upon the fate of forthcoming generations."

The "Report on Work Done" written by the cabinet member Monteagudo at the direction of the Protector and Unanue's administrative report give a complete picture of the reforms which San Martín's rule carried out in the army, the finances, justice, and teaching, thus giving a new life to the Republic of Peru.

The institutional reforms carried out by San Martín in Peru with the intelligent co-operation of his ministers suffice to establish the democratic nature of his enterprise and to understand the reactions that the hero awakened against himself. Those reforms gave the new state its liberal foundations and are worth as much as the landing in Pisco, the victory at Pasco, the entry into Lima, and the surrender of Callao. His work as a reformer and founder was performed, to its greater glory, during a year of threats, obstacles, and dangers.

From the first moment San Martín tried to win over the confidence of the Spaniards, and when he landed he said in a proclamation: "European Spaniards: My announcement is not that of your ruin. . . . Only the freedom of Peru can offer you a safe haven. . . . The close bonds that unite us Americans lack only your good wishes and conduct to create a great family of brothers."

These feelings later inspired his negotiations at the armistice at Punchauca; and when he entered Lima, after declaring the independence of Peru, latent passions were awakened among some of the people against the Spaniards, and this resulted in the following decree from the Protector:

There having come to my notice, gravely wounding my feelings and violating human principles, that some excited individuals assault, persecute, and insult Spaniards, I order that anyone who commits such excesses, which are against American kindness, self-respect, and proper education, be reported to the political and military governor of this city, for the purpose that, upon verification of the facts, the proper penalty against such reproachable conduct be applied.

The Spaniards, meanwhile, were plotting against the Protector, a fact which he himself reported to Miller in 1837:

The promise given by General San Martín to the Spaniards that their persons and property would be respected provided they observed complete neutrality in the war was kept.
When the liberating army entered Lima, the same general decreed that any Spaniard who wanted to leave the country could do so, taking all his property with him, except the slaves, who were to join the army, and they were given three days to do this and sell their possessions. All the wealthy ones, except a few, left for Europe and Brazil, and the proof of the religiousness with which the Government kept its word lies in the fact that the European Spaniards registered, within the specified time and in their own names, more than two million pesos.

This procedure fitted closely with the wise San Martinian methods: exodus of the wealthy Spaniards, which weakened the Royalist party, and retention of their slaves, to increase the liberating army; but this was not an easy task, given the deep roots of aristocratic traditions in the old colony. San Martín's report to Miller continues:

This generous conduct, far from leading those stubborn enemies to keep a simple neutrality, made them think that the governing was weak, and, guiding themselves by this idea, they made use of all the imaginable methods to harass the cause of the patriots. They collected funds to corrupt the soldiers and to pay emissaries, whom they constantly sent to the enemy.

It should not be forgotten that this happened in the midst of war; that political passions were added to selfish motives; that San Martín also undermined the enemy army with similar actions, and that, logically, the defeated ones had to take vengeance against the victor by means of calumnies, although in that general clash of forces the liberating government also committed some abuses.

The government was perfectly aware of their activities, both through the wives of many of the leaders of the plotters (although it should be said, to give them due credit, that all the women demanded, as the price of their informing, that their own husbands should not be harmed) and through one of the Spaniards who had joined the plotters with the knowledge of the Government. The rulers could have imposed an exemplary punishment, but to do so would have necessitated dishonoring the promises so solemnly made and revealing at the same time the means through which they received their information.

Some measures of repression were taken, however, among them the exiling of one Abadía, a powerful and counter-revolutionary Spaniard, about whom San Martín says:

Among the papers taken from an enemy spy in Guarochiri there was a love letter addressed to a lady whom General Miller knew well; this letter was sent by the general to the addressee. The lady, thankful for the consideration of which she had been the object, and being really a patriot, came personally to thank General San Martín, who, taking advantage of this opportunity, learned from her that Abadía and Arismendi had been entrusted by the enemy with the task of keeping them informed; but she thought that the former would not do it because of lack of courage, although she did not doubt that the second would do his part, being a man of a greater firmness of character and lesser knowledge. In consequence of this warning, the general wrote to the correspondent he had in the enemy army, who not only answered in the affirmative but also sent him a copy of a report on the forces of the patriot armies, exactly drawn from the official statement for December. And the correspondent added that although he personally could not say positively that the copy had been sent by Abadía, he harbored little doubt that this man was the means through which the enemy generals received their frequent communications.

I copy this episode both because it is San Martín who tells it and because he lifts a corner of the veil which covered Lima, the city of the women with the covered faces, the palaces with coats of arms and the recalcitrant Spanishness. Up until the moment when San Martín arrived in Peru, this country had been the stronghold of monarchism. And he understood as soon as he arrived that he had to win not only over an army but also over the spirit of the country. The softness of the climate and of the customs was a greater danger there than the arms; therefore San Martín acted with so much caution, which was a proof of genius, but which the masses at the time did not understand. Says the document:

These data decided General San Martín to send away from Peru such a redoubtable enemy (Abadía). It is a fact that San Martín had no personal feeling against him; on the contrary, he appreciated his talent, his energy, and the kindness of his deportment. But he (Abadía) could not be a friend of the independents because he was in opposition to their interests. He had made war against them constantly, not only with his advice but also with his possessions. If to all this is added the imperative law that compels him who unfortunately is in command in times of rebellion to take in some cases violent measures, it will be realized that mere suspicion warrants a commander to act this way; so much more so in the case of Abadía, about whom there was almost proved evidence of his hostile conduct.

That was not the only case. But most of them were blamed on the minister Monteagudo; and San Martín, in his old age, blamed the gravest of them on the Peruvian Torre Tagle, who was his second in political command. San Martín's enemies charged him with cruelties against arrested men, profiting on confiscations, and with annoying people in their homes. Thus the Protector took the blame for the hates that revolutions leave behind and received the affronts that war brings under these circumstances.

The Archbishop of Charcas, and the bishops of Trujillo, Cuzco, Huamanga, and Arequipa as well, plotted also against independence, despite the fact that the lower clerics sympathized with the revolutionaries. The Archbishop of Lima, Monsignor Heras, who was an ally of the aristocrats, secretly harassed the work of San Martín. Archbishop Heras found himself compelled to resign and requested his passports to return to Spain. He was given twenty-four hours to leave the country, in spite of the fact that he was an octogenarian. When he left Peru he confessed that "the independence of the country was assured forever," and declared that he would report this fatal fact to the Crown and the Holy See. Pope Pius VII had published in 1816 an encyclical advising the churches of America to be faithful to the Spanish ruler and recommending to all the faithful "the firmest hate against the seditious ones."

To this struggle against the prejudices, interests, and feelings of old Peru was added the demoralization of the patriot army, caused mainly by Lord Cochrane. In another chapter we shall speak about this curious personage and his relations with San Martín. Here I must limit myself to bringing out the clash of the vice-admiral with the Protector, as the latter tells it in some notes of his Archives, but wholly in accord with historical truth:

Soon after the liberating army entered Lima, Lord Cochrane submitted two bills to the Government: the first one, stating what was owing to the fleet from the day it sailed, which amounted to 120,000 or 130,000 pesos; and the second one, amounting to two hundred and some thousand pesos, for the salaries in arrears and value of the prizes taken, which the Government of Chile owed him. He was told that as far as the first bill was concerned, it was accepted, and that to cover it a draft was being made against the Treasury for 40,000 pesos, and that the balance would be paid the next October; and that as to the second bill, the State of Peru, being entirely independent from that of Chile, could not pay somebody else's debts.

A few days after these replies were made, positive news came about the coming of the enemy. Consequently, the Government ordered that all bullion and other articles found in the Treasury should be placed on board the ships, and the population was warned that although the commander in chief was going to defend the city he could not guarantee the outcome of the fight; and that for this reason the public was informed that all those persons who wanted to protect their funds could deliver them in the port of Ancón to the treasurer and two accountants who had been appointed for this purpose, which several people did.

Precisely at this critical moment, when the enemy was facing Lima, Lord Cochrane sent in a note stating that his crews were near mutiny and were demanding their back pay. He was told that inasmuch as the government bullion had not been coined and was on board ships at the port of Ancón, it was not possible to comply with his request; but that it would have priority over all other matters as soon as the enemy withdrew from in front of the capital.

Without any further ado, this metallic[a] lord, whose conduct can be compared with that of the most famous filibusterer, went on board the ship where the funds were kept, and after expelling the treasurer and two accountants who were in charge of the money, seized it, despite the protests of those men, who wanted at least to deliver the funds properly and take a receipt that would shield their responsibility. Such a just demand was rejected by the commander of the fleet. . . . The amount appropriated by Lord Cochrane was 586,000 pesos. Of these, 153,000 pesos belonged to the Government and the balance to individuals, most of it in metal which they had sent to the Treasury to be coined, and which the Government of Peru had to replace.

After this episode Cochrane set sail for the coasts of Mexico, returned to Guayaquil, quarreled with Blanco Encalada for trivial reasons, and in June 1822 anchored in Valparaiso and after injuring San Martín's reputation left the service of Chile in 1823 and offered his services to the Brazilian fleet.

San Martín's legions had fought without any selfish interest, filled with the spirit of their commander; but the Lima Council, on the advice of Riva Agüero, ordered the liberators to be rewarded with land and money.

San Martín found himself in the position of having to distribute the rewards that had been accorded, and this brought about discontent among the officers, because envy made its appearance. Once again the ancient myth about gold being the curse of heroism had become a reality.

One day in 1821 San Martín heard that the discontented were plotting, and he was even given the names of some Argentine officers who were implicated. On the following day he said suddenly to Las Heras, "Colonel, I have been told that the officers of the Army of the Andes are plotting against me."

Loyal Las Heras exclaimed that he could not believe it, and it was agreed that a secret meeting with the officers would be called the following day for a cross-examination. A Colombian colonel, Heres, had reported the plot; he claimed to have known about it because it was a matter of public knowledge and because the abbot, Echagüe, had heard it from another cleric—but nothing could be proved. San Martín was asked to call a court-martial and pass sentence himself, according to the evidence. He asked the accused for a written declaration, and they either denied the imputations or ratified their obedience to the Protector. At the end of the case nothing could be clarified, or San Martín made no effort to clarify it. It was enough for him to have seen that his legions were not inspired by the same feelings of former years.

A long time later, Las Heras confessed to the Chilean historian, Vicuña Mackenna, that the plot was a fact and that it was nipped in the bud. Similar declarations were made by General Rufino Guido to the historian, Bartolomé Mitre, in Buenos Aires. According to them the plot did not succeed because the lower officers and the rank and file could not be depended upon. Some of the higher officers made fun of San Martín privately, calling him "King Joseph," and complained because Canterac had not been pursued after the entry into Lima. However, the fact is that the pursuit failed because of the disloyalty of the same men who criticized San Martín.

One of those loyal to him wrote, many years later:

As far as the pursuit of Canterac is concerned, the reason for the pursuit not being undertaken as it should was that the higher officers were plotting against San Martín with the idea of having him displaced from command, and they tried by every means to bring discredit upon him, as if any one of them were capable of taking his place; and if they did not dare carry out their plans it was because they never had with them the lesser officers and, still less, the troops.

In some notes written in exile, San Martín himself has explained what happened during the pursuit of Canterac and during other misjudged movements in his Peruvian campaign. He says:

General Las Heras was put in charge of pursuing the enemy with the whole army and the guerrillas, except Battalion Number 4 and thirty horses which remained in Callao with the commander in chief for putting an end to the task of making the Castillos, holders of the various castles in Lima, capitulate. The orders given him were to proceed with energy, but without undertaking a general action; however, with not a little surprise on the part of the commander in chief, a note was received from General Las Heras on the second day of this march, in which he said he had not been able to follow the enemy because he was entirely without food.

About this episode San Martín adds the following:

This note [Las Heras'] is in the hands of General San Martín. In consequence, he was told that if it was impossible for him to pursue the enemy, he should turn back.

General Arenales' division withdrew from the mountains owing to a mistaken order given by Colonel Alvarado, who was in Palpa with the cavalry; when the commander in chief learned about this order, he ordered General Arenales to stop his march; but the latter had already crossed the mountains and his division was in a lamentable condition, both owing to the exertions of the campaign and to sickness, which made it impossible for this general to recross the mountains.

The objective of the division sent to Ica was no other than that of bringing the unit to full strength with the recruits enrolled in that province, as was done. General Tristán, in the instructions he received, was told finally and positively not to undertake any action against the enemy, even if his forces were superior, because his objective was only that of increasing and organizing desertions [from the enemy ranks], and to withdraw at the least sign that the enemy was coming.

As is seen, many and varied were the difficulties confronting the Protector during the year he was at the head of the protectorate. When he took it over in 1821 he had promised "to give his place to the Government which the people of Peru would be pleased to elect, the form and determination of which would be determined by the representatives of the Peruvian nation." A year later he carried out this promise. In the face of this development and of his institutional work in Peru, we must believe that he assumed the protectorate, not because of personal ambition, but because of necessity and in order to overcome so many obstacles to the materialization of his dream.

Thus he was making it materialize, energetically and with lucidity, and taking over the influential nuclei, when the University of San Marcos gave a reception in his honor.

This took place at San Marcos on January 17, 1822, in a most solemn ceremonial, as in the time of the viceroys. Mace-bearers, insignia, university caps added a colorful note to the ancient rooms. San Martín sat at the head place on the platform, with the great figures of the Army, the Church, and the Judiciary. Dr. Justo Figuerola, representative of the bar, professor of law, attorney general, and grand notary of the archbishopric, took his place on the speakers' platform. In a speech full of Ciceronian affectation, he recounted the life of the warrior: "Son of a lieutenant colonel of the Spanish Crown and governor of the Guaranís [Indians]; but rather than that, son of himself and native of America," said Dr. Figuerola, to soothe the aristocratic prejudices of Lima and reconcile them with the homage to a reputation which had not been inherited, such as San Martín's. "There remains for the children without merits to clothe themselves with the garments of their ancestors," added the speaker, quoting a phrase from Plutarch. Speaking of the wars against Napoleon, in which San Martín fought on the side of Spain, he said that San Martín had been imbued with the spirit of the Recaredos (medieval heroes). When he came to San Martín's meeting with Osorio at Maipú, the San Martinian epic became studded with classical names: "But the ruthless Hector was not going to fight against Patroclus, but against Achilles himself, whose weapons, shining as the sun when it emerges from the bosom of the waves, make the son of Priam tremble and seek his health in flight." (Priam was Viceroy Pezuela, Osorio's father-in-law.)

About San Martín's landing in Pisco, he said: "Your Excellency cannot write what Julius Caesar did, '*Veni, vidi, vici,*' but 'I arrived, and at the notice of my arrival the peoples ran to take refuge under the shadow of my banners.'"

The entry into Lima and the defense of the city, threatened by the Royalists returning from the mountains, again awaken the memories of the rhetorician: "Rome does not want the Tarquins, no matter how much they try to occupy the throne from which they have been expelled."

Up to this moment we do not know what San Martín, resigned to listening to such praise, thought of it. We can imagine what he thought, knowing him as we do. Perhaps the most eloquent part of the whole speech were those passages, "South America's Washington," and "Buenos Aires, Chile, and Peru are free because San Martín broke their chains." These sentences are, at least, identical to those which history repeated a century later.

It has been said that San Martín gave way in Peru to the aristocratic suggestions of the Lima atmosphere, and evidence of it has been seen in acts which only reveal—as this one at the university—the adaptation of the great leader to conditions ruling the society in which he acts, in order to control and change it. In the same way one must interpret his creation of the Order of the Sun, which some historians have criticized him so much for, although San Martín himself explained the lofty motives of it.

"The foremost title of nobility has always been that of the protection given to the oppressed," he had said when he came from Chile to Peru, in a manifesto addressed to the Peruvian nobility. Aristocratic tradition was firmly entrenched in Lima, and San Martín, unable to eliminate it, sought to change it. With the Order of the Sun he endeavored "to make hereditary the love of glory, without hurting equality before the law," as "patrimony of the liberating warriors and reward for deserving patriots." With this order he wanted Peruvians to remember the "heroic years." Such was his only thought: civic betterment, as one can see, inasmuch as he established the order in order to stimulate those who had fought for freedom.

Soon after entering Lima San Martín had addressed a manifesto to Lima women, and later he created for them the "Order of Merit," the insignia of which read, "To the patriotism of those most sensible." This political act seems easy to understand in the atmosphere of Lima, where feminine influence was powerful. Rosa Campusano was one of those favored with this decoration.

The pretty Guayaquil girl, Rosa Campusano, who was nicknamed "La Protectora" because of her relations with San Martín, was then thirty-two years old and was ten years younger than San Martín. Ricardo Palma has given us to understand that a love relationship existed between the two, although it seems that she was also his Egeria, because she was a cultured woman and an instrument of his political plans, inasmuch as she exerted a powerful influence upon important men in Peru.

She had come to Lima from Guayaquil in 1817 (when San Martín was entering Chile), and she settled in the Calle San Marcelo with certain elegance. Her salon was visited by the most brilliant figures of Peruvian aristocracy, and it was said that even the viceroy, La Serna, felt attracted to her. Among her visitors were Count of Vega del Ren, Count San Juan de Laurigancho, Marquis Villafuerte, Viscount San Donás, and others of their rank in the last years of the viceroyalty.

Among the friends of Rosa Campusano there were also some secret patriots, like Cortínez, Boqui, Mariátegui, and Sánchez Carrión, who, shortly before San Martín's arrival, were conspiring with him. When the Numancia Regiment surrendered, this lady had something to do with it, in connection with Heres, the commander of the unit; and the same is said of her relations with Commander Santalla, who led the rebellion of the Cantabria Regiment in Callao.

It cannot be doubted, in the face of this evidence, that Rosa could have been an efficient agent for San Martín, and also his Egeria. Rosa Campusano was still young when San Martín met her: of medium height, with a fine figure, the whitest of complexions, delicate hands, blue eyes, small and expressive mouth. Her talk was entertaining, with Castilian phrases and seasoned with Lima jokes. For her reading she preferred some verses by Arriaza and the story of Abelard and Heloise, signs of her times and temperament.

A most seductive woman, she inspired passions and gallantries, because she was beautiful and agreeable. If it is true that San Martín was her lover, it could only be "on the quiet [de tapadillo]," as they say in Lima; and we only know for sure that when the Protector created the feminine branch of the Order of the Sun he decorated her together with other deserving ladies of Lima; and that she had, years later, a son, who, because of his age, could not have been San Martín's child, although he was nicknamed "The Protector" in school, much to his annoyance.

Rosa Campusano lived over half a century, and at that age, ill and poor, Dr. González Vigil, director of the Public Library founded by San Martín, gave her, for the sake of charity, a room on the back courtyard of the building. There Don Ricardo Palma met her in 1847—he had been a schoolmate of her son—and he found only the ruins of her former beauty; she had become prematurely old and walked with a crutch, although she still talked wittily and did not hide her pride on having been known as "La Protectora" in her younger days.

As far as San Martín is concerned, there is no record that he remembered her later; but Rosa Campusano has become associated with his name in the Peruvian tales, and she is the only woman who enjoyed this privilege in the singular and austere life of our hero, as if she were an incarnation of old Lima of the masked women, which San Martín conquered without bloodshed and abandoned without violence.

X. THE NIGHT IN GUAYAQUIL

Hardly had the operations started on the coast and in the Peruvian mountains, which have already been described, when San Martín thought of Bolívar, who was fighting in Colombia with admirable heroism. The two paladins did not know each other personally, although they had been on the point of meeting in Cádiz and in London, before beginning their heroic exploits. In 1820 destiny was taking them to a forced meeting, and San Martín, foreseeing it, sent from Peru his greetings to his brother from Caracas, congratulating him on his victories and emphasizing the solidarity of their common enterprise.

From Bogotá on January 10, 1821, Bolívar wrote to San Martín, answering his greetings:

I had been looking forward to this moment all my life; and only the moment of embracing Your Excellency and joining our flags can be more satisfactory to me. The victor of Chacabuco and Maipú, the first son of his Fatherland, has forgotten his own glory when he addresses his exaggerated praise to me; but it does him honor, because it is the most shining evidence of his goodness and his selflessness.

Knowing that Your Excellency has set foot on the shores of Peru, I have considered them free, and I hasten to congratulate Your Excellency on this third free country which owes its existence to you. I am on my way to fulfill my promise of uniting the Empire of the Incas to the Empire of Freedom. Doubtless it is easier to enter Quito than Lima; but Your Excellency will be able to accomplish with more ease the difficult task than I the less difficult one, and soon Divine Providence, which has so far protected the banners of Law and Liberty, will bring us together in some corner of Peru, after having trampled upon the trophies of the tyrants of the American world.

Six months later San Martín entered Lima, and from there he fraternally helped Bolívar, who was still in Colombia, his troops having been unable yet to enter Quito, despite this being the lesser task, as he had said in his letter.

While San Martín was winning in Peru, the Colombian legions were marching south toward Ecuador, commanded by Sucre. This general of Bolívar's and the Junta of Guayaquil, after the defeat at Huachi, asked the Argentinian for help, and San Martín sent Colonel Andrés de Santa Cruz with 1,622 men, among whom were several Argentine officers and units. These reinforcements left Piura, crossed the Marcara River, arrived at Saraguro on February 9, 1822, joined there the troops of Bolívar, and were present in the victories of Río Bamba on April 21 and Pichincha on May 24. As a consequence of these decisive victories Quito surrendered and Aymerich, shortly before a powerful chief, capitulated. So important in this campaign was the co-operation of San Martín that Sucre, Bolívar's Minister of War, wrote him on February 28, 1822: "When we raise our flag on the tower of Quito, Peru, its government and Your Excellency, who so powerfully have helped our cause, will merit our undying gratitude."

On August 23, 1821, Bolívar had written San Martín from Trujillo:

After the welfare of Colombia, nothing is more important to me than the success of Your Excellency's arms, so worthy of taking your glorious flags wherever there are slaves to come under their protecting shadow. May Heaven grant that the services of the Colombian Army may not be necessary to the people of Peru! But it marches confident that, together with the army of San Martín, there will not be a single tyrant in America that will even dare look at it.

Such was the advantageous position of San Martín in Peru, after the crossing of the Andes and the battles of Chacabuco and Maipú, the repercussions of which were felt by Morillo in the north and are admitted by Spanish historians. In those early months of 1822 San Martín occupied Lima and part of the mountain chain, Callao and the whole coastline, with 8,000 men. Bolívar was the victor only in Colombia, the only land he effectively occupied, and this after several ups and downs of the revolution in his country. Therefore Bolívar, on the eve of Pichincha and Río Bamba, had not the power he later acquired.

When the Colombian arms entered Ecuador, San Martín and Bolívar established clearer and more direct communications. The need for reciprocal help seemed indispensable to both. Without binding himself by treaty, San Martín joined his forces to those of Bolívar, sending him auxiliary[1] troops, and among these the mounted grenadiers, his favorites, who had fought so brilliantly at Río Bamba and Pichincha, victories that paved the way for Bolívar's entry into Quito and Guayaquil.

The Colombian chief was grateful for the contingent sent by those he called the "liberators of the south . . . whom, for so many reasons, we must rate as our best friends and brothers in arms." By decree dated June 18, 1822, Bolívar admits that "the Government of Colombia is indebted in part for the victory of Pichincha" and asked that the troops which have helped him be named "Grenadiers of Río Bamba."

Five Argentine officers were in that battle, and among them was Juan Lavalle, whom San Martín had trained since the latter was a youth, when in 1812 he took him into his regiment in Buenos Aires. The grateful Bolívar showed himself ready to let the Colombian Army go wherever its brothers from the south needed it: so he wrote San Martín in June. San Martín replied in equally brotherly terms:

The triumphs of Bomboná and Pichincha have sealed the union of Colombia and Peru. Peru is the only remaining battlefield in America, and there must gather those who want the honor of the final victory against those who have already been beaten throughout the continent. I accept your generous offer. Peru will receive with enthusiasm and gratitude all the troops Your Excellency may spare, in order to speed up the campaign and leave as little as possible to the hazards of fortune. I trust that Colombia will have the satisfaction that its arms may contribute powerfully to put an end to the war in Peru, in the same manner that Peruvian arms have contributed to raise the flag of the Republic on the south of this vast continent. It is necessary to combine in large scale the interests the peoples have entrusted us with, so that a solid and stable prosperity shall give them the benefits of freedom. I shall go to greet you in Quito. My soul fills with joy when I think of that moment. We shall see each other, and I feel that America will not forget the day we shall embrace.

America has not, certainly, forgotten the day the two heroes embraced, but the results were far from those San Martín had looked for when, during the interview at Guayaquil, he tried to set the bases for the promised co-operation.

Since the beginning of 1822 San Martín had been planning that interview with Bolívar, wishing to achieve a co-operation "in large measure," in order to put an end to the war. He wanted this alliance for shortening the campaign and assuring victory, following the methods of strategic certainty already applied in Chile. In January San Martín, with the purpose of going to Guayaquil and meeting Bolívar, delegated the government of Peru to Torre Tagle and made these notable remarks:

The cause of the American continent makes me carry out a mission which is dear to my highest hopes. I am going to meet the Liberator of Colombia at Guayaquil. The general interests of Peru and Colombia, the energetic finishing of the present war and the stability of the destiny which America is fast nearing make our interview necessary, inasmuch as developments have made us responsible for the success of this sublime enterprise.

There is in these words no reference to any annexation of Guayaquil, which had not yet been discussed; nor to any form of government for America, which San Martín did not even mention. His purpose, in seeking the interview, was not that of a legislator or politician, but that of a soldier. He wanted to end the war with the co-operation of Bolívar, and for that he sought the interview with him.

His intended visit in February of that year had to be postponed, and when in June he embarked in Callao on board the *Macedonia* in order to confer with Bolívar, the latter did not harbor the same cordial purposes of four months before; the military and political situation had changed also. After the triumph of Pichincha and the occupation of Quito, Bolívar entered Guayaquil. He felt stronger and less sympathetically inclined toward his Argentine brother.

The schooner *Macedonia*, with San Martín on board, entered the mouth of the Guayas and sailed upstream to the island of Puná, where she stopped to announce the arrival of the illustrious traveler.

The island of Puná had belonged to the Empire of Cuzco: it had been annexed by the Inca, Huayna Capac, after the conquest of Quito. When a ferocious chieftain named Quinballa reigned on the island, Huayna Capac came to Puná, abolished human sacrifices, and established the cult of the Sun.

San Martín was accompanied by his aide-de-camp, Rufino Guido, and the Protector's flag flew from the top of the mast. It was the end of June, which in that winterless region, hardly two degrees from the equator, is a season of temperate days. The hot sun and the tropical rains keep vegetation luxurious and the air softly warm. Under the equatorial light the water of the river shone in red and golden tones; the fleshy trees on the shore reflected their tropical greenness on the thick current; on the branches of the island perched parrots and other multicolored birds.

San Martín, from his ship, looked with his artist's eye upon that exuberant landscape, so different from the Argentine pampas. Neither the Uruguay— "the river of birds"—nor his native Yapeyú—"that which is ripe"—had such luxurious aspect, despite their names, and the Andes he had crossed to come to the tropics were only a cyclopean pile of naked rocks. The austere soul of the pilgrim had been shaped in those molds, not in these others of luxuriant sensualism and theatrical ostentation.

A few days before the *Macedonia* anchored at Puná, Bolívar had arrived in Guayaquil from Quito, and he had, as in an act of conquest, annexed these Ecuadorian provinces to Colombia. Such an act of arbitrary force was an unforeseen occurrence and contrary to the plans of San Martín. He would have wished that Guayaquil and other Ecuadorian towns could have kept their autonomy, which they recovered years later, or that they could have democratically decided their own destiny, as happened with the peoples of his exploits. The fact was, for the moment, irreparable, and although Bolívar's attitude annoyed him, he had to meet him in order to decide about the most urgent operations of the war, which was the only object of his voyage.

In the *Letters of the Liberator*, published by the Government of Venezuela, there are communications from Bolívar to Santander in which the former admits the military nature of the annexation of Guayaquil, in spite of the appearance of democratic procedure with which it was disguised. Quito and Guayaquil had belonged to the Empire of the Incas and to the viceroyalty of Peru. Their annexation to Colombia was voted in the presence of Colombian troops. San Martín, who had helped free those peoples, would have preferred that the problem of jurisdiction be postponed until after the war, or that it be solved with the proper guarantees. A local party backed San Martín's views. Bolívar did not want to wait; but time has shown that San Martín was right, because Ecuador is now an independent nation.

It is a proven matter that José de Olmedo and other Guayaquil men of prominence had been in communication with San Martín since 1820, for the revolution that was carried out there against the King; that Cochrane helped those movements of the Ecuadorian patriots with his ships in the harbor; that Luzuriaga and Guido had a part in getting military help; and that when San Martín entered Guayaquil he was enthusiastically received by the people, which aroused Bolívar's first jealousies. But Guayaquil belonged to Colombia when San Martín arrived.

When Bolívar entered as a military conqueror in Guayaquil, his secret agents, in order to please his vanity, erected triumphal arches along the street through which he came, and on the arches they painted this legend: "To Bolívar, Liberator of Colombia, Thunderbolt of War, Rainbow of Peace."

Having been advised of the arrival of San Martín at the Guayas, Bolívar sent him on July 25 a letter full of personal compliments, inviting him to come to the city "so that he could embrace him on Colombian soil." These words, in passing, made it of record that Guayaquil belonged to Bolívar's Colombian empire, and the guest could only either refuse the invitation or accept the *fait accompli*. Bolívar's flattering letter has been kept in San Martín's archives, and it reads:

With the utmost satisfaction, most respected friend, I give you for the first time the title which my heart has granted you. I call you friend, and this is the name we should carry through life, because friendship is the only bond that should unite brothers in arms, in enterprise and in opinion. I would regret as much your not coming to this city as the loss of many battles; but you will not leave unsatisfied the wish I have of embracing on Colombian soil the foremost friend of my heart and my country. How would it be possible that you should come from so far away without letting us in Guayaquil see the great man that all are anxious to know, and if possible to touch? It is not possible. I am waiting for you and will meet you wherever you indicate; but without desisting from the honor of having you visit this city. A few hours, as you say, are enough for a discussion between soldiers; but they would not be enough to satisfy the passion for friendship, which is going to begin to enjoy the happiness of knowing the dear object of its affection, which it loved only through opinion, only through fame.

San Martín, who knew men and was not susceptible to flattery, read knowingly those sugary phrases, so different from those that he used. He would have preferred to have the conference on board the *Macedonia*: to go to Guayaquil was to recognize the Colombian sovereignty imposed by Bolívar. He clearly saw in all this the Machiavellian net that had been set for him; but he had come from Peru not to create conflicts but to solve them; and he decided to land, trusting in the simple frankness of his nature rather than in courtly maneuvers.

Once his landing had been arranged, the *Macedonia* weighed anchor in Puná and made her way the following day up the Guayas to Guayaquil, where an enthusiastic multitude was waiting for him at the quay. It was July 26, 1822. Above the green coast the houses of the port shone in the sun; of the port that that visit would make so famous in the history of America. Bolívar sent two aides-de-camp to greet him in his name and offer him the hospitality of the mansion which had been prepared for his stay.

When San Martín and Bolívar met, the latter greeted the former with these words: "At last my wishes of meeting and shaking the hand of the renowned general San Martín have been fulfilled."

Both men embraced among the acclaim of the people, who watched this scene in front of the door of the house that had been prepared for the voyager, and they ascended together the stairway of the building. There were among the Guayaquileans two latent factions: that of the Autonomists, pro-San Martín, and that of the Annexationists, pro-Bolívar, although opinions could not be freely expressed. The annexation to Colombia, already proclaimed by Bolívar, was a *fait accompli* by means of force. The visit of San Martín, the object of which was not known, created however a general expectation.

When they had come into the salon, Bolívar introduced his officers, among them Mosquera,[2] who later became a general. There were also present Admiral Blanco Encalada, the Argentinian who commanded the liberating fleet anchored in Guayaquil; Guido; and the Argentine, Manuel Rojas, secretary of the legation in Peru. Some of these men were able to watch scenes of which they have given testimony for posterity; but none of them was present at the conferences that San Martín and Bolívar later had. The secret of their conversations has aroused the curiosity and the inventiveness of many chroniclers, but history must warn against them, because they heard nothing.

Immediately afterward San Martín received the visit of the aldermen and the city corporations, according to the Spanish-American custom of the time. A delegation came to offer him the homage of the women of Guayaquil, and one of them, a very beautiful young lady, stepped forward and, with her most seductive smile, placed a crown of gold leaves on the head of the serious-looking San Martín. The young lady was Carmen Garaycoa, daughter of a woman who was a close friend of Bolívar. She belonged to a Guayas family, one of whose women Bolívar called "The Mad One" and another "The Glorious One," as may be seen in letters he wrote them.

It cannot be doubted that this untimely ceremony, so suited to the sensual tastes of Bolívar and equally contrary to the ascetic temperament of San Martín, was plotted by the former. These coronations and feminine offers reflect the Bolivarian nature, made up of classical reminiscences and romantic feelings, the theatricality of which excited the imagination.

San Martín, in his austerity, was a new type of paladin, strange to these traditions and this atmosphere. Perhaps, astutely, he thought that this unexpected homage was a trick to test him, suggested by the same Machiavellian spirit that inspired the letter of the day before. Hence San Martín, really disconcerted, could only remove the crown with his own hands; and inasmuch as that might have seemed a discourtesy to the pretty Guayaquilean who had placed it on his head with so much innocence and feminine grace, he could only stammer, "I do not deserve this demonstration. There are others more worthy of it. But I shall keep this souvenir because of the patriotic feeling that inspires it and because of the hands whence it comes, since this is one of the happiest days of my life."

He took off the golden crown—he who after Chacabuco had taken off his head the crown of flowers that other feminine hands had placed there.

It is not known whether San Martín kept the golden crown; at least it has not been found among his relics, nor is there any word that he took it with him when he left Guayaquil. In any event, he did not need it, he who would not be king and disliked Caesarean pomp. He could, perhaps, have traded it, in the years of poverty that followed his days of triumph, for a piece of bread in his exile. . . .

Greetings over, Bolívar and San Martín went behind closed doors to talk without any witnesses. When the door opened again, Bolívar left with a pensive air. San Martín accompanied him to the stairway and a few hours later repaid his visit. On this occasion they spoke again, alone, for a brief moment. On the following day, July 27, San Martín again visited the Liberator at his home, and they talked in secret from one to five in the afternoon. It is possible that in the course of this long conversation they ratified the decisions already discussed during the two brief talks of the day before; but there is no document recording formally what was said there.

Whatever has been said, much later and fragmentarily, by alleged witnesses and partial commentators, lacks all validity as a literal version of the dialogue. It is known, however, and from trustworthy sources, that both men maintained, as far as it was possible for them, the gentlemanly reserve to which they obligated themselves, both in consideration of each other's position and for reasons of patriotism.

This reserve and the passions of the day favored tendentious fabrications, intended to serve regional or partisan interests, and not the least daring in the manufacture of these fables, thirty years later, was General Mosquera, a friend of Bolívar's, when both the latter and San Martín were dead. But General Guido lived at the time in Buenos Aires, who accompanied San Martín to Guayaquil, and he flatly contradicted those versions, saying that neither himself, nor Mosquera, nor anybody else, had heard what was said there.

Although the words that were said there have not been recorded, we can deduce them, because we know the attitude of both men. Also, we have the admissions of themselves, and this the best source to restore the scene. If there was a conflict in Guayaquil, it arose not from antagonism in their doctrines but from the diversity of their temperaments.

From those conferences came the ascent of Bolívar and the elimination of San Martín.

Ever since his conversations of the 26th, San Martín had decided to retire. We must so affirm, because on the 27th, in the morning, he ordered his baggage taken on board; he had decided to return to Peru that same night. The long conference held at Bolívar's house was a farewell visit, and what was said there must have been simply a confirmation of what they had said before, plus the military information that San Martín was able to give, inasmuch as Bolívar was now to remain alone on the American stage, to finish a war without the help of the man he had treated as a rival, not as a brother in sacrifice and glory, as he had craftily written in his letter of the 25th, inducing San Martín to land and be embraced "on Colombian soil," as the letter said.

The shortness of the conference confirms its exclusively military nature. San Martín was not a man to lose himself in academic discussions about systems of government on an occasion such as this. Government systems and even the occupation of Guayaquil meant nothing in face of the previous question of military co-operation. In his conversation with Bolívar he proposed military co-operation again, laconically, on the basis of the strategic situation as shown by facts and figures, and Bolívar refused such co-operation. That was all, as we shall prove later. That was why the interview at Guayaquil was so brief, despite its optimistic outlook.

At five o'clock in the afternoon, at the end of the conference held on the 27th, they entered the dining room. Bolívar had prepared a banquet, followed by a dance, to take leave of his guest. After the dessert, Bolívar, who sat beside San Martín, asked the guest to stand, and, standing up himself, raised his glass and offered this toast: "To the two greatest men in South America—General San Martín and myself."

This toast affirmed a truth that history has confirmed; but it also revealed the unmasked arrogance of Bolívar, which was in marked contrast with the virtuous words of San Martín, when he replied to the toast with these words: "To the early end of the war; to the organization of the various republics of the continent, and to the health of the Liberator of Colombia."

The two men of genius, who had not been able to come to an understanding because of the difference of their temperaments, showed their naked souls in the course of this banquet.

If we did not have any other and more explicit documents, those two toasts would give us the key to decipher the secret of Guayaquil; in them is discovered the arrogance of Bolívar and the unselfishness of San Martín.

One was a Caesar who prolonged in America the race of the European conquerors, from Alexander to Napoleon, warriors of Homeric pattern; the other was a selfless missionary, without any predecessors in history, and in him the American revolution showed its most genuine embodiment. If we could attribute any predecessors to San Martín, they would belong to the class of the saints armed for the performance of a mission.

After the banquet there was a dance; festivities that were never lacking in the unfolding of the American epic. San Martín attended as if absent-minded, absent in spirit. The Dionysiac Bolívar, like his officers, danced frantically. Before midnight, the dance was taking on the nature of a bacchanalia, in a maelstrom of gold braid and décolletés. San Martín called Guido over. "I cannot stand this noise. Let us go."

Courteously accompanied by Bolívar, whom he would never see again, San Martín left without being noticed, and both men went to the harbor. San Martín was also accompanied by his aide-de-camp and by one of Bolívar's. When they drew away, they could still hear, in the tropical night, the music and laughter of the ball.

Bolívar took leave of San Martín and gave him his portrait. That was a gesture from an egocentric, which San Martín repaid from Lima with another revealing gesture: he did not send Bolívar his portrait, but his pistols and his horse.

The group arrived at the deserted quay in the dark. The riding light on the *Macedonia* shone on the dark waters of the Guayas. The sky of Ecuador spread with indifference above the Andes, in the face of that absurd antagonism of North against South. San Martín said good-by to the aide-de-camp who had accompanied him on board. The schooner sailed down the river, bound for the coast of Peru.

While they were going along those luxuriant shores, San Martín said to Guido: *"El Libertador nos ha ganado de mano."*[3]

What did San Martín mean by that? His interlocutor, who told the anecdote, explained it according to his judgment. San Martín was sometimes a man of enigmatic phrases. Did he refer to the matter of Guayaquil, in which Bolívar "had the jump" by annexing it to Colombia? Perhaps. Did he mean that Bolívar had "beaten him to the jump" in connection with the war, which Bolívar wanted to end by himself? Maybe. Both things had just happened, and because of them San Martín had decided to withdraw. Bolívar knew it already, and that was the secret of Guayaquil. San Martín was returning to Peru with this terrible secret: his forthcoming abdication—an attitude that his contemporaries were to misjudge so badly and which was to arouse so many polemics in the future.

But what had San Martín and Bolívar spoken about in that conference at Guayaquil? What had they said to each other, and why had they separated so quickly? Why was San Martín leaving the American scene, apparently leaving his own work unfinished?

The answer to these questions is found in a letter that San Martín wrote to

Bolívar privately. History now knows this letter, which was published by Captain Lafond de Lurcy, of the French Navy. With it the secret of Guayaquil vanishes and the enigma of its denouement is deciphered; about which I will, in another chapter, give conclusive details.

Hardly had San Martín arrived in Peru and solved the first difficulties of his return when he wanted to confirm to Bolívar what he had told him personally; perhaps in order to record and justify his own attitude. From Lima he wrote him confidentially the long letter which follows, and which amazes one both by its lucidity and by its equanimity. Only a superior man could write this exceptional document:

Lima, August 28, 1822.

My dear General:

I shall write you not only with the frankness of my nature, but also with that which is demanded by the high interests of America.

The results of our interview are not those which I foresaw for a quick end of the war. Unfortunately, I am completely convinced that either you have not deemed sincere my offer to serve under your orders with the forces at my command, or that my person is embarrassing for you. The reasons you advanced, that your tact would not allow you ever to give me orders, and that even if that were the case the Colombian Congress would not authorize your separation from the territory of Colombia, have not seemed very plausible to me.

The first one refutes itself. As far as the second one is concerned, I am convinced that if you expressed your wishes you would find unanimous approval, since the object is to end this campaign, which we have started and in which we are engaged, with your co-operation and that of your army, and that the honor of bringing it to an end would fall upon yourself and the Republic over which you preside.

Do not indulge in any illusions, General. The news which you have about the Royalist forces is wrong: they number, in Upper and Lower Peru, more than 19,000 veterans, who may unite within two months. The patriot army, decimated by illness, will not be able to send to the front more than 8,500, and of these a great part are raw recruits. General Santa Cruz's division (the casualties of which, this general writes me, have not been replaced despite his insistence) on its long march overland must experience a considerable loss, and it will not contribute anything to this campaign.

The division of 1,400 Colombians which you are sending will be needed to garrison Callao and keep order in Lima. Consequently, without the backing of the army you command, the operation which is planned by way of the Intermediate Ports will not have the advantages which could be expected unless powerful forces could draw the enemy elsewhere; and in this way the struggle will be indefinitely prolonged. I say indefinitely because I am deeply convinced that, be what may the difficulties of the present war, America's independence is irrevocable; but I am also convinced that the prolongation of the war will be the ruin of its peoples, and it is a sacred duty for the men in whose hands lies its destiny [America's] to prevent a continuation of such evils.

Be it as it may, General, my decision has irrevocably been made. I have called the First Congress of Peru for the 20th of next month, and on the day after its installation I shall embark for Chile, satisfied that my presence is the only obstacle which prevents you from coming to Peru with the army at your command. For me it would have been the acme of happiness to end the war of independence under the orders of a general to whom America owes its freedom. Destiny orders it otherwise, and one must resign oneself to it.

Having no doubt that after my going the Peruvian Government that may be established will request the active co-operation of Colombia, and that you will not be able to refuse so just a demand, I shall send you a list of all the officers whose conduct, both military and private, may commend themselves to you.

General Arenales will be left in command of the Argentine forces. His honesty, his courage, and his knowledge, I am sure, will make him deserving of your every consideration.

I shall say nothing to you about the annexation of Guayaquil to the Republic of Colombia. Allow me, General, to say that I did not believe it behooved us to decide this important matter. At the end of the war the respective governments would have decided it, without the troubles that now may result for the interests of the new states of South America.

I have spoken to you, General, with frankness; but the feelings expressed in this letter will be buried in the deepest silence. If they were known, the enemies of our freedom could take advantage of the fact to our sorrow, and the intriguers and the ambitious would sow discord.

With Major Delgado, the bearer of this letter, I am sending you a shotgun and a pair of pistols, together with my personal horse, which I offered to you in Guayaquil. Accept, General, this souvenir from your foremost admirer.

With these feelings and with the hope that you may have the glory of ending the war of independence of South America, I am,

Your affectionate servant,
José de San Martín

As may be seen in this letter, the matter between San Martín and Bolívar boiled down to military co-operation to end the war. Bolívar refused it, and even refused San Martín's offer to fight under his orders. San Martín then decided to resign in order to avoid a conflict, and he went away without a single gesture that did not reveal his magnanimity.

All that has been said about a disagreement on constitutional forms is, therefore, simply a fabrication.

San Martín's posthumous enemies have pretended to find something to mar his glory in the monarchical feelings attributed to him. If the hero of independence had seriously thought such things, that would be an error which we could forgive him for, because he would have simply followed some trends of the times, and that would not detract at all from his heroism, because he did nothing to impose such opinions.

It has been said that in Peru he tried to have himself crowned emperor; and this is alleged by the same people who accuse him of seeking the crowning of some European prince. How could both intentions be reconciled? The monarchical suggestion which he made to Viceroy La Serna at the Punchauca meeting was, as San Martín himself said later, simply a trick to end the war.

We shall see later that San Martín called the Peruvian Congress before leaving the country, when he resigned his protectorship. He did then, as a founder of that republic, what he had done in Chile when the latter country established its democratic government, and as he had done before that in the Plata, when he promoted the Liberal Assembly of 1813 and the declaration of independence by the Congress in 1816.

The alleged disagreement with Bolívar in Guayaquil on constitutional matters lacks any evidence, and it is absurd to attribute it to the monarchism of San Martín, when the same charge was made against Bolívar later. The truth is that San Martín always showed disinterest about his personal predominance, and that in the three nations his sword liberated he always served the principles of democracy.

If there is any document wherein San Martín may have suggested the creation of a monarchy, we know already that it has as its only meaning a diplomatic or military stratagem, as he himself says. On the other hand, there are abundant acts and opinions of the hero's which prove his respect for free institutions and his absolute personal disinterest. But, should these thoughts not be convincing in themselves, we should remember the version of the Guayaquil conference written by Bolívar himself to Sucre, in a letter in which he says of San Martín: "He does not want to be king." On this point I shall insist, with abundant evidence, in another chapter.

On his return to Lima, San Martín issued a proclamation relating his meeting with Bolívar in terms which hid the truth of what had happened, in order to save the prestige of the man who was going to succeed him:

"I had the satisfaction of embracing the hero of South America. That was one of the happiest days of life. The Liberator of Colombia is helping Peru with three of his brave battalions. Let us all show our eternal gratitude to the immortal Bolívar."

It was only a small help—1,400 Colombians promised by Bolívar as reciprocity for the men San Martín had lent him for the Quito war.

This help, however, was offered under embarrassing conditions, such as that the troops would depend directly upon Colombia, so that the latter could at any moment withdraw them; and even then the promise took long to be fulfilled.

How different had been, a few months before, the generous attitude of San Martín, when he sent his troops to the battles of Río Bamba and Pichincha! If he had known the *Comentarios,* by Garcilaso, the last Inca of mixed Spanish and Indian blood (Garcilasco de la Vega), he would have remembered the maxims of the sage Inca, Pachacutec: "It is better that others envy you for your goodness, rather than you envy others for your badness." "He who tries to count the stars, not knowing how to count his own fingers, should be laughed at." But if San Martín did not "remember" these phrases of the Inca's, we must believe, in view of his conduct, that he knew them.

When leaving for Guayaquil, San Martín had delegated his authority to the Peruvian Torre Tagle, and when he returned he heard the disagreeable news that his minister Monteagudo had been deposed in a recent mutiny. Monteagudo, his life threatened, left Peru and took refuge in Quito. These events, while they weakened San Martín's political position in Lima, cannot be considered as the reason for the Protector's withdrawal, inasmuch as he had, ever since Guayaquil, decided finally to retire.

Much has been argued about all this, since those days of 1822. Passions and fancies have fed the century-long intrigue, giving to the conjectures the dialectics of a lawsuit and the interest of a novel. But the enigma is no longer. The abdication of San Martín is an act of laic sanctity so without precedents in history that complicated explanations are sought for it, because its simple greatness exceeds the usual measurements of military heroism.

The reason for the disagreement between San Martín and Bolívar was neither the occupation of Guayaquil nor the constitutional plan, but solely the military co-operation between them. The elimination of San Martín, who left his troops to Bolívar, and the cordiality shown by San Martín to Bolívar both during and after the interview, explain the joy with which the Liberator wrote to Santander after the meeting, as we shall see in another chapter.

The alliance between the northern and the southern armies was indispensable for the early ending of the war. This premise is evident, but Bolívar did not accept its consequence; not even under his own command, as San Martín suggested. There remained under the circumstances no other prospect than an isolated action, ineffectual, or a conflict between both chiefs, or the elimination of the more selfless, who left his army to the other. The latter is what happened.

The hero of the sword has traditionally been a man tending to exclude others, with an egocentric will and imperious passions. San Martín was not that, because he sought neither Caesarean powers nor personal glory. He said it when just arrived from Spain in 1812, and he repeated it several times in 1820 and 1821. He came to serve South America's independence, and that was his mission. His was not the quarrelsome patriotism of several regions of the continent, but a vast, continental love.

A fighting man in fighting times, he served fighting; but his Pythagorean intelligence protected him from spurious passions, and he did not want to resemble Alexander, or Alcibiades, or Philip, or Darius, or Xerxes, or Solon, or Caesar, or Pompey, or Charlemagne, or Napoleon. In America he did not want to be the conqueror or the satrap of the old epics or legends.

His is not a Homeric type, but something new and greater: San Martín welds together the spirit of Marcus Aurelius with the fiber of the Cid. He is the interpreter of a new continent, of a new genius, of a new creation. He is rather a Brahmin than a Shatriya (Hindu warrior caste); but he partakes of the two, because he is an "initiate"; a master who rules his appetites and beyond his own self and his times. He is an ascetic of patriotism, a stoic of victory. Therefore his attitude after Guayaquil was not understood. But today we understand it: it crowns the heroic deed with that act of virtue which marks the beginning of San Martín's third journey in life—that of renunciation, which does not belong to the epic of America but to the teachings of mankind.

PART III
(1822–1850)

𝕽enunciation

"I am, and shall continue to be, in retirement from the world."

—SAN MARTÍN

———◆———

I. THE STANDARD OF PIZARRO

THERE WERE THREE BREAKS which in San Martín's life pointed to his singular destiny: the first, in 1811, with Spain, with his family, and with his racial past; the second, in 1820, with Buenos Aires, with Dionysiac America and its nascent demagogism. At each break his genius appeared greater and purer. With the first break the old man died that the new might be born for greater things: thus he severed the umbilical cord that bound him to Spain, the old mother, and he ceased to fight in the Peninsula against Napoleon because it was better to fight in the Plata against Ferdinand.

With the second break he gave a greater context to "Argentinity" through his vision of Americanism as a whole: thus he cut the accidental ties that bound him to Buenos Aires, and he refused to fight against the local chiefs because it was necessary to fight against the Royalists of Lima, in order to save not only his regional fatherland but all the fatherlands of the American brotherhood.

With the third break he placed himself above vain antagonisms, when, on meeting Bolívar and finding in him a rival, he lifted himself above ambition through renunciation; thus he cut the soiled bonds so common to all men in power, and he refused to fight against his rival because he preferred to teach his America the universal lesson of the man who battles in silence against all the passions until he has triumphed over himself.

Of the break with Spain, the racial mother, we have already spoken, as also of his break with Argentina, his homeland in anarchy. Now we have seen, after Guayaquil, his supreme break. These are not really breaks, except in the sense that something breaks when from the seed comes the tree, and from the tree, the flower.

Being stages of his spiritual growth, those breaks of San Martín's were real mystic transitions, possible only in a man of genius, as he was, through the holiness of his charitable action and through the amplitude of his secret wisdom.

San Martín, who on his arrival from Chile with his army had created the Peruvian flag at Pisco and proclaimed Peru's independence in Lima, inaugurated the first Congress of the new nation on his return from Guayaquil, as he had promised the year before; on September 20, 1822, on his convocation, the democratic representation of the country had been established.

He attended the inauguration in person, and before the Assembly he took off the red-and-white sash that crossed his breast as a symbol of the supreme power which, under the significant title of "Protector of Peru," he had held until then. "Protector," not Dictator or Liberator, was the title he had given himself, as if he had foreseen that his destiny reserved for him, even for his mysterious voyage, something of the mission of the holy paladins sent from Monsalvat on a mission of justice.

When the chorus asks, in front of the King, who is the pilgrim and what is his mystery, Lohengrin answers:

"There is, far away, an inaccessible world, a sacred place called Monsalvat; there an eternal temple arises, the splendor of which has no equal on earth. Within its walls, as in the Holy of Holies, an august vase is kept, which the angels entrusted to the pious custody of the purest man. A dove, crossing space, comes every year to renew its splendor. It is the Holy Grail! It gives knights their inextinguishable ardor. He who obtains the glory of serving it becomes vested with superhuman power, and with victory sure in his power, he holds in his hands the fate of the wicked. Even if it is necessary to go to distant lands to protect rights and virtues, his power subsists and his strength is sacred, while nobody in the world knows his title. But such a sublime and wonderful spectacle cannot be offered to the eyes of mortals; nobody escapes the severe law, and if his secret is discovered, he must go. The thick veil has been drawn aside, and I must obey the law of the Holy Grail. Parsifal is my father, and his is the crown."

Such is the ancient mystery.

And when San Martín—the Protector—had placed his insignia upon the table, deeply moving everyone, San Martín—the Protector—spoke thus:

"When I return the insignia of the Supreme Ruler of Peru, I only carry out my duty and the dictates of my heart. If the Peruvians have anything to thank me for, it is the exercise of the powers which circumstances placed in my hands. Today, on resigning, I pray to the Supreme Being for the wisdom, the enlightenment, and the prudence which are needed for the happiness of the governed. From this moment the Sovereign Congress is installed and the people reassume the power in all its manifestations."

He knew well that his enemies called him ambitious and attributed monarchist plans to him. His attitude at that moment was a flat denial of those insults. When he arrived from Europe in 1812 he had taken part in the revolt against the Triumvirate in order to demand peremptorily the convening of the National Assembly which was late in meeting after 1810, and which, when installed in 1813, gave the peoples of the River Plate their most liberal laws. In 1816, from his Cuyo residence, he had also inspired the meeting of the Congress of Tucumán, which declared the independence of the "United Provinces of South America." In 1817, after beating the Royalists in Chile, he had resigned the supreme power which had been given him by the Assembly he had called, keeping for himself only the military power, with the purpose of continuing on the Pacific coast his liberating enterprise, while Chile, under O'Higgins, began its democratic organization.

Now, five years later, with Peru liberated through his action, he was again renouncing power before the Congress he had created, and through this action he was proclaiming the sovereignty of the people. Such were the liberal principles and the civilian conduct of this warrior during the ten years of his predominance in America. His luminous life did not, however, escape the calumnies of those who tried to darken his virtues. But such acts speak for themselves with incontestable truth.

Before leaving the hall, he left several sealed documents for Congress, which were later opened and read before the Assembly. One of them said:

To a warrior who fights for the happiness of peoples, the pleasure of victory is only a means for persuading him to let the people enjoy their rights; moreover, his wishes are not fulfilled until the liberty of the country has been definitely assured, because the changing fortunes of war often alter the most promising perspectives. A prodigious chain of circumstances has already made the future fate of America indubitably secure; and the fate of the Peruvian people needs only a national representation in order to become permanent and prosperous.

My glory has reached its limit when I see the Constituent Congress installed: to it I deliver the supreme authority which necessity made me assume. If my services to the cause of America deserve the consideration of Congress, I mention them today with the sole purpose that there may not be a single voter to favor my continuance at the head of the Government.

This speech and message moved the Congress and the nation deeply. Their rough eloquence painted vividly an ascetic and virile attitude, in its hard lines.

Only in Washington had a similar personality been revealed before; but that of San Martín is the more amazing, because all this happened in South America. The war of independence was the lair from which emerged the big and small bosses who, with Bolívar at their head, created a demagogic Caesarism. Their type of individualist domination could be traced back to the arbitrary heroism of the Conquistadores. If there is any Hispanic atavism in San Martín, whose parents were born in Castile and León, we would have to trace it to the Christian legends of St. James the Apostle (Santiago) and Don Quixote, or to the Castilian chivalry of Ruy Díaz de Vivar (El Cid), with his sword and his Ximena, or to the last representatives of medieval democracy: Padilla, Bravo, and Maldonado,[1] drowned at Villalar and sacrificed at Segovia by the Germanic imperialism of Charles V. Those democrats of Old Castile acted and spoke like San Martín; but they represented an ideal that at their time was dying, while San Martín anticipated, with his original genius, the destiny of our republican America, which, through him, entered virtuously into the political history of the world.

The Congress, moved by those gestures, proclaimed him "America's First Soldier of Liberty"; it gave him a vote of thanks for his services, with a yearly pension of 12,000 pesos, and it appointed him commander in chief of the land and sea forces of Peru. San Martín declined those honors in the following words:

Being firmly resolved not to betray my own feelings and the great public interests, allow me to say that the distinguished rank to which the Congress has raised me, far from being useful to the nation, would frustrate its own purposes if I accepted it, and my action would alarm those who long for true liberty; it would divide the opinions of the peoples and decrease their confidence which Congress can only inspire through the absolute independence of its decisions. My presence in Peru, in view of my relations with the Government which I have just left and with the armed forces, is inconsistent with the morality of a sovereign body and with my own opinion, inasmuch as no personal isolation on my part could deflect the shots of gossip and calumny. I have fulfilled the promise I made to Peru: I have seen its representatives meet. The enemy force does not any longer threaten the independence of peoples who want to be free and who have the means to become free. The army is ready to march in order to put an end to the war for ever. I have now only to express my most sincere gratitude and my promise that if ever the freedom of the Peruvians is in danger, I shall fight for the glory of joining them, as a citizen.

This was the same man who in 1812, newly arrived in Buenos Aires and without any personal fortune, had given up half of his pay as a colonel of grenadiers to the public treasury; the same one who gave up his emoluments in Cuyo; the same one who, being rewarded with 10,000 pesos by the Congress of Chile, donated the prize toward the foundation of the National Library; the same one who in 1815 refused his promotion to brigadier in his own land; the same one who sacrificed everything, including his health, his peace of mind, and his home, to organize the forces which liberated America.

After the meeting at Guayaquil and the revolution in Lima, nothing had changed in him. His army in Peru had at the time 9,000 men, and he expected a reinforcement of 1,000 men from Chile. These forces could have tempted an ambitious mutineer or a bold Praetorian—or also a general of his technical ability and public antecedents. But he did not let himself be tempted, not even by his wounded amour-propre. That did not seem a renunciation but a lesson. There is something magisterial in great sacrifices, and all sacrifice is divine in essence.

As the Congress insisted in its resolution and San Martín in his renunciation, the national representatives, moved by that unbribable virtue, accorded him new honors. He was given the title of "Founder of Peruvian Liberty"; he was authorized to wear for life the bicolored sash which he had given up; the erection of his statue in Lima was ordered, and the placing of his bust in the National Library he had founded; and the Congress decided that whenever he was in the country he should be rendered the honors paid to the President.

But those were not the things he loved best. He had come to Peru to free it from its two secular tyrannies, the temporal and the spiritual, and he merely wanted to take with him, as sole spoils for his deeds, the Inquisition inkstand and the flag of Pizarro, symbols of those two tyrannies and relics of whose possession this humble man was to be so proud.

At the time these things were happening San Martín was already preparing his voyage to Chile—a kind of voluntary exile after his abdication. He was leaving Peru forever, without any resentment and with deep emotion. From his place of retirement at the camp of La Magdalena he addressed his farewell to the Peruvians, the words of which deserve to be engraved in bronze:

I was present at the declaration [of independence] of the States of Chile and Peru; I have in my possession the standard which Pizarro brought with him to enslave the Empire of the Incas; therewith I am more than repaid for ten years of revolution and war. My promises to the peoples in whose lands I have conducted warfare have been fulfilled: to obtain their independence and to leave the election of their governments to their own will. The presence of a fortunate soldier, be he as selfless as it may be, is to be feared by the states which are newly formed.

Besides, I am bored with hearing that I am trying to enthrone myself. However, I shall always be ready to make the last sacrifice for the freedom of the country, but only as a private individual, and nothing else. So far as my public conduct is concerned, my compatriots (as generally happens) will be of divided opinions; *their sons will reach a true verdict.*

Peruvians: I leave you with your national representation established. If you give it your full confidence, be sure of victory; otherwise anarchy will devour you. May Heaven protect your destiny, and may your destiny give you every happiness and peace.

San Martín, thus, left Peru bearing the titles of "Protector" and "Founder" which the Republic he had liberated had bestowed upon him, and taking with him Pizarro's standard as a symbol of his victory.

Legend says that Joanna the Mad, daughter of Isabella the Catholic and mother of Charles V, was the one who embroidered the standard which Pizarro took to Peru in 1526. He who despoiled the Inca Atahualpa died at the hands of his companions, in a fight over power and loot, as punishment for the disloyalty with which the Inca was treated by his conquerors. When Pizarro landed with that flag the cycle of colonization began in America; when San Martín took it away with him, the cycle came to a close and a new one in history opened. Such was the meaning of the relic, and San Martín knew it.

On April 3, 1822, Don Felipe Antonio Alvarado, mayor of Lima, had written San Martín as follows:

I have the honor and great pleasure to send to Your Excellency the proclamation approved by this illustrious Municipality, together with the Royal Standard which will never again fly in Peru. Please keep it and, with it, the gratefulness of the Municipality, which takes glory in seeing that the individuals it represents are now free, through the protection of Your Excellency.

The proclamation to which the note refers, signed by the city's authorities, evidenced the background of the trophy.

San Martín asked the Lima Council about the authenticity of the standard whose ownership was attributed to Pizarro, and the Council replied that "having acquired trustworthy information and having carried out all the investigations deemed opportune," it appeared that it was the same royal standard with which the Spaniards enslaved the aborigines of Peru.

These documents and the origin of the donation give this flag an undoubted symbolical value. San Martín was pleased to have it, but the envious did not even allow him to enjoy that peace. Years later Sucre "discovered" another Pizarro standard for Bolívar; later too, a President of Peru asked San Martín to give it back; finally, it was said that the one in the possession of San Martín was not genuine, and that he had stolen it. Whether or not the flag was genuine, the symbol was, and Peru had given it to him as such.

Having handed back the insignia of Protector of Peru, San Martín left Lima and went to La Magdalena, which he called "The Town of the Free," with symbolical intention. La Magdalena was his country residence; it had belonged to the viceroys, and Bolívar used it after San Martín had left it. There he found his brother in arms, Tomás Guido, who listened to him in those confidential hours. To that place of retirement came then the delegations from Congress to demand that he accept the post of generalissimo, which San Martín refused.

"My task is ended," he told them. "My presence in the Government would be not only useless but harmful. It is for the Peruvians to finish this task."

When the delegates withdrew, San Martín closeted himself in his room to pack his baggage and his papers. Late in the afternoon he asked Guido to have tea with him. Guido had heard him say shortly before, while he was walking along the corridor of the house: "Today is really a day of happiness for me. I have got rid of a burden which I could not carry. The peoples we have freed will take charge of their own destinies."

Despite these words, the occasion did not call for gaieties. He had already decided to leave Peru, although he hadn't told anyone yet. That afternoon, while talking in his room, he suddenly said to Guido:

"What can I do for your wife in Chile?"

Guido looked at him, surprised.

"The traveler who will take your parcels will deliver them personally," added San Martín.

"Who is that traveler?" asked Guido.

"It is I," he answered. "My horses are ready for the trip to Ancón. I am embarking this very evening."

Guido, dumfounded, burst into objections. How could he expose his work to the hazards of a campaign that had not been finished yet, when he had the backing of public opinion and the army? How could he leave the political fate of the country to the turbulent reactions which his absence would surely arouse? How could he leave orphaned those who had accompanied him from the River Plate and from Chile?

These objections from his brother in arms were a forerunner of the resentment the Argentine commanders would feel in the face of the unexpected retirement of their chief, under such circumstances. San Martín, after listening to Guido with deep emotion, which he tried to hide, added calmly:

"I have thought it all over carefully. I know both the interests of America and my own duty. I leave with grief my comrades, whom I love as if they were my own sons and who have so generously helped me. But I cannot delay my departure one single day. I am going!"

The vision of his labors during the last ten years must have passed before his eyes at that moment, and in that procession must have been the images of so many young men whom he had taken from their homes to those adventures.

"Nobody," continued San Martín, "will take from me the conviction that my presence in Peru would bring to it more misfortunes than my separation. For many reasons I cannot keep my position without violating my feelings and my convictions."

These vague allusions seemed more enigmatic in the solitude of that house in La Magdalena, surrounded by the silence of the country night. He who thus spoke was the same one who had crossed the Andes to throw out of Lima the last viceroy of America. Pizarro's standard was already in his baggage, among his papers and his clothes. What reason had he to go away?

"I am going to tell you," he added. "To maintain the discipline of the army I would have to shoot some commanders, and I have not the heart to do it to men who have been with me through thick and thin."

Colonel Guido listened to him with amazement. To whom could he refer? Not to him, surely. Perhaps to some who had conspired against San Martín himself, as we have told in preceding pages. . . . More powerful reasons could be guessed. Guido thought of Guayaquil. . . .

Something had made the military fiber of San Martín's army sag, whatever the reasons. The Pacific Fleet had become undisciplined because of the evil temper of Cochrane and the delinquency in paying the crews. The action of Güemes on the Upper Peru border had failed, because of the civil war and the tragic death of this leader. Disease had decimated the patriot army, and although new levies had been made, it was far inferior in numbers to the army of the viceroy, which had taken refuge in the mountains. To move against this army and fight the last battle he lacked enough horses and mules, and he could not expect fresh help from Chile or Buenos Aires. None of this, however, was the reason for his departure. Despite the revolt against Monteagudo, Peru's public opinion continued with San Martín, as we have just seen; and the troops were also with him, despite the conspiracy of 1821, which boiled down to the disloyalty of some commanders, as has been shown in a former chapter. Bolívar's military co-operation would have solved the difficulties, but Bolívar had just refused it—and that was the reason for his attitude.

"There is a greater difficulty," affirmed San Martín; "a difficulty which I could meet only at the cost of the fate of the country and my own reputation: Bolívar and myself cannot be in Peru at the same time. I have penetrated his thoughts; I have understood his annoyance at the glory that could be mine for ending the war. He would use any means to enter Peru and perhaps I could not avoid a conflict, giving a scandal to the world, and the only ones who would profit by it would be the enemy. That, never! Let Bolívar come into Peru, and if he makes safe what we have gained, I will be happy, because America will win in any event. It will not be San Martín who will give a day of joy to the Spaniards."

At the time nobody could have realized the greatness of those words. San Martín did realize it. We also realize it, now.

If they are checked against the calm letter which he wrote Bolívar after the meeting at Guayaquil, saying farewell, and with the austere manifesto he had just addressed to Peru to justify his retirement, those words, pronounced that memorable evening at La Magdalena, reveal in the voice of

San Martín the genuine pitch of an exceptional soul. The confidences he had been making in his letters since 1814, the consistency of his repeated renunciations, his disinterest in power and money, his ascetic sufferings when he prepared his expedition, his horrors of civil war, his mystic love for America, his lack of personal vanity—all that made of his latest attitude the logical climax of his destiny. The soul of this hero had the quality of civilian sanctity, and in that it differed from other military heroes.

The room at La Magdalena filled with a cosmic silence, comparable only to that which sometimes pervades at night the highest Andean heights.

An orderly came in to say that everything was ready for the march. San Martín, who knew where he was going when he left Buenos Aires, was now leaving Peru without knowing where he was going. It was the hour for returning, the hour of the sad journeys. After having filled the continent with his action, when he came from the Atlantic to the Pacific across the Andes, he would go now from the Pacific to the Atlantic, and even farther. He was leaving America to enter into the history of mankind.

Outside the house the fields smelled of spring. He took leave of Guido with a silent and strong embrace. Above the black Peruvian soil the night rose to heaven, sprinkled with a thousand stars. Which of those was San Martín's star, the one he cursed in Cuyo one day in 1816, in a moment of anxiety? Perhaps it was that one, so bright, about to set. . . .

At the gate of "The Town of the Free" San Martín mounted his horse and started for the Peruvian coast, followed by his servant and his orderly. It was September 20, 1822. That same evening, at ten o'clock, he went on board the brigantine, *Belgrano,* whose name reminded him of the old friend who had died in poverty and solitude. San Martín ordered the master to set sail to the south. He who had come by sea was returning by sea—but this time without his arms, dressed in black civilian clothes.

Thus Parsifal, in the poem, divests himself of the arms with which he has roamed the world, because he is about to enter the mystic temple of renunciation.

Three military encounters had San Martín in Chile, and in them he showed plainly the moral and technical qualities of his military genius: the geographical names of Chacabuco, Cancha Rayada, and Maipú point to the places of those three encounters.

Chacabuco was the first battle fought by the Army of the Andes after descending the western slopes toward the Chilean capital—a battle mathematically prepared in Cuyo and foreseen as a victory which would assure the independence of Chile, at the same time giving a fulcrum to the campaign for the liberation of Peru. The battle of Chacabuco took place in February 1817, completely in accordance with San Martín's plans, as far as date, place, and outcome are concerned, with a certitude which shows the maximum ability of the strategist. From Chacabuco the triumphant legion moved on to Santiago and created the Chilean national government that has endured until now and which then presided over the formation of the United Army, a military alliance of Argentinians and Chileans for the expedition to the Peruvian coasts.

Cancha Rayada was a surprise in the dark of the night, one year after the triumphal entrance. A new Spanish army, sent by the viceroy of Lima, had reached Talcahuano to join the defeated Royalists. San Martín's army, swollen with pride at the first victory or perhaps absent-minded with thoughts of the march to Peru, was surprised near Talca and defeated without fighting, in the midst of an appalling nocturnal confusion. San Martín, who was with O'Higgins at the theater of the surprise, withdrew with the other commanders to the desperate capital. This happened in March 1818. The unforeseen setback placed San Martín's warrior temper on trial, because he made of it a moral victory over himself and over a people which had fallen upon tribulations. At that very moment of failure he restored all the forces and retook the offensive.

Maipú was the revenge for Cancha Rayada, a few days after the disaster, on April 5, 1818, memorable day of lasting victory, which saved four years of previous sacrifices and opened the door for the eventual outcome of the San Martinian cause in America. Maipú was a victory not as lengthily prepared as Chácabuco, but an improvisation of genius, born of an outburst of courage and carried through with amazing tactical ability upon a battlefield imposed upon San Martín by circumstances. The magnitude of the two armies, the importance of their losses and booty, the consequence of their results on continental emancipation, all of these make of Maipú the greatest of San Martín's feats as a warrior. The Royalist armies were there smashed forever. All the victories later achieved over the Royalists in South America were simply a consequence of that battle and of the following, until Pichincha, Río Bamba, Junín, and Ayacucho, in which were present the Argentine grenadiers, his favorite disciples.

The three military actions of San Martín in Chile have been individually studied by the technicians of war, but they must be joined together in a biography of San Martín as three episodes of a single personal enterprise, the forerunner of which was the preparation in Cuyo, until the crossing of the Andes, and the corollary of which was the Lima expedition, until the emancipation of Peru. San Martín was present at the three episodes of Chilean history: thoughtful strategist at Chacabuco, stoic soldier at Cancha Rayada, intrepid tactician at Maipú; and on all three occasions, an indomitable paladin. In the rhapsody of the hero, those three moments must be shown together, as in a monumental triptych. And so they were remembered, undoubtedly, by the warrior who came from Chile and who was returning to Chile, shorn of his weapons.

But this strong warrior who closed his epic in 1822 was at the same time a missionary of love.

When war was going on in the south of Chile, after Maipú, when the patriot Freyre was fighting against the Spanish chief, Sánchez, San Martín had addressed himself to the latter offering peace:

Nothing honors a general more than keeping his serenity in danger and facing it when there are chances of winning; but nothing so much eclipses his name as the useless shedding of the blood of his men. Whatever be the method of war which Your Excellency proposes to use in that province, I am going to call upon it and finish the war. It is not my intention to bring you through the force of my armies to a dishonorable position; my intention is to prevent the calamities which are devastating Chile. Let Your Excellency make the proposals which you deem honorable.

The Spanish commander answered impudently, rejecting this invitation, and he was defeated after a bloody campaign, which San Martín had tried to avoid. But San Martín knew how to keep serenity in the face of danger, and he didn't want to shed uselessly the blood of his men; he tried to avoid the calamities of war. Similar humanitarian suggestions were made by him in 1817 to Viceroy Pezuela and in 1821 to Viceroy La Serna. He waged war only for charity and as a duty.

When landing in Pisco, San Martín had said to his legions in a proclamation:

We have already arrived at the place of our destiny, and now courage must finish the labor of constancy. Remember that your great duty is to console America and that you are not here to make conquests but to liberate peoples. The Peruvians are your brothers. Embrace them and respect their rights, as you respected those of the Chileans after Chacabuco.

And in a manifesto addressed to the peoples of Peru he had explained the philosophical nature of the colonial conflict and of his own mission:

The revolution in Spain is of the same nature as ours; both have freedom for their aim and oppression as their cause. But America cannot look upon the Spanish Constitution except as a fraudulent means of keeping the colonial system, which is impossible to keep any longer by force. We cannot expect any benefit from a code written 2,000 leagues away, without the intervention of our representatives. The last Spanish viceroy is making an effort to prolong his decrepit authority. . . . The time of oppression and force is past. I have come to put an end to this era of suffering and humiliation.

The hero who in 1820 left his homeland insulted did not harbor any rancor against it; on the contrary, he addressed himself from Peru to the City Council of Buenos Aires, reporting on his campaigns and inviting the people to give themselves a constitution and restore national government, "so that the fratricidal struggle may come to an end and the brother peoples may give the nation a degree of splendor and solidity which may attract to it the respect and consideration of Europe."

Those are the days of Punchauca, and the Argentine civil wars "are embittering the triumphs of those who fight against the enemies of America. . . . I speak to Your Excellency as an American who from an immense distance keeps the destiny of those promises at heart, without any other pretentions than that of seeing them free and happy."

These feelings of love toward Argentina found their clearest symbol when, victorious in Lima, San Martín offered to the Buenos Aires Government the trophies of his victory:

> In the course of the campaign which has sealed the independence of Peru, the Liberating Army has taken, among various other trophies, five flags and two standards which were in the hands of the enemies of America. I beg Your Excellency to accept them as an expression of the homage of the troops under my command, and to order that they be deposited wherever Your Excellency deems fitting.

Buenos Aires received with pride these trophies of victory, and the poets celebrated San Martín's glory with lengthy odes:

> *From today on to the future*
> *Thine is the marble, Thine are the bronzes.*

Esteban de Luca, who had already sung to Maipú, celebrated in Buenos Aires the entrance of San Martín into Lima. The Government, by a decree signed by Martín Rodríguez and his minister Rivadavia, ordered the printing of Luca's poetry and presented the author with the works of Homer, Virgil, Tasso, Voltaire, and Ossian. The poet sent San Martín his *Canto a la Libertad de Lima,* as he did before with the *Canto a Maipú.* San Martín replied with an affectionate letter, but so laconic that it almost boiled down to the following:

> I can assure you that the successes which have crowned this campaign are not due to my talent (I well know the limits of it) but to the determination of the peoples to obtain their freedom and to the courage of the army I command. With this kind of soldiers, anybody could undertake anything with success.

Let this letter be compared with that of Bolívar to Olmedo on the *Canto a la Victoria de Junin* and it will be seen to what degree these two warriors were different.

Neither glory, nor infamy, praise, insults, victory, or defeat ever disturbed the clear water of San Martín's spirits. Before Argentina, before America, before Spain, he keeps unperturbed his moral equilibrium, as he kept his mental lucidity in the accomplishment of his destiny. When in 1822, after Guayaquil, he resigned his command and went to look for his daughter, he did only what he had determined to do since 1820, as he told his father-in-law in a confidential letter as soon as he had victoriously entered Lima:

> My beloved father, if our success can calm the passions and anarchy of the United Provinces, I shall have completed the work which I have undertaken. I

long to find a corner and live the rest of my days dedicated to the education of my daughter; but the sacrifice of a few months is necessary in order to leave Peru sufficiently buttressed so as not to expose it to the vicissitudes which Buenos Aires and its provinces have suffered.

This simple letter illumines also, with a serene light, the soul of the hero in his renunciation.

He who in 1814 was already speaking of the crossing of the Andes and the maritime expedition against Peru—the plan of action later carried out—is the same who in 1820 planned his retirement to private life in order to educate his daughter, as he did in the years that followed the interview at Guayaquil, according to the plan made for his life.

In August 1821, after having the independence of Peru sworn, San Martín had said to his legions:

For eight years I have commanded you, and at the end your virtues and constancy, under the auspices of Heaven, have brought about the independence of South America; on the ice of the Andes, on the waters of the Pacific, and on the deserted coasts of Peru, your homeland always saw you contented. Hunger, nakedness, fatigue, and death you have faced with enthusiasm. Zealously trying to spare me annoyances, you have given the world the first example of the closest brotherhood between the armies of two nations. Rivals only in your search for danger, firm in the face of misfortune, moderate in victory, ferocious in combat, and helpful to the unfortunate—such has been the mark of the Army of Liberation.

Comrades: My gratitude will have for a model your heroism: you will see me at your side as long as there are dangers. Once the enemy is thrown from this country, I shall descend to the category of a plain citizen, delivering the destiny of Peru into the hands of a sovereign Congress. I shall seek retirement in the midst of peace, and each day that I can embrace an old soldier of the Army of Liberation I shall receive the reward for all my labors.

San Martín, then, did not leave Peru because he was weakening in the face of the military struggle, nor because he did not have the adhesion of his troops or the friendship of Buenos Aires or the civilian backing of the Peruvian Congress. Neither did he leave because he had harbored monarchist illusions or had been awed by the greatness of Bolívar, at whose orders he offered to place himself. The refusal of Bolívar on this point gives the clue for the renunciation of San Martín, and this is explained by the nature of his genius, and because ever since his arrival in Lima he had decided to retire, as he told his father-in-law in 1820, and as he told O'Higgins, Basil Hall, Lord Cochrane, and Peru itself in a manifesto on taking on the protectorate. On retiring, in 1822, he gave up personal command, but only because he knew that Bolívar, with his genius, could be his successor in the great undertaking.

The warrior of Chile is already the man capable of honor in battle, capable of stoicism in defeat, capable of kindness in the armistice, according to the moral complexity of his extraordinary soul. With the Peruvian undertaking, begun in 1820 and closed in 1822, San Martín had reached the highest degree of mastery; but he is the same singular and selfless man of the former times. The capture of Lima without any bloodshed and the taking of Callao without a battle are new forms of the victorious genius at his best; but Guayaquil is the culminating victory of his lofty soul. He who broke his pact with the Spanish kings in 1811 had come to Lima to recapture the standard of Pizarro, and the symbolic trophy was already in his hands. With this his mission was at an end.

Serenely, with amazing virtue, he gave Bolívar the military command and gave back to Peru the insignia of its sovereignty.

From his ship San Martín wrote a brief farewell letter to Guido and another to Alvarado, both full of noble feelings and justice, inseparably characteristic of his conscience.

Napoleon also experienced this fatal moment of the finished undertaking, when the hero survives his feat. But Napoleon was the defeated man of Waterloo, the captive on the *Bellerophon,* the exile of St. Helena, and his pride of Prometheus in chains did not allow him to understand in full the esoteric lesson of the outcome. San Martín, on the other hand, understood the denouement of his action because he played his part with Pythagorean lucidity and because he himself created this denouement in a gesture of evangelical renunciation.

In this he stood apart from almost all the famous warriors—because he did not belong to the Dionysian line of conquerors. His background was not that of the warriors who founded kingdoms for themselves, subjecting peoples for the benefit of their dynasties. San Martín was not similar even to Bolívar, who pretended to unite the whole continent under his sole authority and who gave his own name to a nation—Bolivia—formed with remnants of peoples dismembered by his sword.

San Martín felt neither the pleasure nor the glory of war. He fought through duty and for service. During his epic he never felt himself to be a demigod, but a man—and in that is the novel greatness of his heroism.

II. THE RETURN TO MONSALVAT

San Martín ordered the captain of the ship to sail for Valparaiso, next port for his return. He was now sailing alone through the Pacific—the same man who two years before had come through that very sea at the head of a numerous fleet, with five thousand soldiers.

He was taking with him, besides his modest clothing, only 120 ounces of gold for his expenses. This was his only money, and when he thought of that he remembered the many times his enemies had called him a thief. His life's destiny had been realized. That was the mission of his paladin's soul. Nothing else did he need now. Those things were what his inner self came to seek in the City of Kings, the city which others would enter later, in a fratricidal war, to seek theatrical pomp and ephemeral powers.

The mysterious traveler arrived in Valparaiso October 13, unexpectedly, accompanied only by his orderly, Eusebio Soto. The news of his arrival spread quickly. It was said that he had escaped from Lima, fearful of becoming the victim of a major attempt at assassination, as Monteagudo had been. His enemy Cochrane was near by at the time, and some malicious souls enjoyed themselves thinking of an encounter between them. Also, the infamous rumor spread that San Martín had tried to smuggle a large amount in gold. Irresponsible voices said that San Martín, the liberator of Chile, was going to be arrested in Chile. Many hated his name in that country. The hour of power was past.

Fortunately, the noble O'Higgins, his loyal companion, was still Supreme Director. Upon learning of his arrival, the guns of the port fired a salute to the flag on the *Belgrano*. The Director sent his carriage to take him to the city. His aides, General Prieto and Major O'Connor, greeted San Martín officially.

The traveler had come with the idea of going to the baths at Cauquenes, because he was ill, with stabbing rheumatic pains in one arm. It was his purpose, besides, not to take any part in public affairs and to seek a place for rest either in Chile or in Mendoza. The spirit of what O'Higgins called "the Carrerist gang" was undermining O'Higgins' regime, which was near its fall, and this made the fate of the solitary traveler sadder still.

A few days before, the following mocking verse had circulated:

> *Your glory, O San Martín,*
> *Has reached its top and warns you*
> *For your own good to avoid*
> *Any action of uncertain ending.*

The Protector's retirement gave rise to hostile comments in Peru. His mysterious voyage and the silence he kept about the Guayaquil meeting fed all kinds of rumors. The time was not favorable for him, after the revolt against Monteagudo, and his old enemies encouraged gossip. Some said San Martín had gone because he had failed in his plans to crown himself emperor. Others affirmed he had left because the patriot legions no longer had any confidence in him. Some averred that cowardice was the reason; that San Martín feared equally the Royalist foe in the mountains and the local reaction coming to a boil in Lima. And as if all this were not enough, some added that San Martín had absconded with 30,000 pounds taken from the Peruvian Treasury. An ambitious man in disgrace, a leader who had lost his prestige, a timid soldier and a thieving ruler—that was San Martín in the eyes of many, in the sublime hour of his misunderstood greatness. Such insults were heard all along the Pacific coast when the silent pilgrim landed in Valparaiso.

Said the overthrown Monteagudo a year later:

> I cannot estimate the weight of the circumstances which precipitated the withdrawal of General San Martín. However, I think that he could not resist the calumnies of the ungrateful, and that, having lost confidence in many of those who were then on the stage, he thought he could not continue there without lowering himself to the point of negotiating with the new passions and interests that had arisen in his absence. Thus it was not long before they took off their masks who only believe in the freedom of the press when it allows them to defame others. General San Martín, the hero of Chacabuco and Maipú, he who became still more of a hero when he undertook to liberate Peru with a handful of braves, he who without placing upon his brow any crown of laurels soaked in blood, won over numberless obstacles by means of wisdom, he who saved Lima from the catastrophes everyone was presaging for the hour when the old resentments came to a head, he who lifted with his own hands many of his present enemies from the depths of misery, has been insulted in some newspapers of that city, with impunity and in face of the scandal felt by the honest people. But his brilliant services to the cause of America since the year XII [1812] and those rendered to Peru, opening the doors to its destiny, are the property of history, which cannot be defrauded.

Monteagudo wrote those just and noble words at Quito, where, a refugee after his downfall, he published his *Memoria,* in which he replied to the Peruvian attacks and set forth the principles he upheld while a minister in the cabinet of the Protector at Lima. The exile was to return later to Peru with Bolívar, where he was treacherously assassinated.

Former minister Unanue, in November 1822, wrote San Martín a letter, soon after the latter's departure, giving him interesting news about Monteagudo, suffering from poverty in exile: "Monteagudo writes me requesting that his salary for July be paid, because he finds himself in the direst poverty. His enemies are many: they blame him for things in which he had no part. I have had to defend him several times, for things that had occurred because of me and not of him." This letter reached San Martín's hands upon his arrival in Chile, when he was under the weight of similar calumnies and similar poverty.

On his return voyage San Martín received many letters telling him what was gossiped and printed about him. Thus he learned that in a secret session of the Peruvian Congress, at which titles and honors were conferred upon him on his departure, Deputy Mariátegui had said: "Peru has suffered greater tyranny and excesses in one year of freedom in Lima than in three hundred years of Spanish domination." On the same occasion Deputy Colmenares had opposed the planned honors: "Peru has obtained its freedom without needing the help of San Martín and his troops. The sash is a symbol of sovereignty, and sovereignty is vested upon the Congress. It is enough, as a reward, to give him the title of generalissimo." How could such ingratitude be possible? And the worst of it is that many of those he had formerly favored also turned against him.

But nothing so vexed San Martín as the version that he had tried to establish monarchical regimes in America. He protested against it with sarcasm at the time, and with anger later, when he wrote from Europe:

I know the efforts that have been made to make believe that General San Martín had no other objective in his trip to Europe than that of creating a monarchy in America. The wretches who circulate such miserable impostures do not know that the feelings I have so frankly expressed (because I am a free man) on that point have nothing to do with my feelings concerning the masses in general, and that I would give my life a thousand times over to uphold the republic.

As to the other insult—that he was leaving the political stage for fear of his adversaries or because he did not dare give decisive battle to the Spanish in the mountains, the facts were an eloquent enough reply. His military plan in Peru had been as skillful as in Chile, with the differences necessitated by adaptation to local conditions. Like a knight in love, he wanted to conquer Lima through love, not by force, and Lima surrendered to him without a struggle. He preferred to sow the seeds of revolution among the people and of desertion among the enemy, and the results were completely satisfactory. Cochrane on the sea, and on land his generals, Las Heras, Miller, Arenales, and others, had won victories such as that of Pasco, in accordance with his plans. Moreover, he found a way to help Sucre at Río Bamba and Pichincha, despite the fact that San Martín's army had been decimated by disease. His agents had promoted the republican uprising in Guayaquil long before Bolívar's entry into the city. Callao and the coasts were under the flag of the homeland, through the work of his genius. To judge his military ability and his civic courage there was enough with that; but besides it there was also his campaign across the Andes, and Chacabuco and Maipú, his Chilean victories.

The Chilean epic had as a precedent, in San Martín's career, twenty years of warfare in Spain and the battle of San Lorenzo in Argentina; and it had as a corollary in Peru the occupation of the coast, the mountain campaign, the victory of Pasco, the capture of Callao, and the entry into Lima, which is the cornerstone of his triumphs. All this seemed to be worth nothing in those days of his return, when San Martín was called a coward and incapable.

During his stay in Valparaiso, when he returned from Peru, he was constantly in the company of Zenteno, D'Albe, and other comrades. This also gave rise to a rumor—that they accompanied him because he feared an attempt on his life. Under the burden of so many insults, he sought solace in the harbor and in the beautiful scenery near it,

There lived at the time in Valparaiso an English widow, Mrs. Mary Graham, a witty woman of the world, who in 1824 published in London a book on her South American travels. She herself tells us that a few days after his arrival San Martín visited her at her home, being introduced by Zenteno, who was governor of the port, together with other gentlemen who accompanied him. The chronicle left by this writer is interesting, not only because it is one of the few testimonials known to have been left by a woman about the personality of San Martín, but because she met him in those days of adversity. The Englishwoman, besides, was a friend of Lord Cochrane's, and in her book she does not conceal her partiality for her countryman, an enemy of San Martín's, from which there arises a studied aversion from the American hero.

Mrs. Graham received her visitors in a small room. The talk became general. The Englishwoman began to observe San Martín, her mysterious guest, "a very tall, fine-looking man, dressed in plain black clothes," as she says herself. "San Martín's eyes," she adds, "possess a peculiarity which I have only once before seen in somebody else, a famous woman: his eyes are black and handsome, but restless; they look fixedly only an instant, but in that instant they tell you everything."

San Martín's manner struck her as easy, as did his speech. "He speaks French passably," she says, "and he understands English." During the visit, which lasted four hours, San Martín monopolized the conversation. "I am not a woman to repeat private conversations, which I always consider sacred," says Mrs. Graham. "But San Martín is a public man, and his talk was of a general nature." They spoke of government, philosophy, religion, American affairs. His political ideas did not seem very clear to the Englishwoman. It would seem that the guest revealed an equal fear of demagogy and despotism. His wish to protect his reputation as a liberator and his principles of law and order made a strange contrast in his opinions. When the talk turned to philosophy and religion, San Martín and Zenteno showed themselves somewhat skeptical. They considered religion as a state machinery, good for the priest and the crowd, but unnecessary for the learned. "Allusion was made to the superstitions of the Roman Church, which in South America are seen in plain nakedness, without the prestige given them by Italian art."

It is easier for a Catholic than for a Protestant to fall into skepticism, it was said. And this seemed to the lady to be San Martín's state of mind. Apropos of the Reformation and scientific discoveries, the talk turned on the political revolutions of modern times. The times of Louis XIV were mentioned as a cause of the French Revolution, and the conversation veered toward the revolution's effect on America, the intellectual progress of Europe, and again the Roman Church. Zenteno, who was called "The Philosopher" (a rationalist Liberal in the French mode of the "century of light"), attacked Rome, and to show off his reading, said solemnly:

"Rome crowned Petrarch but jailed Galileo."

Someone commented:

"Exact science can become an instrument of tyranny; but not poetry, nor oratory, nor history."

The conversation was becoming pedantic when the maid brought in tea. Mrs. Graham excused herself for not being able to offer maté to her *criollo* guests. San Martín, who took his tea without cream, resumed the conversation while he sipped and smoked his cigar. He spoke of physics, languages, climate in connection with health, and finally fell upon the subject of Peruvian antiques, which was what interested the Englishwoman most, describing the tombs and mummies of the Incas. "That was the best part of his talk," says Mrs. Graham. Then he told her about his own life in Lima. He related that in order to discover the true feelings of the people he walked the streets in civilian clothes, and, as Caliph Haroun al Raschid, went into barrooms and markets. Sometimes, among the populace, he heard talk about himself, and understood that that people did not need him any longer. . . .

"After a life of so many worries," said San Martín, "I also need some rest. I have taken leave of my political career, being happy to have accomplished my part in the task. I have with me only the flag of Pizarro, the banner under which the conquest of the Inca Empire was carried out. That flag was flown in several wars, not only against the Indians but also among the Spaniards themselves."

And after a pause, he exclaimed with moving solemnity:

"The possession of this flag has always been considered a symbol of power and authority. I have it now." And he sat up and looked around, with a dominating gesture. He knew that his inner self was listening.

Mrs. Graham, who so tells it in her book, says that that was the most characteristic thing that happened in the four hours that San Martín spoke with her, and she writes, "That was the only moment when San Martín was himself." We must believe her: Mrs. Graham told us more in that phrase than she thought. . . .

The mention of the Incas and his pride in having rescued the flag of Pizarro was, as that perspicacious woman noted, the most characteristic and the most intimate revelation of that predestined and long-suffering soul. San Martín did not speak like that out of rhetorical affectation, which was not in his nature. That was only a naïve confidence of his inner self. The Incas and Pizarro were esoterically remote causes of his heroic destiny. Perhaps San Martín was an avatar of Atahualpa, the sacrificed Inca.

Mrs. Graham noticed in San Martín a certain wish for pre-eminence in conversation, due no doubt to his long exercise of command. She heard from him some gallant words, which she glosses over with pretended irony, as she later confesses: "He was extremely courteous; his words, as much as his manners, seemed to me full of gracefulness, and now I believe what I have so many times heard about him: that few can best him at a dance."

Mrs. Graham admits in her book that he was a man of talent, but she does not consider him well read.

> He has the ability to show what he knows, but few have in the same degree *l'art de se faire valoir.* . . . His handsome personality, his smooth manner, notable in someone who for so long has handled men, give him decisive advantages. He aspires to a universality like Napoleon's, of whom he speaks as a model, or a rival. . . . I believe he wanted to pose before me because I was a foreigner, if it is true that Zenteno told him I would write about him. But the truth is that on that evening he spoke to show himself off. . . . At nine o'clock the visitors left me, and I felt very happy to have known one of the outstanding men of South America.

Who would believe that this simple, quiet, and affable man is the same one who had just left Bolívar, talked of pathetic things with Guido at La Magdalena, and closed in Lima a destiny of glory in the face of selfish rivalries? It cannot be doubted that this man whom Mrs. Graham knew in Valparaiso in the most admirable hour of his life was a unique personality.

Two days after this visit San Martín left for the baths of Cauquenes. His chronic ills became worse in Chile, and he had to spend two months in bed. He could make no decision about his future until the end of 1822. He stayed in Santiago, worried at the latest quarrels of Cochrane's and at O'Higgins' political situations, as well as at his own economic situation in face of an uncertain future. In the midst of these new trials he left, at last, in search of peace, to live on his Mendoza farm.

San Martín crossed the Andes on muleback, this time alone and without any illusions. Those peaks must have seemed to him as austere and desolate as his own soul. That mountain was the twin sister of his genius; they had both been born of the same cosmic genesis. He had crossed it in 1817 with a legion of 5,000 warriors, bound for glory. He had crossed in again in 1817, in 1818, in 1819, and in 1820, when he left behind his homeland in the throes of civil war, having before his eyes as a guide his enormous continental undertaking. Now he was going back over the road of his return, as Don Quixote after the battle, his lance broken. "Destiny so orders it," he must have said to himself while his mule plodded on, repeating the phrase of his letter to Bolívar. Everywhere the mountain showed its frozen peaks and its dry abysses. Mount Aconcagua, in the shadow of which he slept the eve of Chacabuco, seemed to recognize him from its immaculate heights. Thus he went on, remembering the stages of the old journey, until, when reaching La Cumbre (the name of a place, not "the summit," the meaning of the words in Spanish), he had a happy and unexpected meeting.

Manuel de Olazábal, former cadet of grenadiers, initiated in 1813, had left Mendoza, where he lived, to meet on the way his former "colonel" as soon as he learned of his return; and he himself tells in his *Episodes of the Independence,* what I wish now to tell.

San Martín was coming through La Cumbre riding a fat mule, with a Hungarian-type saddle, the stirrups lined with cloth against the cold. He was dressed in a short blue pea jacket and trousers, yellow gaiters and gloves; a Chilean poncho covered his body, and on his head he had a large hat of Guayaquil straw. In his sad face "shone those eyes that nobody could describe." He was accompanied by a captain, two servants, two helpers, four muleteers, and three freight carriers with the baggage and food.

Upon seeing his chief, young Olazábal, who stood waiting for him, ran to embrace him. San Martín placed his right hand on the youth's head and said, "My son!"—shocked by the emotion of finding him there.

After dismounting, the traveler rested on a saddle on the floor, while they prepared him a maté. When he had drunk it, he thanked them:

"It has been a long time since I had such an exquisite delicacy."

Then he gave the order to continue the trip and mounted again; he looked at the mountain range and exclaimed, as if talking to himself,

"Well, perhaps it is better that we come down from this eminence, where in other times America looked upon me."

It was a fresh, bright day of January. The tiresome descent exhausted him.

They spent the night heavily blanketed at El Manzano and rested the next day at El Totoral, a farm of Don Juan Francisco Delgado.

There he was reached by a courier sent by O'Higgins, with the mail from Lima. San Martín looked at the envelopes, read one of the letters and said:

"Oh, if Alvarado follows the campaign plan I left for operations against the Intermediate Ports, he will be victorious; otherwise he will fail."

Then he opened another letter and said:

"This is from Riva Agüero, the biggest scoundrel there is in Peru."

When he had read it his face shone with anger:

"Rogue! Now he calls me to go back, otherwise Peru will be lost! The intriguer!"

He continued reading his correspondence; he took an envelope and after looking at the writing and the stamp he recognized the handwriting:

"This is from a *matucho*,[1] my brother Manuel, who, still believing me the 'Dictator of Peru,' writes me for the first time since we parted in 1811, never having answered the many letters I wrote him calling him to my side."

He tore up the letter without reading it and threw it away.

Perhaps if Manuel and his other brothers, creoles and soldiers like himself, had come to help him in his enterprises of America, his life might have been less sad.

He spent three days at Delgado's farm; with that rest his strength improved and he continued.

On February 2 he slept in a place called La Estacada. On the 3rd, while walking, suddenly he said to Olazábal:

"Do you remember what day this is?"

"At this moment, no, sir."

"Well this day in 1813, more or less at this hour, the Regiment made in San Lorenzo its first attempt. The matuchos must not have forgotten; neither have I, because I was somewhat worried."

They arrived at Uspallata and afterwards descended to the "plain of Mendoza," the familiar settlement where he started his military career. They could see the white houses between the green of its fruit gardens. Don Quixote was returning to his village, thinking about the Knight of the Mirrors or the magician Merlin; and perhaps like the Knight of La Mancha murmured to himself: "I know who I am."

When he entered the city, by the alameda (poplar-bordered avenue) he himself had planted, his appearance was a surprise. The good people of long ago came to greet him. Nobody understood why he was returning; not even he himself could explain it.

San Martín had always been a man of unexpected or disconcerting attitudes. He only could tell them he had entered Lima victoriously, as he had announced; that America was free; that he brought the flag of Pizarro; that his Dulcinea was rescued and that his task was finished.

If before he had come to prepare the war in his "Insula Cuyana" (Mendoza), now he was returning to it to find rest in his last days. This was his Arcadia, where in 1816 he dreamed his vocation of farmer, or the refuge that his saintly asceticism wished for when, from Europe, he wrote during his long exile:

"I expect to remain two more years in Europe, the time I believe necessary to finish the education of my daughter; if by that time the United Provinces are quiet, I will return to my country, to go to my refuge in Mendoza."

San Martín, upon arriving at Mendoza, lodged in the home of his good friend Doña Josefa Ruiz de Huidobro, who received him happily and gave him every possible care.

The first thing the traveler did upon entering his new home was to order his scanty luggage to be brought home. They took down from the pack mule the bag he had brought from Lima. He started to look at it with some wistfulness; inside was his saber of Maipú, Pizarro's flag, and the inkstand of the Inquisition.

At night when he was alone, he opened his leather suitcase and took out the most varied objects: a brass sundial, some chintz pillows, an English rifle, some paintings on tin, a white sword belt, a gilded spade, some napkins, binoculars, bridles, tablecloths, a powder flask, and also a few pieces of wearing apparel; the saber, the flag, and the inkstand, his favorite possessions. From these priceless relics came a contradictory suggestion of pride and sadness. . . . In another bag that he didn't open were his papers. . . .

During these days, knowing that O'Higgins had also left the Government, he wrote to his companion these revealing words: "Millions and millions of congratulations for your separation from the Government. . . . Now you will enjoy peace, without the necessity of creating ingrates every day. . . . Enjoy the peace that the memory of having worked for the welfare of the country will give you."

San Martín had reached that unavoidable hour which sometimes comes to great leaders of historic action; when the enterprise is finished the hero returns to the darkness of his human condition. The mystery of the theater, which presents kings, heroes, and demigods incarnated in human actors, have sometimes similar moments. When the tragic poem is finished the artist returns to his daily reality, shorn of his crown and his symbolic ornaments. When Shakespeare said that all the world is a stage and men only actors, he referred to that hidden similarity between the real and the esthetic life.

The character created by art is a momentary reality and then disappears like an illusion, as happens in history with men who were bearers of a message of the inner self.

San Martín, who was a real initiate, knew as Shakespeare, who was an initiate, too, the meaning of this deep truth.

The climate of Mendoza gave him back his strength. "He had recovered the activity of twenty years ago. . . . Neatly dressed in black, he frequented parties and danced." With his good humor he made simple jokes which revealed his candid soul. Olazábal found him one day in his room pasting on some wine bottles labels which read: "Málaga," "Mendocino." Then he explained:

"When we were going to the campaign of Chile in 1817, I left in a basement of my farm, Los Barriales, in care of honest Don Pedro Advinícula Moyano, some dozens of bottles of delicious wine. You will understand that, after so many years, I had forgotten this, but Moyano has brought me a few bottles, telling me that he still has the rest, Now it occurs to me to put Mendoza labels on these two bottles of Málaga wine, and Málaga labels on mine. As Mosquera and Arcos will dine with me today, after dinner you will see!"

At four o'clock the dinner began, and after teasing Arcos because he could not cut a baked cake, San Martín uncorked his bottles, served the Málaga wine with the Mendoza label; they found it good, but not of first quality; then he served, in other glasses, the Mendoza wine labeled Málaga, and the guests, who thought themselves connoisseurs, said:

"Oh, there is a big difference! This one is exquisite! What fragrance! What taste! There is no comparison between them."

Upon hearing them, San Martín revealed his secret, laughed like a youngster and teased them without mercy, finally admonishing them:

"Gentlemen: you do not know anything about wines, and you are fooled by foreign labels."

The "Cuyo" wines were, since the Independence, a topic of political pre-occupation: *El Centinela*, a Buenos Aires newspaper, had published in 1823 an article signed by "A Friend of the Country," sent from Mendoza, regarding this industry, requesting tariff protection.

Since 1815 San Martín had devoted himself to promoting the wine industry in Cuyo. He used to talk to his Mendoza friends about European wines and the way they were made. Because he talked like this, his enemies invented stories about his liking to drink.

San Martín moved from the home of Doña Josefa to his Mendoza farm, Los Barriales, five leagues from the city. The farm was not very large; besides the modest house it had a field of corn, a vineyard, a place to raise horses, and a mill. The master hoped to occupy himself with these things. As Alonso Quijano, shorn of his arms, he had accepted Sancho's advice, of not dying and, instead, of becoming a shepherd. . . . For the present he would be accompanied in his new adventure by Pedro Núñez, overseer of the farm; Eusebio Soto, a page with whom he came from Peru, and the creole cook, who would be housekeeper. The healthy climate of Mendoza would complete the picture of the eclogue, an illusion of happiness. . . . "Happiness is not real, but only imaginary," San Martín said once, showing, by those words, the poet that lived in his stoical heart.

What worried him now was the new angle in his life: after the first part, which had been one of apprenticeship to know himself, and the second part, which had been one of realization to perfect his heroic deed, he had reached the time of the third part: renunciation, which San Martín sought for his inexhaustible virtue as the new expression of his extraordinary life. What San Martín now dreamed of was to make his farm an Arcadia for his body and a refuge for his spirit. To fulfill this dream he would have had to forget the world; but the world came to seek him in his solitude.

The Peruvian Santiago Campos, from Lima, congratulates himself because San Martín has reached Mendoza safely; "which congratulation, transmitted through all of America, at the same time flatters our hopes for the future and paralyzes Spanish pride"; and with the same emphasis he added that "the prosperity of his country cannot but become a reality, as long as the hero and liberator of old Peru is interested in it."

The chaplain Don Pedro José de Tramarria, also from Lima, extends wishes for the health and peace of San Martín at Mendoza, "completely convinced that the liberty my country enjoys is due to the efforts of Your Excellency, and this will prolong indefinitely my thanks to you, to whom I owe my life, and while I live I will not fail to pray to the Lord."

All these friendly letters could have changed San Martín's pessimism about men; but, even if he read them with pleasure, they were not sufficient to take him out of the indifference with which he viewed certain things in life.

But not all the letters were pleasant. His friend Salvador Iglesias, who had gone from Chile to Peru, informed him from Lima:

What clamor there is in this city about the absence of Your Excellency! The majority want you with anxiety; my coming here makes them hope that perhaps Your Excellency may come back here someday, and especially in the present circumstances, which seem uncertain and poor. There is absolutely no money, except the revenue from the Port of Callao. The present state of affairs is diabolical.

On October 21, 1823, he was given a letter, one that pierced his usual indifference. It was another from Riva Agüero. Dated at Trujillo, it took sixty days to reach him, forwarded from Chile. Riva Agüero was the scoundrel of the intrigues of Lima who was responsible for the fall of Monteagudo and the local suspicion of San Martín. He was now in a fight with Congress. He again asked San Martín to return to Peru, to bring arms and command an army in the war against the Congress, which had already begun.

San Martín, master of calm, lost his patience upon reading this insolent communication. Trembling with anger, he crushed the paper, read it again, and wrote the deserved answer, which left for Lima on the next day. He answered that never would he stain his sword in civil wars and said strong words against Riva Agüero. Regarding the consequences of this answer, I will speak in a later chapter.

In November 1823 José Orbegoso and other Peruvian chiefs wrote him together in the name of the people and the army, requesting him to return to Peru and saying that, as he is "the Founder of its Liberty," they asked him to save the State, which had begun to fall into anarchy.

San Martín would not return to Peru; his decision was irrevocable; but he was not indifferent to the suffering of the nation he founded, and he wrote to Orbegoso an answer for all of them:

You know intimately my feelings for Peru, for America, for its independence and happiness, for which I would sacrifice a thousand lives.

Because he would not return to Peru, he gives his last advice upon saying good-by:

Peru is lost, yes, it is hopelessly lost, and perhaps the cause of America in general. You have the power of saving it, and it is in your hands, and in those of Guisse, Soyer, Santa Cruz, Portocarrero. It is said: these people can be the redeemers of America, or its executioners, there is no doubt; you will decide which. Without losing a moment take care of the complaints you may have, respect the authority of Congress, good or bad, or whatever it is, because the country has elected it, unite as necessary, and thus drive the Spaniards from Peru; otherwise let us kill each other, if this is the unhappy destiny that awaits the patriots.

Meanwhile Bolívar remained on the Colombian border, cautious and alone. Later he entered Peru, where he first was crowned by victory and where afterwards his work was destroyed by anarchy.

How could San Martín have peace in Los Barriales if there he was reached by the lowest passions? His soul wished to retire from the world, and the world came there heavy with its burdens. He renounced the war at Guayaquil and power at Lima; he did not wish to live in Peru or Chile, and when he sought refuge on his farm at Mendoza, he could not find it. The way to Buenos Aires also presented itself full of dangers and shadows, as we shall soon see.

Where would he have to go? Would he have to leave the Dionysiac Continent, because the Saint of the Sword now returned through the road to Monsalvat, the mystic mountain of wisdom? And would he reach it?

The "knowledge" and the "power" will conquer "love," surrounding the heaven of this life with a synthesis of spiritual mastership, as in the life of the great initiates, masters of humanity. The transition of the epic myth and the tragic pathos of the ascetic solitude will be accomplished in silence, which is the "way to perfection" for superior souls.

III. PATH OF SOLITUDE

Upon his return from Lima, San Martín hoped to go immediately from Mendoza to Buenos Aires to see his wife, who for some time had been very ill. He wants to "take advantage of the safety offered by an expedition against the Indians, which will leave from there," as he informed her in a letter. The Araucanians of Chile and Patagonia used to assault the outposts and farms of the Argentinian pampas, endangering travelers; however, if that danger seemed forgotten, San Martín encountered a greater one when he decided to undertake the trip.

A guerrilla sent from Buenos Aires went to seize him; on the road he was informed in time. When in later years, justifying his conduct in those dark days, he wrote to Guido, a relative of his wife and his faithful companion:

Perhaps you don't know that in the year '23, when, persuaded by my wife to come to say good-by to her, I decided in May to come to Buenos Aires, there were guerrillas on the road to seize me like a villain; a thing they could not accomplish, because I was warned by a good man from the same administration. And at what a time, when no government of the revolution has had more regularity and stability!

These confidences show the hostile political attitude towards San Martín, on his return, and the intimate drama of the hero, who, when returning from Lima, could not recover the peace he had promised himself because an adverse fate was against him in his country and in his home.

The married life of San Martín has been a topic of slanderous tales born in the days of contemporary hate, which have been maintained until today with unpardonable levity by the gossipers. It has been said that San Martín separated from his wife in Mendoza and gave her back to her parents, displeased with her, because he suspected her faithfulness; that this separation was followed by the anger of the Escalada family and that when the hero returned from Lima in 1823 he did not want to go to Buenos Aires, on account of the alleged offense, to see Doña Remedios, who was dying.

All this is nothing but a malicious lie, one of the many with which San Martín's enemies embittered his life, and it is a knightly satisfaction for this narrator of his life to show the falsity of such tales, that I would not tell here had they not been repeated in a society of wise Argentinian historians, and if I could not draw upon documents to clean such stains from the home of the hero.

In previous chapters I have told how in February 1813, after being married four months, San Martín left his wife in Buenos Aires to undertake the mission that ended with the battle of San Lorenzo; at the end of that same year he left his home again for Tucumán to command the Army of the North; from there he came back to Córdoba, sick; whence he went to Mendoza to take charge of the Government of Cuyo, at the end of the year 1814.

Just as in those first two years of his marriage, the years following were perturbed by the circumstances of war and frequently interrupted by military events affecting a man who, as I said when I told of his marriage, was not a man of idyls. Doña Remedios, in spite of being very young, knew to what tremendous destiny she had united her life, and did honor to him.

When San Martín was appointed governor of Cuyo, Doña Remedios came to be with him at his home in Mendoza, and there we saw her during the years 1815 and 1816 as the intelligent collaborator of her husband; while San Martín prepared his army, she embroidered the flag of the Andes and donated her jewelry for the enterprise. In the month of January 1817, on the eve of the crossing of the Andes, San Martín decided that his wife and daughter should return to the home of her parents in Buenos Aires, for greater safety in that critical moment of the war, and because the health of his wife was not good.

It was a wise decision, and they separated on the best of terms, to such extent that Doña Remedios was recommended by her husband to the Government, and Director Pueyrredón immediately wrote him from the capital: "You can be sure that she will not lack the eighty pesos that you give her, as well as anything else that could be granted, depending on my ability." Under these circumstances the lady returned to Buenos Aires, and when in 1817, after Chacabuco, San Martín came from Chile to the River Plate he joined his wife at his in-laws' home.

In those days, after Chacabuco, Doña Remedios was able to witness in the capital the honors rendered to her husband, the austere victor; and when the Argentinian Government granted a pension to the daughter and her heirs, she thanked them for the gift, showing her wifely pride "at my husband's efforts crowned by a happy event" and "at the applause in honor of my husband." In those same days she was ill perhaps with the first symptoms of the malady that killed her. "I would have liked to thank you in person," Doña Remedios says to the Supreme Director, "but as I am not able to do this owing to my poor health, I am doing it through this note."

During the winter of 1817, when San Martín returned to Chile to continue the war, he left his ill wife in Buenos Aires. Director Pueyrredón, who used to write him very often informing him of politics, used also to inform him in each letter about Doña Remedios' health. "Margarita thanks you and returns the good wishes; she is gaining weight very much, and she has not given me children, but she is a good companion. Yours is completely recovering." Pueyrredón talks thus of both "companions" in August 1817, when San Martín has already left for Mendoza.

Before and after that, in other letters from the Director, he read in one of them: "Yesterday I had the pleasure of seeing Doña Remedios; it is obvious that she has been ill, but she continues to improve, and you can be sure you have a companion"; and in another: "Madame Remedios continues to be very well, and I congratulate you on her good health."

Doña Margarita Arias de Correa, a friend of both, wrote to the victor: "May heaven keep you as an instrument of our happiness and as a whip to the proud Spaniards, until you finish the great enterprise you have begun, and then return with tranquillity to spend happy days together with Madame Remedios and the child, whom I wish you have the pleasure of seeing in perfect health." San Martín wished hard that such a hope could be fulfilled, but his destiny cost him the sacrifice of his domestic life.

San Martín returned to Buenos Aires in 1818, after Maipú, and when his wife had recovered, he took her with him to Mendoza. They traveled together; and because the days were very rainy during that winter season, Pueyrredón wrote him soon after his departure: "It has not stopped raining since you left. If these rains followed you in your trip, they must have certainly been very annoying for Doña Remedios." The letter ends with this cordial greeting: "Regards to Madame and a happy trip."

Some references to the letter files suggest that San Martín, after Maipú, talked of taking his wife to Chile but gave up the idea, perhaps because Doña Remedios and his daughter would be an obstacle to the soldier on a campaign, and Doña Remedios accepted her situation with resignation.

San Martín stayed in Mendoza with his wife the second part of the year 1818, and then went alone to Chile, whence he returned to Mendoza. Here he found Doña Remedios again very ill, and in March 1819 he decided to send her again to her parents' home.

During those days he writes to Guido:

"I don't know anything about Buenos Aires since the last communications you sent; but the most certain news we have is that the way to the capital is entirely clear. This has made me decide that Remedios should go tomorrow morning to be with her family, because the opinion of the doctors is that if she stays in Mendoza her life will be very short.

On April 30 of that same year, San Martín announced to O'Higgins: "Remedios left for Buenos Aires, because this country did not agree with her. Here you have me a widower."

Belgrano was returning from Tucumán to the south in those ungrateful days, when he met Doña Remedios and Merceditas in Rosario, who were on a trip to the capital, and San Martín's good friend writes him from Rosario in April 1819, giving him reassuring news. "Madame Remedios, with the precious and vivacious Merceditas, passed through here happily, and from what the conductor of the stage tells me, she continued well to Buenos Aires." On that same trip Belgrano met, in the center of the pampas, the traveler, Haigh, an English merchant, who was returning from Valparaiso to London, and talking about the difficult situation in which America found herself, on account of the war. While they ate in an inn, Belgrano said to him in English, "What can you expect from us? We must commit blunders, for we are the sons of Spaniards, and no better than they are." At this unfortunate moment Doña Remedios and San Martín's daughter crossed the pampas for the last time, while the hero prepared to continue his errant adventure along the Peruvian coast.

In 1819, before going to Chile, San Martín had made the necessary arrangements for his family expenses, and to this effect informed Pedro Advíncula Moyano, the overseer of his farm of Los Barriales in "La Villa Nueva," and his resigned wife. In 1820 Doña Remedios, from Buenos Aires, wrote to Moyano: "San Martín tells me in one of his letters that owing to his absence you must deal with me regarding the farm and the mill. . . . Mother, Father, Manuel, and the girls thank you for your regards, and wish to know you, because I have talked so much of you. . . . Merceditas asks me to send you a million kisses for the little ones."

It is not known which would have been better for that lady, whether to live in that distant corner of Los Barriales or in Buenos Aires, where the climate also did not agree with her, and where San Martín's disobedience in 1820 caused great anger against him, and extended to his family the hostility.

San Martín had sailed from Valparaiso with the liberating expedition in August 1820, and two months later his father-in-law, Señor Escalada, sent him news of everything happening there. "My beloved son," he says in the beginning of the letter, "who gives so much glory to my home, in spite of so many envious enemies you have here . . ." Then he tells him the state of revolution in the city, the fights where Rodríguez and Dorrego are involved, the part taken in these disorders by the restless Hilarión Quintana, his brother-in-law, the unjust suspicions the Government has against Mariano, his son. Then he talks of the liberating expedition to Peru that has just begun:

> Zañartu [minister of Chile in Buenos Aires] does not expect results from your expedition until the end of this month. If they are favorable, as we so much wish for, we have decided to show our resentment at home by refusing to receive congratulations, which would change into disdain and insults if the results were adverse, because, this being the order of the world, it is to be expected of so many Pueyrredonistas, Sarrateistas, and Soleristas.[1]

All these figures of the directorial or unitary party, built around the former friends of San Martín, were then irritated with him, because he did not bring the Army of the Andes to defend them against the federalists.

His father-in-law's letter ends with news of the family:

> As Remedios will tell you in the enclosure about our *chiche* [jewel], I end by saying that this one will be taken by Mr. Basil Hall, captain of the war frigate *Conway*, who has visited us and wants to have the pleasure of telling you he saw us. He has been in Manila and has met Bernabé, and he expects to go back there. In that case write him a few lines calling him and offering him a better position and fortune.

Your affectionate father,
ANTONIO JOSÉ ESCALADA

It is in effect an affectionate "father" of San Martín's, this old *porteño*.[2] The *chiche* to whom he refers is Merceditas, Bernabé is a brother of Doña Remedios who is in Manila, the restless Basil Hall is the English sailor who talked to San Martín on board the *Moctezuma* in front of Callao, and who afterwards wrote his personal impressions of the Protector.

Señor Escalada died very soon after writing this letter, while his son-in-law continued in the Peruvian epic. At this time Doña Remedios became very ill and went to live in a villa of the family in the present Calle Caseros. With grief for the death of her father and the delay of her husband who did not return, her illness was aggravated.

As if this were not sufficient, posthumous malignity has sought a pretext for slander in the unfinished paragraph of a letter sent by San Martín to Guido in April 1819, when his wife, ill, left for Buenos Aires: "I am sure you will say I was born to be a real *cornudo* [cuckold]." This phrase, which has been maliciously interpreted, refers to his situation as commander of the Army of the Andes, as is shown by the complete text of the sentences preceding and following:

> Tagle has been very courteous in separating me from the command of the army. God will pay him for the benefit he has done me.

This refers to the order to leave with the Army of the Andes for Tucumán (which was afterward revoked), and then adds:

Would there be time for the Army of the Andes to cross the mountain range and reach Tucumán, in order that the newly appointed chief could stop the enemy and organize the army? Whatever it is, I will do nothing else but obey, wash my hands and follow the decision I have already taken.

This was the time when anarchy was beginning and when San Martín saw all his enterprises of the Pacific crumbling. The letter continues:

I have told you previously that my spirit has suffered what you cannot imagine. Someday I shall inform you of certain things, and then I am sure you will say I was born to be a real *cornudo*.[3] But I would even sacrifice my life before staining my public life for ambition.

We can see by this document what depths the calumny has reached.

The letters quoted show that there was nothing true in the stories of a disagreement between San Martín and his wife. Their separation in 1817 is explained by the impeding crossing of the Andes and in 1819 by his wife's health. After the first separation they again unite, in 1818, and after the second separation the correspondence between them continued, as can be proved by the letter of Remedios to Moyano, and the letter Basil Hall took from her to him during the expedition to Lima, and on his return in 1823, when she called him from Buenos Aires.

Neither is it true that the family was angry with him, as can be seen by his father-in-law's letter and San Martín's answer from Lima, a letter mentioned in a previous chapter. And still more false is the statement that he did not want to go to Buenos Aires to see the ill one who called him, as can be seen by the letter he wrote to Guido.

Such was the state of affairs in 1823 for San Martín; he was uncertain, lonely, and sad, with Riva Agüero in Lima and with Doña Remedios dying in Buenos Aires.

The man acclaimed by the crowds in the palace of the City of Kings was now alone, at his farm, Los Barriales, without a command and without health, family, or riches. But he did not complain; he who did not want to govern others knew how to govern himself and to overcome adversities.

In those melancholy days of Los Barriales, San Martín was visited by some friends from Mendoza, who kept him company in his solitude. Good Pedro Advíncula Moyano talked to him about Doña Remedios and showed him her letter, remembering the friendship of his (Moyano's) children with Merceditas. Sometimes Doña Josefa Ruiz also came, and the conversation was about her sick friend and the child. Perhaps if Doña Remedios had stayed at Los Barriales when her husband left for Peru, the good climate of Mendoza would have been better for her than the humid climate of Buenos Aires, and she would have had fewer worries.

Those who smeared his reputation as a public man, calling him a hypocrite, assassin, ambitious, a deserter and a thief, also struck him in his private life. Somebody even published an apocryphal "love correspondence of San Martín," claiming this correspondence had been lost in the flight from Cancha Rayada.

Manuel Olazábal, officer of the army, says in his memoirs:

From 1817 to 1823, when General San Martín withdrew from the theater of his unfading glory and departed for Europe, nobody can testify to having seen him showing a preference for any woman, even when being surrounded by so many goddesses in high society. However, he managed this matter with the same impenetrable reserve with which he carried out his plans for victory and conquest. In 1818 there was in Santiago, Chile, a lady who drew attention to herself not only for her beauty, but also for her wit. There is no doubt that she was tempting. Nobody knew that the general ever had any private affair with her.

I do not know if these secret affairs reached Doña Remedios' ears.

In January 1823 Salvador Iglesias had written him from Magdalena, sending him the staff of Pizarro's flag and a copy of La Abeja Republicana (The Republican Bee), in which the former Protector was insulted without mercy:

Your Excellency, read very carefully La Abeja Republicana of Saturday the 11th: It could not talk in more insolent terms. It is necessary to endure it, or go out with a pair of pistols and assassinate the vile editor. This and also what the dissatisfied may do is one of the reasons for Cabrera to leave. I am only awaiting orders from Your Excellency to do the same thing, when Your Excellency finds it convenient, because it is impossible to stand so many villains.

Several friends of the hero in Lima answered these attacks, and the noble answer is still in the Archives.

San Martín denounced the writer of La Abeja and wrote to Lima in February 1823:

When I finished my career, I made up my mind not to answer the criticisms of my enemies, which every public man, even being just, is bound to arouse, specially during a revolution; but the editor of La Abeja compels me to break this intention, when the most sacred thing a man possesses is attacked; I have remembered that I am a father and that honor is the only heritage I leave my children; yes, sir, the only thing left by the one who has been absolute arbiter of the destiny and fortune of great states.

Allow me, Your Excellency, a word that will not fail to merit your consideration: that the name of General San Martín has been more esteemed by the enemies of the independence than by the many Americans whom I snatched from the vile chains they dragged.

It was bitter for San Martín, this moment of 1823, when he began to travel a new path of silent pain. He could not think any more of Peru, where the civil war was beginning. The house of Magdalena had been assaulted by the mob and plundered of the furniture San Martín left.

Neither could he think of Chile, where O'Higgins had left the Government, overturned by a revolution, and where Cochrane and Carrera's followers worked against him, forgetting his services in the Chilean epic. He believed that his "island of Mendoza" could be the shelter of renouncement, as six years before it had been the site of the heroic deed; but to that corner jealousy and grudge come to seek him. In Buenos Aires they did not forgive him for the disobedience of 1820, when he departed for Peru with his army, leaving the country in the throes of civil war, of which he wanted no part; but, furthermore, the suspicious politicians of 1823 believed that the warrior, idle after his abdication in Lima, came to his native land to seize the Government, through a military coup, as other South American generals were doing. All this is absurd to think of San Martín, but that is what the ignorant believed. San Martín sought a retreat for his soul; he believed he could find it at his farm, Los Barriales; but he could not take his wife there because she was very ill in Buenos Aires; he could not even go to see her to say good-by for the last time in Buenos Aires, because political intrigues prevented it. Some of this talk in the provinces must have reached the Government, because in the ministerial newspapers there was allusion to a conspiracy to give the country to a lucky soldier; and San Martín was subject to watching; his mail was intercepted and spies were sent among his own servants, as he himself relates:

I believed that my ten years of public life would have protected me, in the eyes of my countrymen, from any suspicion of harboring ambitions for any kind of command. . . . Two months after reaching Mendoza, the Government ruling Buenos Aires at the time not only blockaded me with spies, among them one of my servants, but conducted a little, ignoble war against me in the public papers of its devotion, at the same time making me suspect to the other governments in the provinces. . . . The men of the opposition, whom in general I had not even seen, circulated the absurd version that my return from Peru had no other object but to overthrow the administration of Buenos Aires; and to corroborate this opinion, they showed with unusual insolence letters they claimed I wrote.

Such miseries, which alone were sufficient to embitter the patriot, were aggravated by the misfortunes of his domestic life, already referred to.

When in 1823 San Martín decided to continue his trip to Buenos Aires to see the woman who was calling him, he could not realize his wish, because in May, when he was ready to leave, he was advised that there were people armed on the road to seize him, on account of the suspicions fostered against him by the internal strife of the parties.

San Martín had said good-by to his wife in 1819 to go to Peru, on an occasion that reminds us of the Cid in romance:

> *"Enjugad, señora," dice,*
> *"Los ojos hasta que torne!"*
> *Ella, mirando los suyos*
> *Su pena publica a voces:*
> *"Rey de mi alma y d'esta tierra, conde,*
> *¿Por qué me dejas? ¿Dónde vas? ¿Adonde?*
>
> *"Dry, my lady," he says,*
> *"Your tears until I return."*
> *She, fixing her eyes on his,*
> *Her pain reveals, exclaiming,*
> *"Lord of my soul, and of this land, ruler,*
> **Why dost thou leave me? Where dost thou go? Where?"**

Remedios died in Buenos Aires, August 12, 1823, without her husband's having been able to be at her side at the hour of her death. San Martín had not seen her for four years. Thus ended the life of that selfless woman, far from her husband, at the start of her married life.

With Doña Remedios dead in Buenos Aires, San Martín's friends sent him their condolence. From Santiago, Chile, his good friend José Rivadeneira sent his:

We knew the bad state of health of Doña Remedios; blows like these come to the men who by their virtues should stop them, but we are mortals and it is necessary to suffer. How true is what you state, that you know how to find women in quantities, but it is very hard to find a friend.

As can be seen, San Martín said that he had not only lost a wife, but "a friend," difficult to replace. Other companions who knew San Martín's home sent him condolences in similar terms. Colonel Manuel Rojas, who accompanied him on his campaigns, wrote about the death of the kind and virtuous companion, "the person that was a half of his soul and whom he chose in society to make his best friend":

She will always be missed, by all the people that knew her merits, and in many years her family will not find a matron to take the place of the one you have just lost. . . . I hope Your Excellency will be somehow comforted by the general sympathy, by the thought of being a father and that a young daughter awaits advice and education from Your Excellency, and hopes that this excessive pain for this mortal blow will not be the end of him.

On his part Don Tomás Guido, faithful friend of San Martín and familiar with his intimate life, and also a relative of Doña Tomasa de la Quintana, his mother-in-law, writes him thus:

What could I say to you about the unfortunate Remedios? I believe that if that girl had been more methodical in her cure, she would have saved you the sorrow of losing a friend; seeing my aunt Tomasa will aggravate your grief, because her ailments have come back.

Guido had advised San Martín not to make the trip to Buenos Aires and said it would be better to send for Merceditas, the child, "and bring her to Madame Ruiz, whose advice and respect would certainly be of use." Madame Ruiz was none other than Doña Josefa Ruiz de Huidobro, the lady from Mendoza who had been a good friend of Doña Remedios during the years she lived with her husband in Cuyo. San Martín understood that he should go to Buenos Aires, with the purpose of getting his only daughter, to educate her as he had planned in 1820, and to go with her to Europe, if he could arrange it with his small means.

It can be seen that not even at Los Barriales could he find full peace. The ungrateful news from Peru, where Riva Agüero was excited, and from Chile, where his friend O'Higgins had had to emigrate to Callao, did not balance the notices that came from Buenos Aires. In the United Provinces civil war broke out again; the local regime of the capital sank in reputation; the Government, inspired by Rivadavia, distrusted San Martín; the dissatisfied had their hope in the solitary one of Los Barriales, and Dr. Pedro Vidal wrote him on September 1, 1823, presenting the present picture, and calling him to help the country:

It is not a problem any more now that its mistakes have defeated this administration, and that it has disregarded with criminal indifference the general interests of America, prolonging the war at the very time that it should have ended; Your Excellency is the only column that can hold up the majestic edifice raised by your courage, and the patriots share our only hope, placed on the magnanimity of Your Excellency, who, forgetting just resentments and the many proofs of ungratefulness, might devote yourself again to saving us from the shipwreck that threatens us.

In October 1823 Captain Manuel Guevara, who came from Buenos Aires, visited San Martín to give him a letter from the governor of San Fe, Don Estanislao López. The letter had been given to the traveler at the post of La Candelaria, and read as follows:

I know positively, through my agents in Buenos Aires, that on the arrival there of Your Excellency, you will be court-martialed by the Government for having disobeyed orders in 1817 and 1820, carrying out, instead, the glorious campaigns of Chile and Peru.

To avoid this unheard-of scandal and as proof of my gratitude and that of the country I rule for Your Excellency's patriotic refusal in 1820 to shed the blood of brothers with the main bodies of the Army of the Andes which was in the providence of Cuyo, I have the honor to assure Your Excellency that, at one word from you, I will be, with the whole province, waiting for Your Excellency at El Desmochado, to take you in triumph to the Plaza de la Victoria.

If Your Excellency would not accept this, it will be very easy to take you with entire safety through Entre Ríos to Montevideo.

San Martín was very worried by this letter; next day there came to visit him Colonel Manuel de Olazábal, and San Martín handed him the letter and said:

"Read it."

When Olazábal had read it, he showed his surprise and his indignation; but San Martín calmly said:

"I cannot believe in such behavior. I will go, but I will go alone, as I crossed the Pacific, and as I am among my people of Mendoza. But if destiny wishes it to be that way, I will give for an answer my sword, the freedom of a world, Pizarro's flag, and the flags of the enemies conquered with those arms that I did not want to stain with Argentinian blood. No! Buenos Aires is the cradle of liberty. The people of Buenos Aires will do me justice."

On November 20 San Martín left his Mendoza retreat to come to the River Plate, but he was coming with the intention of embarking for Europe, leaving the country for at least two years. He would have liked to avoid crossing the capital, but he had to do it, because his only daughter lived there, whom he had to get from her grandmother's house to take with him. In that hour of solitude the man of iron felt the need of affection.

He had crossed the Andes and liberated a continent, but the liberated countries paid him with ingratitude. That did not matter to his great soul; what mattered now was to find a shelter in which to await death, and meanwhile to fulfill his paternal duties.

That father of America had another daughter. To this one he must dedicate his new life. But where to go? That giver of countries had no country. To Spain, where his own parents were buried, he could not return, even if his sister lived there. In Buenos Aires, his wife and father-in-law already had died, while his brothers-in-law, Escalada, Mariano, and Manuel, who had learned how to use arms from San Martín, were still generously following their military adventures. Besides them, he had no other relatives. He could not stay in Buenos Aires, nor did he desire to do so; antagonized by the Government, his friends were leaving him. . . . So he had no hope of love, except from the innocent heart of his daughter, who was only seven years old. Upon her mother's death she had been taken by her grandmother, Doña Tomasa de la Quintana, then a widow, who took a great fancy to the child, but who spoiled her completely without trying to educate her.

San Martín had to quarrel with his mother-in-law to get her back, using as a pretext the need of giving Mercedes a good education in Europe, though the truth was that he did not want to leave without her, because he was compelled to go.

The sad paladin, in his misfortune, raised funds as he could, made his scanty baggage ready, picked up the girl, and embarked at the port of Buenos Aires, bound for Europe. He had no other alternative; the lands of Chile, Peru, and La Plata were forbidden to him: the nations he had liberated. His expatriation had begun and would not end until his death, twenty-six years later.

Upon leaving, on February 10, 1824, the traveler left to his friend, Colonel Federico Brandsen, of French origin, the following farewell note: "In an hour I will leave for Europe, with the purpose of accompanying my daughter and placing her in some school of that continent; and I will return to our country during this year or before, if the sovereigns of Europe should decide to dictate our future to us."

San Martín, who was a very good friend of Brandsen (his companion), as he was of Luzuriaga, Olazábal and others, ended the short letter with "A million regards to your wife and a lot of kisses to my godson." To a few other countrymen he left similar notes. With his friend Goyo Gómez he had talks and left him in charge of his interests in Buenos Aires; and he had a long conference with Don Vicente López about the political situation of the country.

During his short stay in Buenos Aires, San Martín ordered a grave to be constructed in the Recoleta Cemetery for the remains of Doña Remedios, and placed on the grave of the wife an inscription that has the unmistakable accent of his spirit:

HERE LIES REMEDIOS ESCALADA
WIFE AND FRIEND OF GENERAL SAN MARTÍN.

It was the last homage of the gentleman without blemish to the selfless woman who sacrificed her youth to join her name to that of the paladin who, fascinated by another love, that of America, lived so few hours at her side. Her married life, like that of Ximena of Gómez, the wife of the Cid, was a continuous sigh in his absence, while the husband traveled far from his native land, fighting against so many "infidels."

The political passions had come to hound him even in his distant corner of Los Barriales, and he knew very well that neither in Buenos Aires, center of so many hostile passions, nor in any other part of America could he find the quiet he wanted.

San Martín had reached that sad hour in the life of a hero when glory is nothing but the heavy load of fame; when, prestige and power lost, enemies are merciless and friends leave; an hour of universal cowardice, when all exterior circumstances join in a conspiracy to make more bitter the solitude of his conjugal home. There was no place for the dialogue of the Cantares, nor for the happiness of the bourgeois. The affronts which made the hero the target of everything hateful had the model wife suspected of unfaithfulness; and to make it worse it was said that the husband was an adulterer and had a mulatto son by the Negress Jesusa, a slave of his wife's.

Nothing of his fame was left untouched or unblemished in the driveling and foul mouths of his slanderers. All of this should be wiped out by the history of the austere inscription which the gentleman left on the grave of his beloved: "Wife and friend of General San Martín." And that is what Doña Remedios had been to him, the naïve girl of fifteen who on marrying such a man had married the pain of so much glory, and who ten years later, when dying, called for the absent one in her agony.

That posthumous homage to Remedios was owed by the paladin to the wife whose patrician hands had embroidered the Flag of the Andes. She had offered to the hero's enterprise her worldly jewels, thus leaving her youthful body bare of splendor, as if prepared for death.

The woman whose grave was in Buenos Aires had given him his only daughter, the one he was now coming to get from the home in mourning, with the purpose of making her his joy in the uncertain days that had begun for him.

Alone with that seven-year-old daughter, the hero of America went to seek refuge in the lands of Europe. Upon his return to France, the Ministry and the police placed obstacles to the landing of the soldier enemy of kings and liberator of countries. He went immediately to England, were he stayed a few months, and then to Belgium, where he made his home, countinuing like this in the solitude and the path of perfection for love that he began to tread in Guayaquil with his renouncement.

IV. TEACHER OF HIS DAUGHTER

On February 8, 1825, San Martín, living in Brussels, wrote to O'Higgins:

Since the end of last year I have been established here. Seeing how cheap it is here, and the freedom to be enjoyed, I have decided to live here until I finish the education of the girl; then I shall return to America, to end my days on my farm, far from any public duties, and if possible from the society of men.

San Martín had said in 1816, when he sought land for the farm in Mendoza, that a farmer's life was best suited to his nature. But he contradicted his misanthropic plans in the following paragraph: "I am awaiting the developments of the campaign in Peru. May luck be favorable, so the ailments of America may end!" Those were the days of Ayacucho. The generous liberator continued thinking of our America and of the lot of his fellow men. He would never leave them out of his thoughts.

The same year 1825, he writes to Chilabert, his former companion on the *Canning*:

I have had the honor of crossing with you the stormy Atlantic. Without thinking, I give myself again to its fancy, believing that in its inscrutable waters will drown the ignoble passions of the enemies of an old patriot; but, against all hope, the *Argos*[1] of Buenos Aires shows up, continuing the attack of its brother *El Centinela*,[1] and protected by Neptune, crosses the ocean, and in the month of the storms, arrives in this hemisphere with the declaration of a new war. And here I am not knowing what decision to make. In my refuge of Mendoza I promoted a military federation of provinces. I come to Europe, and a month after my arrival an agent of the Argentinian Government in Paris (who undoubtedly attends the private meetings of the French cabinet) writes to some South Americans living in London that they are trying to carry (inside of a pocket) a little king, to form with him a military government in America. Thus General San Martín was shown that, having been brought up in the barracks, he had been deprived of the opportunity of studying other systems more appropriate for the real needs and will of the people.

The journalistic hostility which followed him for so many years worried the soldier: "In this war of the pen made on me, I cannot defend myself with the same weapon, as it is unknown to me." This was why he had abandoned his Mendoza refuge, Los Barriales, in 1823, and now shunned the big European capitals, regretting his inability to be protected against such repeated attacks "on a general who, at least, has not made his country shed tears."

He did not even have time to read the letters from his best friends, "because he was preparing himself for death," not as Chilabert, but as a good Christian who, owing to his age and ailments, cannot sin any more." In this situation he gives his fervent thanks to the One who rules over the fortunes of soldiers and politicians, for having separated him from them. He said these things without bitterness or solemnity, but rather in jest.

At the beginning of his residence in Europe, former "Emperor" Iturbide of Mexico had tried to have an interview with San Martín; but there is evidence that the latter eluded it, because his decision not to interfere with the politics of America was definitive.

San Martín's economic situation was becoming difficult, and in 1827 he wrote to O'Higgins, exiled in Peru, these confidences:

I will talk to you about my situation, which is very sad today. On my arrival in Europe, I invested in the Peruvian Loan, not only the 15,000 pesos granted me as pension, but 6,000 more pesos of my own money; so that with the interest, together with the revenue from my house in Buenos Aires, I would be able to keep myself in this country until the completion of my daughter's education. Peru has stopped payment of its dividends; the income from my property in Buenos Aires is nominal because, owing to the circulation of paper money, the exchange on London is 16 pence instead of 50 as it was before. In such a sad situation, and to be able to support myself modestly, I have had to sell at a vile price the title to the 21,000 pesos risked. As a result I have hardly anything to live on, except the annual pension of 9,000 pesos granted me by the Congress of Peru. As you will see by the attached memorandum, by the end of December of the present year 31,000 pesos will be owing me. I know the dark situation in which that Republic finds itself, and it would be a lack of consideration on my part to request payment of what they owe me.

Amid the difficulties of his poverty, the exile placed his daughter in a boarding school and established himself in Brussels, 1422 rue de la Fiancée. There he led a sad and poor life. During the holidays and vacations he brought Mercedes to spend a few days with him. When she was at boarding school he used to make short trips to London, to see English friends, or he sometimes went for personal business to Liége and Antwerp, or to Aix la Chapelle, to take the cure at the baths. To his comrade Miller, who was in England, he explained some of these things in his letters. In June 1828 he wrote: "I will return to Brussels on the 12th of next month to bring Mercedes back, because on that day her school closes until August 1, when the summer vacations end." He wrote Miller from Aix la Chapelle and told him of his trip and his ailments:

On the 27th I left Brussels to come to these baths, fairly well relieved of my rheumatism; perhaps the movement of the carriage or the humidity of the day was the reason that upon my arrival in Liége on the 28th I found myself in such a state of prostration that it was impossible to continue my trip until the 11th of the present month, when I arrived here suffering in an inexpressible way, especially from pain in my right arm, which had swollen in an awful manner. On the 6th I started taking the baths, and in spite of the season, which has not been of help to me on account of being so cold and humid, I find myself today very much relieved.

His only joy in such situations was his daughter, who was growing healthy and studying successfully. Much was due to the good disposition of the child and not less to the schools which taught her arts and languages, and which adorned her spirit with new graces; but San Martín was the real molder of her moral conscience. When he freed her from the indulgence of her grandmother in 1825, he wrote these

RULES FOR MY DAUGHTER

1. Humanize her character, making it sensitive, even toward the insects which do not injure. Sterne had said to a fly, opening the window for it to go: "Go, poor animal: the world is large enough for both of us."
2. Instill in her love for truth and hate for lies.
3. Inspire in her confidence and friendship, but with respect.
4. Encourage in Mercedes charity towards the poor.
5. Respect for other people's property.
6. Get her used to keeping secrets.

7. Inspire in her a feeling of respect toward all religions.
8. Gentleness with servants, the poor and the old.
9. Let her talk little and say only what is necessary.
10. Get her used to being quiet and serious at table.
11. Teach her to love cleanliness and to have contempt for luxury.

If these rules, worthy of being taught in all homes and schools, are admirable as a doctrine, more admirable still was the touch of authority and love with which the widowed father succeeded in making of the "undisciplined rascal" he brought from Buenos Aires a model woman, a Parisian for her culture and distinction, and a respectable matron, in the Spanish manner, for her sound domestic virtues, as was seen through the rest of her life. Don Tomás Guido was right when, in 1827, he wrote from Buenos Aires: "You never had a happier thought than when you took her [Mercedes] to Europe; our women here remain in a sad state of education." How secretly proud was the middle-aged father with the success of his girl! She was his in the flesh and in the spirit. And when sometimes San Martín let himself be carried away by paternal joy in the contemplation of his loved one, he restrained his weakness, trying to recover his serious air, as when he said: "A father is too partial a being to give his opinion; however, my observations are those made with the indifference of a stranger because I know that from a wrong opinion may come a bad education."

Poor San Martín! He was doubtless a severe soldier, but he was also a man of fine sentiments and a teacher of sound pedagogical intuitions. Those rules he had written to read secretly and to be guided by them in the education of his daughter, enlightening her growing conscience, throw a light for us into the darkest corners. The warrior who quoted Seneca, Epictetus, and Diogenes, the ruler guided by the spirit of Marcus Aurelius, was a disciple of Pythagoras, a real initiate.

In the rules for the education of his daughter, he showed his admiration for all religions, worshiped nature even in the humble form of the insects, was gentle with the poor, the old, and the servants, kept secrets, practiced cleanliness and held luxury in contempt, appreciated good manners, valued silence, joined friendship to respect, and clasped life in a large circle of mystery and unity.

Sterne's phrase to the fly, "The world is large enough for both of us," explains his own renunciation. Such were the teachings of his private life, and such were the rules disclosed by his public life. He was a teacher, this man of the lodge (Masonic initiate), this liberator, this missionary, who did not miss the most painful experiences of calumny and injustice, who knew the bitter savor of life.

No wonder then that at the time of his long American agony he seemed to many a mysterious being who inspired suspicion and distrust. No wonder there were people who hated him and who loved him with equal tenacity.

No wonder he was capable of so many victorious efforts over his own thin flesh, over a hostile land, until he calmly fulfilled his mission, going from renunciation to renunciation, from pain to pain, surviving his accomplishment in a miraculous old age which is as surprising as his heroic youth.

He was absorbed in his fatherly thoughts when he received a letter from Mendoza, from the talkative Don Salvador Iglesias, containing news which surprised him:

"Here it is said with certainty that you have married the daughter of an English lord; others say, a girl of the Bourbon family. And they are so sure of it that they even mention the name of the Englishman who reported it, which I don't recall."

How could he marry! Neither the daughter of a lord, nor a Bourbon princess, nor anybody. The tale came from the remote village in Cuyo which he so loved, and perhaps was born from the jest of an English traveler. The credulity with which the version was accepted reveals the princely esteem in which he was held. He was not a Spanish grandee, but he was an American grandee. And why not? However, he had no fortune, and he lived in retirement. Once in a while, to amuse himself, he attended a concert in Brussels. At one of them he saw, on an evening in 1827, the beautiful Lady Cochrane, wife of his enemy, and he found her "quite desirable" and stouter than when he first met her on the Pacific.

But he kept a silent memory of Doña Remedios, "San Martín's friend," and he was already ill and in his fifties, with all his hopes firmly placed upon the future of his daughter. His life as a widower would last until his death, and all his love would be bestowed upon his child.

To Pedro Advíncula Moyano, who was looking after his interests in Mendoza, he wrote in 1826: "Don't spend anything on the farm; let it pay its own way with its products." If the revenue was not sufficient, he would sell the farm. If business was good, he would build a house on a less nitrous site.[2] Let Moyano tell him about the condition of the property, and especially the mill. Let Moyano make an inventory, aided by San Martín's brother-in-law, Mariano Escalada, of the farm and of the objects he left in the care of Doña Josefa Ruiz. If the house was in bad condition, it would be wise to transfer the furniture, in order to avoid its being destroyed, to the house of Don Manuel Molina. And Merceditas sent her regards to Anita and Pedrito.

He also wrote his brother-in-law, Manuel Escalada, in April 1826, concerning his private business: he approved Escalada's having rented Merceditas' house for 2,500 pesos a year; he advised him to collect his confidential papers, which he left with Doña Josefa Ruiz, and his books, which were held by Don Miguel Riglos; he asked him to apply for a pension for the girl and for a three-year furlough he had formerly requested of the Government; he requested Escalada not to hide from him the unpleasant news about the Government's attitude toward him, because he would "receive it with the calm which experience and knowledge of men give me"; and he ends by telling Escalada he is sending a toy for San Martín's little nephew.

In the same letter, next to this tender message, are found these melancholy words:

Since I last wrote you, I have only experienced ills and misfortunes: the carriage in which I was going to visit an acquaintance in the country having overturned, my right arm was dislocated, and on top of that I contracted an attack of erysipelas from which I have not yet entirely recovered. My brother Justo, who unwisely guaranteed a loan for the Marquis of Vignola in Paris in the amount of 68,000 francs, was sent to debtors' jail at the death of Vignola, and I have had to pay 33,000 francs to complete his bail and release him. My sister, who recently lost her husband, whose property was confiscated by the ruthless Spanish Government because he emigrated, being a Constitutionalist, finds herself now in the uttermost poverty. In fine, I assure you that were it not for the consolation I get from Merceditas' company, my life would be unbearable.

In 1827 Mercedes fell gravely ill of the measles, which caused her father great despair, inasmuch as he thought the girl was going to die.

The lonely San Martín one day in Brussels saw his brother Justo Rufino, referred to above. He kept him in his house for several years. Justo was the youngest of the brothers, and they had not seen each other since 1811, when José set off from Spain for London, en route to his America.

All his brothers had embraced the army career, followed by Don Juan, their father. Justo had reached the rank of colonel in the Almanza Regiment. Juan Fermín, major of the Luzon Hussars, had died in Manila in 1822. Manuel Tadeo, a colonel of infantry, died a bachelor in Valencia in 1851. All of them, despite their Argentine birth, remained faithful to the King's banner, except José. What was the mystery of his soul, which had dragged him to a destiny so different from that of his brothers?

Memories of childhood fed the conversations between José and Justo, reunited in Brussels after so many years. Their parents, Don Juan and Doña Gregoria, had died already: he in Málaga, she in Orense. She died the year after José left Spain. Could it be that José's adventure in leaving Spain to fight in America against his brothers and his king had quickened her death?

Fateful changes of homes and families! María Helena, the only sister, lived in Madrid and had married a revenue clerk. José would have liked to see her; but, how, if she could not go to Belgium? The Liberator of America could not go to Spain. He would never return there. It was not that he did not love Spain and the Spaniards. It was simply that his destiny had so dictated.

The two brothers talked, after an absence of fifteen years, one about youthful adventures in Madrid, Seville, and Paris, and the other about his life in Chacabuco, Maipú, and Lima. Justo Rufino, their mother's pet, had had an inclination toward love affairs and luxury when young. Not so José

Francisco; he was always the same, both as a child and as a grown-up: reserved, tenacious, austere.

"I can assert that the one who gave me the least trouble was Don José Francisco," their mother said in her will, in 1803. In the smoke of cigars the most distant and varied memories floated in the saddened minds of the two brothers.

The year after San Martín's departure for America, and a few days after the battle of San Lorenzo, when her son had defeated the Royalists for the first time, the mother had died in Orense, where she was living with María Helena. The latter had married Rafael Menchaca; the son-in-law (Menchaca) had taken charge of the funeral, and it was he who presented the will to Father Santana, at the Church of Santa Eufemia del Centro.

When the last rites were administered and the last wishes of the lady had been carried out (as related in a former chapter), Doña Gregoria was buried, March 29, 1813, in the Convent of Santa Domingo. There lies forever, in Spanish soil, the Spanish mother of the American hero.

In their talks at Brussels, the brother who came from Spain must have told the one who had returned from America about those details concerning the death of their mother, whose memory was a secret link between San Martín's heart and the land of his elders. San Martín could then tell his brother how he had waged war without hate and without cruelty.

In 1817 there arrived in Buenos Aires General Milans and other Spanish officers who had fled Barcelona to escape King Ferdinand's cruelty, and the Supreme Director wrote San Martín: "They have been welcome, as will be any one who comes as a friend to live with us." The same sentiment had been expressed in a *cielito* (Argentine melody) by the gauchos. As far as his own feelings were concerned, how could he forget that at the Punchauca conference, when the Pacific war was going full tilt, San Martín had toasted Viceroy La Serna and the reconciliation between Spain and America? Perhaps San Martín was thinking that he could return to Spain when his mother's and his daughter's motherlands had been reconciled, as he had wished in his toast at Punchauca.

For San Martín, his daughter's and his brother's company were the best possible entertainment those days. He had almost no dealings with strangers. "In the eyes of these people," he said, "I am a real recluse. I do not see or talk with any living person, because, as a result of the revolution, I have become bored with people." This was true, and even though later he reached extremes in misanthropy, he did not lack further voyages and dreams.

Sometimes he dreamed and made plans:

Once Merceditas' education has been completed, I plan to go to Buenos Aires. If they leave me alone and let me enjoy life, I shall set my general headquarters one year on the shores of the Paraná, which I like very much, and another year in Mendoza, until old age prevents me from traveling. But if they do not want to leave me alone, I shall sell what I own there and I shall return to die in this corner of the world. So my enemies would have the satisfaction of having spoiled my old age's last days.

Why did he like the shores of the Paraná? He had been born on the shores of the Uruguay, which he never saw again after the days of his childhood. On the banks of the Paraná, at San Lorenzo, he had won his first American victory, charging himself, sword in hand, against the invader. Could it be that this was the memory which made him love the Paraná River as he grew old? Could it not also be the memory of an artist, the remembrance of a painter, that vision of the deltas and the barracks?

One knows already why he remembered Mendoza—there he had had his "island," and there he now wanted to have his Thebaid of renunciation; there had been forged the weapons of his glory; there he lived the only home days of his married life; there Mercedes had been born; there he could again live on his farm, in a delightful climate, eating tasty fruit and listening to the water run through the ditches among the elms, until the day came when death would take him from the foothills of the Andes, a name which for him was the key to his exceptional destiny.

In that retrospective vision (his plans were now only so many manifestations of his nostalgia) San Martín remembered the ingratitude of men, the calumnies of his enemies, the persecutions of which he was the butt—and, suddenly, among the shadows gathered by the passage of time, there appeared, far away, the image of his America and his own image in front of her. The truth is that in spite of everything he loved those peoples, as he confided: "What do you want me to say, my dear friend, except that despite having been treated as an *Ecce Homo* and greeted with the honorable names of thief and tyrant, I love them, and am very much interested in their happiness?"

Poor San Martín! "As an *Ecce Homo*," he says. He was that. He was "the man of suffering," the anxious missionary of liberation through renunciation; and he knew it. His sacrifice was a mission of love consciously carried out. He who had given a fatherland to others went on loving the fatherland that was his only in his dreams.

Whatever his pessimism about men and his nostalgic memories of Mendoza, San Martín found in his life a source of happiness which he had not known before, his daughter's love. The middle-aged father saw beside him his growing daughter, who had arrived now at the age of her mother when San Martín first met her. The girl's slender figure had acquired already the outline of a woman, although her father kept on calling her "my little one" when he spoke of her.

The physical and spiritual changes which Merceditas had gone through after her college years filled her father with surprise and happiness. "Every day I congratulate myself on my determination to take her to Europe and away from Doña Tomasa. This amiable woman, through the excessive love she showed her, had spoiled her to the point of making her a little devil."

But that happened in 1824, when he took her from Buenos Aires to Europe. Now Mercedes spoke French and English fluently; her advances in drawing and music were surprising; her discretion and charm captivated everyone. She entertained her father in the evenings, and when he was ill she was like a precocious mother for the patient. Never did the old man understand better than on those occasions what a treasure of happiness he had near him. Visitors congratulated him on his daughter, and from America he often received letters from friends, speaking of the praises his daughter received from strangers.

She was still a little girl when she placed this postscript at the bottom of a letter her father had written to O'Higgins:

My dear Sir:
Knowing that you are my daddy's best friend I have begged permission to add these lines as a greeting—not only to you, but equally to your mother and your sister whom I am anxious to know.

Your attentive servant,
Mercedes

O'Higgins, founder of the Chilean Republic, who lived in exile at an estate in Montalván, Peru, answered with emotion, congratulating the father of such a girl and recalling the days in Mendoza when he had more than once held her in his arms. Mercedes grew up among heroic memories evoked from other times. Her father would tell her who had been his companions in the fight and which ones were still his friends, O'Higgins among the best.

In 1828 San Martín, after much hesitation, decided upon a trip to Buenos Aires to offer his services to the Argentine Government in the war with Brazil,[3] and to see if he might establish himself once more in his own country now that the scantiness of his resources certainly no longer allowed him to continue in Europe. Shortly before this trip he was aware that he had not yet visited Paris, and he excused this negligence to his friends by saying that he would surely do so before sailing for America: "It may be that this winter I shall see Paris, as it would be a shame not to see it, being so near, in such an interesting country, and especially before returning to America. Otherwise they might say I was just trying to be different."

There came a day when he finally left for Buenos Aires, after placing Mercedes in a boarding school under the guardianship of his brother Justo. This voyage had a profound significance in the life of San Martín, one that must be explained in a separate chapter. It is sufficient now to say that the purposes of his trip were frustrated and that he quickly returned once and for all to Europe.

In his letters of those days, we find him suffering the indispositions of age. He complains of the cold, he who eight times had crossed the Andes' towering heights and slept in subzero weather:

What can I tell you about the horrible winter we are having? In human memory there hasn't been another like it. For three months I haven't stirred from my house, thanks to my wound, and in such circumstances I have come to appreciate the worth of my daughter's tender consolation. She is enjoying the best of health, and the wonderful personality she displays gives me reason to hope that she will be a loyal wife and loving mother.

The wound to which this letter referred was one suffered in an accident returning from America, between Falmouth and London in 1829.

His trip to Buenos Aires a failure, San Martín established himself in Paris, taking Mercedes, whose schooling had been finished, to live with him. His brother Justo also accompanied him to this new residence. San Martín rented a three-room house, richly hung with tapestries, in the suburbs. A garden and some outbuildings were included, and he paid an annual rental of 1,000 francs, or about 200 Argentine pesos. As he happily confided to his friends, it was a small enough sum.

San Martín was not receiving any salary at that time from Argentina. The pension which Buenos Aires granted to his daughter after the victory of Chacabuco was cut off during the regime of Rivadavia; the life pension granted him by the Peruvian Congress was not materializing either, and what he got from Chile did not amount to much. The farm in Mendoza had been sacked by revolutionary bands in 1831, and the overseer had fled to Chile. As a result of all this he could only count on the rent from the house in Buenos Aires, gift of the Argentine Government to Merceditas in the triumphal days, since the father declined in Argentina as in Chile all pecuniary gain from his victories. Nevertheless the house in Buenos Aires rented now for $5,000 (Argentine) a year, which sufficed for the expenses of the old exile, in view of the modesty of his life and the sobriety of his customs.

Mornings San Martín occupied himself cultivating the garden with his own hands or working in his little carpenter shop; afternoons he strolled, going to visit parks and museums with his daughter; nights he read the newspapers and "happy books," as he called novels and books of poetry.

He told his faithful friend, Don Tomás Guido, about this peaceable life, and that companion of another and so different life in Chile and Peru was often asked: "Would you think I am happy? Yes, my friend, I truthfully am!"

And truly he must have been, because that reserved and ascetic individual had never, till now, let such a confession escape him. He was not completely happy, however. Something was lacking in this life in Paris:

Would you believe it, there is an empty space which my soul finds in its very happiness. Do you know what it is? Not being in Mendoza. Oh, I know you'll laugh. Go ahead, laugh, but I say that I prefer the life I knew on my farm to all the advantages of cultured Europe, and above all of this Paris, which, thanks to the liberality of its government and the security one enjoys under it, is a gathering place for an immense number of foreigners.

San Martín had an assiduous correspondent in Mendoza, one Salvador Iglesias, who sent him picturesque letters full of gossip and information about the farm:

If you would only sell it and keep nothing but the mills! I have a good reason for saying so because the farm doesn't produce a thing; on the contrary it costs like the mischief. Nuñez, poor fellow, industrious and all that, is tired of the thing if the truth were known, because he can't get ahead with it. Quite the contrary. It's all expense and setbacks, partly because you insist on handing out to those poor folks whatever they happen to need, and the worst of it is they haven't the capacity to appreciate anything, believing the world owes them a living. . . . Your horses are doing well and being well cared for! Everyone has obtained horses from you, and only I have been left without, but until you give the word I don't intend to take any for my pleasure. . . . The Alameda place is about to fall into the street because they're removing its adobes [sun-baked bricks] to make some benches with.

What follows from Iglesias appears a bit selfish. At one place he says: "You know I am fond of horses, and I am the only one without a horse from your herd." Again, "If you want to sell the Alameda place, I myself would like to buy it." The insinuations of the loquacious Iglesias are usually inter-larded with the most variegated gossip: "José Aldao is not your friend." Is there no mention of friends tried and true? "Beruti is abominable." But who is respectable? And in other places, various reports and opinions: "The 30th of last month a few remnants of the Army of the Andes passed through here, one hundred and two grenadiers commanded by Colonel Bogado. . . . El Callao is always occupied by the enemy. . . . Your friend Tagle and his wife died natural deaths at the El Callao place." Another time he writes: "The Republic [of Peru] has suffered a continuous upheaval of evil since you left. . . . You have won the contest completely and have confounded all your miserable rivals."

In his modest Paris house he gave Mercedes one of the tapestried rooms, kept another for himself, and reserved the third for his guests. Don Tomás Guido wrote him that if he had the wherewithal he would come to visit him in Europe, "determined not to speak of revolutions." San Martín answered his faithful friend, with an invitation: "No matter in what part of the world you find me, a room and a cooking pot will always be shared with you." Don Tomás couldn't come, but one day his uncle showed up, a Don Hilarión de la Quintana, a relative of Merceditas and a companion at arms of her father— so quite naturally he lodged in the guest room. What a hospitable home! He had other guests, and to many friends San Martín offered his roof and his bread: "I am not given to caprice, I live frugally, and with my income I am the most powerful man in the land." His income! We know how little it was; but even so, it was enough for his needs and for his generosities. But this happiness came to an end.

In 1831 he writes:

From the first of March of this year until the current October I haven't had anything but tribulation. The cholera hit us at the end of March, and my daughter was attacked in a particularly severe manner; I fell sick of the same epidemic three days later. Imagine! Imagine our situation, not having a soul around except one maidservant; fortunately the day before the sickness struck Mercedes, the eldest son of our late general Balcarce had come from London and was with us at our country house two leagues and a half from the capital. He was our salvation. If it hadn't been for his careful attention, both of us would have died. Mercedes recovered within the ensuing month; but I was seized, just as I was beginning to convalesce, with a gastrointestinal ailment which has had me at the edge of the grave and which has made me suffer inexplicably for seven months now.

That casual meeting between young Balcarce and Mercedes was to decide the destiny of both, and from the moment he noticed the inclination of his daughter, San Martín encouraged the engagement because he saw in the young man a lot of fine character. He says to O'Higgins:

He is the eldest son of our honored and deceased friend already mentioned, and attaché of the Buenos Aires legation in London. His good judgment is greater than his twenty-four years warrant; likable, informed, and industrious, he has a knack of making all who meet him love him; he hasn't any fortune beyond his honor, which is great. Here is everything I have wished for Mercedes' happiness. I had planned for her to marry upon my return to America, in other words, two years from now; but in view of the bad state of my health, I have anticipated that time, thinking of what a state my daughter would be in if she should lose her father. So it is that her marriage occurred nine days ago.

The wedding day of Mercedes San Martín and Mariano Balcarce was the 13th of December 1832. The witnesses were Don José Joaquín Pérez, Chilean minister to France, and Colonel Iturregui, diplomatic agent of Peru. At the end of December the young married couple departed for Buenos Aires to see their relatives and arrange certain domestic affairs. Their absence was to be prolonged two years.

San Martín wanted to accompany his children on that voyage. How proudly he would have presented Mercedes at her grandmother's house, showing off his own handiwork as father and educator! Although the two newlyweds insisted, he refused to go with them. His health was bad, and traveling would hurt him. The last season of mineral baths at Aix had been a nightmare, because they brought on nervous attacks which were scarcely allayed later by a stay on the beach at Dieppe, although the salt air did strengthen him some.

But the real reason for his staying behind was his fear of the political passions of Buenos Aires. Members of both contesting parties continually summoned him to "save the country." San Martín feared these men of Buenos Aires: "I know well their long career of revolutions and knaveries. . . . They want me to serve as a screen for their ambitions. . . . They impudently believe they can gain more advantage from me than from the Government itself." San Martín said these things then, and perhaps he was right. He had been through all that in 1829.

Furthermore one of the very men who now summoned him was none other than he who, when San Martín was in Lima and a rumor circulated in Buenos Aires that he was dead, had commented in *El Centinela* that he was "a tryant of the first water and assassin of his fellow citizens." San Martín answered his present summons with sarcasm: "A tyrant and assassin is not fit to rule free men." Amid such recollections and perspectives, San Martín watched his children go and leave him, although he was secretly anxious to return again to Argentina and find there a corner of peace and die in his own land.

The newlyweds were graciously received by their numerous kin, the Escaladas, the Quintanas, the Oromis, the Guidos, the Balcarces. But this last family had fallen on bad times following the differences that arose between the ex-governor Balcarce and the now-all-powerful Rosas.[4]

The marriage of his daughter was for San Martín the realization of an intimate dream. He profoundly liked young Balcarce, whose very name drew him closer to his heart, since it was that of an old-time comrade. The two witnesses of the wedding (Perez, Chilean minister, and Iturregui, Peruvian minister) brought the names of the two nations most intimately linked with the creation of his genius into association with that ceremony. His public life had already been closed. He could now write "finis" to his parental mission in life.

V. JOSE MATORRAS' GHOST

Five years had elapsed since San Martín left Argentina to live in Europe, closing his career of public service. These meager and obscure years had been dedicated to his daughter's education and to eking out a living. He had felt a definite nostalgia for his homeland in spite of his disappointment over its leaders, and when war broke out with Brazil the voice of duty impelled him to embark upon a new adventure.

For some time his good friend and most indefatigable correspondent, Don Tomás Guido, who had never stopped rebuking San Martín for his departure from Peru, had sent news about the internal disorders of the United Provinces, insisting that San Martín's presence would be useful in Buenos Aires and advising his return. The old expatriate's unfailing answer to these letters was "No," and once he wrote in this sharp and profound manner:

I confess that the outline you send of conditions makes me sad, but it does not surprise me. I say it does not surprise me because, knowing our America's situation so well, I could have predicted accurately nearly all that is happening and will happen without any great amount of foresight, as you will readily agree. The final consequences are determined, although it is hard to say just when they will run their course. You surely have not forgotten how often I have told you that our great crisis would come upon the conclusion of our independence. This crisis was made inevitable by the backward, wayward masses of our population. And their individualistic, provincial inclinations have been whetted by the revolution itself. These evils would have been largely remedied if the men in positions of leadership had realized that while the cause of independence merely needs a certain national pride for its support (and even the primitive savage has that), true liberty and all its rights need a solid foundation of stanch citizens, not "spit-and-whittle" idlers, but men of high purpose and knowledge capable of appreciating the intrinsic, not arbitrary, values which representative government brings. You were with me five years. No one knows better than you my antipathy for all that luxury and privilege represent, my hatred of all that aristocracy stands for. By inclination and principle I love the republican form of government, and no one is more republican than I. But my predisposition has not kept me from seeing that this form of government could not be realized in America except as an aftermath of horrible anarchy, a genuine trial by fire. However, it would be worth the price if the attainment of our goal could be guaranteed, but the experience of centuries has shown us that the consequences are always tyranny and a despot.

These words confirmed in the presence of known facts what San Martín had prophesied eight years before in the manifesto which he gave the United Provinces upon his departure from Valparaiso on his way to Peru. He had declared once again that he was republican by conviction and that if occasionally he had despaired of democracy in America it was not because he preferred an aristocratic regime; it was just that citizens of the necessary caliber were lacking, and he could see that from the inevitable demagogic struggle only barbaric dictatorship, the curse of South American life, could arise. Not even the supporters of a centralized power, the unitarians, escaped his censure, especially since he himself had suffered unjustified vexations under the government of Rodríguez and Rivadavia[1] in 1823. He referred to them in paragraphs which I have already cited from his replies to Guido:

In '23 when I yielded to the importunity of my wife and came to bid her good-by for the last time at Buenos Aires in May, they posted squads along the road to apprehend me like a common criminal, and had it not been for the warning given me by an individual within the administration itself, I would have been caught. Imagine such a thing happening during the most stable of our revolutionary governments! After this don't you think I ought to shelter myself, not to save my life (because you know I scorn that), but to avoid an outrage that would put a blot on my public honor?

Upon the outbreak of war with Brazil, when Rivadavia occupied the presidency, Guido insisted upon calling San Martín, using a new motive expressed seductively:

Can you presume that just because you become a hermit, the hopes of your friends and the persecutions of your enemies will not follow you to the ends of the earth? . . . I thought you had abandoned that stoic philosophy which impelled you away from the theater of your fame. . . . I see the war with Brazil as a new theater opening to the glories of General San Martín.

That war was like a trumpet, shaking the inmost fibers of the old soldier's being. San Martín saw in the Portuguese empire of Brazil a survival of the European colonial regime. Perhaps the task of continental liberation, which was the mission of his life, had not been finished at Ayacucho in view of the fact that there still existed in Rio de Janeiro a Portuguese Court linked by blood and institutions to the Old World's dynasties. That empire under the impulse of colonial traditions had obstructed the revolution in Uruguay, and still had intentions of pushing to the River Plate by means of conquest, just as in the time of the viceroys. It was essential to protect the integrity of Argentine territory in Uruguay, stop the invader, and sow republican ideas in the province of Rio Grande, carrying them clear to Rio de Janeiro as he had carried them to Lima years before. The plan was grandiose and worthy of his genius. He had, meanwhile, studied geographic and social details of the empire (Brazil), perhaps with a view to formulating a campaign. But he nevertheless well knew that the conflict had come at an inopportune moment for Argentina, disorder being rampant in the provinces of the River Plate.

From afar he followed anxiously the course of the war.

Upon learning of Alvear's victory at Ituzaingó he writes in a letter: "I have enthusiastically celebrated the triumphs of Buenos Aires. These blows will soften up the Emperor."

At the very start of the war with the empire of Brazil, San Martín wished to send an offer of his military services from Brussels, where he lived, to the United Provinces of the River Plate. But he refrained because of a personal aversion to Rivadavia, who was president of the nation.

Once Rivadavia had fallen and his old friend Don Vicente López was elected president of Argentina, San Martín addressed himself to the new official on the 7th of December 1827, offering his services "in the just, although imprudent, war in which our country finds itself." López didn't answer, perhaps because his term of office was very brief, or perhaps because San Martín's offer did not gain a favorable official reception. Perhaps also his frankness in calling the war against Brazil "imprudent" had offended. But San Martín could not help calling it that, because the empire had dynastic connections in

Europe which were dangerous when provoked, and also because the war in the River Plate could not help being prejudicial to Argentine interests, given the external pressure of British interests and the separatist tendencies of certain Uruguayan elements. In spite of all this, however, San Martín decided to embark for Buenos Aires, as he had done in 1812, in order to defend his country, of which Uruguay, invaded by the Brazilian Empire, was an integral part.

In October of that year, 1827, he wrote to his friend, O'Higgins, explaining his previous abstention and his new plans:

You have probably learned of the resignation of Rivadavia. His administration has been disastrous and has only served to divide us. He has conducted an underground war against me with the sole purpose of turning opinion against me, as if my only purpose in going to Europe had been to build up political power in America! I have ignored his gross imputations and his ignoble person. With a man like this at the head of the administration I did not deign to offer my services in the war with Brazil, feeling sure they would have been refused. But with the change in administration I have believed it my duty to do so, in whatever capacity the Government at Buenos Aires sees fit to employ me. If my services are accepted I shall embark without loss of time, and will advise you.

Feeling such resentments and hopes, San Martín decided upon his trip to Buenos Aires. He left Mercedes at a boarding school and sailed on the *Countess of Chichester,* weighing anchor from Falmouth at the end of 1828. Although he had resolved in 1824, after his voyage from Buenos Aires in a cargo ship, never to subject himself to the erratic and slow navigation of such a ship in the future, he wrote to his comrade General Miller who lived in England, asking him to find out the necessary procedure for embarkation and to reserve passage on the *Chichester,* one of the best packets in that line. But the crossing lasted seventy-five days and even entailed an atrocious storm in the River Plate, which caused a delay near Montevideo.

On this voyage San Martín traveled incognito with a passport in the name of José Matorras.

His servant, Eusebio Soto, a young man of twenty-four years who had been with him since the days of his residence in Peru, accompanied him in the new adventure. Soto had served as his valet during his exodus following abdication, when he arrived without pomp or official escort at the port of Valparaiso. Soto had also accompanied San Martín at the baths of Cauquenes, on the farm in Mendoza, and the various other stopping places of his expatriation period. This creole youth was one of the few faithful friends the great man had left in the solitude of his disasters, when he reached the extreme expedient of adopting a pseudonym. San Martín had sailed under a fictitious name, taking the surname of his mother which had appeared in his records at the start of his career in Spain. Perhaps the adoption of this assumed name was to avoid being molested as he passed through Rio de Janeiro, or it may have been due only to his propensity for the mysterious. Nevertheless San

Martín was indubitably a man who outlived his fame, and José Matorras was just the specter, almost posthumous, of the military hero of other years.

Without having stopped at Montevideo, San Martín arrived at Buenos Aires the 6th of February 1829, in the month of the victories of Chacabuco and San Lorenzo and of his own birthday. This coincidence must have aroused melancholy emotions, mixed with the remembrance of those generous hopes with which he had arrived on the *Canning* seventeen years before. He had been young then, and the future had smiled upon him when in 1812 he came to offer his sword for American liberty. And although the fights of the past had come out gloriously for him, now he must perforce look back upon them with that nostalgia reserved for tasks that are finished. He was getting gray. Ill health continued to bother him, and he was poor. In short, one thing was clear: he must put his old sword away. Preoccupied with the news of Lavalle's revolution which he received in Rio de Janeiro, he learned in Montevideo of the creation of a Uruguayan flag for the new nation that had just come into being on the other side of the River Plate. Portugal and England had triumphed, thanks to our squabbles along the Plate. Artigas,[2] the defeated leader, had shut himself up in Paraguay. Ramírez of Entre Rios province was dead and Quiroga of the province of La Rioja was in the ascendency. Meanwhile the United Provinces of the war of independence were less united with each passing day and continued to be torn by internecine fights leading to the dictatorship foretold by San Martín in his manifesto issued in Chile in 1820 upon his embarkation for the campaign in Peru. Now that the cycle of wars against Spain was closed, other actors with other flags occupied the field with the civil wars which San Martín abhorred so much. His old officers were now the confused protagonists in a cruel struggle begun by that young cadet Juan Lavalle, who had been initiated into the old grenadier regiment by San Martín himself. These men, now ascended to the rank of generals, had taken over the Government. The River Plate area had fallen upon evil days, and upon his arrival at Rio de Janeiro the old traveler learned that the national picture had changed since he left Falmouth. The war with Brazil was over, and in Buenos Aires a new revolution had broken out. His "unlucky star," as he had termed his fate in 1816, had once again made its appearance on this voyage. A terrible discouragement invaded his spirit. This trip was becoming another failure, and even before arriving in his country he thought of turning back to the foreign soil of his enforced exile.

San Martín considered the peace with Brazil "shameful" just as obstinately as he had thought the war inopportune and brought on by "fear instilled by the loud-mouths of the capital." Certain it is that in 1814 a war on Uruguayan territory frustrated his early plans, and now in 1829 on coming from Belgium another war in Uruguay was equally frustrating his present plans. One might say that Uruguay was reserved by destiny for the victories of Alvear. In the first war he took Montevideo from the Royalists, and in the second he defeated the imperial troops at Ituzaingó. Destiny reserved other plans for San Martín.

He had no way of knowing to what extent chaotic conditions then existent would allow the realization of his aims in coming to his country, but not once did he imagine that Buenos Aires would receive him as badly as it did. It would be more accurate to say that it did not receive him at all, because the traveler did not even care to disembark. On that same 6th of February (the month seemed to be designated by his horoscope no less for pain than for glory) the sad pilgrim found at the very gates of Buenos Aires this jeering handbill:

AMBIGUITIES

General San Martín has returned to his country after an absence of five years, but only after learning that peace has been concluded with the emperor of Brazil.

Full of mockery, indeed, but more for the Argentine hand that wrote it than for San Martín!

The news spread like wildfire through little groups of gossip-mongers scattered about Buenos Aires, arousing his old rivals and filling them with meanness—stirring up past envies.

San Martín well knew the quarters from which he was harried, much as dogs bark at strangers, but this, far from being any consolation, only made him sadder as he thought of the absolute disinterest with which he had served the country that was now besmirching its own glory.

The packet which brought José Matorras also brought English merchandise to Buenos Aires and was scheduled to return to Falmouth with suet, hides, woolens, jerked beef, and other Argentine products. The business of unloading and taking on cargo would take some time, and San Martín neither wanted to wait nor to disembark. He determined to return to Montevideo, and for this he needed another ship and a new passport. He therefore hit upon an appeal to the Minister of Government of Buenos Aires, one José Miguel Díaz Vélez, of whom he solicited a passport "for myself and a servant who wish to return to the capital of Montevideo, at which point it was impossible to disembark upon arrival previously on account of the haste of the captain's order to sail." Together with this official appeal he sent ashore a personal letter to this same Díaz Vélez, former subaltern of his, as were all the men who then held office in Argentina. In the letter, dated February 6, San Martín addresses the minister as "My esteemed friend" and continues:

After exactly five years of separation from my country I have come home with the firm hope of spending the rest of my days in the peace of a retired and private life. However I counted on tranquil conditions which I supposed existed in our nation—and upon finding these not prevalent I knew it would be impossible for any man who had taken part in the Revolution to promise himself tranquillity, no matter how strictly neutral the course he steered through the clash of opinions. So, in view of the state of things here, and furthermore not belonging nor wishing to belong to any of the parties in question, I have resolved to look for my peace in Montevideo, from which point I shall raise my prayers for the speedy re-establishment of harmony.

The letter went on to mention the recent appointment of Díaz Vélez to the ministry, expressing a certain disdainful note: "for me no public employment is worth much, especially in such agitated times." And as if to soften this aspersion with a more cordial expression, he reminded him that on leaving Buenos Aires in 1824 he had left orders that a colt from his stables in Mendoza be presented to him. On the following day, February 7, Díaz Vélez answered San Martín by sending him the requested passports along with a letter in which he addressed him as "my old and worthy friend," expressing surprise at his "unexpected arrival at anchor" and lamenting his inability to embrace him on account of his decision to go on to Montevideo. It was courteous enough, but it did not invite him to set foot on land.

As for the political conditions in Argentina, he was sorry that San Martín should have obtained his information in Brazil, "where the recently concluded peace has not served to lessen their nationalistic hatred or their displeasure at changes of government not deemed favorable." "Moreover," (Díaz Vélez adds, slightly piqued by the rather Olympian abstention of our traveler from internal questions), "there is no such thing as a political party, unless you want to dignify with such a term the rabble and bands of savages." The latter were the federalists, and nothing could better show the existence of irreconcilable factions than this very wording.

As the arrival of San Martín was known in Buenos Aires, the true name of the supposed José Matorras was discovered on board the ship where for seventy-five days the authentic personality of the greatest American of his age had been hidden.

Argentine social life was buzzing, and the politicians began to discuss the mysterious voyage of San Martín, some with doubts, some with much conjecture, and others with enmity. Many old friends who had hoped to see him thought it well to remain in fearful, watchful waiting. But a few among them, moved by sincere friendship, dared to go to the roadstead to greet him.

San Martín, who was much hated, was at the same time much loved by those who really knew him. One of the old companions-at-arms who came aboard to offer his services was Colonel Olazábal. No sooner did he learn of San Martín's arrival than he arranged for the emotional visit in company with a friend, Major Alvarez Condarco. On their way through the market, going to the port, they bought some handsome peaches as a gift for the guest, and at the shore they hired a whaling boat to approach the ship. When some fifty meters away, they could see San Martín leaning on the rail with his gaze fixed on the city. Upon coming aboard they as well as San Martín were filled with extraordinary emotion.

"My son!" exclaimed the voyager as he recognized Olazábal. They embraced, their eyes filled with tears. Olazábal describes it thus in his memoirs:

"San Martín was in slippers and was dressed in a frock coat of cheap cloth that reached his ankles. He had become grayer and fatter, but he still retained a magnetic sparkle in his eyes and that martial posture from the days when he led his legions to victory." This is the picture he presented to Condarco and Olazábal, who had served as officers under him in the campaigns of the Andes.

"And how did you leave your daughter, Mercedes, Excellency?" asked Olazábal.

"Well," responded the traveler. "She stayed behind in a boarding school. What a girl! Confound it, she's very willful and hard to manage. Why, you'd think she'd been reared by her grandmother! When she sailed with me to Europe she actually had to spend most of the voyage 'imprisoned' in her stateroom!"

It appeared that he was trying to hide with rough soldier talk the real tenderness he felt as a father, the exceptional affection he gave Mercedes, making her the sole object of his life in the somber declining years that were already beginning.

Olazábal brought a letter from Guido, and San Martín invited him to his stateroom, where they could talk after the message had been read. It was a long letter in which Don Tomás Guido painted a picture of disastrous anarchy reigning in the nation and argued that since only a strong government could save the country it was evident that no one but San Martín could command the situation in moments like these.

When San Martín had read Guido's message he was thoughtful a long time, holding the letter in his hand. He finally spoke gravely:

"I learned of Lavalle's revolution when I was in Rio de Janeiro, and I heard of the execution of Dorrego when I was in Montevideo. I consequently decided to do nothing more than drop anchor at Buenos Aires, to take care of a few matters and then return to Europe without disembarking. My sword? No! Never will it be unsheathed in civil war!"

He was the same austere patriot of old, just as in his greatest years.

The younger men, Olazábal and Condarco, heard him with emotion. Who was right? Guido and those who believed that San Martín ought to mix into internal conflicts and settle them, or the soldier who in 1812 hadn't wanted any political influence; who in 1814 had sought retirement in Cuyo in order to get away from Buenos Aires' political factions; who in 1820 had sent the United Provinces the warning which foretold present disasters and a bloody dictatorship for whatever adventurer came along? Would those who refused to listen then respect his opinion now? A vision of dark and fateful portent arose before the hero who had been scorned and mocked.

While they were talking in the stateroom, Colonel Espora entered with Minister Díaz Vélez' reply. And when Espora took his leave, San Martín, shaking hands, added these words to his good-by:

"Tell Díaz Vélez to be happy, if he can."

San Martín had always been a most cautious man. From youthful days on it required no less than a heroic mission to draw him into contact with the world. When the hour of his destined task had passed, his innate asceticism asserted itself and he sought in solitude that silence beloved of wise men.

Olazábal's visit on board lasted four hours. San Martín had been his grooms-man, as he had often been for many other young officers he had molded. And as this young man was about to leave, San Martín handed him a letter for Guido, exclaiming with feeling:

"Embrace me, son!"

The two men embraced in parting and were seen sobbing.

"And embrace your dear wife for me," said San Martín.

Young Olazábal could scarcely bring himself around to saying good-by to the chief, the master.

"Ah, who knows if we'll see each other again!" sighed San Martín.

Olazábal and Condarco were grief-stricken as they lowered themselves into their boat. San Martín was accurate in his presentiment: they would never see each other again.

Was it for such as this they had fought for their country?

On the 12th of February the newspaper El Tiempo inserted a "correspond-ence" signed by "several Argentines," reproaching San Martín for his de-parture. These "patriots" have the "sublime courage to live in their country" while San Martín is leaving at a time when "no man, regardless of his great-ness, should allow himself to be separated from his land." According to the authors of the article, the old hero ought to stay and perish with his fellow countrymen in the political turmoil; rather than flee and publish before the world the ignominy of Argentina. The Government ordered an explanation inserted in the same paper, stating that the Government had by no means prohibited San Martín from disembarking and that neither were conditions such that he would find it impossible to live in his country.

On the 13th, the day the Government announcement appeared, the Gaceta Mercantil published the following laconic notice: "The brigantine-of-war, General Rondeau sailed from the roadstead at 2 P.M. of the 9th. Aboard was General San Martín, who had been on the English packet, Countess of Chi-chester, en route to Montevideo."

Thus did San Martín depart from Buenos Aires for the last time, finding, on the very anniversary of the Chacabuco victory, that the coasts of his own land were inhospitable.

The following day, in the same newspaper, an article on the exploits of San Martín in the wars of independence was published, "by a companion-at-arms." This was suspected to be the work of Tomás Guido. With this, the whole affair was dropped.

Martí remembers that when Bolívar, wronged and sick, was leaving Caracas for the last time as he was on his way to the coast to die, he said to his servant, José, who accompanied him:

"Let us go, José, they are throwing us out of here."

So, likewise, as San Martín left Buenos Aires forever, going to the lands where his previous expatriation had sent him, he might have said to José Matorras, his "double":

"Let us go, José, they are throwing us out of here."

San Martín spent a few less disagreeable days in Montevideo. That beautiful Uruguayan territory was also his country, intimately involved in the continental brotherhood of his America. The political and diplomatic mistakes that had brought about its separation from the United Provinces could be imputed to certain oligarchies and leaders; but Uruguay's "Argentinity" could be reconstructed in the future. In his work of liberation, San Martín had not fought for Argentine hegemony, but for American brotherhood; and he respected the right of each liberated people to self-government. What he could never understand about the American Revolution was regionalism à la Artigas, or domination à la Bolívar. But all such was passing in 1829 and would pass completely until liberty alone remained in America, enduring for as long as that "river of birds," the Uruguay, should flow through the land, the Uruguay River which gives its name to that republic along the River Plate and which saw the birth of our knight-errant. The Uruguay River borders the territory of Las Misiones in Argentina, thus bathing the shores of Yapeyú, San Martín's birthplace. On its eastern shore it kisses the native land of Artigas, Uruguay, and across its waters the two nations commune in close friendship.

San Martín stayed in Montevideo from the middle of February till the middle of April, enjoyed the finest hospitality of that land's leading men. Thanks to the effort of Dr. Vidal he obtained offers of lodging and several families gave receptions in his honor.

The pilgrim must have thought in these days about his birthplace of Yapeyú, which always beckoned him. From Montevideo he could see the deep hollows of his native town, now lying in ruins. Portuguese monarchist hordes had sacked Las Misiones in 1817 at the time San Martín was fighting the battle of Chacabuco and gaining his place in continental history. What coincidences of time and place! José Matorras remembered his mother and the times when she had led him by the hand through the native woodlands.

Ten years before, at the outset of the federal crisis, San Martín had written from Mendoza in February 1819, to Francisco Ramírez and Estanislao López, Argentine leaders, asking them to adjust their quarrels for the sake of unity so that outside enemies might be dealt with. In a similar way he addressed Artigas, saying among other things:

Each drop of American blood that is shed because of our battles touches my heart. . . . At such time as the nation shall find its freedom I shall renounce all posts and retire; . . . my saber will never be drawn from its sheath on account of

political opinions; . . . finally, my countryman, let us resolve our present troubles
and unite against the Spaniards.

Artigas answered that December: "I am resolved to defend this nation as
long as the perfidious Brazilian coalition exists. Believe me inexorably bound
to this duty." But in 1829 the proud Artigas, now defeated, was a refugee in
Paraguay.

On April 4 Lavalle, from his headquarters in El Saladillo, commissioned
Don Juan Andrés Gelly and Colonel Eduardo Trolé to go to Montevideo for
a conference with San Martín. "I have authorized them to speak with you in
my name," reads the short letter from Lavalle to San Martín. The interview
took place with great cordiality, but nothing came of it. San Martín answered
on April 14: "I am sorry to tell you that the means you propose cannot have,
in my opinion, the effect you hope for in ending the evils which afflict our
unfortunate nation." What were the proposed means? He doesn't say, but he
infers what they are in this other paragraph: "In your present situation, even
one single victim whose life you can save for our country will prove an in-
estimable consolation to you, regardless of the results of the campaign to which
you are dedicated." The leader of the unitarian faction had already shot
Governor Dorrego; the retaliation of the federalist faction wouldn't be long
delayed. This could lead only to the extermination of one band by the other.
Was it San Martín's duty to mix himself into the conflict and assume the
dictatorship? Both unitarians and federalists[3] wished to see him in their ranks
and make use of his prestige as a hero to further their stupid hatreds. San
Martín gave Lavalle the advice he needed (although it was not heeded), but
San Martín refused to play the part of assassin of his fellow citizens.

Almost the same day on which San Martín answered Lavalle, he wrote
O'Higgins all about these negotiations: "Lavalle's object is to have me take
command of the army and the province of Buenos Aires and then effect settle-
ments with the other provinces. He aims to see the authors of the December
first coup accredited through the offices of myself and the other governors."
That was the movement which Lavalle led against Governor Dorrego, and
which culminated in the shooting of the latter.

Days later a friend in Buenos Aires sent him the following news about the
politics of the moment:

Don Bernardino Rivadavia embarked May 1 for France with a passport from the
French consul. Lavalle remains in Flores with his column, and Rosas and López
are in Luján with their forces. Some of the army chiefs have joined them. Unless
reason intervenes there will probably be a battle very soon. This is the way our
unhappy country is being desolated!

Such were the dramatic circumstances in Argentina when San Martín saw
himself obliged to leave the country for the second time, unable to countenance such anarchy. And so he saw in 1829 how his predictions of 1816

and 1820 were beginning to be fulfilled. The tyrant Rosas already was appearing on the horizon of the bloody plain, just as San Martín had foreseen in the first years of the emancipation. It seemed to be the unavoidable fate of this Bacchic land, because the same bloody tragedy overtook the nations liberated by Bolívar, and Bolívar himself was a victim. Bolívar had assumed the dictatorship; San Martín had no desire whatever to do so.

Thus San Martín was obliged to return to Europe, although the reduction of his income by the paper-money depression in Buenos Aires did not really leave him enough to live on in Europe. His daughter's property in Buenos Aires yielded him six thousand pesos a year, but on the continent this sum shrank to only $1,500. He wanted to go to Mendoza and collect a part of his Peruvian pension, now that it did not appear he could obtain any sort of salary in his own country. He would have liked to remain there and lead a life of retirement to prove to the people "that my ambition amounts to nothing more than to live and die peacefully in this benevolent land." But civil war frustrated these hopes.

The agitations of nineteen long years spent in search of liberty and the social crises he had witnessed seemed to San Martín to argue powerfully for "a vigorous government," and he came to this conclusion "like a drowning man grasping at straws. . . . It is necessary that one of the two political parties disappear," and the Argentine provinces were coming to that.

San Martín left Montevideo en route to Europe. The newspaper *El Tiempo*, in its April 23d edition, said good-by to him with these laconic and malicious words:

"Last week General José de San Martín departed from Montevideo in the direction of Rio de Janeiro. It is thought here that he may be going to Europe, but we have been assured that he will establish himself in the Brazilian capital. We wish the former were true rather than the latter."

San Martín had told his friends in Montevideo and had written to O'Higgins and Guido that he was leaving to complete his daughter's education in Europe and that if, at the end of two years, the nation had calmed down, he would return to the refuge of his farm in Mendoza, with the intention of spending his last years there.

The editors of *El Tiempo* lied knowingly when they published the false notice of San Martín's passage to Brazil. But worse than the plan to create prejudice against San Martín was their confession that they preferred to see the great patriot far away from America.

In Uruguay San Martín had exchanged notes with General Rivera (he was the leader who had just concluded a successful campaign in the territory of Las Misiones) about the negotiations of the federalist leaders and unitarian leaders offering him the Government, notes in which he expressed his just motives for feeling obliged to remove himself from civil wars. He was again animated by the same ideal that he had expressed in Valparaiso upon leaving for Peru, the same ideal that had motivated him in Guayaquil when he scrupulously avoided a bloody and useless rivalry with Bolívar. In the Argentine chaos, which was but one episode of the continental chaos, San Martín saw once more his America torn by the absurdities of forces that knew no law. What had been a prophetic vision before was now actual experience. His perceptive power again pointed out the evils and foretold the future, as if the master statesman had perforce returned just at that grim moment to give a new lesson to his bewildered countrymen.

A short while before leaving the River Plate forever, José Matorras, the specter of catastrophe, spoke thus:

What is needed is a savior who will combine the prestige of victory with respect for all the provinces, and who, with above all a strong arm, will rescue the nation from the evils which menace it. There is a consensus that presents San Martín as a candidate for this, and I base this observation on innumerable letters and conversations I have had with respect to this particular matter. I also find myself in accord somewhat, in view of the circumstances of the day. Very well. Granted that it is absolutely necessary that one of the contending factions disappear from the scene, since the presence of both is incompatible with the public peace, would it be possible for me to make myself the one chosen to be an assassin of my countrymen and, like another Sulla, burden my country with proscriptions?

No, never! I would a thousand times rather perish in the turmoil that threatens her than to be the instrument of such horror. It is a foregone conclusion that I would never be allowed to exercise the clemency which the situation would demand, judging from the sanguinary vows of the factions, at the moment when one of them becomes victorious. I would be obliged to be the agent of unbridled passions which know no other principle but vengeance.

The present national situation is such that the man who becomes its leader has no alternative to a complete dependence on one single faction, save the complete renunciation of authority. This last is what I choose. . . .

These were the things San Martín said in 1829 when he refused the dictatorship, and when he learned that another Argentine, Juan Manuel de Rosas, would undertake complete power.

The attitude San Martín manifested in 1829 had no influence on events that followed, but it is highly significant to the biography of this hero because it reveals his personality. His newest renunciation might appear to be egoism or cowardice, had it not come from a man who had already completed fifty years of life, and who had sacrificed so much in the service of his country. He departed from the theater of civil war because he felt a premonition of tragedy in forces that were beyond his individual power to control, forces that would certainly lead to mass murder.

Ambition did not influence him in the least, and he governed himself by a clear comprehension of all that happened, a comprehension which embraced the most minute details and the profoundest depths. His perception of events and men was extraordinary. His sharp intelligence had furthermore been nurtured on books of applied science (architecture, fortifications, agriculture, irrigation, mechanics, and meteorology) and in books of geography, history, and philosophy and ethics. Contrary to the general impression, he was a man of serious reading, albeit seldom given to literary expression. His spelling was bad, so bad that it is usually necessary to correct the excerpts cited from his letters, but his thought is always clear, thanks to an exceptional intelligence, accustomed to meditation.

Just as in 1816, an epic year, he had prophesied anarchy, in 1820, in the midst of civil war, he prophesied bloody dictatorship. But in 1829, surrounded by so many shadows, his spirit saw a glimmer of patriotic hope. After tyranny, the dreams of May 1810 would begin to be realized:

"Mankind will be able to take advantage of the lessons taught by past experience and save their country from evil. This is my hope. Without hope and without a dream, as a philosopher once said, man would cease to exist."

San Martín was no longer a warrior, he was a seer. He who had disarmed himself in Lima seven years before, now experienced his fourth and last renunciation. He was fifty years old, and was pursuing his third journey in search of spiritual perfection. "Stripped of all that is carnal," as Thomas à Kempis puts it, devoid of all earthy desire, he was like "the man of sorrows" of the Scriptures. His country's mystic, liberty's ascetic, he saw about him the world's desolate panorama. The saint had disarmed himself forever, and, as in the myth of the Holy Grail, after having shed the blood of the Swan, the valiant knight talked with his guide:

"Where do you come from?"

"I don't know," answers Parsifal.

"Who is your father?"

"I don't know."

"Who has sent thee hence?"

"I don't know that, either."

"And what is your name?"

"I had many names, but I no longer remember them."

San Martín, the Saint of the Sword (José Matorras, the Specter of Catastrophe), now sailed through the turbulent waters at the mouth of the River Plate toward the open sea, the ocean of the Atlantides, from which he had come.

VI. THE RECLUSE OF GRAND BOURG

In the middle of 1829 José Matorras, who had fleetingly appeared in the harbor of Buenos Aires like a specter of Argentina's catastrophic hour, found himself once more in Europe. The portals of his country were closed to him, and they were not to open again until thirty-three years later, when they received his ashes in one of those deifications by which a people give posthumous compensation for the unjust suffering they have imposed on their noblest servants as the fatal price of glory. The pilgrim returned with his soul full of uncertainty, and an adverse fate followed him as he renewed his expatriation in Europe.

Established anew in Brussels, he wrote to the good O'Higgins: "As the old maxim has it, 'When it rains it pours.' On my trip back from America, between Falmouth and London, my coach overturned and broken glass from one of the windows cut my left arm deeply. But not wanting to be dragged into the public eye by the papers, I carefully remained incognito."

In this manner the hero took up his European "dog's life" anew, a life full of calamities and constant vigilance in avoiding the curiosity of the public.

He lived in Belgium two more years, and in 1831 he moved to France with his brother, Justo, and his daughter, Mercedes, who was married a short while later. He took lodgings near Paris, in the country, "to get away from the unbearable hubbub of the great city," as he says. Poverty, infirmities, and nostalgia begin to afflict his existence with a dull rancor.

Meanwhile he continued to think about his country and about the fortunes of America. He continued to correspond with his old friends. Don Vicente López wrote him lamenting that he had not disembarked at Buenos Aires, because it would have been most pleasant "to talk of the nation's affairs with her true founder." San Martín answered, saying: "I would rather endure my voluntary exile than to witness the afflictions which my country still is suffering." Letters also came from the faithful Guido, asking if it was true that San Martín had been called to Peru, and San Martín replied that if such a thing should occur, and he were to return to Peru, he would advise his old friend "just in case you are disposed to undergo new hardships and adventures." O'Higgins also usually wrote to him, philosophizing about the ingratitude of the peoples they had liberated and about the virtues of Chile's restorer and the victor of Lima. San Martín answered with the familiarity of a bosom friend, counting the Chilean, O'Higgins, among his favorites. In retirement he sadly followed the course of South American anarchy. He learned how the Dionysiac Bolívar had met his end, devoured by the very flames he had kindled.

In December of 1831 Bolívar had died in Santa Marta, poverty-stricken, prematurely old, relieved of power, expelled from his country, repudiated by the peoples he had governed. In fine, with his fantastic exploits as conqueror and legislator submerged in the ruin of failure. If only Bolívar had not been so drunk with illusions of personal glory and ambitions for political power, had he united his genius with the genius of San Martín, as the latter had suggested in Guayaquil, America would have had a more pleasant fate. Our surviving hero saw with great pain, from his exile in Europe, that all his prophecies had come true in the Argentine provinces and in the rest of the continent.

As if this patriotic grief were not enough to burden his existence, the fates piled sickness and poverty upon him to such a degree that he would have been able to repeat in those years the phrase uttered by Quevedo while imprisoned in the Tower of Juan Abad: "My life is no longer life, but a prolixity of death."

With his soul in such a state, filled with suffering and stringent need, San Martín chanced to meet Don Alejandro Aguado, Spanish nobleman and friend of his young manhood, who had come to be a powerful banker in France. That meeting was a lucky accident in the life of the old expatriate.

Both had belonged to the Regiment of Murcia in the Spanish Peninsula. Almost a quarter-century had passed since then, and drastic changes had come over them both, so they had many good and bad things to tell each other in going over their diverse careers.

They proceeded from La Rue Neuve Saint George, where San Martín lived modestly, to have lunch at Aguado's hotel near the Place Vendôme, where they were luxuriously attended.

"So you are the great banker Aguado!" San Martín exclaimed to his old messmate and comrade of many a revel.

"Man, if a person can't get to be liberator of half the world, it seems to me he ought to be allowed to be just a banker," replied Aguado jestingly.

Who would have thought in those days in Madrid and Cádiz, when they were both young, that this would come to pass! How time changed things! What dramatic surprises destiny held in store! Here is the paladin of America, exiled from America, an old, sick, poor, and lonely man who, after having fought against the kings of Spain (not against Spain), was now to have the aid of a generous and rich Spaniard!

The old friendship blossomed vigorously anew amid a variety of such feelings. San Martín said, years later, that had it not been for that noble Spaniard he would have ended his days in a hospital. It was Aguado who financed the purchase of a property near one he owned, so that San Martín could live with befitting dignity, and near to him. In San Martín's old age Aguado was his provider.

The great banker lived in the Château de Petit-Bourg on the Seine, about two hours outside Paris by the Orleans railroad. It was a potentate's rural residence, and besides he had another house and office in the city. Right in front of Petit-Bourg, on the other side of the river, San Martín acquired the Grand Bourg place on the advice and with the help of Aguado. This property consisted of a two-storied house with white walls and a steep dark-tiled roof, plus one hectare of ground planted with both fruit and shade trees, and also a garden where multicolored dahlias grew. San Martín lived there for fourteen years, from 1834 to 1848. Aguado ordered a hanging bridge over the Seine between the two places, thus facilitating the exemplary intimacy in which the two friends lived.

To attend to family matters or to his business, Aguado occasionally visited Spain. On one of these trips, the last he was to make to his native land, he invited his friend San Martín to accompany him. How well this old alumnus of the Seminary of Nobles would have liked to return to Madrid after so many years; this son of a Málaga captain would enjoy seeing again the city in which his father served; this son of Doña Gregoria would enjoy returning to Castile, home of the Matorras', and continuing to Orense in Galicia to visit his mother's tomb. The two old comrades of Murcia wanted to satisfy their nostalgia for the gallant and warlike days of their youth in Seville and in Cádiz.

San Martín loved Spain, and in the thick of war he said that he fought not because of a hatred for the Spaniards but for his love of America and her liberty. During the interview at Punchauca with the viceroy of Lima he toasted the reconciliation between Spain and America at the time when they were locked in conflict and he was the leader of the rebellion. But how could he return to Spain? It was there he had broken off his career when he was a cavalry colonel, and if he returned now he, a rebel general, would surely meet some of the military officials against whom he had fought in America. Tireless Aguado smoothed out all the obstacles. He obtained passports and a declaration from the Madrid Government that San Martín would be received with all deference but without any military character.

María Helena, San Martín's widowed sister, lived in Asturias, and naturally he wished to see her. It was clearly seen throughout the negotiations that the war he had fought had been a civil war. Riego's[1] frustrated revolution at Las Cabezas de San Juan was nothing less than the Spanish version of a revolution which also embraced the Spains of the New World. The mutiny of the fleet commanded by O'Donnell, which refused to sail for America, had been fomented by agents of Buenos Aires. How could he enter Spain without his rank of Argentine general, hiding his title as founder of the Hispano-American republics? In Paris he well enjoyed an obscure life. But in Madrid such an obscurity seemed a cowardly and, in a sense, clandestine thing. He was intransigent. Aguado left for Spain in 1842 without his friend.

During that trip Aguado died suddenly in Asturias, and on opening his will it was learned that he had named San Martín executor of his estate and guardian of his children.

The total benefit of Aguado's appearance in 1833 and of his influence in San Martín's life cannot be fully estimated unless one contrasts the miserable loneliness of his former life with the consolation he found in the refuge of Grand Bourg in the company of such a noble friend.

For his living expenses San Martín could only count on the rental of his daughter's house in Buenos Aires and his Peruvian pension, after his return from the Plate in 1829. His brother-in-law Escalada looked after the scant amount yielded by the Buenos Aires rental, and Dr. Mariano Alvarez of Lima, or the good O'Higgins, who lived as an exile in Peru, looked after the pension, which was always in arrears. This money, certainly not an abundant sum, arrived late and with losses because these countries' constant revolutions caused the money to depreciate. At times he was paid with customs due bills or papers of credit whose value diminished upon being negotiated. And still San Martín went through torture each time sheer necessity compelled him to claim what was coming to him, for he well knew the bad economic condition of the Peruvian Government. Finally his pension was included in the budget, which facilitated more regular payment, but which ignored the arrears. On top of this the crisis cut his pension in half. With such means San Martín had to bear the expense of his daughter's education, his own support, and the care of his health. There were times when money was lacking, a horrible experience for a man so full of dignity and scruples.

In 1831 O'Higgins wrote him from Peru:

I had been delighted, thinking they would have handed me perhaps fifteen hundred pesos cash this month, but yesterday I was disillusioned: there isn't any hope. I plan to use my modest influence to see if they won't deliver two thousand pesos in customs due bills which might lose 15 or 16 per cent. If I am successful I shall remit what I get to you in care of Baring Brothers and Co. of London, as you have instructed me in your letters. As for your pension, Alvarez will continue collecting whatever he can each month, and sending it to you.

The subject of pecuniary assistance runs like a dark thread through the correspondence: San Martín was full of embarrassment, and his friends in America showed their good will. He continued to live in a country house away from Paris, for his health and "because the hubbub of a great capital is unendurable." When he contemplated the possibility that destitution might oblige him to abandon his exile and become involved in the civil wars, he exclaimed: "My bile is aroused and I get into a vile humor." He suffered indescribably "on witnessing the ills which afflict our unfortunate America." Meanwhile, the crisis of the Plate grew worse: "The latest news from Buenos Aires doesn't leave the slightest hope for a peaceful settlement between the unitarians and the federalists, and the question must be decided with rivers of blood." And this is exactly what he had foreseen ten years before.

His economic situation became more stringent each day, and he said he would not be able to go on living in Europe "unless you help me by collecting my pension, a thing I believe to be impossible if Escobedo's revolution is a reality." This is what he wrote to O'Higgins concerning his Peruvian pension. Then he remembered Mercedes: "If I did not have a daughter I could endure the direst need, but my responsibility to her obliges me to follow a different course." So lived the patriot who had been called a robber, and so spoke the man who had been judged insensitive. "Truly," he exclaimed with bitterness, "when you consider that so much bloodshed and sacrifice have only served to perpetuate disorder and anarchy, it fills one's soul with cruelest disappointment and sadness."

Such was the state of his purse and his spirit when Mercedes fell ill of cholera in 1832, and when he contracted the disease from her soon afterwards. Without money and with no one but a maid to care for them in their modest house, San Martín could truthfully say that he had been on the point of dying in a hospital. And while he was convalescing from cholera he suffered a severe gastric complication. "All old houses are leaky," he had written five years before, referring to his old ailments. But the illnesses of 1832 were much more dramatic in form.

During these evil days there appeared, as if brought by some mysterious helping angel, young Mariano Balcarce, who married Mercedes, and old Alejandro Aguado who stretched out his friendly hand to his poor comrade. These two developments made a welcome change in San Martín's life. His daughter's future, which so preoccupied him, found its best solution in her marriage with Balcarce, and when the latter needed to go to Buenos Aires to work, Aguado provided $14,000[2] for the trip. As for San Martín himself, we already know how much Aguado did by giving him a roof for his head and comforting friendship. Argentines too little remember the debt of gratitude they owe to the memory of the noble Spanish gentleman who made it possible for the life of America's Liberator to be lived in a serene old age that was like clear twilight at the close of a long autumn afternoon.

Shortly after having moved to Grand Bourg, and just as he was beginning to find consolation for his misfortunes in the friendship of Aguado, San Martín became a terrible vexation to Manuel Moreno, Argentine representative in London.

This trouble with Moreno arose from San Martín's knowledge that Moreno had insinuated that he had made a voyage incognito to Spain and suspected that he had been involved in machinations against the governments of America. San Martín was indignant and wrote him a violent letter from Paris addressed to London, a letter which was a challenge to a duel. Did the intriguer perhaps think that he had gone to Madrid in search of "a job as valet to His Catholic Majesty"? Didn't his previous public service merit protection now from such foolishness? Manuel Moreno answered respectfully, denying any accusation and adducing documents, "because the time has come to cease arguing and allow letters to testify." But in spite of all this San Martín continued resentful. He spoke of going to London to give Moreno a "cudgeling," and he wrote to Guido that all the American diplomats did in Europe was "to be deceitful and to gossip." He writes to Guido:

Who would have thought that, with all the distance which separates me from my land, the only countryman who is in Europe should come to disturb my peace, the sole good I was able to enjoy separated from all I love best; and that at over fifty years of age I should have to be embroiled with a bully and with sword and buckler should have to defend myself from knaves and scoundrels?

A poet-priest, taking advantage of his sacerdotal character, pursued an honorable paterfamilias with mordant verses. And although by tradition the person of a priest is sacred, the offended man caught the clergyman, hanged him by his heels, and gave him a sound beating. The poetic friar never again wrote satiric verses.

San Martín refers to the story, and then adds this comment:

What a rascal! If I ever dig my nails into him he'll have to be made over again! And now I remember that he once offended you in a lodge session. Just leave him to me. I swear by the honored spirits of my forbears that I'll avenge the insult of this windbag if it's the last thing I do. But enough of joking, and let us confess that a man like that is a stigma on the State he represents.

San Martín had come to know Manuel Moreno in London in 1811. One of them was arriving from Spain to embark for America, and the other, still a very young man, had just buried his brother at sea, the illustrious secretary of the Junta de Mayo (revolutionary committee of May 1810). This memory did not extenuate the unpleasantness at all. We see by this episode of 1834 just how great was San Martín's indignation at being suspected of a supposed monarchical intrigue. But at the same time, once the thing blew over, he wrote his confidential commentary with a certain Cervantine humor. The theme of the supposed monarchism of San Martín (which we can call the theme of Punchauca, the true significance of which San Martín himself made clear long before) continued to furnish material for his intriguing enemies. And we have already seen how this offended him.

The nobility of the patriotic ideal which animated San Martín's deeds had not died within him, and during his old age he repeated on several occasions the profession of his American faith, republican and liberal. He constantly meditated upon the course of European politics in relation to America's future, and his correspondence contains opinions on the subject. In 1831 he wrote to O'Higgins:

If, as is not probable, absolutism is triumphant, there is no doubt that Spain will be aided by the Holy Alliance in her effort to reconquer her old colonies. *I do not fear all the power of this whole continent so long as we are united; but if we are not united, our dear country will suffer incalculable evils.*

"Our dear country" was, for San Martín, all of America as he spoke with his Chilean companion. He made this statement when the absolutist reaction reappeared in France.

From Paris in April of 1833, a short time before the incident with Moreno, he wrote to Mariano Alvarez of Lima:

The horizon is growing alarmingly dark again for this continent, not only because of the critical position of Turkey after the setbacks of her armies, but also because of the influence Russia has exercised in Near Eastern affairs, an influence which alarms the rest of Europe. If to this one adds the conflicts of interests between the representative and the absolutist governments, governments which can't exist side by side for very long without settling the question of liberty or oppression, a question no human foresight can predict an answer for, you have an inevitable struggle from which our America could gain infinitely [the letter is mutilated at this point, but it is possible to reconstruct the paragraph: ". . . gain infinitely if her governments conceived the idea of attracting the emigration of capitalists as well as workmen who could seek in our beautiful countries the tranquillity which this old continent would deny them."]

As time goes on, the peace he found in his home lent an impressive transparency to his ideas. Grand Bourg was like a monastery to his soul. There he meditated upon America and upon mankind. He cultivated American plants, practiced manual arts, and lived an ascetic and humble life.

"I am and shall remain in retirement from the world."

He wrote this from his retreat at Grand Bourg to his children, Mercedes and Mariano, in Buenos Aires in 1835.

In this manner he lived, in retirement from the world, until the end of his days, meditating upon America as in a long prayer for the future of his beloved continent.

After the cholera and the complications which followed had subsided, San Martín spent a season bathing in the mineral waters at Aix in Savoy during the month of September 1832. The following summer he returned to Aix in order to continue the hot baths which had done him much good, with the attendance of Dr. Soligny. This gentleman, doubtless at the suggestion of his illustrious patient, decided to undertake a scientific trip to America. Possessing a sizable fortune, he wanted to perfect his botanical knowledge and get away from his monotonous European life, as he put it. San Martín recommended this traveler as a learned philanthropist and an honorable man, mentioning in passing his gratitude for the careful way he had attended him during his stay at the baths.

In winter his indispositions grew worse again, because cold weather did not agree with him. Retired from intercourse with other people, he allowed a pessimistic note to creep into his letters. He was already coming to be the old man who had outlived the things which were the objects of his desire.

"The cold of winter has obliged me to leave my country retreat, but tomorrow I return to it, never again to leave my nook until the prospect of Buenos Aires is such that I may be allowed to return there to rest my bones."

In a letter to Mariano Alvarez of Peru, in April 1833, he complained of his misery:

This winter hasn't been as hard on me as might have been expected because of the weak state I was in at the end of autumn. Three or four new inflammatory stomach upsets have disappeared thanks to a few days spent in bed and a severe diet. If I haven't gained any ground, at least I have enough strength for a long trip to the baths upon which I fasten all my hopes of recovery.

The children of men who were his companions-at-arms in America paid him frequent visits at Grand Bourg. Daniel Guido Spano, a son of Don Tomás studying in Paris; Florencio Balcarce, brother of his son-in-law, a young Argentine poet now living in France; Francisco and Antonio Tocornal, sons of Don Joaquín, Chilean boys who were on a trip through Europe; one of General Prieto's sons, and Prieto says in a letter of presentation: "He is the 'little fellow' who sat on your knee so many times when you honored us with your welcome visits," and the father remarks that he is glad that San Martín can now see him as a grown man. One day a son of the Chilean general Pinto comes to see him, bearing a letter from his father: "Be so kind, my general, as to bless my son. It is my only ambition for him, and it will serve as a powerful stimulus to keep him in honor's path. . . ." San Martín was now the American Patriarch who gave his blessings to the new generations.

The one who most frequently visited the house at Grand Bourg was, of course, Florencio Balcarce. He writes to his brother who lives in Buenos Aires:

I have the pleasure of seeing the family now and then on Sundays. I would go there every Sunday if the steamships ran on regular schedules. The general enjoys to the utmost this solitary and peaceful life he so desires. One day I find him serving as armorer, cleaning his pistols and shotguns. Another day he is a carpenter, and so he spends every minute in some occupation that distracts him from other thoughts and gives him good health. . . . Mercedes spends her days battling with her little ones, more and more mischievous all the time. . . . Pepa understands French and Spanish, but doesn't talk yet. And of little Merceditas the grandfather reports he has never seen her quiet even one second.

One day this little granddaughter came crying to her grandfather's study, and in order to quiet her he gave her a medal tied with a yellow ribbon for her to play with; it was nothing less than the Bailén decoration. The little girl carried the toy away happily, and the grandfather forgot what he had given her just as the child forgot what she was crying about. Her mother recovered the medal and kept it. Today it is in the Museo Nacional of Buenos Aires. San Martín never once asked about it. The man who knew so well how to deserve medals valued them lightly.

Merejkovsky, biographer of Napoleon, says of Bailén that it "resounded throughout Spain, in France, in all Europe, as a loud slap in the Grand Army's face, in the Emperor's face. Bailén evens the score for what happened at Bayonne."

"Once honor is lost there is no way of recovering it; wounds suffered by honor are incurable," murmured Napoleon upon learning the news, turning so pale he seemed about to faint. And in the Council of State he sobbed as he spoke of Bailén.

"The spell of victory," adds Merejkovsky, "is broken; Napoleon can be beaten!"

Such is the importance of the battle of 1808 for which San Martín was decorated and promoted to lieutenant colonel. So he spoke with truth when he announced in his manifesto of 1820 that upon his departure from Spain in 1811 he renounced his fortune and an auspicious beginning. "Destiny," as he said in that manifesto, took him then to America to found our liberty. And thirty years after Bailén San Martín scorned his medal, giving it into the irresponsible hands of his granddaughter.

It was said at Aguado's house that Louis Philippe, the French king, had heard of San Martín's deeds in America and of his modest life for some years at Grand Bourg. So it was planned that San Martín should be presented to the King, but with that accustomed modesty which was based on wisdom, he skillfully avoided the realization of that plan by courteously putting it off. Was he to be considered a favor-seeking courtier? Was he nothing but an object of curiosity? It was a life of solitude and silence that he had gone to France to find. It was only just, then, that they should allow him to live as he wished, in silence and solitude.

In 1841 his friend General Miller proposed that he take a trip to Constantinople, Iran, Cairo, and Jerusalem, returning to Europe by way of Calcutta, Canton, Panama, and New York. It was an itinerary worthy of an English tourist, but San Martín, old and infirm, was just not interested. How could he be interested? Only a short time before, he had started south from France, and when he had traveled only one post stage he preferred to come home again on account of the heat. The same year, nevertheless, he visited Vendée, "with Rochejacquelein's book in my hand," seeing the historic places of the terrible war, where he "still encountered many people who had witnessed it."

The things of war had not vanished from San Martín's memory; in his bedroom he had a clock with a bust of Napoleon on it, and also some nautical scenes depicting the battle of Abukir, acquired in London and water-colored by San Martín himself, who, as is known, was something of a painter.

His love for painting must have been stimulated in 1845 when he went to Italy, going as far as Rome and staying a brief season during the winter in warm, bright Naples. But these trips were rare, and as a general rule he traveled only for his health. After 1834 his serene life was lived almost entirely in the quiet house at Grand Bourg. From time to time the house was visited by young writers of the new generation who had heard in America the echoes of his deeds and who wished to know the illustrious old man.

One day in 1843 young Juan Bautista Alberdi left the siege of Montevideo and came to Paris, where he saw San Martín for the first time at the home of Don Manuel José de Guerrico. San Martín had come from Grand Bourg for the interment of one of the daughters of the Spanish poet, Don Manuel Ochoa. San Martín entered Guerrico's drawing room dressed in a black frock coat, silk vest, and high collar, carrying his hat in hand. Alberdi was surprised to find him so different than he had pictured him. His modest air, civilian clothes, and unaffected speech, how different from the conventional type of warrior! He wrote:

I thought he'd look like an Indian, as so many times he had been described; but he is brown, like a man of rather bilious constitution. . . . I found him lively and facile of gesture; . . . his heavy, virile voice attracted my attention. . . . I had heard that his health had suffered much, but was surprised to find him looking younger and more agile than any of the war-for-independence generals I have known, not excluding General Alvear, the youngest of them all. . . . General San Martín suffers when he is inactive, and gets relief only when he is in motion. . . . His handsome, well-proportioned head has kept all its hair, although it is now almost entirely white.

Alberdi scrutinized him minutely: "his aquiline nose," "his small mouth," "his gracious smile," "his pointed chin," and also "his huge shoes." He did not wear side whiskers or mustache in spite of the fact that it was the style for old men. However, he wore a mustache later when his hair was all gray.

As a result of the casual encounter in Guerrico's house and a conversation with Balcarce, a visit to Grand Bourg was arranged for young Alberdi. It took place on September 1. He left the Jardin des Plantes district at eleven o'clock in the morning and arrived by the Orleans railroad at the Ritz station at one in the afternoon, somewhat frightened by his first experience with train travel. The trip from the station to San Martín's house required half an hour. He passed by many mud walls along rather sad-looking streets, admiring the trees and flowers of the park. He was greeted by Mercedes, Balcarce's wife, and he saw in her a marked resemblance to her father. She showed him the upstairs rooms where San Martín had his study, "worthy of a philosopher for its simplicity." Alberdi saw hanging on the wall the curved saber of the American campaigns. . . .

The conversation turned, naturally, to these campaigns, although San Martín spoke of them only on rare occasions.

What struck Alberdi most was San Martín's austerity, the modest way in which he spoke of himself. Although second-rate men become vain even about things they have never done, this distinguished person seemed interested only in asking pardon for his glory. The letter to Bolívar after Guayaquil, which Lafond published in 1840, had been given to Lafond by Bolívar's secretary, not by San Martín. Whenever anyone proposed that he reply to censure or amend facts in his favor he always refused to furnish the documents. He did not believe in taking advantage of polemics: he left his conduct and his papers to the judgment of the future. His only affirmation was that he did not "abandon" his Peruvian campaign; he merely left it for Bolívar to finish with the help of his Argentine soldiers, and this was accomplished actually. The peace of the continent required such a procedure. On leaving Peru with the title of Founder of Liberty, granted by the Congress, he carried Pizarro's standard as a symbolic trophy. He kept it in Grand Bourg. At the insistence of the young visitor from Tucumán Province, Argentina, San Martín himself showed him the 300-year-old discolored cloth. And Alberdi left Grand Bourg meditating:

"San Martín is Pizarro's conqueror."

Certainly he was. But Pizarro was the cruel conqueror of the noble Atahualpa. And was not San Martín an embodiment of the vanquished Inca, returned again to Peru to fulfill the eternal law?

In 1844 Florencio Varela moved from Montevideo to Paris in order to influence French opinion in favor of the unitarian faction's cause. This editor of the *Comercio del Plata*, elegant journal for Argentine *émigrés*, spoke with Thiers and others whom he impressed by his gentility and intelligence. On Sunday, April 7, he visited San Martín at Grand Bourg. In his "Travel Diary" he refers to that visit. San Martín invited him to dine at his home, and over their dessert the young Balcarce said to his father-in-law:

"Father, with your permission let us drink to the pleasure of having Señor Varela with us, and to his family's safe return."

San Martín agreed and, raising his glass, he directed some pleasant words to the guest, who was seated on his right.

Varela, much pleased, answered:

"I shall die happier now that I have known the man to whom our country owes most of her triumphs."

San Martín, full of emotion, began to cry, and amid his heroic tears he sobbed: "Cannot those barbarians be satiated with so many years spent persecuting decent men?"

Was he referring to himself, exiled because of partisan passions? Perhaps he referred to Varela, who shortly afterwards was assassinated in Montevideo? Did he refer to Rosas and to all the blind men of the civil war?

A short time after Alberdi's and Varela's visits, another Argentine youth came to the house at Grand Bourg from Chile, bringing a letter of introduction to San Martín signed by General Las Heras, written in Santiago on October 18, 1845:

This will be presented to you by Señor Don Domingo F. Sarmiento,[3] one of our compatriots who was precipitated to this side of the Andes by the torrent of misfortune in our country some time ago. Here he has been occupied in literature and in perfecting our educational system, and with the object of gaining greater knowledge for this task he turns toward the land where you now reside.

Señor Sarmiento, an enlightened patriot who because of his extreme youthfulness could not have known you during the epoch of your grand deeds, ardently desires to approach you now, esteeming you as one of the few living monuments of our history.

San Martín finished reading the letter, in which there were other phrases of friendly personal recollections, and fixed his black magnetic eyes on the young countryman in front of him, who likewise scrutinized him, anxious to begin the conversation as soon as possible.

Sarmiento was thirty-four years old. His rugged head and electrifying expression formed a contrast to his interlocutor's smooth old head and serene countenance.

They talked of Las Heras and O'Higgins, his companions of the Andes crossing; of Rosas and tyrannized Argentina, of Montt and Chilean progress, and of America's emancipation and education. Sarmiento told him of his life in San Juan, and these reminders of the province of Cuyo aroused San Martín's sympathy. Sarmiento's father, Don Clemente, was the one who had carried the news of Chacabuco to San Juan. The boy was only six years old then. The youthful visitor expounded the doctrine of "Civilization and Barbarousness" and finally confessed that his main reason for coming was to learn a few facts about American history from San Martín's lips. Relentlessly pursued by his aggressive guest, San Martín felt restrained.

"My papers are in order," was his only answer.

That great soldier did not wish to speak further, signifying that with those papers his history would be written later. And meanwhile he did not care to discuss himself.

"San Martín scarcely enjoyed talking about the past," Sarmiento said many years later, "and those who desired to hear him were obliged to use the greatest skill in getting him to touch the subject. A portrait of Bolívar which was in his room served me as a pretext to induce him to explain about the interview of Guayaquil."

Sarmiento used to brag about having a special gift for pulling all a man knew "right out of his craw," and in truth he proved with San Martín that he did have such a gift.

The fact is that a few days later the author of *Facundo*, a member of the Historical Institute of France, discussed the Guayaquil interview before that society. He even brought the stubborn protagonist of the interview to hear his discourse. What Sarmiento said at that time about the supposed mystery of that interview is just what is verified by the letter which San Martín sent to Bolívar when he returned to Lima; a document which I have copied in a preceding chapter.

Sarmiento was to succeed San Martín in another of America's epics of liberation. He went to Grand Bourg to receive the sacred torch from the Patriarch.

The Argentinians who visited the hero at Grand Bourg were, in the majority, enemies of Rosas and his system. Alberdi, Varela, and Sarmiento spoke ill of the tyrant. San Martín also censured Rosas' tyranny, as many of his letters clearly show; but the Confederation's international policy drew him toward the governor of Buenos Aires for reasons that demonstrate the temper of his spirit in old age.

San Martín was unable to view Rosas in the impassioned manner of the young fighters, not because he was old, not because he was removed from the scene, nor because he had never been offended by the tyrant, but simply because he had foreseen this marriage of revolution as something fatefully inherent in the peoples' lack of culture. As early as 1816 he had said, at the very first sign of regional grudges, that if things continued in such fashion the federation would be "a den of lions"; in 1820, that civil war would give rise to a new servitude; and in 1829, that political warfare would result in bloody extermination. He had not wished to use his saber in 1812 to seize power, nor had he wished to stain it with American blood in 1819, nor had he wished to fight personally against Bolívar in 1822, nor had he wished to accept the Argentine dictatorship in 1829. If all the men of the sword had followed his example, the democracies would have had another and better fate. No one followed his example, however; no one listened to his prophesies and teachings. It was as though some fatal destiny dragged these people toward tragedy. From his retirement following his renunciation at Guayaquil he commented in his letters about Bolívar's march toward the abyss, and expressed presentiments of Rosas' advent. Upon his return from the Plate in 1829 San Martín wrote concerning the Argentine revolutions:

In my humble opinion, the thing that prolongs this series of revolutions is the lack of guarantees backing our governments. In other words they depend upon three or four military chiefs who require a degrading sort of adulation, they depend upon the masses of the lowliest people in the capital, fickle, easy to direct at the whim of four demagogues like Tagle and a few rogues.

The focus of all the revolutions has been Buenos Aires. There one finds the cream of anarchy, dissatisfied and vicious men who live off the upheavals, men who, because they have nothing to lose, expect to gain everything in disorder. They make possible the preponderance of the three or four chiefs who wield power, those who in collaboration with one another depose or sustain the Government at will.

These things leading to disorders which grip the capital must disappear, without its being necessary to shed a single drop of blood. A couple of regiments of the militia of the countryside would oblige an unconditional surrender in fifteen days simply by preventing a single head of cattle from entering the city, as they have done before. Someone will say to this: "In such a case, the one who controls the surrounding country will be the real chief of the State." Yes, doubtless, Señor Don Tomás, and I too am of that opinion.

With the help of the rural element it won't be necessary to have a single soldier in Buenos Aires, because the civilians will be careful not to make any moves under penalty of starvation.

San Martín wrote this in 1833 with an absolute understanding of reality in the pampas region, a situation which was beginning to find a deity in Rosas, because Rosas was another Dionysiac son of the soil.

"I prefer," he adds stoically, "the voluntary ostracism I have imposed upon myself, to the enjoyment of such license."

In speaking this way he was doing nothing else except to describe actualities and to predict the fatal bunglings wrought by passions which for twenty years were indifferent to the high example of San Martín.

But in 1838 the River Plate was attacked by a European power. Rosas in Buenos Aires resisted this aggression, and San Martín considered this conflict as a problem of sovereignty.

Upon learning of the French blockade of the Plate in 1838, he offered his services to the Government in Buenos Aires. He knew which were his "duties as an American" and he only awaited orders to march. He did not think himself an "indispensable man," but if they deemed him useful he would depart immediately to lend his military services in whatever capacity designated for him. And once the war was over he would retire into a corner of his country "to leave his bones in the land which gave him birth," or he would return to Europe again if he could not live in his own country. He attributed France's blockade to a "peculiar fickleness of this nation," and he could find no justification for "any Americans who would join with a foreign power to humiliate their country, motivated by a contemptible partisan spirit." So spoke San Martín in a letter to Rosas when the Liberator of America was already sixty years old.

Rosas answered, thanking him for his offer and congratulating him on his attitude. But the suspicious tyrant very astutely advised him to stay in Europe where he could be useful to the Confederation in the conflict. A short time later he named him Argentine minister to the Government at Lima, a post which San Martín did not accept for very good reasons.

He would have liked to return to Peru, but he would not do so as Argentine minister: "the Peruvian Congress once named him generalissimo of that nation, and he created many personal connections during the exercise of his power in Lima." His situation would not be at all comfortable, and he would see himself involved in intrigues prejudicial to his own welfare and to the good friendship of both the sister nations.

In 1845, upon the outbreak of another aggression by England and France, who combined against Rosas, San Martín wrote to his friend, Don Federico Dickson, the Argentine Confederation's consul in London, a letter which expresses his censure: "They have planned the conquest of both banks of the River Plate, but they will never achieve it." They might be able to take Buenos Aires, but the level plains, their cattle and provisions, would remain in the hands of the natives. The city could be isolated by two hundred leagues of desert. Rosas had prestige in the plains country, and 8,000 gauchos with thirty artillery pieces were enough to blockade the capital by land if it should fall into the hands of the invaders. Buenos Aires did not fall, and the Argentine Confederation came out victoriously in this second aggression which San Martín censured. The old expatriate continued to defend American independence, proving himself to be a strategist who adapted his plans to the reality of each new American circumstance.

San Martín's letter to Mr. Dickson was published in *La Presse* of Paris four years later, when the question of the River Plate was restated in connection with the Lepredour treaty. This letter and another which San Martín sent to Minister Binau (whose acquaintance he had made at the home of Aguado's widow) were influential in the French cabinet and parliament in curbing the imperialistic policy. Saldías, the historian, has perfectly explained San Martín's patriotic intervention in that conflict which so preoccupied his epoch.

In 1846, a fugitive from the northern cold, San Martín had gone to spend the winter in Naples, and from there he wrote to Rosas: ". . . In the circumstances in which our country finds itself I would have been very pleased to be able to offer my services anew as I did at the first French blockade." Perhaps his services would not be found useful, but they would serve to demonstrate "the most unjust character of the aggression and abuse against our country by England and France, and also that our country yet possesses an old defender of her honor and independence. . . . Now that the state of my health deprives me of this satisfaction, at least I take pleasure in sending you these sentiments, along with my boundless confidence that the justice which assists us will triumph."

Rosas answered San Martín's letter:

"The moral influence of your patriotic American prayers in the present circumstances, as in the earlier French blockade, amounts to a distinguished service to the independence of our nation and of the American continent, to which you consecrated with such glorious honor your best days."

San Martín's generous attitude during the two conflicts between his country and the European powers had established between him and the governor of Buenos Aires a ceremonious and cordial correspondence. Rosas, for his own part, showed a very appreciative attitude towards San Martín which warmed the old man's heart. And one has to look here for the sentimental motive which prompted the leaving of his saber to Rosas.

Rosas had written to him: "The gratitude of the Argentine Confederation and of America can never forget you: it will follow you into retirement and always honor your memory."

When young Mariano Balcarce, recently married to San Martín's daughter, came to live in Buenos Aires, he was named an official in the Ministry of Foreign Relations by his uncle, Governor Balcarce. But upon the latter's fall from the Government, Mariano lost his position, an event which profoundly embittered the father-in-law. Rosas himself repaired this injury by naming

Mariano to a post in the Argentine legation in France. San Martín thanked Rosas for making amends.

In 1849 the Restorer paid official homage to San Martín in his annual message to the Buenos Aires Legislature of that year, pointing out those merits which made him worthy of the national gratitude. San Martín, who was now blind, caused that allusive passage to be read twice, and he thanked Rosas for his thoughtfulness with the emotion of an old man who in so many years of activity had received so many affronts from the Argentine governments. To these grateful expressions from San Martín, expressions no less surprised than sincere, the tyrant of Buenos Aires answered:

"How do you expect us to act otherwise when your heroic accomplishments live among us, made greater still each day by your civic virtues?"

Rosas was on the eve of his downfall, and San Martín was on the eve of his death.

Thus the stoic old man spent fourteen years in the house at Grand Bourg, which was like a monastery for him, and in which he stated, "I am and shall remain in retirement from the world."

Following a voyage on the Seine in 1841, a Captain Lafond of the French Navy wrote San Martín:

"Twice I have passed your cottage on my way to and from Fontainebleau by steamboat, and I have saluted the modest dwelling place of one of the greatest of men. You are the Cincinnatus of America."

In spite of the long period of time he spent in that retirement, his nostalgia for America was never diminished in the old man's heart. A visit or a letter would always awaken his desire to return there before he died.

Referring to Chile, he says to José Ignacio Zenteno in 1842: "I have had, and now possess, more good friends in your country than in any other spot in America." And then he mentioned those Chilean friends: "O'Higgins, yourself, Generals Prieto, Cruz, Pinto, Borgoño, and Blanco; Señores Salas, Palazuelos, Barra, Pérez, Cáceres, Quinta Alegre, Tagle, Larrain, Zañartu, Sánchez, Aldunate, and others." There is, in that long list and in the following reflections, an old man's satisfaction: "From no country has he received more demonstrations of sincere affection," and he recalls the attentions showered on him when he was ill in Chile on returning from Peru; the announced appointment to the Council of Agriculture; and the invitation given him to come live there, an invitation patently disinterested since "it is directed to an old sick man whose services are absolutely nil in value." In 1843 he received a decree from Chile which was the finishing touch of satisfaction: "General San Martín will be considered as in lifelong active service with the Army, and he will receive the entire salary of his rank even when he lives outside the territory of the Republic." The decree was signed by President Bulnes and his minister, Santiago Aldunate. Upon reading it and seeing those names at the bottom, he imagined that perhaps Chile could be the refuge for his dying days, and then he spoke of "how awful it has always been to live in Europe" and how pleasant it would be for him to return to the Chilean land of his past victories. And he let his old man's fancy wander: "to live there a retired life in company with a few and old friends, surrounded by the memories of our past endeavors to make old age more bearable."

Along with the Argentine Confederation and the Republic of Chile, the Peruvian Government also was courteous to San Martín during his last years at Grand Bourg, which were the most tranquil of his long exile.

San Martín scarcely ever left his residence, except for some exceptional visit or for most urgent business, or to take brief trips for his health. His great feats were over, and he was in the renunciation stage, like a great master of wisdom, in solitude and in the silence of a great, loving heart. His life was now completely in the realm of the spirit, as though he did not exist save in memories and in dreams. It was a contemplative life that unfolded in Grand Bourg during the fourteen years that San Martín spent there.

The old house still stands, and in one of its parlors there is a portrait of the hero. On the wall is a plaque which tells of that virtuous dweller of other times. The historic lodging is now an asylum for children cared for by a religious order of sisters who are accustomed to offering prayers for the soul of the saintly man who lived there from 1834 until the revolution of 1848. In that year San Martín, now a septuagenarian and almost blind, moved to Boulogne-sur-Mer, stunned by the social unheaval that was beginning to stir the world.

From Boulogne-sur-Mer the following year, San Martín wrote to President Castilla of Peru, describing that European revolution of 1848 in terms that seem to have been written today, and which show how he kept even till the last hours of his long life his clear comprehension of social phenomena. He says:

The passage of time, which should have brought improvement in France's condition following the revolution of February, has not produced any change, and things are the same, or worse, as much because of the events of May 15 and of July as on account of the lack of public confidence inspired by the men who are now heading the administration. The maxims of hatred for the rich which have been instilled into the working class by the demagogues; the sundry and powerful factions into which the nation is divided; the uncertainty brought on by the likely imminence of a general European war; the paralysis of industry; the increasing cost of an army of 550,000 men; the marked diminution of revenue and the lack of business confidence, have done away with security, the basis of public credit. And this sad picture is not the most alarming one for the nation's politicians: the great difficulty is *in feeding in the midst of industrial stagnation* a million and a half or two million workers who will be without work next winter and deprived of all means of existence. This future evokes a great attitude of distrust especially in Paris, where all the people who have something to lose ardently wish for the continuance of the

present state of siege, preferring a government of the sword to the alternative of falling into the power of the socialistic parties.

To sum up: France and a large part of Europe are in such a state of disorder and
tumult that one cannot discern the final outcome of this immense revolution. But
what is most probable today is a civil war, and it will be very hard to avoid unless,
to distract the contending parties, there is recourse to a general European war accompanied by revolutionary propaganda. Regrettable expedient, but the partisans
do not think of consequences.

San Martín who, in his youth, had passed through the Napoleonic catastrophe in Spain, and during his maturity had lived through the epic of
American emancipation, was now witnessing, in the declining hour of his old
age, the epiphany of the proletariat, whose revolution continues today, the
result of the previous two upheavals. Aged and blind, he left Paris in great
distress and abandoned the house at Grand Bourg to look for one last refuge.
For the last time he thought of America; but he paused at the shore at
Boulogne, hesitant and homesick, facing the stormy sea. . . .

VII.   ECCE HOMO

One day, from his exile, San Martín wrote in a confidential letter some words
which I have cited before, and which I now repeat because they reveal all the
serene compassion of his soul for the peoples among whom he carried out his
mission:

"They have saluted me with the honorable titles of thief and tyrant, and
in spite of their having treated me as an *Ecce Homo,* I love them and am
interested in their happiness."

Human life is not solely a chronology of deeds, but also a configuration
of thoughts and a plot of passions. San Martín felt the call of mercy and
Christian sacrifice, and that is why so many of his contemporaries did not
understand him. Opposed to his disinterested heroism there was destined to
be a sort of aloof lack of understanding and the aversion of those who move
only in the shadowy circle of primitive instincts.

San Martín encountered the Carreras in Mendoza, Lord Cochrane in
Chile, and Riva Agüero in Peru, and all of them later became his enemies.
They fomented the injurious propaganda which, through perverse libel, contributed not a little toward discrediting the great man. The Carreras were
later joined by such international adventurers as Brayer, whom San Martín
expelled from the United Army; and Cochrane was joined by others of his
nation, such as Stevenson, who accompanied him in the Pacific; and Riva
Agüero was joined by the malcontents whom the paladin left in Peru, and

who expressed themselves most virulently in Pruvonema's famous book.[1] The meeting with Bolívar at Guayaquil generated continental rivalries which were added finally to these other animosities. The acts of violence which war obliges such as the persecution of the Spanish Royalists of Peru and certain executions such as were meted out to the Carreras in Argentina were used as charges against the good name of the Argentine statesman. The Spanish histories written by Camba and Torrente presented him as a cruel man, and the memoirs of his personal enemies considered him the most detestable man as well.

A caricature of the period shows San Martín disguised as a tiger grasping in its claws the heads of Manuel Rodríguez, Mendizábal, Prieto, Conde, Morillo, and the Carreras, with this caption: "Look at his victims and deduce the fate that awaited you. Have fear still!" But the deaths of those people were imposed by the exigencies of the revolution and can be imputed to others with more justice than to San Martín.

History has demonstrated with documentary evidence that he was far away from the countries in which they were executed, or that he even interceded in some cases to save the criminals, or that he simply fulfilled his military duty in the heat of war. They have called him a cruel assassin on this basis with no more reason than those who called him incapable and cowardly because he refused to set fire to Lima and delayed his entry into the city while planning to gain the support of public opinion first, in order to enter without bloodshed a city he had previously won over by his moral genius.

Another caricature presents him with a large sword and spurs, riding on a burro (O'Higgins) and driving before him a herd of sheep which represents "The People of Chile," according to a placard. The burro is dropping dung in the form of coins which a man with two faces is catching (Pueyrredón), while San Martín brandishes a bottle labeled "Rum" and carries some more bottles in a kind of haversack.

History has demonstrated, also with documents, the complete abnegation of Chileans and Argentinians in the Andes campaign, the disinterest of San Martín and O'Higgins, and how the former carried out the campaign so sick that he had to take opium in order to allay his pain and sustain his efforts. For all of this his enemies called him a thief and a drunkard, as evidenced by the sketch.

A third caricature represents San Martín on a throne, disguised as a bloodthirsty cat stepping on some cadavers beheaded by his butchery, and stretching out a claw to receive the imperial crown offered him by a kneeling soldier, again the noble O'Higgins. San Martín is saying: "I will make you prince of the blood and you will be next in importance to the King." In the background an orator addresses a multitude of blindfolded people, exclaiming: "People, remove the bandage from your eyes! You are victims of a traitor, slaves of a tyrant!"

Nevertheless history has proved that if San Martín ever countenanced monarchy it was only diplomatic artifice or military strategy, for he founded democracies in Argentina, Chile, and Peru. San Martín never had ambitions for personal power, nor did he exercise power harshly.

Although the sympathizers of the restless Carrera brothers promoted hostility against San Martín in Chile, the noblest Chileans spoke in his favor: Blanco Encalada, Zenteno, Cruz, Freyre, Pinto, Prieto, Bulnes, and—the greatest of all—O'Higgins, his best friend. Chilean history, through the investigations of Barros Arana, Vicuña Mackenna, and many others, has reestablished the truth; and Chilean gratitude has raised statues to glorify him.

In 1817, on coming to Buenos Aires after the victory at Chacabuco, San Martín decided to talk personally with José Miguel Carrera, imprisoned in the Cuartel del Retiro. Unexpectedly he went to see him on the twelfth of April. As he entered he stretched out his hand to him, but Carrera refused to give him his. In spite of this rebuff, San Martín went on with what he had to say. He advised Carrera not to attempt to return to Chile, since O'Higgins was resolute in his intention to suppress the slightest disorder. The prisoner answered insolently that he would not go without counting on means for resisting violence. Overlooking this defiant attitude, San Martín persisted in telling him that the United Provinces could name him their minister plenipotentiary to the United States, out of consideration for the services he had rendered toward his country's independence. Carrera was obstinate and refused to come to terms. San Martín was still patient, advising him to reconsider, and he "left as he had entered—grave and stern." This is what is known about the visit, from Carrera's own admission and the account of historians.

After the interview, San Martín returned to Chile and José Miguel escaped to Montevideo, from where he plotted a conspiracy that was discovered. His conspiracy, in 1818, planned a series of assassinations in which certain French adventurers were involved, one Robert chief among them. A few were shackled and thrown into jail in Buenos Aires. "These I know are secure," said Director Pueyrredón,[2] and the others "I have ordered brought in dead or alive." It appears that there was a design against the lives of San Martín and O'Higgins. Pueyrredón adds:

"The Javiera woman and other Chileans are involved. Ask O'Higgins whether I should send this wretched woman to Chile or just deport her. All the others are my own affair."

When in 1818, after the battle of Cancha Rayada, Luis and Juan José Carrera, convicted of conspiracy against the Government of O'Higgins and accused of other crimes, were shot in Mendoza under the supervision of Luzuriaga, Monteagudo, Vargas, and other functionaries, San Martín intervened to ask mercy for the criminals. Nevertheless the responsibility for their execution was imputed to him, and their brother, José Miguel, now fled from his Buenos Aires imprisonment and, taking refuge in Montevideo, promoted a campaign of abuse against San Martín, inspiring the cartoons cited above, and the diatribes of *El Hurón*, which he printed on his own press acquired for the purpose. In the face of these attacks, San Martín considered issuing a manifesto explaining the origin of his differences with José Miguel Carrera, and in his rough draft the following can be read:

El Señor Don José Miguel Carrera will allow me to draw comparison between his conduct and mine: through his own fault he sacrificed the Chilean Commonwealth, and I twice have gained its liberty. He only wants to dominate his country as though it were an entail of his property, and I desire nothing more than to see it independent.

In reference to the death of Luis and Juan José he said simply: *"I have not ordered the execution of your brothers."* And: "After the battle of Maipú I interceded before the Chilean Government with all my influence in behalf of the Carreras and won their pardon. But it was too late."

This is true, and the letters by which San Martín made his appeal, as well as O'Higgins' reply, are known.

The young wife of Juan José Carrera, passionately in love with her consort, to whom she sent fervent letters while he was imprisoned in Cuyo, went to see San Martín to plead for her husband's life. Although his enemies said that San Martín received her discourteously, the truth is that he interested himself in her cause and wrote O'Higgins, asking clemency for the criminal: "If the small services I have rendered Chile merit any consideration, I place them in the balance, asking that the action against the Carreras be quashed. These individuals may someday be useful to the nation, and Your Excellency will have the pleasure of having used clemency for the public benefit."

O'Higgins reluctantly acceded to this petition, upon San Martín's responsibility:

Your Excellency's worthy mediation in favor of the Carreras can't help but produce fully the results which Your Excellency proposes, and even though the existence of these men should endanger the nation, Your Excellency, upon whom rests the salvation of this State, will know how to reconcile the risks involved with the object of your pretension.

The news of the pardon arrived too late at Mendoza.

San Martín added, addressing José Miguel in the planned, but not published, manifesto:

I have held your brothers' lives in my hands, and I assure you that if, instead of being only an auxiliary general, I had been born in Chile, I would have saved the governor of Mendoza the trouble of having executed them; and even though, I repeat, not having had the slightest part in the execution, had I been governor of Mendoza, it would have taken place long before.

The execution of the Carreras was, then, necessary in the judgment of San Martín; and he himself would have carried it out had he deemed that his birth and rank warranted it. But he did not order them killed, and, on the contrary, he interceded in their favor.

The shooting of José Miguel took place in 1821 while San Martín was in Lima; and neither can this execution be imputed to him, in spite of the fact that San Martín held an unfavorable opinion of this Carrera. In a letter to Sarratea, written in Europe many years after those disagreeable events, he admirably describes José Miguel: *"An imprudent man, he sacrificed everything to vengeance,"* he says. And later he adds: "Carrera, although having much native talent, was an assassin and an immoral man by education and character. He boasted of his vices, allowed himself to be dominated by his passions, was ambitious out of vanity and not for any noble purpose, and all his political moves were errors."

After the battle of Rancagua, Carrera, sheltered in Cuyo, wanted to exercise there his authority as a Chilean official, which San Martín did not allow him to do, and this was the beginning of the enmity between the two, aggravated later by Carrera's rivalry with O'Higgins, whom San Martín always supported.

As did the Carreras and their gang of thugs, Cochrane and his friends abused San Martín later for motives equally personal and impassioned.

San Martín being detained in Mendoza for reasons of health and for the recall of the army from Chile, ordered in 1819 by the Government of Buenos Aires, Cochrane endeavored to take over the command of the expedition to Peru and to give Freyre, a Chilean soldier, the command of the land forces. San Martín returned to Chile in January of 1820 at O'Higgins' call. Cochrane's attempt rebuffed, he renounced his command of the fleet. But San Martín tried to dissuade him, not foreseeing the vexations which the presumptuous lord would cause him in Peru. These arose in 1821 over the fleet's pay, and over Cochrane's criticism of the military inactivity of his chief or the ambition he supposed him to have. Mitre says concerning Cochrane and his relations with the Protector:

Later, on seeing his adventurous schemes destroyed, he concluded that San Martín's prudence was timidity, and his *sang-froid* was indolence, until he underrated him as a general with his accustomed haughtiness and tried to eclipse him out of jealousy, through prodigious exploits such as those involving his frigate *Esmeralda*.

The generalissimo, who in his equanimity did not force himself to punish the heroic and skilled mariner, endeavored instead to bind him to his own destiny, faithful to the promise he had made him in Valparaiso that their fortunes would be identical, when he saved him, as the admiral himself admitted, from the ignominy of dismissal by the Government of Chile on account of his imprudent actions. However, San Martín always withheld from him his confidence and even his esteem.

Before the taking of Lima, Cochrane had asked San Martín for money to finance Lady Cochrane's return to London. The Chilean Government had already paid him something, and Cochrane had 23,000 pesos in paper money besides, which he didn't want to convert into pounds sterling because of the unfavorable rate of exchange. But after Lima's capture his financial negotiations involved larger sums: he wanted 110,000 pesos for his frigate *Esmeralda*, 150,000 pesos for back salary, and in addition the expedition's pay roll, which amounted to more than 400,000 pesos. He asked to have this sum paid in Peru, or to be allowed to return to Chile to make collection, as it was becoming impossible to manage the crew. These constraints caused a serious unpleasantness between San Martín and Lord Cochrane, and because of this Cochrane was later one of his detractors.

The interview between Lord Cochrane and San Martín took place in the Palacio de Gobierno of Lima on August 5, 1821, in the presence of Monteagudo and García del Río, the Protector's ministers. Cochrane came to demand the pay owed to the fleet, and it was common knowledge besides that he was resentful of the omission of his name from the medals commemorating Peruvian independence. He also complained about San Martín's having assumed the protectorship. Since he presented his demands for money with a certain acidity, San Martín interrupted him to command respect for his authority:

"Don't you know, milord, that I am the Protector of Peru?"

"No, señor," Cochrane answered.

"I have ordered my secretaries to inform you of the fact."

"Well, that is not necessary now that you have told me personally; I hope, however, that this will not interrupt the friendship which has always existed between San Martín and me."

According to Cochrane's view, San Martín had been unfaithful to the instructions of the Chilean Government in assuming control of the nation and had broken his promises by not paying the fleet as he had said he would on embarking at Valparaiso. San Martín justified his protectorship on the basis of military necessity, which would not forbid the next convocation of the Congress; and as for what was owing to the fleet, he explained that by the condition of the exchequer, although assuring Cochrane that he would fulfill his earlier promise. Cochrane seemed to speak in defense of Chile, holding San Martín as a rebel chief in relation to the Government of that country, and he threatened to withdraw his fleet from the authority of the Protector. Irritated by such insolence, San Martín exclaimed angrily:

"You can take your fleet wherever you please, and you can leave whenever you please: all I need is a pair of brigantines."

Under the circumstances, with a reply like that, San Martín was literally burning his ships.

In view of the unpleasant turn which the conversation was taking, the ministers retired from the salon together. Cochrane remained in silence and then got to his feet to leave.

"Forget, milord, what has happened," San Martín said to him on bidding him good-by.

"I shall forget it when I am able to do so," the admiral replied.

Days later Cochrane began correspondence with San Martín about the payment of the fleet and about the disagreeable incident, lamenting its occurrence:

Would to God that Saturday, August 5, had been erased from the days of my life. . . . The painful remembrance of it makes me very unhappy. How could San Martín, honorable and just, have been capable, even in a moment of exasperation, of expressing feelings that should never have been found in his liberal spirit? But has he not done just that? Has not San Martín, whom I thought to be my friend, said to me with cold indifference that I could order the fleet wherever I pleased; go anywhere that occurred to me? Hasn't he told me: "You can go whenever you like"? Ah, General, that was a regrettable day for me. I shall never be able to see you again until I feel I can do so without a tear in my eyes. I feel desirous of avoiding human society. I shall retire where Lady Cochrane's gentle friendship will augment the comfort I long for. I have never hurt any man or committed acts for which my conscience reproaches me. . . .

With the exception of yourself there hasn't appeared a single man capable of elevating himself above the crowd and commanding the political horizon with an eagle's glare. But if you trust to the wings of chance, like another Icarus with wax wings, your fall could smash Peru's liberty and involve all South America in anarchy, civil war, and despotism. If kings and princes only had one single man in their councils who on all occasions would tell them the naked truth, many errors would be avoided, and humanity would suffer less evil. . . .

I have valued your interests more than my own, even at the risk of incurring your lifelong disfavor. And that would have happened had not your talent for seeing things in their true colors intervened, a talent which you have fortunately acquired, *not having been born a king, but having been born to govern, nevertheless.*

He tells him that he can be the Napoleon of South America, or at least one of the greatest men who figure in the world of that day; and that he has the power to choose his career. San Martín answers:

I know very well that one can't fly on wings of wax. I distinguish the course that I must follow, and confess that, great as are the advantages gained up to now, many reefs still remain which, without the help of justice and true faith, cannot be avoided. No one covets more than I do the skill with which to finish the work I have begun. Dragged by the imperious dictum of circumstances to occupy the position of leadership, *I wish to return with honor to the simple status of citizen once the nation is free of her enemies.* . . .

I am ready to receive whatever counsels you may wish to give me, milord, because perhaps the splendor which is deliberately placed in front of my eyes dazzles me without my knowing it.

This correspondence throws clear light upon the incident concerning the fleet and upon the character of both the antagonists. Just as on other occasions analogous to this, San Martín speaks like a master of serene calm facing a neurotic person. Several days later Cochrane seized the bars of silver bullion on board his ships and sailed away from Peru to become a detractor of San Martín in his memoirs.

Nine years after the death of the Protector, *The Times* of London, referring to Lord Cochrane's memoirs, published this partial and lamentable judgment on February 13, 1859:

The brave admiral proves that San Martín, his companion-at-arms, was a monster. To say that he was a fraud is not enough. With the most extraordinary seriousness he told lies that were obviously absurd. He was, at the same time, a coward, a braggart, and totally incompetent, although he somehow always managed to come out all right. But what he did was worse than doing nothing at all, for he betrayed every interest except his own.

This posthumous newspaper squib in *The Times* has no basis in history. It is merely a trifling echo of Cochrane's abuses, and Cochrane certainly is incapable of being a judge in history's courts, since in life he was a detractor of San Martín over questions of money. An impressive man with a piratical soul; a man who was mercenary and a romanticist at the same time, Cochrane said equally harsh words about his country, England, when he left to travel the world like one of Byron's characters.

After having served in the European wars, Thomas Cochrane was expelled from the House of Commons and sentenced to the pillory on account of some questionable manipulations on the exchange. In that critical moment Alvarez Condarco of Tucumán Province, Argentina, the Chilean Irisari, and Alvarez Jonte of Buenos Aires, who were in London as agents of San Martín to organize a fleet, persuaded Cochrane to go to Chile and serve American independence in naval expeditions being prepared by the Argentine liberator. He accepted the offer, and upon saying farewell to his country he pronounced, at a banquet, these words which show his flair for the dramatic:

They say that I am ruined. I am not ruined in spirit, for I resist all oppression. I am going to absent myself from my country, but I do not regret leaving those who build churches with the money they take from others; I am not sorry to leave the religious propagandists, because I know they are a bunch of scoundrels; I am not sorry to leave the inventors of new taxes, because they are a plague on the nation and are good for nothing except to be destroyed like harmful insects; I am not reluctant to leave behind the government spies, nor those who cut off the heads of Englishmen in order to justify government measures.

Such words are sufficient to define Cochrane's character, but that does not alter the fact that he was a daring seaman who lent important naval services to the cause of American independence. He commanded the Pacific squadron under the leadership of San Martín, whom he wanted to supplant, and with whom he quarreled over the delay in paying the fleet's crews. The noted adventurer, after having served republican America in the Pacific, went to Brazil to serve the Portuguese monarchy in the Atlantic. Several of Cochrane's admirers, among them Stevenson, the Englishman, in his memoirs, took up his animadversion to San Martín, portraying the latter as an inept soldier and an ambitious failure. From such envenomed sources, during a long period, certain publicists have taken sustenance and have continued to attack San Martín's glory.

And as for the great London journalist who slandered San Martín in 1859 on account of the atrabilious lord, we remind him that other Englishmen such as Lord Macduff, Robertson, Haigh, Basil Hall, Miller, and Mary Graham, who knew the Argentine hero personally or who were qualified witnesses of his deeds, had a more just estimate of his merits. He was estranged from Cochrane by the curse of gold, the curse that haunted the heroes of Germanic epic poems. In spite of those quarrels with the "metallic lord," as San Martín himself called him, San Martín refused to retain any vengeful rancor against him. Once the affair was concluded, he scarcely ever thought of it again. Lady Cochrane, the admiral's beautiful wife, told Miller in London in 1827 that while she was passing through Brussels she had seen San Martín, but that he had not greeted her.

San Martín was greatly afflicted on learning of this, and he answered Miller:

You have done well to assure Lady Cochrane that I have never seen her in any Brussels street; once I saw her, I believe it was at a concert, but at a great distance, and truly she was pleasing to the eye, although she appeared a little heavier than before; had I encountered her, you may be sure that I would have paid her my respects, because the differences that have come between her husband and me should never include his charming wife. Should you see her, please give her my regards and return the compliment of her affable remembrance.

In these words gallantry is found, but no rancor.

The case of Riva Agüero is analogous to that of Cochrane and of Carrera. That Peruvian patriot was envious of San Martín from the moment the latter arrived in Peru, even though he calculatingly supported him. In San Martín's absence he engineered the downfall of Minister Monteagudo. When San Martín left Peru he promoted a revolution against the Congress and wrote to San Martín, calling on him to take part in the civil war. San Martín indignantly replied from Mendoza in 1823 in words which follow:

In writing me such a message you doubtless forgot that you were addressing a general who has the title of Founder of Liberty in the country to which you have brought nothing but misfortune. If I offered my services to the government council and to you, with the necessary provision of being under the command of another general, it was in fulfillment of a promise I made to Peru when I left there, a promise to help her with my efforts if she should find herself in danger, as I believed she was after the setback at Moquergua. But how can you possibly have persuaded yourself that General San Martín's offers (to which you have not deigned to reply) were ever made to any individual, and much less to such a contemptible person as yourself? Your audacity in making this proposal that I should wield my saber in a civil war is incomprehensible.

Knave! Don't you realize that this saber has never been stained with American blood? And you invite me to stain it at the same time that you proscribe Congress and declare it traitorous in the newspaper of the 24th of August, which you send me. You do this to the Congress in whose formation you have supposed yourself to have had the principal part. Yes, you had a large part all right, but it was in the low intrigues which you concocted for the election of deputies, and which you continued for the purpose of discrediting, through the press and through your despicable henchmen, the allied armies and a general from whom you had received nothing but benefits. That general will always be held responsible by Peru for not having rid her of a scoundrel such as you, loaded with crimes. . . .

You say that you were going to lead the army that is in Huaraz. Is there one single officer who can bring himself to serve against his country, and above all, under the command of a cur like you? . . .

Impossible! I am writing to Colonel Urdininea, giving him a faithful description of the black soul that is in you. Oh, enough! A rogue shouldn't occupy the time of an honorable man any longer!

So he ends, unceremoniously, his terrible reply. San Martín must have written it during one of those trances in which, as he used to say, "my bile is agitated." Such moral reactions were the only things that usually exasperated him and caused him to abandon his serenity. The harshness of this reply was the cause of Riva Agüero's loathing, and he inspired the attacks against San Martín published in Peru after 1822 by the *Abeja Republicana* ("The Republican Bee") and other publications.

San Martín replied in 1831 to José Rivadeneira, one of his correspondents who usually sent him all the bad news from Peru:

In Lafuente's manifesto there are some highly curious fragments, of whose existence I was completely ignorant. For example, Riva Agüero's letter to one Zubiate y Falcón, in which he announces my arrival in Montevideo, at the summons of yourself and others, with the design of being crowned king. As for Pezet's writing (or *Treasure*, as it is called) which is printed for the charitable purpose of discrediting a general who has had the good fortune of contributing to the liberty of the nation which engendered, unfortunately, such a despicable man, I know nothing of its contents, but I do know that said Pezet was a man whom I honored and with whom I had not the slightest differences. It wouldn't be at all strange if this

Treasure is the legitimate brain-child of Riva Agüero himself, and is attributed to Pezet who, I have been told, is dead.

Analogous to the case of the *Treasure* is that of the famous *Pruvonema* (anagram for *Un Peruano*—"A Peruvian"), attributed to this same Riva Agüero, and which carried the defamation of San Martín to the extreme.

The book written by Pruvonema (two volumes of "memoirs and documents of Peruvian independence") has pages that pertain to San Martín. They refer to the earlier epoch when he fought in Chile: "The period of San Martín's stay there in Chile's time of mourning." On the victory at Maipú the following is read:

San Martín was far away from his army during that battle, stretched out on the ground and so intoxicated that he didn't give one small command. . . . Drunkenness [it adds] is a vice that is firmly rooted in San Martín, and it can be said that he spends a great part of the day sleeping off its effects.

Concerning the Peruvian epoch, the insults are worse:

San Martín was a scoundrel. . . . He did not fulfill what he promised in his decrees. . . . He wished to be crowned Emperor of Peru. . . . He forcibly took over the command, plundered estates (farms, ranches) jewels and money. . . . He pounced upon the jewelry and wrought silver of the pawnshop dedicated to the widows' and orphans' gratuity fund. . . . The memory of such rapine as that, among so many other examples, makes his name more execrable each day that passes. . . . He burned the Archives in Lima, conniving with Monteagudo to cover up his systematic robbery. . . . He annoyed women and committed murders . . . this adventurer who only sought his personal fortune. . . . San Martín's conduct, it is said, was so detestable that it can only be compared with that of the barbarian chieftains who come armed to sack the nations they invade, and who leave behind them horror, death, and desolation. . . .

At the time he left for Guayaquil, he gave Monteagudo an order to have six leading Peruvian patriots assassinated treacherously. . . . The perfidy and cruelty of San Martín can only be compared to that of Nero and Caligula.

Such are the judgments of Pruvonema regarding San Martín; but later it is seen that he judges Bolívar with no more benevolence:

The coarse vices of a wild soldier were perfected in him; the army had handed the empire to a monster; it was enough to look into his face to know the atrociousness of his soul; his glance was that of an outlaw.

This description of Phocas, a tyrant of Byzantium, written by the Count of Segur, serves Pruvonema as a description of Bolívar. And then he adds regarding both liberators: "The atrocities of Pizarro himself in the conquest disappear from sight when compared with the execrable crimes of San Martín and Bolívar." In the case of this writer we deal not with a simple case of anti-San-Martín "Cochranism" like that of Stevenson, but with a much more profound wickedness, and it is hard to believe that "a Peruvian" would write such things, in view of the fact that not even the Spanish chroniclers such as Camba and Torrente went to such extremes.

Riva Agüero's hatred found a propitious atmosphere among a part of the Spanish population of Peru and among the aristocracy of Lima who were injured by harsh provisos or by war taxes imposed by the revolutionary government in 1821 and 1822. Some of those acts were, nevertheless, not sanctioned by San Martín, or were done while Torre Tagle exercised delegated power and the Protector was away. Let us see what San Martín himself wrote with reference to this in Paris several years after the events. He says:

At this time the Marquis of Torre Tagle was at the head of the administration: he came one afternoon to La Magdalena to consult with the general about the necessity of expelling the Spaniards from Lima, for they not only undermined public opinion, but they were influencing the heavy desertion the army was experiencing. This was proved by two deserters from the light infantry battalion, captured the day before. They testified that an unknown man had invited them into a saloon to take a drink and had urged them to desert, giving six pesos to each one and clothing for disguising themselves. They carried out his suggestion at ten o'clock that night, near the Plaza de Toros. To these facts was added the accusation of several patriotic friars who, by means of the confessional, could corroborate the conduct of the Spaniards.

In view of this, General San Martín immediately agreed upon the measure for their expulsion, but imagine his surprise when in the following day's *Gaceta* he read the decree of expulsion with an added proviso that the Spaniards would be obliged to hand over half of their possessions! This was a measure first of all impolitic, because it gave rise to the impression that not only was the administration unjust, but also was bent on despicable rapine; and second, unrealizable because the European Spaniards who remained in Peru were absolutely destitute, and even in the case of those who had some money, it was easy for them to hide it with the infinite number of sympathizers they had, and in this way laugh at such a dirty and inopportune measure.

"A dirty measure," indicative of "despicable rapine"—such is San Martín's qualification of that abhorrent decree which cost his own reputation so dearly.

But he was not at that juncture in the bravely revolutionary Argentina of 1812, nor in austerely patriotic Chile, but in that old City of the Viceroys in which there were still viceroys ten years after the revolution of May 1810, and where the counterrevolution was based on three centuries of courtly venality and prejudice.

Years before there had already circulated a couplet about the uncertainties of the revolution in Peru:

> *Arequipa ha dado el sí,*
> *La Indiecita seguirá:*
> *La Zamba vieja ¿qué hará?*
> *Sufrir jeringas de ají.*[3]

Gold, which in Germanic myth was the damnation of gods and men, was so for this hero, San Martín, in Peru, the land of fabulous mines. Confiscated ranches were given to government men; it was decided to give rewards of money to the officers, and this aroused regrettable rivalries among them; finally came the quarrel with Cochrane, likewise over a question of money. Poor San Martín! So indifferent to gold, and yet he had to bear this infamous cross until the ancient ill fate of the heroic myths was realized in its entirety for him!

When San Martín went to Paris for the first time from Brussels, he went to visit an academy on Mi-chaudière Street, where several young Spanish-Americans were being educated. It was an establishment founded by illustrious Spaniards expatriated for their liberal views, among them, Moratín, Silvela, Vallejo, and Salvat. The students were Argentinians, Peruvians, Colombians, and especially Chileans. When they learned of San Martín's presence, they came running and surrounded him with much ado, like grandsons crowding about their grandfather. The visitor wore a gray frock coat, rigorously buttoned, and he was leaning on a thick cane. He surprised them all by the clear memory with which he recognized each one by his father's name.

Among the Chileans there were Soler, Lastra, Toro, Larraín, Borgoño, and also young Vicente Pérez Rosales, who refers to the episode in his memoirs, together with a recollection of walking under the trees of the Tuileries with San Martín on another afternoon. On that occasion, Pérez Rosales recalled things associated with his infancy, and with his family, and San Martín, treating him like a comrade, induced him to talk about the opinions that were held about him in Chile.

"What was being said about the Argentinians in Chile at the time you left? Did the Chileans remember the Army of the Andes?"

"There are certain events which cannot be forgotten," answered Pérez Rosales, "and the crossing of the Andes is one of them."

"Good. But are the few sincere friends I had when I left still there in Chile? Friends in name only, my young friend," the exiled hero went on, placing his hand on the shoulder of his interlocutor, "flock in great numbers around anyone who has jobs at his disposal, but there is a scarcity of sincere friends."

Pérez Rosales explained that upon the downfall of O'Higgins, his friends, who were also San Martín's friends, were either obliged to keep silent, or suffered persecutions. . . .

"So that my poor reputation doesn't find the atmosphere too healthy there for similar reason?" commented San Martín briskly.

"That is the truth," responded the young Chilean, "because—oh, I don't dare——"

"Have courage, young man; just keep in mind that you are speaking with one of your fellow students. As you were saying, because . . . ?"

"Because, just as O'Higgins has enemies," Pérez Rosales timidly answered, "they are not lacking for you; actually among the sons of the Old Chile [the Chile which endured Rancagua] there are very few who do not attribute the unfortunate death of the Carreras to you and Don Bernardo [O'Higgins]. And neither is there a lack of evil tongues which say funds placed by Chile in your hands for the liberation of Peru were mishandled."

"On hearing that, San Martín pressed his face violently between his hands," relates Pérez Rosales, "and he remained such a long time in this agitated state, it was evident that it signified painful recollections and the bitter sorrow which human ingratitude always causes in the hearts of upright men; I was already beginning to repent of having been so utterly frank in my answer, when, straightening up and drawing a quick breath, with his bewildered gaze fixed in the treetops, he exclaimed in a low voice, as if talking to himself:

" 'Good-for-nothing gringo [foreigner]! Little admiral, who considered any money he couldn't pocket for himself, as stolen by someone else! Excuse me, my dear colleague, I don't know what has happened to my senses. . . . So they are saying all those things yonder? Well, they must have reasons for that . . .' "

And so, having recovered his habitual serenity, San Martín continued, explaining all about the affair of the Carreras; and as for his own intergrity, he smiled sarcastically, pointed to his well-worn clothing, showed his old gloves, and added only:

"There it is at a glance!"

Don Vicente Pérez Rosales adds to the account of that doleful scene, written in his memoirs during his maturity, the recollections of the many generous deeds with which the victor of Chacabuco marked his passage through Chilean history.

San Martín, who knew the human passions so well, and who considered them with wise equanimity, wrote during his exile a reply to Guido, who was urging him to explain his conduct publicly and to defend himself against his calumniators:

The average man judges the past with true justice, and judges the present according to his own private interests. . . . Five sixths of the world's inhabitants are stupid, and the rest are rogues, with the exception of a few good men. . . . I will be in no hurry to satisfy such people, because I am sure that the men who matter will do me the justice which I think I well deserve.

And he was not mistaken then, just as he was not mistaken in 1822 when he said in his manifesto on leaving Peru that the sons of his contemporaries would give the true verdict regarding his conduct. And that verdict was given, half a century later, by Señor Paz Soldán, the erudite Peruvian historian:

> . . . He was confident that the sons of his contemporaries would give the true verdict. It is certain that many of those contemporaries abused the memory of that hero; but we, sons of theirs, whose judgment is the true one, declare before the universe that San Martín is the greatest of all heroes, the most virtuous of all public figures, the most disinterested of all patriots, and the humblest in his greatness. We affirm that Peru, Chile, and the Argentine Provinces owe their life and their political being to him; that San Martín injured no one; that he suffered with Christian resignation, even in the simple retirement of private life, the most undeserved attacks; that nothing was ever revealed by his speech that would have stained another's honor; and that there never came from his pen any of the corrosive venom of defamation. In all this he is greater than Bolívar and Washington.

San Martín was completely right in saying while he was exiled that his enemies in America had treated him as an *Ecce Homo*. But these offenses, as he foresaw, have been rectified by posterity.

The executive board of the International Bureau of American Republics,[4] on a motion by Elihu Root, Secretary of State of the United States, resolved that a bust of San Martín be placed in the Hall of Nations alongside that of Washington. Referring to this project, Mr. Root said:

> San Martín died in exile without having been understood. For those generals and politicians who plunged the American republics into bloody revolutions for their own egoistic ambitions and for their followers' benefit, the flourish of audacity which power and fame engender has the appearance of desirability, while the spirit of abnegation in favor of a cause appears to be weakness. But the people of these nations, raised to the heights of duty and honor, have finally understood that the great South American, the only one worthy of being compared with Washington as an example of patriotism, was the modest soldier who cherished his cause more than his position and who was motivated only by his interest in the welfare of his country, as much while exercising power as when giving it up.

That is America's judgment, the judgment which San Martín expected posterity to accord him all through the long and arduous years of his old age—years spent in the philosophic serenity of his long exile.

VIII. "THE DIONYSIAC CONTINENT"

From the very time of the events themselves, San Martín's contemporaries considered that his entry into Lima was his crowning achievement, but that his abdication following Guayaquil was an act that would need to be explained by history. Both episodes mark the zenith of San Martín's life: one in the military realm, the other in the realm of spiritual perfection. In the comprehension of them both lies the accurate posthumous evaluation of his genius.

But a comprehension of these episodes was not immediate, on account of San Martín's desire to make the Peruvian campaign a bloodless one; on account of the enigmatic silence he preserved in the face of strangers who censured him; and later, on account of the wanton passions which Bolívar left behind him as a fatal expression of a regrettable South American peculiarity.

Following the conference of Guayaquil, Vice-admiral Blanco Encalada had written a confidential letter to O'Higgins on September 9, 1822, containing his impressions of Bolívar, whom he had just met:

Guayaquil is united to Colombia by Bolívar's wish and by his bayonets. Bolívar's moderate ambition extends much farther than you and the world have imagined. The many conversations I have had with him, and the frankness he has shown me, plus my observation of his conduct, have enabled me to know him. It is sufficient to say to you, as a Chilean and as a friend, that I consider him a dangerous enemy against whom we must necessarily guard ourselves well.

Perhaps Bolívar's personal traits justified such judgments. Doubtless these judgments found fertile soil in the regionalistic passions of our peoples and in the traditional fanaticism of Hispano-American culture.

From Lima in 1823, a friendly correspondent wrote to the absent San Martín: "The Chileans and Argentinians are fraternally regarded in Peru, but not the Colombians." However, it is certain that many Peruvian leaders were taxed by the arrogance of the Argentinians, and also that there existed suspicion between the Argentinians and the Chileans and between the Colombians and Venezuelans. These regionalisms became extremely virulent later on, taking on really tragic proportions throughout the South American continent. Ecuador had been the battleground for two hegemonies, personified by the elemental imaginations of their followers in San Martín and Bolívar. Calumnies were also hurled at San Martín in Chile and Argentina and at Bolívar in Colombia, and both were threatened with death. Such was the curse of the dionysiac continent upon which both heroes moved, different in character, but identical in their mission, and both subjected to the same destiny.

The victory of Pichincha, in which the grenadiers of Buenos Aires sent by San Martín to the aid of the Colombian Army took such a brilliant part, was celebrated with a banquet in Quito, at which Bolívar presided, and to which came Colombian, Peruvian, Chilean, and Argentinian leaders in cordial fellowship. This marked the de-facto alliance between the two liberating armies, that of the North and that of the South. To celebrate it, Bolívar, in one of his many toasts, indiscreetly said:

"The day is not far away when the triumphal banner of Colombia will reach Argentine soil."

Perhaps Bolívar, in his Caesarean enthusiasm, wished this to be a demonstration of affection for the Argentinians who were seated at the table, but it was not so interpreted, and it is said that Major Juan Lavalle, one of the grenadiers of the crossing of the Andes, and an energetic campaigner at the battle of Río Bamba, asked for permission to make a toast, and replied to Bolívar's imprudent statement:

"The Argentine Republic is independent and free from Spanish domination, and has been so since the day on which she declared her freedom, May 25, 1810. The Spanish have been defeated in all their attempts to conquer her territory. Our national anthem commemorates our victories."

This was the first public sign of the suspicion that was beginning to be manifested between these two regions, the North and the South, a suspicion awakened by the martial lust of the Venezuelan captain who was soon to create, with pieces of Argentine and Peruvian territory, a new state which he named with his own name, congratulating himself on becoming an eponym after the fashion of the classic conquerors.

Well known are the fervent words with which Bolívar, in an official paper, celebrated the adoption of his name as the national title of Alto Peru[1]:

"Only God had the right to call that land Bolivia. What does Bolivia mean? An unbridled passion for liberty. God's rapture could find no other adequate expression for its sentiments, so He took away your name and *gave mine to all your generations.*"

Following what happened at Quito, an analogous episode occurred in Guayaquil during a banquet. Bolívar was seated across the table from Colonel Manuel Rojas of Argentina, secretary of the Peruvian Legation. He kept staring at him, trying to force the colonel to lower his glance, but not succeeding. Finally the Liberator grew nervous and asked him patiently:

"Who are you?"

"Manuel Rojas."

"What is your rank?"

"Colonel," and he showed his epaulets.

"What is your nationality?"

"I have the honor of being from Buenos Aires."

"It is well known for its insolent air."

"It is an air befitting free men," the Argentinian calmly replied.

Both men were then silent. Their table companions were apprehensive. And the comments began to scurry about.

All these rumors created an anti-Bolívar feeling which was a dark contrast to the brilliance of his military genius. Talk of it reached the ears of San Martín, but he did nothing to foment it. He too knew opposition, and he felt himself above dealing in such misery. San Martín was more fully aware than anyone else of Bolívar's defects, or better, of his ill-starred destiny, since his defects were but part of his greatness, as abysses are necessary to make mountains impressive; but he also knew better than anyone else what Bolívar's greatness consisted of, and we shall know later what his true opinion of him was. In spite of that opinion, the South American atmosphere was propitious for all kinds of schismatic intrigues, and San Martín was even forced to defend himself from them during his exile and old age, because he had no desire to foment them.

In 1823 the biography of San Martín, published in London by Gaul y Jaen (pseudonym of García del Río), arrived in Peru. And with reference to it, Salvador Iglesias wrote San Martín, enclosing one of Bolívar's letters. San Martín was still in Mendoza, and Iglesias was in Lima:

I send you the Bolívar enclosure. Bolívar has told me that he has been very pleased to see your public life written about, and that although some of your enemies attempted to prevent its coming to light, he had exerted his influence somewhat to keep it from being suppressed.

But the correspondent adds: *"I know the contrary to be true, from what I have heard."* San Martín reads this and is silent. Perhaps he smiles.

Notwithstanding the mutual esteem of Bolívar and San Martín, the discord between these two supreme leaders grew, and the passions of their subalterns were polarized in their names.

General José Rivadeneira tells San Martín in 1829 about the condition of Peru following the retirement of the Protector:

. . . A Council of three imbecilic, useless, cowardly and ignorant individuals who are good for nothing. The army deposes and manages it shamefully. They put that cur Riva Agüero in power, and he is succeeded by the infamous Torre Tagle. Then comes Bolívar. What meanness! What adulation! And how this man terrifies everyone! Santa Cruz is the only one who has performed well. La Mar succeeds him and is a useless, false, hypocritical man, a nonentity perfectly suited for doing no good. He himself has said that he is not a good leader. In war he might prove to be so-so, but we have already begun to lose. God grant that the results may not be that the Colombians should dominate us as colonials, and may He grant that Bolívar's portrait, which used to be hung with that of Columbus and your own in the salon of the Palacio, be returned to the place where it was. It was Bolívar who ordered his portrait to be put in the place of yours. La Mar ordered Bolívar's picture removed. . . . But La Mar is no friend of yours, since Luna Pizarro, one of your avowed enemies, is his angel and his director.

Salvador Iglesias paints a picture in 1826 of Chilean anarchy, which is just as bad as it is in Peru and in all America:

Chile is completely disorganized, her Government is discredited, without public support, and without money. Last month a revolution against Freyre was attempted, but came to naught. And as a result, Colonel Sánchez, Zañartu, Soler, Argomedo, his son, Fontecilla, Don José Antonio Rodríguez, Don José María Palacios, Dr. Marín, Father Oro, and others were banished to Lima; Zenteno has fled with his family to England (so they say); Boyles, Viel, and other leaders are stigmatized, and Freyre is suspicious that they may attack him. Freyre has gone to Chiloé with an expedition, leaving the Government to his three ministers.

Freyre had taken office following the ouster of O'Higgins, and the latter wrote San Martín long letters full of affection and stoicism from his exile in Peru.

José Rivadeneira, already mentioned as one of San Martín's friends, wrote him several anecdotes about Bolívar from Lima.

At Bolívar's invitation, Rivadeneira went to visit him one morning in his Lima palace, just as the Liberator was on the point of leaving for Alto Peru.

"General," Bolívar said to him, "I told you from Huanuco that you could count on being the governor of El Callao. It is the key to Peru's defense, and were I not so positive of my election, I would not offer this post to you. Here is the official notification, and I have already told Heras to include all the honorary titles and an expression of my confidence."

"I reiterate my thanks to Your Excellency," responded Rivadeneira, "but before I accept the appointment it will be necessary for us to come to terms."

"What terms are you referring to?"

"There are two of them: first, I have enemies without having offended anyone, and should someone out of ill will spread gossip about me, promise not to take action without first hearing me. And second, you must understand that I am an intimate friend of San Martín, so much so that should we by misfortune find ourselves in hell, I would still love him and be loyal to him. On account of this loyalty, my enemies will surely slander me and say that San Martín must be coming back to Peru and that I am probably planning to hand the fortress over to him."

"I have nothing against San Martín," Bolívar answered. "He laid the foundation stones of liberty and independence, although he has been ill rewarded. He went away and left the work unfinished, and I have been called to save Peru. He has been defamed in every manner, with gross injustice, even in the public press. In Quito one of his mortal enemies told me that San Martín had not stolen even one maravedi, and that 30,000 pesos which had been given to him for his services by the governments of Buenos Aires and Chile were invested in a London firm that has gone bankrupt, and now he doesn't have anything but the income of his daughter, in her own right. I am glad to hear of your loyalty to San Martín, because such a trait is found only in a decent man."

Several days later Rivadeneira went to visit Bolívar at Magdalena and found him entertaining Alvarado, Unanue, Larrea, Salazar, and others. Bolívar showed Rivadeneira one of his portraits which he had commissioned for the purpose of sending to London. Rivadeneira didn't like it very much, and so Bolívar, half joking and half in earnest, said:

"It's easy to see that, since it isn't your friend San Martín's portrait, you don't like it."

Bolívar then asked that a portrait of San Martín be brought from inside. It had been dropped, and the painting of the face was torn from ear to ear. In that condition it had been displayed in public in Santiago, and Salazar had brought it to Bolívar in order to ingratiate himself with him. On seeing the mutilation, Rivadeneira protested:

"Only Chileans are capable of showing their gratitude in such an infamous manner to the man who made them independent and for whom the true patriots retain love and esteem. My General," he added, "we have already come to an agreement regarding San Martín, and I remind you that Your Excellency has confessed his merit. All that has been said against him is slander, and I reaffirm to Your Excellency my loyalty and friendship for San Martín, which I shall cherish even in hell."

A few days later Bolívar said to General Salom:

"My esteem for Rivadeneira is based not only on his conduct, but also on the loyalty he has for San Martín in the midst of so much envy and rivalry."

Bolívar ordered a portrait of San Martín hung in the Palacio at Lima beside his own and that of Columbus, and others were responsible for removing it once the Liberator had fallen.

San Martín for his part, always valued the portrait which Bolívar himself had given him as they parted at Guayaquil. In his bedchamber in France the portrait of the great Venezuelan was side-by-side with his own, and both are preserved today in the Museo Nacional of Argentina.

General Tomás Guido wrote San Martín from Buenos Aires in 1826, telling him that he had been forced to leave Peru, exiled in direst poverty, and with no place to go. This was the fate suffered by several others among San Martín's Argentinian comrades, following Bolívar's entry into Lima. "My only crime," writes Guido, "must have been a frank declaration I made to General Bolívar that I would never make common cause with your enemies." According to Guido, Bolívar told him that San Martín, at Guayaquil, had expressed a bad opinion of the secretaries of the delegation he had left in Peru in charge of the Government when he left for Guayaquil. And besides, Bolívar complained that San Martín did not write him from his exile.

San Martín answered:

I am finally driven to believe (and only by your assurance) that all the men who have refused to blow a defaming trumpet to discredit the ex-general San Martín have been persecuted by General Bolívar. I say that it is necessary to believe this because, since I have seen so much, so much, of the low and dirty gossip which unfortunately abounds in our America, I had hesitated to believe several anonymous letters which have been written to me about this. Besides, I was unable, and am still unable, to understand the motive for such strange conduct. It cannot be rivalry, since the successes I have had in the wars of independence are very subordinate in comparison to those successes which Bolívar has given to America's cause. Furthermore, his own letters (the originals of which are in my possession), up until the time of my departure for Europe, show a sincere friendship for me. I can't find any other motive than friendship for his complaint that I have not written him any more since my departure from America. And frankly I will say that my failure to do so has been occasioned by an excessive scrupulosity, or call it pride, on my part, because having been granted a pension by the Congress of Peru, and finding Bolívar at the helm of that State, I concluded that to continue writing him would be considered as a stratagem of selfish interest, especially had I done so after his latest triumphs. If my failure to write him is causing him displeasure (and I don't find any other reason for it), I say with feeling that smallness of spirit does not befit the great name he has acquired.

As for the criticisms they have assured you I made to the general concerning the secretaries of the delegation, I shall only say that this can't be anything but plain gossip invented by one of his hangers-on. The secretaries of the delegation were my own, those whom I had chosen. To discredit them would have been to make myself a party to their bad conduct, or at least would have shown a shameful weakness in having kept them on if they were not capable to discharge their duties. You will bear in mind that, upon my return from Guayaquil, I told you the opinion that I had formed of General Bolívar, to wit: a man of extreme fickleness in principles and full of childish vanity. But I have never thought that he deserved the title of impostor, for that is a defect not worthy of a personage of such elevated rank.

At this point his pen seems to stop out of sheer nausea:

Enough! To delve further into such base gossip is unthinkable.

Actually, what preoccupied Bolívar in 1826 were the rumors that San Martín was ready to return to Peru. And Guido's preoccupation was that San Martín would not come back, and that he had abandoned the Peruvian scene in 1822 for good.

"I will never forgive you," Don Tomás Guido tells him, "if you should retire from Peru, and history will be hard put to give favorable interpretation to such a step."

San Martín was moved by the censure of his faithful friend. He answered:

When I am dead you will find among my papers (in my last will there is a clause which expressly requires that they be delivered to you) original and highly interesting documents. These, and the notes I have made, which you will find in order, will show my public conduct and the reasons for my withdrawal from Peru. You will tell me that in the public opinion and in your own, these documents should come to light during my lifetime. There are several reasons why I do not share this view, but I shall cite only one of them, which to me is conclusive: the average man judges the past with true justice, and judges the present according to his own private interests. With respect to public opinion, are you perhaps unaware that five sixths of the world's inhabitants are stupid, and the rest are rogues, with the exception of a few good men? After positing this axiom of eternal truth, you will see that I will be in no hurry to satisfy such people, because I am sure that the men who matter will do me the justice which I think I well deserve. As for history's being hard put to give favorable interpretation to my separation from Peru, I shall say with Lebrun:

> *En vain par vos traveaux vous courrez à la gloire;*
> *Vous mourrez, c'en est fait, tout sentiment éteint:*
> *Vous n'êtes ni chéri, ni respecté, ni plaint.*
> *La mort ensevelit jusqu'à votre mémoire.*

These reflections of San Martín when he was already in exile and when Bolívar's successes might have awakened his envy demonstrate the rigid moral discipline of his spirit. He gave a noble explanation of his epistolary silence in regard to Bolívar during his exile. He put a stop to intrigue, scorned South American gossip, and he spoke of that glory for which others were so vigilant with the serenity of a just man who trusted only in posterity. That understander of men well knew that contemporary passions are not usually conducive to the discernment of true merit, and that it is necessary to depend upon history, because only she is able to re-establish justice. Glory, as a sensual possession of applause, did not interest him, and Lebrun's verse came to his lips like an expression of his own wisdom. Tribulation and the passage of the years had brought his genius to maturity, and he spoke with the words of the poets and meditated with the thoughts of the saints. He added in his long letter to Guido:

Notwithstanding these principles and the scorn I may have for history, knowing the partisan spirit, the low flattery, and the sordid selfish interest which usually motivates writers, I cannot overlook the fact that I have a daughter and friends (even though precious few) whom I must satisfy. With this object, and for that which they call glory, I have worked two years in making extracts and arranging documents. I do not do this for self-justification, but so that the deeds and motives upon which my conduct has been founded during the time I have had the misfortune of being a public figure may be verified. Yes, my friend, I say misfortune because I am convinced that *one will be what one must, or he will be nothing.*

In fine, if you, as you say, will never forgive my separation from Peru, wait until the next packet sails and you will rectify so terrible a sentence. At the present it is not possible for me to go into the necessary details of this interesting matter, because the mail leaves this afternoon for England and I must take advantage of it in order to make sure this reaches there in time to catch the packet that leaves for Buenos Aires this month. When you see my exposition, it may be that you will change your opinion, because I am sure that you will know things that you do not now know, and that will surprise you in spite of the many things you have seen during the revolution. You will understand that I shall have to take certain precautions, being obliged to entrust this interesting exposition to the risks of the mails; nevertheless I shall tell you enough so that you may form an idea.

The confidential exposition which San Martín promised to Guido is unknown today. Perhaps it was lost, since in that epoch the Buenos Aires postal service intercepted his correspondence. In any event, the papers and other confidential information which he left furnish all the truth we need to know.

Scarcely having returned to Europe from America, San Martín dedicated his leisure time and good will to the documentation of his historic actions, and he wrote his friend, Don Mariano Alvarez of Peru, from Paris in 1833, telling of his intellectual tasks:

The absolutely private life which I have lived without variation since my arrival in Europe gave me the idea of writing the record of my campaigns from the year 1813 to 1822, for two reasons: first, these memoirs might be of some use to our country, and, second, to occupy my time, since I can't bear idleness. This work, begun for my own entertainment, took on greater scope than I had intended, with the help of my papers I had left in Buenos Aires and which I picked up during my trip to Montevideo in 1829. These documents, gathered at first out of mere curiosity, include a complete collection of all the public papers and pamphlets published in Peru, Chile, and Buenos Aires from 1810 to 1812; authenticated copies which I had made of the secret orders of the Spanish Government, and other interesting documents found in the archives and secretaries' offices of Chile and Peru; transcripts of original records of the principal trials of the Lima Inquisition, of the secret correspondence of the commanders in chief of the Royalist armies with the viceroys of Peru, and of the latter with the viceroys of Nueva España [Mexico], Santa Fe de Bogotá and Quito, and of my correspondence with the independent governments of America.

Don't think that these memoirs will see the light immediately. No, my friend, they will not be printed until after my death. First, because with this safeguard they will be written with the most severe impartiality and veracity, without self-justification; and second, because my own knowledge is not sufficient to present them to the public in a sufficiently finished style. The work done to date is simply the arrangement of the facts in their chronological order, together with the corroborating documents, year by year, beginning with 1813 and continuing to 1822. After my death, if my son-in-law thinks that this organized material may be of some use to our America, as I believe it will be, he and his friends will seek a skilled pen that can bring these memoirs profitably to light.

In this revelation several characteristics are found that should be underlined: the amplitude of the plan, the manner of documentation, the hero's evaluation of his life's importance, his desire to be useful to his country with these memoirs, his intellectual honesty ("without self-justification"), and finally his modesty in leaving the publication to the judgment of his family, and the definitive editing to pens more skillful than his own.

This collection of papers is without doubt the one which San Martín once offered to Guido, and the one which the Balcarces[2] presented to Mitre, which has been since published in twelve volumes, and which I have utilized in writing this Life, searching through and behind the anecdotes for the hero's true spirit. These papers, together with his personal correspondence, document the deeds and the thoughts of the paladin, apprehended in his deepest intimacies.

On April 9, 1827, General William Miller, from London, asked San Martín, who still resided in Brussels, the reason for his split with Bolívar. The Englishman perhaps wished to write a few words about it in his memoirs in answer to certain rumors that he gathered in Peru. Miller was a friend of San Martín, and of the truth.

"According to some insinuations I have heard from a *certain person*," he says, "he is seeking to give people the impression that you wished to be crowned king in Peru and that this was the main purpose of the conference at Guayaquil."

San Martín held General Miller in high esteem. The preceding year, upon learning that he was traveling in Europe and was thinking of going to Brussels to visit him, San Martín answered that it would be for him "a pleasure to embrace him and especially if you should wish to come stay in my house, where you will find a soldier's quarters, a roast, a bottle of wine, and absolute independence."

We know what San Martín thought of Miller from this same letter of 1826: "If I had had the good fortune to have only six men in my army who had possessed your knowledge and virtue, the war in Peru would have ended two years sooner than it did." In another letter, on learning that Miller is thinking of returning to Peru, he was pleased, "because you are the only soldier who has not been involved in the political antagonisms of the local factions." Had he not so highly esteemed him, San Martín would not have invited him to stay in his home, since he lived frugally in a gloomy misanthropic mood. On account of his liking for Miller, and the fact that the humbug about the coronation had offended him, he was going to talk of Guayaquil, in spite of his habitual silence upon that episode of his life, due to his consideration for Bolívar and the American cause. He never spoke of it publicly. Now, at the request of Miller, and so that a lie wouldn't have a leg to stand on, he was ready to lift the curtain slightly and show the truth about the meeting, although not knowing who the "certain person" might be to whom Miller alludes. At any rate he was not interested in knowing the slanderer's name, only the slander itself, and it is worth noting that San Martín and Miller both had the decency not to name the person:

If, as I do not doubt (and only because General Miller says that it is true), the certain person has spread these insinuations, I say that, far from being a gentleman, he only deserves to be called a notorious impostor and despicable rogue, since I can assure you that had my intentions been as he says, he was not the one who made me change my plans.

As for my trip to Guayaquil, its sole object was to procure from General Bolívar whatever help he could spare for the termination of the war in Peru, aid that, even ignoring the interests of America in general, was just and necessary compensation for the help which Peru had lent for the liberation of Colombian territory. My confidence in achieving good results was greater than ever, since the Colombian army had grown in size with prisoners after the battle of Pichincha, and now numbered 9,600 bayonets. But my hopes were in vain, since the Liberator, in my first conference with him, declared that, making every possible effort, he could spare only three battalions with a total force of 1,070 men. This help did not seem enough to bring the war to a close, since it was generally agreed that success in the campaign could not be expected without the active and effective co-operation of all the Colombian forces. And so it was that I made my decision on the spot, thinking it my duty to make every sacrifice in behalf of the nation. On the following day, and in the presence of Vice-admiral Blanco, I told the Liberator that, having allowed the Congress to be convoked the following month, the day of its installation would be the last day I would stay in Peru, and I added:

"Now you possess, General, a new field of glory in which you will set the final seal on American liberty."

I authorize you to write to General Blanco to verify this. At two A.M. the following day I embarked, and *Bolívar accompanied me to the boat and gave me his portrait inscribed with a statement of his sincere friendship.* My stay in Guayaquil was not more than forty hours, enough for my purpose.

At this point, San Martín brusquely stopped as if he disdained to continue speaking further of the imputed charges against him, and casually turned to other subjects:

"Let us leave the topic of politics and proceed to something of greater interest to me. I thank you for the news you send of Commodore and Mrs. Bowles." And thus he turned his back on the disagreeable humbug.

It seems likely that at Guayaquil they may also have talked, incidentally, about forms of government for America. But this topic, we repeat, could never have caused an estrangement between the two leaders. San Martín told the Chilean envoy in Paris, Don José Pérez, in 1832, that Bolívar did not think monarchy possible unless the kings were Americans, to which San Martín would have responded that the people would not be able to respect "those whom they had known as *naranjos* [orange trees]," referring to the nun who saw an image of Christ carved from the wood of an orange tree on the convent grounds, and who was unable to worship it, because of this.

Bolívar repeated, in a letter to Peñalver in 1822, that phrase of Voltaire's on the divine right of kings: "The first king was a successful soldier." According to these letters, San Martín's thoughts were far removed from any idea of coronation, since he had been known as a "naranjo"; but Bolívar's case was different, since he was a "successful soldier" and could have, like Napoleon, founded a dynasty. Bolívar did not establish an empire, but he did create a lifetime presidency in the constitutions he drew up, and he exercised a dictator-

ship. San Martín did nothing like that; he renounced the power of government and left the choice of each liberated people's destiny to popular suffrage.

One of Bolívar's letters to Santander, concerning the famous meeting, says
of San Martín: *"He does not wish to be king"*; and a report of his secretary to
the Colombian Government in 1822 on the same subject, says: "If the Protector's statements are sincere, no one is farther from occupying a throne." So
San Martín told the truth in his reply to Miller in 1827.

It is true that in the last days of his protectorship he commissioned his
minister García del Río to make a diplomatic move of ambiguous nature in
London with the purpose of gaining England's support for America in the
struggle against the Spanish kings. This move was never carried to its conclusion, and for corroboration of this, let us see what García del Río himself
wrote to San Martín from Santiago, Chile, on March 21, 1822, while on his
way to England:

> In one of the bulletins you will note that Abreu [commissioned by Ferdinand VII
> to negotiate acceptance of the Spanish Constitution in America] was a prisoner
> here. I am glad, because this gentleman has been imprudent enough to tell about
> what took place at Punchauca, adding besides, the *horrible imputation* that we
> were going to Spain in search of a little Bourbon for Peru.

García del Río's move must have been analogous to that which Bolívar made
later with Campbell, in other words, like San Martín's gesture at Punchauca,
a new diplomatic stratagem.

M. Lafond de Lurcy wrote to San Martín in 1839 asking for information for
his book *Voyages* about the events in Peru during the independence period,
at which time Lafond visited the ports of Guayaquil and El Callao as an officer
of the French Navy.

I have no knowledge of any of San Martín's letters containing the solicited
information; but, judging from certain indications in the correspondence which
is preserved in his archives, it appears that San Martín may have talked with
Lafond about the questions he had propounded, and that from this talk comes
much of what the book published by Lafond in Paris in 1844 says, in the
second volume, about the conference at Guayaquil:

> Stevenson, Miller, and Baralt confess in their works that they are ignorant of
> the matters discussed by the two liberators of Spanish America and that they have
> been unable to raise the veil which covers them. More successful than they, I
> have been able to go back to the sources. Here are the data I have obtained from
> General San Martín and from Bolívar's aide-de-camp, who served as his secretary
> on that occasion. . . . San Martín wished to deal with three major points: first, the
> return of Guayaquil to Peru; second, replacements for his division; and third, some
> means of bringing the war to a close quickly. This last point was the one which
> interested him most. He foresaw the difficulties of ending the war soon, without
> the aid of Colombian forces. The divisions of Chile and Buenos Aires were re-
> duced to half their strength.

As can be seen, there was nothing at all about a monarchy or a republic. Guayaquil's annexation to Colombia was already a fact, so nothing remained save the military question of bringing the war to a close. Lafond adds:

Until then, San Martín had done much more for Spanish America's independence than had the Colombian liberator. He had helped organize the republic of Buenos Aires, had established the Chilean Republic, and had almost entirely freed Peru of Spaniards, who now retained no more than the interior. On the other hand, Bolívar had just finished the war in Colombia, thanks more to his generals than to his own efforts. Páez at Carabobo, even though Bolívar was personally in command there, had been the hero of the battle, and Sucre had won the battle of Pichincha at the head of Colombian and Peruvian troops. But Bolívar did not let these considerations perturb him, in view of the profound and sincere love which San Martín had sworn to Colombia.

"I will fight under your command," he told Bolívar, "with the noblest abnegation. There are no rivalries as far as I am concerned when the independence of America is at stake. Be assured, General; come to Peru; count on my sincere co-operation. I shall be your lieutenant."

Lafond, the Frenchman, comments in his interesting book: "Bolívar could hardly believe such sincerity."

San Martín's retirement, his renunciation of the protectorship of Peru, and his withdrawal from America grew out of this attitude. He recognized that the triumph of the arms of emancipation was assured. But Ayacucho would not have been so long delayed, nor would America have suffered so tragically from anarchy, as Bolívar later saw it, had Bolívar accepted the proffered co-operation. San Martín's proposal rejected, a bloody rivalry was possible, but San Martín preferred to remove himself in order to protect America from such a shameful thing. Lafond says:

General San Martín's enemies spread the absurd rumor that he aspired to the crown: San Martín was deeply shocked and made a radical decision which all loyal friends of America regretted, thinking *qu'il avait eu l'orgueil de sa vertu*, and his enemies slandered him, saying that he was leaving Peru because of lack of confidence in his troops. The truth is that the Protector, seeing in his own presence the real cause for Bolívar's having refused to come to Peru with Colombian troops, thought it his duty to sacrifice his own interest for that of his country. He convoked Congress, handed over his power to it, and, in spite of the urgings that he stay in Peru as generalissimo of land and sea forces, he departed for Chile, taking with him only the standard of Pizarro which the Council presented to him as a token of public recognition.

Captain Lafond publishes the letter which San Martín sent to Bolívar from Peru following Guayaquil, which the reader remembers from an earlier chapter, and which came to Lafond's hand through the intervention of Bolívar's secretary. That document illumines the very depths of the matter, stripping it of the fantasies which contemporary obloquy had woven about the secret which the participants of that conference obliged themselves to guard.

The letter written to Guido in 1826, in which San Martín cites a verse by Lebrun, shows us what heights of serenity our hero had reached in his renunciation, just as the letter written to Miller in 1827 shows how deeply he had been offended by the lie that he had attempted to have himself crowned in Lima and that the failure of this purpose was the cause of his withdrawal from Peru. In both instances San Martín maintains his appearance of imperturbable dignity. Captain Lafond's book, published years later, uncovers the whole truth, thanks to the letter which San Martín wrote to Bolívar upon his return from Guayaquil about the matters they had just dealt with in the conference and about the reasons for his retirement. It is not just today, in the face of those documents, to insist on the fable that he tried to assume a royal crown and that he abandoned the scene, vanquished by the overpowering genius of his supposed rival. That is not the significance of Guayaquil: when Bolívar withheld his co-operation, he committed the greatest of all his errors, so damaging to America. And when San Martín retired he silently performed the most heroic act of his life.

The charges that have been made against San Martín by certain writers have centered about his retirement from command and his monarchical intentions, but I say that these very charges could be made against Bolívar. The latter, after having exercised a dictatorship in the nations he governed, including Venezuela, abandoned the theater of his old triumphs when outraged public opinion arose against him. And it is known that finally he was forced to leave his own country. As for the monarchy, there is a letter of his which Restrepo[3] published, in which, addressing Mr. Campbell, Great Britain's chargé d'affaires in Colombia, Bolívar says to him:

Considering the very serious difficulties that were encountered in organizing the republic, perhaps the only solution would be the establishment of a monarchy, calling a foreign prince who professes the Catholic religion; but for this it would be necessary to count on the help of a power like France or England.

San Martín, on the other hand, had feigned monarchist aims as a cunning device and retired from America in abnegation.

The letter published by Restrepo has lately been included in the collection of *Cartas del Libertador* (Letters of the Liberator) published in Caracas by the Venezuelan Government, which confers a special authority to its text; and in it Bolívar declares, addressing himself in 1829 to Campbell, the British representative:

In fine, I am far from opposed to the reorganization of Colombia with the well-tried institutions of wise Europe. On the contrary, it would make me infinitely happy and would revive my strength to support a project that might be termed our salvation and that could be achieved, not without some difficulty, with the help of England and France. With their powerful support we would be equal to any difficulty, but without it, no. For this reason I reserve my definite decision until we know their attitude toward the change of system in question and the choosing of a dynasty.

While Bolívar was engaged in these dynastic moves, San Martín ratified his democratic faith by several declarations and was aggrieved by the news of anarchy created by just the kind of political militarism which he wished to avoid. The generals who were thirsty for political power arose to follow the seductive example set by Bolívar, but they were undeterred by any qualities of genius or heroism.

On the anniversary of one of his triumphs, Bolívar was celebrating with a banquet, and someone proposed in a toast that the Omnipotent should forever protect the Liberator. The latter got to his feet and, raising his glass, said:

"Yes, gentlemen, today marks thirty-nine years in which time I have been born three times: once for the world, once for the republic, and once for my own glory."

In 1823, as he brooded over his next campaign against La Serna, he wrote to Santander from Lima: "In spite of everything, believe me, the force of my character will make itself felt, and I will begin my campaign the day it is least expected, for I am as prodigal of soldiers as those who, when they have money, don't know anything else to do with it but spend it."

When he arrived in Alto Peru (later Bolivia) two years later, drunk with military success, he dreamed of the "conquest" of Paraguay, a war against Brazil, and a Napoleonic march upon Argentine territory, as he declares candidly in a communication to the Colombian Government: *"The demon of glory must carry us clear to Tierra del Fuego."*

San Martín foresaw these coming deliriums at Guayaquil: he offered his co-operation for the rapid conclusion of the war against the King of Spain; Bolívar refused it, and later, to avoid a regrettable clash, left him his troops:

"It will not be San Martín who will give the enemy a day of merrymaking," the self-denying paladin said to Guido.

A few years later Salvador Iglesias wrote to San Martín, who was living in European exile:

"Current news, originated by the *Gaceta de Chile,* says that Bolívar, on arriving in Colombia, was received with gunfire and had to leave that republic somewhat hurriedly, and that in Peru the same reception awaited him. We shall see what comes of this."

When San Martín learned of Bolívar's final failure in Peru, he wrote these reflections to Guido:

The Lima movement does not surprise me. Neither has Bolívar's conduct in Peru. Recall the opinion which, upon my return from Guayaquil, I told you I had formed of that general: unfortunately for America, I have not been obliged to revise that opinion. I am convinced that a passion for ruling is what dominates him, and very few men can overcome such a passion. I do not have the slightest doubt that this general has honest intentions in attacking my opinion, but it would be ungentlemanly of me to take advantage of the situation in which he finds himself, a situation which I am sure will be made worse by his character. . . . I will not publish secrets which only you know and which will only be revealed after my death.

Such confidences are only for Guido. He will publish nothing, especially now that Bolívar is in trouble. All this had been foreseen by San Martín at Guayaquil.

As early as 1827, from Brussels, San Martín had written a letter to Miller, foretelling Bolívar's failure: "The man is marching with long strides toward the precipice."

Later Bolívar had to leave Peru. His lieutenant, Sucre, was assassinated; they tried to assassinate the Liberator in Bogotá, but he was saved by his mistress Manuela Sáenz, who shared his bed that night in the Palacio de Gobierno. It is known that his tempestuous career began with dictatorship and ended with a feeble gesture toward bringing in a European prince. Then came the rebellion in Caracas against the old idol, and the great Venezuelan fled to die dramatically in the solitude of Santa Marta.

Because San Martín knew men, and because his soul was sublimely enlightened, a brief conversation was enough to enable him to penetrate to the depths of Bolívar's soul when he met him in Guayaquil. There and then he wrought, without violence, the most sublime deed of his life. The noble warrior's task was concluded, and the Brahman within him appeared to overcome antagonism with renunciation.

From Paris in 1833, when Bolívar had already died, San Martín wrote to Dr. Mariano Alvarez of Lima:

I refer to the assassination of Monteagudo: Not a single person has come from Peru, Chile, or Buenos Aires that I have not asked about this matter; but each one has given me a different version. Some attribute it to Sánchez Carríon, others to certain Spaniards, another to a colonel jealous of his wife, and some say that this deed is hidden by an impenetrable veil. In fine, even Bolívar himself has not escaped the wicked imputation, especially wicked because, ignoring the fact that his personal character was incapable of such a low deed, it is clear that he could have removed Monteagudo without committing a crime, had his presence been embarrassing. In my opinion such a crime is never committed without some particular object.

With San Martín's habitual sense of justice and his mental serenity, he declares there that he does not believe his glorious companion capable of criminal baseness. He knows very well what Bolívar's defects were: a deformity in his grandeur, a lack of balance in the very strength of his genius. But he did not wish that pettiness should be attributed to the man to whom he had entrusted America's liberty at Guayaquil, because he knew him to be his twin in the heroic mission.

But that which gives the best key to the mystery of the two heroes is the silhouette of Bolívar written for Lafond by the sexagenarian San Martín when he was living in exile and Bolívar was in his tomb; in it the same glorious light illumines both souls, that of the personage silhouetted and that of the supposed rival, now old, who pictures him just as he was:

I saw General Bolívar for only three days, during the conference I had with him at Guayaquil. Consequently, in such a short time, it was impossible, or at least difficult, for me to evaluate a man whose looks, at least upon first sight, did not predispose one in his favor. Be that as it may, here is the idea I have of him from my own observations, compared with those of impartial persons who have lived in intimate association with him.

General Bolívar seemed to have *excessive pride,* which would be in contradiction to his habit of not looking squarely in the face of the person with whom he was talking, unless it were someone greatly inferior to him. I was convinced of his lack of frankness during the conferences I had with him in Guayaquil, since he did not respond in a decisive manner to my propositions, but always evasively. The tone he used with his generals was extremely haughty and hardly of the kind to win affection.

I noticed, and he himself told me, that the English officers serving with him received most of his confidence. To continue, his manners were distinguished and showed the fine education he had received.

His speech was at times vulgar, but this defect was not natural, only affected to give himself a more military air. Public opinion accused him of *excessive ambition* and a burning thirst for power, which he later proceeded to justify. *They* [the people] *likewise attributed a great disinterestedness to him, which is just, since he has died in indigence.*

Bolívar was very popular among the soldiers, to whom he granted liberties not sanctioned by military laws. But he was severe with the officers, whom he sometimes treated humiliatingly.

As for this general's military deeds, one can say that they have earned him, justly, the fame of being considered as *the most astonishing man South America has known.* What characterizes him best, and is in a certain sense his special property, is his perfect steadiness which *fortified him in his difficulties* and refused to allow him to be overcome by them, no matter how great these dangers were which his flaming spirit brought on him.

Such was San Martín's enormous antagonist at Guayaquil, such were the questions debated at that famous conference, such were the passions which have swarmed around about it, and such was the purity of soul with which San Martín disdained all the intrigues which followed, until, after the death of the man who had presented him with his portrait, which he cherished, he publicly proclaimed the disinterestedness, the courage, and the glory of the great Venezuelan. San Martín well knew that upon them both, upon Bolívar and upon himself, had weighed the tremendous burden of genius and the responsibility for an entire continent.

The silhouette written by San Martín in France, ten years after Bolívar's demise, was published in Lafond's book. Old age, exile, and approaching death give to those words the accent of history. They sum up what San Martín thought of Bolívar, and in the following chapter will be seen what Bolívar thought of San Martín. The two judged each other, reciprocally, on the high plane upon which they both lived. Far from both of them are those in America who have converted that epic into a tangled quarrel of dialectical sophistry, regional pettiness, and unjust defamations. The passion of the present debaters does not resemble the passion of those who died in the undertaking, when the whole continent was a single nation.

José García, the Tucumán-born officer of the Guayaquil army which was defeated at Ambato, went with the remnants of his troops to avenge this disaster at Tanizahua, at the foot of Mount Chimborazo. Defeated again in November 1820, he was captured and beheaded. In the town of Machangana his head, enclosed in a cage, was displayed on the pillory in the plaza. The head of the beheaded Argentine officer symbolized, at the foot of Chimborazo, the popular spreading of the Argentinian revolution to all the regions of the continent, fraternally uniting them.

On the occasion of the visit the Argentine training frigate *Sarmiento* made to the port of La Guayra in 1900, the Government of Venezuela, Bolívar's country, ordered a portrait of San Martín placed in the capitol in Caracas. Years later, in the same city, a statue of San Martín was erected, continental justice being re-established in this manner, since Argentina has paid similar homage to Bolívar. One of the cities of the Argentine pampas carries the great Venezuelan's name.

IX. CHILD OF THE SUN

San Martín decided one day, a year before his death, to sketch an autobiographical résumé in a letter to President Castilla of Peru. It is excellent for the dignified simplicity with which it presents his beginnings and his achievements and for the clarity with which it expresses the motives of his renunciation:

Like you, I served in Spain's Peninsular Army from the age of thirteen to thirty-four, reaching the rank of lieutenant colonel of cavalry. We Americans, meeting in Cádiz, learning of the first movements taking place in Caracas and Buenos Aires, resolved that each would return to the country of his birth to offer his services in the fight which we calculated had to be undertaken. I arrived at Buenos Aires at the beginning of 1812. I was received by the Governing Junta of the period, one member being favorably inclined, but the other two expressing a marked lack of confidence in me. Furthermore, with very few relatives in my native country, and without any support save my own desire to be useful to my country, I bore this antagonism with steadiness until circumstances placed me in a position to overcome all opposition. During the ten-year period of my public career, in various ranks and commands, the policy which I proposed to follow was inflexible on only two points. Luck and circumstances favored my calculations, especially in regard to the first point, which was: Never to become involved with the parties which were alternately dominant in Buenos Aires during that time, a fluctuation partly occasioned by my absence from the capital for a space of nine years.

The second point was to look upon all the American states into which forces under my command penetrated as brother states, all united in their efforts toward a single, sacred end.

As a consequence of this most just principle, my first step was to order the declaration of each state's independence and to set up its own military forces for security's sake.

This, my dear General, is a short analysis of my public life in America. It would have afforded me the greatest satisfaction to close my career by terminating the war of independence in Peru, but my conference with General Bolívar at Guayaquil convinced me, notwithstanding his protestations, that the sole obstacle to his coming to Peru with his army was nothing but General San Martín's presence, in spite of the sincerity with which I offered to place myself at his command, with all the forces at my disposal.

If America owes me gratitude for any service, it is for that which I rendered in retiring from Lima, a move in which not only my honor and reputation were involved, but which was much more appreciable since I knew that, with the joint forces of Colombia and Peru, the War of Independence would have been completely over in 1823. But this costly sacrifice, and the considerable sacrifice of having to maintain absolute silence, so essential under the circumstances, about the motives which obliged me to take this step, required an effort which you will be able to appraise but which not all have the ability to appreciate.

Upon returning from Lima I went to live on a farm I own near Mendoza. Neither this absolute retirement nor the studied manner in which I had cut all my old relationships, nor above all the guarantee offered by the record of my detachment from all factions and parties in public life, could protect me from the suspicions of the Government which then existed in Buenos Aires. Its ministerial papers attacked me continuously, claiming that a successful soldier was planning to subject the republic to a military regime, substituting this system for the free and legal order. On the other hand, the opposition to the Government used my name, without my knowledge or permission, declaring in its press that I was the only man capable of organizing the State and reuniting the provinces which were at odds with the capital. Under these circumstances I was convinced that, unfortunately, I had figured more prominently in the revolution than I had desired, a fact which would prevent me from being able to continue an impartial course between the parties.

Consequently, and to dissipate all idea of any ambition for any kind of command, I embarked for Europe, where I remained until the year 1829, when, at the invitation of the Government as well as various friends who expounded the guarantees of peace and order which the nation offered, I returned to Buenos Aires. Unfortunately, upon my arrival there I was confronted by General Lavalle's revolution and, without disembarking, I returned again to Europe, preferring this renewed exile to seeing myself obliged to take part in its civil discords. At the advanced age of seventy-one years, with my health completely shattered, blinded by cataracts, I considered, although against all my wishes, ending a sickly life in Argentina, but the events which have occurred since February have placed me in a dilemma as to where I shall go to leave my bones. Although personally I would not be afraid of remaining in my country, I cannot expose my family to the vicissitudes and consequences of the revolution.

So transparent is San Martín's life that it can be simply summed up in that brief autobiography. I have already told in preceding pages how extremely irritated he was by injustice and how he disdained, or forgave, offenses.

Every man lives under two judgments, that of his own inner self and that of other people. Between these two poles the social activities of the historic man unfold. What others think of him wraps itself about a man's being like a web of destiny. History later unwinds the threads which bound his life, and the hero's soul regains its liberty. Only then, when the veils are lifted, can we comprehend all the spiritual beauty which his contemporaries saw so imperfectly.

San Martín had many enemies during his lifetime. One who did so much and was so great could not help having them. The bitterness which these enemies cruelly dealt him explains the pessimistic reflections on mankind which he occasionally expressed during his long expatriation.

In letters to various friends, chiefly to O'Higgins and Guido, the old man writes stoic thoughts about human life, or melancholy reflections about his personal circumstances:

Men differ as much in opinion as they do in physiognomies. Many have called me a tyrant and a despot, and I have scorned them. But I have not been able to overlook those who called me an enemy of my country or accused me of a lack of probity in the management of the public interests. . . .

A veteran in the revolutionary movement, and in the position of leadership in which I was placed by it, my acquiring a profound knowledge of men was inevitable, unless I had been an imbecile. . . .

During the time I have had the misfortune of being a public figure I have looked upon my enemies with indifference or scorn, attitudes I have found impossible to apply to my friends. . . .

The labels of thief and ambitious man which they gratuitously attached to me have not been erased from my memory. I am not able to forget insults, but at least I know how to forgive them. . . .

They think we have stolen right and left. Ah, knaves! If they only knew our situation they would have something else to admire us for. . . .

Don't try to cover up the censure against this old sinner, for you can be sure that twelve years of revolution have injured me to such an extent that nothing makes any impression on me. . . .

Nothing provides a better chance to know what men are like than a revolution. It offers examples by which to measure the immensity of their perversity. . . .

I have become a misanthrope, because, for every virtuous man I found, there were two thousand evil men. . . .

In the midst of a life of absolute isolation, I enjoy a peace which twelve years of revolution made me desire. . . .

Ambition is conditioned by a man's position and circumstances, and there are village mayors who do not feel inferior to a George V. . . .

If the future condition of our country is sufficiently reassuring, I shall come with my family to rest my old carcass in a country house. If not, then "better let well enough alone," as the saying goes.

He loved his ungrateful country and wished to return to it. Men vexed him, and he had lived to serve them.

But while his enemies molested him, San Martín received from gentle folk, intelligent women and appreciative men, comforting words. In those lofty realms of the sensitive spirits shines the praise of his virtues.

A lady of Mendoza told him:

To have merits, my General, and not to have enemies, that is impossible. Scipio the elder saved Rome from utter ruin, and he had to retire to his country residence where he died, tired of the ingratitude of his fellow citizens. . . . Columbus was driven to death by sorrows caused by envy. . . . There is no way of avoiding these evils common to all centuries. . . . Friend, be above them, and in this way you will laugh at your enemies.

Doña Josefa Morales de Los Ríos wrote all this to him from Mendoza on August 28, 1820, in reply to a letter from San Martín "that made her cry." It is at the time of the hero's departure from Valparaiso with his expedition to Peru, when the storm of slander was at its peak against him in Buenos Aires, with no respect for even his family. The man to whom Doña Josefa sent such wise advice in such elegant phrases was worthy of her homage.

Two years before, Doña Margarita Arias de Correa wrote from Córdoba to her "dearly beloved countryman, the most virtuous man of the century," calling him "the tutelary angel of the innocents of the New World," a phrase in which feminine sensitiveness expresses, perhaps unconsciously, the angelic mystery of a guardian soul.

When San Martín entered Lima, Mrs. Torre Tagle personally handed him a letter from Doña Manuela Noriega, a lady who was grateful for the protection given by the victor to a son of hers, and who said: "Patriots place their hopes on the one whom they justly call their liberator, as the man best suited to fulfill the Almighty's purpose for America."

The epic task had ended when a son of General Prieto arrived in Europe from Chile and presented himself to the old hero with a letter from his father:

"This young man is going to fulfill an obligation incumbent on every Chilean, that of kissing the hand of the one who gave us a nation." So reads the distinguished Chilean soldier's letter, which concludes thus: *"Please be so kind, my General, as to give him your blessing."* And San Martín generously blessed the young Chilean, like a patriarch. The youth of America is his posterity.

In the Bhagavad-Gita, one of the sacred poems of India, Krishna the Enlightened teaches Arjuna, the soldier, the mystic doctrine of the essential struggle: "Every necessary act, Arjuna, is achieved by saying, 'It is necessary to do this,' and if the author of the act has suppressed sensuality and renounced the fruits of its works, that is the essence of abnegation." Krishna also teaches that vigor, firmness, skill, intrepidity, generosity, and dignity in command are virtues of the Kshatriya, the warrior; and that those of the Brahman, the priest, are peace, conscience, austerity, purity, patience, rectitude, a knowledge of the diversity of things and of the divine unity. San Martín possessed both kinds of virtues: the military and the priestly. And referring to him, one could remember what Arjuna's teacher said to him: "Oh, warrior without blemish, I have expounded to thee the most mystic of doctrines; he who understands it is wise, and his work must achieve perfection."

Such is the code of ethics for the saints of the sword, and examples of Brahmanic virtue abound in the life of our warrior.

When San Martín was governor in Cuyo, he secretly ordered José M. García to leave Mendoza because it was alleged that García had plotted to assassinate him. Some time later the exiled man wrote him, professing friendship and asking permission to return to his family. San Martín acceded with a letter in which, after reminding the conspirator of his attempt, he added simply: "but my nature takes no pleasure in vengeance."

Seven days after the victory at Maipú, San Martín made another of those magnanimous gestures which were so frequent in his life. Osorio had left behind his briefcase of secret correspondence when he fled, and it fell into O'Brien's hands. The latter turned it over, unopened, to his chief. That briefcase contained the letters of spies and traitors, who from Santiago informed the Royalists of the patriots' movements. San Martín could have used them as a basis for legal prosecution and for the purpose of his own revenge, but he chose to burn the documents.

On April 12 he went with the faithful O'Brien to a ranch in El Salto, in the outskirts of the capital, and there, hidden from imprudent eyes, he ordered a bonfire lighted, into which he threw those infamous papers with his own hand. San Martín, seated on a rustic chair in the shade of a tree, and with the scenic panorama of the Andes spread about him, watched the red flames twisting in the air, while the letters were burned to ashes and the names of the traitors were buried in them. On that very site, years later, O'Brien built a resort cabin in which he kept the chair San Martín had used, with a sign in English, "San Martín's Chair," in memory of this magnanimous gesture.

San Martín, after Maipú, on passing through San Luis, listened while Dupuy was given a detailed report on the mutiny of the Spanish prisoners, in which Ordóñez, Morla, Marcó, and several other officers had been killed. Upon learning that a nephew of Ordóñez survived, he went to the jail to see him and found him in chains so long they wrapped about his waist, and so heavy they did not allow him to move. San Martín sent for a blacksmith to file the chain and fetter in two, and then he called the governor to order that the prisoner be decently dressed and treated more considerately, transferring him to the barracks in simple custody. This man, forty years later, referred to this episode with words of gratitude for his protector. His reference was in a letter to Balcarce, written from Barcelona following San Martín's death. "This gentleman," he says, "seated me in a chair and calmed me, and with kind words asked what had happened." In that letter, young Ordóñez protests against the defamation of San Martín on account of the deaths which resulted from the mutiny of the Spaniards, and he then added:

"General San Martín was a generous conqueror. . . . I cherish a feeling of gratitude in my heart, a feeling which has become esteem and good will, for what this man did in sparing my life.

"His Excellency Don José de San Martín," the nephew relates as an eyewitness, "had been one of my uncle Don José Ordóñez' companions in Cádiz, and when my uncle was taken prisoner in the battle of Maipú, they recognized and embraced each other." And this is all true. In September of 1818, Ordóñez, imprisoned at San Luis, wrote to San Martín calling him "a man I regard with all my affection," and thanking him for favors. The other Royalist chief who was a prisoner at San Luis, General Primo de Rivera, did the same: "I am filled with gratitude which I so justly feel toward Your Excellency on account of the many favors I have received from you, and of the favors which my companions-at-arms have also received with equal good fortune." Along with Ordóñez, those companions are the ones who were later killed as a result of the mutiny of Royalist prisoners in the San Luis jail. Their deaths were scurrilously imputed to San Martín by the passion of the enemy. Ordóñez' nephew exclaimed in 1867, with posthumous and disinterested gratitude: "It is slanderous, and the foulest infamy, to claim that San Martín had a hand in the deaths at San Luis." Not only did he have nothing to do with them, but we have already seen how that gentleman dealt with his vanquished enemies.

During his years of exile the misanthropic San Martín constantly inquired about his friends in his letters. He sent remembrances to the humblest of them and to their children. Once he sent a money gift out of his own scarce funds to help an old comrade who was in dire need, in the same manner that he once had told Moyano, the administrator of his estate, Los Barriales, that he should feed the poor with the produce of the farm. When one of his favorite comrades was coming to Europe, he offered him a place in his house and at his table. He writes to Guido: "Wherever I may be, a room and a meal will always be shared with you." He wrote to Miller: "It will be a great pleasure to embrace you, and much more so if you will come to my house, where you will find a soldier's quarters."

San Martín was a friend who is faithful in the expression of appreciation: "What can I ask you to tell your dear mother and sweet Rosita? Give them both a million regards, and tell them that I shall never forget the wonderful care they gave me while I was gravely ill." Thus he concluded one of his letters to O'Higgins. In 1842 Don Gregorio Gómez emigrated from Buenos Aires to Lima "on account of the circumstances in which that unfortunate country finds itself," and San Martín recommended him effusively because "he is a man of unsurpassed honor and loyal and sincere." Gregorio Gómez was one of the few people with whom San Martín uses the familiar "tu" form of address, "the first friend I had in Buenos Aires." Thirty years had passed since 1812, and San Martín did not forget him. Neither did he forget his Scotch friend, Fife, who aided his escape from Spain in 1811. He had scarcely returned to Europe from America when he went to embrace him at his home in Dublin.

This warrior had within his being an ingenious tenderness, and his noble heart was made up of such sensitive chords as loyalty, gratitude, and generosity. Dispossessed of his arms, the kindliness hidden in his bosom became visible, and as he grew older he became more affectionate, as if the love of his grandchildren softened his nature. He could then have been termed a majestic lapacho[1] in full flower.

San Martín's life so clearly demonstrated his austerity, purity, patience, rectitude, knowledge of the diversity of things and of the divine unity, that a priestly conscience plainly motivated and directed the warrior's will. But to this background of spiritual asceticism are added other mysterious signs which perhaps may be merely apocryphal but which cannot be overlooked when one wishes to contemplate the hero's fullest greatness.

Before 1810 a conspiracy of liberation was plotted at El Cuzco by José Gabriel Aguilar, the miner. To his associates in the conspiracy (according to Mitre's story) Aguilar related this vision one day:

He had had an apocalyptic dream in which he saw an eagle flying from the Pacific toward Peru, and another that flew out to meet him from the heart of the mountains, with four men brandishing flaming swords, riding between his wings. When the two eagles met head on they plunged downward through space, and below them legions of soldiers sprang up, acclaiming their new leaders.

That conspiracy was discovered and came to nought, but that premonitory vision, when interpreted, seems to be prophetic of San Martín, the eagle who fifteen years afterwards came from the Pacific, and of Bolívar, the eagle who went out to meet him from the heart of the mountains, until they met and came to earth, giving rise to legions of soldiers in Peru.

That Aguilar of the prophetic vision is mentioned, together with other precursors of independence, in a "Manifesto to the Peruvians" sent from Chile on the eve of San Martín's expedition, and a proclamation of Director O'Higgins called the Peruvians "sons of Manco Capac," inviting them to "seal American brotherhood" on the tomb of Tupac Amarú, announcing the forthcoming departure of San Martín with his liberating legions.

Also on the eve of the expedition to Peru, San Martín sent from Chile a manifesto to the Indians of Tawantinsuyo (the Indian name for Peru) written in the language of the Incas. Its heading read:

Llapamanta accllasca José de San Martín sutiyocc, Maeeanacocunacpa Apunya Apunmi; chay Llcclay quichila cutichaynassuiquipacc, ppuyo hina llantasca maccanacoccunacpa camachecniecunataguan pay sapallan camachic Chilepis Atuchoc cargoyoquanamanta hasguan, acllas cacunamanta ueñia cacmi [etc.].

This leader's document is worthy of him who was called an Indian on account of his brown coloring and because he had been born among the Indians of Yapeyú. He it was who in 1812, upon beginning his career, asked that three hundred young Guarani Indians be brought to him in Buenos Aires to form the first cadre of his grenadiers, and who, in 1816, upon parleying with the Araucanian Indians in Cuyo, said to several of the chiefs, justifying his war of recovery against the conquistadores: "Because I, too, am an Indian."

As San Martín's forces entered Lima, there was a big earthquake in Peru, as if the earth were stirred up at his presence, and referring to this coincidence, Torrente, the chronicler, says:

. . . A night marked by the Author of nature with an earthquake of the severest magnitude and of the greatest duration that has been felt in those countries where earthquakes are so frequent. Fateful night in which the Supreme Creator showed with signs of unmistakable grief and horror His divine displeasure at the unfaithful and impious vassals of the Spanish monarchy. Terrible night which pricked the criminal consciences, even of the least credulous, and made the most arrogant among our republicans reel, while it gave new hope and consolation to those who had not strayed from the path indicated by loyalty and virtue to see that tacit approbation from heaven for the nobleness of their cause.

The Bishop of Santiago, on February 12, 1818, in blessing Chile's independence before San Martín, stated that he did so "because he was convinced that this was God's will." The fact is that Peru's earth trembled when San Martín entered the City of Kings, founded by Pizarro, the Conquistador.

On Monday, October 8, 1821, at Lima, an Indian ditty was sung in celebration of the Protector:

Palomita hermosa
De todo mi amor,
Hagamos memoria
Del Inca Señor:

*Vuela, vuela alegre
Aplaudiendo al fin,
Y dale las gracias
A mi San Martín.*

which literally translated reads:

*Beautiful little dove
Of all my love,
In memory of the Great Inca:
Fly, fly happily
With applause in your wings
And gives thanks
To my San Martín.*

San Martín suppressed this song because his enemies wished to see in it a monarchistic intention. But in reality it sprang from one of those naïve intuitions of the people; the subconscious mind of the race "remembered" the Inca in the Protector's presence, because San Martín seemed to the Indian troubador's mind to be the Inca returning in a dream merely to recover Pizarro's Standard, once he had established in Peru the Indians' freedom and the liberty of the new City of the Sun.

On December 12, 1821, San Martín invited Captain Hall (Basil Hall, the traveler) of the English Navy to lunch with him, and his guest saw in the drawing room an indigenous mummy recently discovered, which had been presented to the Protector. Hall says:

The figure was a man seated on the ground with his knees almost touching his chin, his elbows pressed against his sides, and his hands pressed to his cheekbones. The half-open mouth showed two rows of beautiful teeth. The body, although shrunken to an extraordinary degree, had all the appearance of being human, with skin intact everywhere except on the shoulder. The face carried an acute expression of agony. Tradition concerning this and other similar bodies has it that in the time of the conquest many Incas and their families suffered such persecution that they actually allowed themselves to be buried alive rather than submit to the fate the Spaniards had in store for them.

This mummy, perhaps that of an Inca, was sent to the British Museum on board the *Conway*, the ship captained by Hall, and who knows whether or not that mummy had once been the body of the Protector whose praise the Indian troubador sang "in memory of the Great Inca. . . . And give thanks to my San Martín."

Colonel Federico de Brandsen, French soldier in the service of America, wrote concerning "the revolutions in Peru," after San Martín's departure, the following words which assume special importance:

A man of extraordinary genius came from the banks of the River Plate to break the Peruvians' chains and to re-establish freedom in the land of the magnanimous

Incas. Brave, generous, skilled, and confident like those children of the Sun, he conquered by love and force of arms the most beautiful provinces of that vast kingdom. Fortune smiled on his wishes. A few steps more, and Peru would see the Sun of the Incas rise over the tomb of her tyrants.

The poets of the revolution, Cayetano Rodríguez, the Franciscan friar, and Crisóstomo Lafinur, liberal professor, call America "daughter of the Sun." Rojas and Varela call the Americans "children of the Sun." López and Luca allude to the Incas as forbears, children of the Sun, and the above-mentioned Luca himself, in an ode to the triumphs of San Martín in Lima, says with true inspiration:

> El valiente guerrero argentino
> Llevó al Templo del Sol sus banderas
>
> (The brave Argentinian warrior
> Carried his banners to the Temple of the Sun.)

This Sun of the pre-Colombian cults, the "God of the Fatherland," is indistinguishable from the Sun of the Hellenic cults, the "God of Delos," in the songs of emancipation so abundant in the two kinds of reminiscences, the classic ones of Homer and Vergil and the American ones of Ercilla and Garcilaso.[2] But all this literary imagination is expressive of the national spirit's true feeling in those days. San Martín was only the enlightened interpreter of a continental mystery, and perhaps this mysterious tradition was the reason for the founding in Peru of the Order of the Sun.

When the restorer of Chile decided to begin "the journey of destiny," the expedition to Peru which crowned his career, he explained, in a manifesto to the Peruvians, the high purposes of his mission with these magnificent words:

The independent states of Chile and the United Provinces of South America send me to enter your territory to defend the cause of your liberty. That cause is your cause and *the cause of humanity*. The means I am depending on to achieve your salvation are efficacious in conformity with a goal so sacred. . . . My proclamation, then, *is not that of a conquistador* who attempts to perpetrate a new slavery. The power of the universe has fashioned this great day of your independence, and *I can be nothing else but the accidental instrument of justice and an agent of destiny*. Justice and the public security oblige me to adopt the final recourse of reason: *the use of protective force*. The blood shed will be solely the crime of the tyrants.

Who is this man who was a warrior and still repudiated conquest and bloodshed, invoked protective force as the final recourse of reason, identified America's cause with the cause of humanity, and wished to be, with pride or with modesty, an instrument of justice and an agent of destiny?

"A simple and pure man, made a seer by his ideal, will bring you liberation. . . . And when he must go to far-away regions to protect right and virtue, his power subsists and his force is sacred while his name is unknown to the world, because so sublime and marvelous a mystery cannot be rightly appreciated by mortal men. No one evades this severe law, and when his incognito is discovered, he must leave."

These words which illuminate Lohengrin's destiny in the Wagnerian version of the ancient myth could be applied to San Martín, "the simple and pure man, made a seer by his ideal, who brought us liberation." He had come from the sea of the Atlantides, who were children of the Sun, and traveled as though carried by the power of fate to the land of the Incas, who were also children of the Sun. The hero felt in his spirit the force which led him: "I must follow the destiny that calls me," he said upon leaving Chile for his last enterprise, and when he disembarked on the shores of Peru he said anew: "We have arrived at the place of our destiny." On that spot he addressed this message to his legions: "Your duty is to console America. You do not come to conquer, but to liberate peoples." And to the enslaved people he addressed this other message: "The time of oppression and force has passed. I come to put an end to that epoch of pain and humiliation." Guided by such inspirations, he put the crowning touch on his career, and "when his incognito was discovered" he knew that he must leave.

This was the reason why he departed, following Guayaquil, leaving his America which he had served ten years with humility and abnegation. He departed to return to Monsalvat, from where he had come, a truth made evident by the wise serenity of his old age. Because of this, the stage of "renunciation," the third period of his life, is so important to an understanding of the mystic meaning of his "beginnings" and of his "achievements."

And perhaps that Monsalvat of the Christian legend may be none other than the symbolic mountain called Paccari-tambo in the America of the Incas: Paccari-tambo, "the dwelling place of the dawn," from where came the Ayar brothers, children of the Sun, according to the legend of the Andes, heroes and teachers, Atlantid founders of the first continental civilization.

In order to consummate his titanic work San Martín had to bear the cross of an extremely sickly body. We have already seen him suffering from many and continuous maladies in the middle of battles. By force of spirit and with medical assistance he stood erect under exhausting labors on his mission of mercy, because "he knows" that "his work must achieve perfection," and so he perfected it, conquering illnesses, poverty, and abuses, in the service of humanity.

During the long solitary hours, the old man remembered in silence the names of those who collaborated with him in the undertaking: the Argentinians Alvear, Pueyrredón, Güemes, Belgrano, Balcarce, Las Heras, Guido, Monteagudo, Godoy Cruz, Lavalle, Necochea, Arenales, Alvarado, Blanco Encalada; the Chileans O'Higgins, Zapata, Zañartu, Freyre; those of other American nations, such as Bolívar, Santander, Sucre, Torre Tagle, Olmedo, Unánue, Del Río, La Mar, Santa Cruz. Then the names of the Royalist leaders passed in review: Pezuela, La Serna, Marcó del Pont, Osorio, Valdez, Monet, Rodil, Ramírez, García Camba, Primo de Rivera, Maroto, Atero, Canterac, Goyeneche, Morla, Aymerich, Ordóñez, important figures of the Spanish army. Many Europeans had also served with San Martín on land and sea: the Englishmen Cochrane, D'Evreux, O'Farriar, O'Leary, Miller, O'Connor, O'Brien, O'Carroll, Guisse; the Frenchmen Brandsen, Raulet, Beauchef, Soulanges, Soyer, Bruix, Viel, D'Alve; the German Althaus; the Portuguese Abreu Lima; veterans of the Napoleonic wars and Nelson's battles before they fought in America. The old man's memory wandered among those names, evoking the epic past. Thus he spent the sad years at Grand Bourg, arranging and annotating his papers so that posterity might one day know what we now do know.

As his long exile passed, the truth was becoming as unmistakably clear as the light of a new day. It was for this that San Martín lived so long, in order that his soul might mature in its destiny of love. Before his death he was able to see how justice was being done for his name in all parts of America, even in those which could appear most hostile to him.

In 1830, Santander,[3] who had been governor of Colombia at the time of the Guayaquil conference, went to visit San Martín in Brussels. There he spoke with him for the first time, and upon returning from Europe he took his leave of the great exile with these effusive words: "I don't believe that time has yet closed the door on the prospect of your offering further services to America; on the contrary, I look forward to the day when you will make new sacrifices for her, guided always by your love for the fatherland and by your charitable experience."

But no one in America knew who San Martín really was better than Bolívar. San Martín was first to cross the Andes, while Bolívar came later. San Martín first carried the war to the Pacific. Bolívar followed after. San Martín was first to enter Lima. Then came Bolívar. San Martín was first to abandon his power to avert anarchy, and Bolívar abandoned it later, defeated by anarchy. Only then could Bolívar comprehend the error of not having accepted the co-operation which San Martín offered. And then, despairing, he, also, committed the monarchical gesture as did his companion-in-glory seven years before, at the expense of much condemnation. Because of this, Bolívar's comments about his supposed rival are profoundly significant, and I wish to cite some which praise San Martín, "because all that survives on the other side of the tomb," as Sarmiento says, "ought to be beautiful and harmonious with the divine forms which the new man puts on."

Bolívar was still in Angostura, from where he wrote to Briceño on October 20, 1818, upon learning the news of Maipú:

The English papers contain the details of the glorious battle of the fifth of April in the vicinity of Santiago. . . . General San Martín beat and completely destroyed there 7,000 Spaniards, took 3,000 prisoners, among them 190 officers, killed more than 2,000 men, until only Osorio, the commander in chief, with 200 cavalry soldiers, survived. San Martín ordered their immediate pursuit. This Royalist army was the last remnant of the Spanish forces in Peru, and this battle has produced the absolute liberty of Upper and Lower Peru. This victory of San Martín's makes it inevitable that independence movements will break out in the southern provinces of Nueva Granada.[4] The Spaniards, powerfully invaded from the south by victorious troops which they cannot resist even by making astonishing efforts, must necessarily concentrate their forces and leave all the entrances and exits of the kingdom in all directions unprotected. I therefore deem the liberating expedition to Nueva Granada a sure success.

Bolívar understood, then, what that victory of San Martín was worth to continental emancipation, and in fact his own expansion after 1818 had its beginning in it. Because of this, he added to this same letter: "America's day has arrived, and everything appears to herald the termination of our glorious and terrible struggle."

When San Martín had entered Lima, Bolívar wrote him, from Trujillo, a letter dated August 23, 1821:

My first thought on the field of Carabobo, when I saw my country free, was of Your Excellency [San Martín], of Peru and of Peru's liberating army. On contemplating that now not a single obstacle stood in the way of my flying to embrace the Liberator of South America [San Martín], I was overcome with pleasure. Your Excellency must believe me that, after Colombia's welfare, nothing preoccupies me so much as the success of Your Excellency's arms, so worthy of carrying their glorious flags wherever there be slaves who take shelter in your shadow.

Bolívar wrote this to San Martín one year before their differences concerning the annexation of Guayaquil, which arose during the conference at which they met for the first time.

From Quito, on June 22, 1822, Bolívar answered a note of San Martín's regarding the Guayaquil problem and the forthcoming conference:

I give my thanks to Your Excellency for the frankness with which you speak to me in the note I now answer. Doubtless the sword of liberators should not be used unless it be to make the rights of the people stand out. . . . But overlooking all political discussion, Your Excellency, with the noble and generous tone that befits the commander of a great people, assures me that our first embrace will seal the harmony and union of our states, without there being a single obstacle that cannot be definitively removed. This magnanimous conduct on the part of the Protector of Peru was always anticipated by me. No such thing as the interests of a small province can disturb the majestic march of South America, which, united in heart, in interest, and glory, does not fix its eyes on the niggardly faults in the revolution, but lifts its gaze to the most remote centuries and contemplates, with pleasure, free generations happy and flooded with all the good things which Heaven distributes on earth and blessing the hand of their protectors and liberators. The conference which Your Excellency has been so kind as to propose to me, I desire with the greatest impatience, and await it with certainty on the strength of Your Excellency's assurance.

Following the conference, Bolívar wrote to Santander, President of Colombia, from Guayaquil on July 29, 1822:

Day before yesterday, at night, General San Martín left here after a visit of thirty-six or forty hours; it can appropriately be called a visit, because we have done nothing more than embrace, converse, and say good-by. . . . The Protector has pledged me his eternal friendship for Colombia; his willingness to take part in the settlement of boundaries; not to become involved in the negotiations concerning Guayaquil; that there shall be a complete and absolute federation, although it includes only Colombia, and that Guayaquil should be the seat of Congress.

He has agreed to send a representative of Peru to negotiate in common with ourselves over the affairs of Spain, with her envoys. Also he has recommended Mosquera to Chile and Buenos Aires to negotiate their recognition of the federation. He desires that we combine garrisons in Chile and Argentina. In fine, he wishes everything to proceed with the appearance of unity, because he knows that peace and tranquillity cannot be had without it. . . . I will say that he does not wish to be king. . . .

His character has seemed very soldierly to me, and he appears very active, alert, and far from dull. . . . He has correct ideas, the kind that are pleasing to you. . . . Good heavens! I don't wish for anything more: this is the first time that I have nothing left to desire and am content with my fortune.

On December 14, 1822, when San Martín, after having renounced his protectorship, had already departed from Lima, Bolívar wrote from Guayaquil to La Mar, who was appointed governor of Peru by that country's Congress:

The loss of General San Martín cannot be repaired except by you and General Alvarado. Believe me that the satisfaction I have felt at the wise decision of Congress in your appointment has been mitigated by the sudden departure of the Protector. Public figures are just as valuable as the opinion the people have about them. General San Martín was respected by the army, which was accustomed by this time to obeying him; the people of Peru looked upon him as their Liberator. However, he has been fortunate. You know that the illusions which good fortune brings sometimes are more valuable than merit itself. Peru has lost a good captain and a benefactor.

When O'Higgins took refuge in Lima after his downfall, Bolívar honored him with a banquet. And in paying tribute to the ex-Director of Chile, he remembered San Martín with a eulogy. Guido sent his pleasing news to the ex-Protector, who still was in Mendoza. El Centinela, Buenos Aires newspaper, published the story of the banquet that same year of 1823, including the phrase of the toast: "To the good angel of America that brought General San Martín with his liberating army from the banks of the River Plate to the shores of Peru." For Bolívar, then, the destiny that brought San Martín to Peru was "the good angel of America." We may add that the very same "good angel" is the one that took him away from the American scene.

I do not overlook the fact that in other letters of Bolívar's expressions less favorable to San Martín are found, but it is passion that speaks in those letters. Bolívar was misled by jealousy of glory, by the licentiousness of power or the necessity of achieving power; when he was inspired by his love for America and the ideal of liberation, his words are accented with fraternal spirit and justice.

It is for this reason that I affirm that no one in America knew better than Bolívar who San Martín was, the real significance of his escape from Spain, his efforts in the region of the Plate, his crossing of the Andes, his inspired idea of carrying the war to the Pacific, his victory at Maipú, his entry into Lima, and his renunciation at Guayaquil.

Political whims during the emancipation and the diversities in temperament of the two men could have created antagonism between San Martín and Bolívar, magnified by the passions of that period and by the mistaken posthumous opinions of those who were unable to see how much of solidarity and unity there was in both destinies. These two had departed from London to return to their native countries, and they moved through tribulation in the interior of America until they met at Guayaquil. That is why, in 1823, when San Martín had already retired from the scene, Bolívar proposed a toast in Lima to "the good angel of America that brought San Martín from the banks of the River Plate to the shores of Peru."

The toast of 1823 is more than a mere rhetorical phrase; it is one of Bolívar's astute intuitions, as we see now that the life of San Martín, child of the Sun, is, like that of his twin brother, marked by mysterious Inca-like signs.

These two worked in harmony on this legendary America, which imbued Bolívar with all the passion of the race and the fire of her lands and imbued San Martín with the Atlantid "beginnings of her children of the Sun." Bolívar began to carry out his dream when, as a very young man, he swore on one of Rome's hills that his country would be free, seemingly already possessed by the Caesarean demon of Rome, and he later came to have "the exaltation of flags" on Mount Chimborazo.

San Martín, for his part, had his beginning secretly in the lodges of Cádiz and London, all that remained of the mysterious Atlantis, and in possession of the Sun Laws with their divine truths he came to have, at the foot of Mount Aconcagua, among the silence of the rocks, his mystic dream. Both died in exile and in poverty, after having lived through heroic anguish. And if one died younger, it is because he was consumed with greater ardor, like one of the logs in the American woods. And if the other survived him, it is because our America demanded it thus, to be able to see more clearly that sublime astral light, prolonged through the calmness of afternoon.

complete, and he was happy in his home in spite of his continuous illnesses. His family was reduced to Mercedes, the daughter happily married to the good Balcarce (another brilliant choice made by her father), and two grand-daughters whom the grandfather adored. He did not have a large patrimony to leave to his heirs, but he was not burdened with debts. In these circum-stances he wrote with his own hand the will and testament which is dated Paris, January 23, 1844 (a short while after Aguado's death) and which re-flects, as do all of San Martín's documents drawn up in his decisive hours, the serene greatness of his soul.

San Martín's habitation at Grand Bourg was, as Alberdi said when he went to visit him, "worthy of a philosopher," and "philosopher" its master had been called, as he began his heroic career, by that Lord Macduff who was his friend in Spain and who foresaw at that time the great destiny which forty years later was in its denouement.

Near the wall of his room was the iron bed, with a coverlet of white and sky blue matching the curtains, a lamp table, a washstand, several chairs, and a desk. On the walls were hung, as austere ornaments, a lithograph of the battle of Maipú, other lithographs of naval episodes of Nelson's campaigns, and an old Peruvian canvas. Two portraits stood out among all the figures: one of San Martín himself and the other of Bolívar, together in a proximity that eloquently put to silence the ignoble passions which tried to separate them in their glory. In that atmosphere the austerity of a life and the saintli-ness of a soul were disclosed.

The winter night was raw, and the fireplace, on whose mantel was a clock with a little bust of Napoleon costumed as a Roman consul, had a roaring fire. Near the fireplace there was a Morocco-leather easy chair and another of red velvet. In the center of the room was a table with a green cover and writing materials.

That night the old man sat down first near the fire to warm his long, bony hands. Then, pensive, he paced the room awhile. He looked at Napoleon, who reminded him of Bailén, and at Bolívar, who reminded him of Guaya-quil, the beginning and end of his career. Finally he sat down to write:

In the name of Almighty God whom I know as the Creator of the Universe, I, José de San Martín, Generalissimo of the Republic of Peru and Founder of her liberty, Captain General of Chile and Brigadier General of the Argentine Con-federation, say that in view of the poor state of my health, I declare in this testa-ment . . .

Then he reread:
"In the name of Almighty God, whom I know as the Creator of the Uni-verse . . ."

He did not include any other allusion to the Supreme Being or to religion. He omitted the ecclesiastic invocations and the importunities for the salvation of the soul that were so traditional on such occasions. If San Martín's will is compared with that of his mother, one can see the difference between two epochs and two religious conceptions. The son believed in God, and even though he had been married by the Church as his parents had been and respected the Catholic faith in the states he governed, we know that his religious belief was that of a liberal Christian, a confirmed and resigned deist. But he saw in the Church an instrument for social discipline. Such are the ideas which, on returning from Peru, after his abdication, he was led to expound to Mrs. Graham, who interpreted them wrongly, thinking him an atheist. San Martín had subjected the clergy in Cuyo, in Chile, and in Peru to his authority, at times exercising episcopal functions himself or exiling Royalist clergy. His enemies had branded him as heretical, as did that Friar Zapata of Santiago, Chile, who, before Chacabuco, compared San Martín to Martin Luther in a sermon, saying to the faithful that they should call him simply "Martín" and not "San Martín" because he was not a saint but a heretic, like the German whose name he shared.

He had exiled the Archbishop of Lima in Peru, and also various bishops, because they were Royalists, refusing to respect the ecclesiastic hierarchies. A few, knowing of his lodge activities, thought him to be a Mason, as were General Balcarce and other officers of his army. But if he was not a Mason, his ideas about the Supreme Architect and man's duties draw him close to the purest teachings of the ancient rituals. He had taught his daughter, in his "Maxims," to respect all religions alike. San Martín did not receive the Holy Communion at his death, and in his will he ordered that he should be buried without any ceremony:

I forbid that any kind of funeral be held for me, and ask that I be taken directly from the place of my death to the cemetery, without any procession. But I would like for my heart to be deposited in the cemetery at Buenos Aires.

He does not wish ecclesiastic rites over his bier, nor worldly pomp at his interment. But one thing he did wish—that his heart return to Buenos Aires, the city which so many times had treated him harshly. He took his leave, then, of life without any rancor. His love of country, which had been his religion, was resplendent in the hour of his departure, and he sent his noblest organ to Argentine soil, of which he was made, although his bones had to remain in the land of his enforced exile. Minister Tagle told López, the historian, that San Martín did not love Buenos Aires, but this clause disproves the statement. San Martín loved Buenos Aires, and because of this he willed his patriot's heart to the City of May[1] on the eve of his death.

Then he wrote this other article:

I declare that I do not owe, nor have I ever owed, anything to anyone.

The brief document containing San Martín's last requests refers more to his family sentiments than to his modest possessions:

My only daughter, Mercedes de San Martín, wife of Mariano Balcarce, I designate sole heiress of all my present possessions and all I acquire in the future. . . . Although true it is that all my desires have had only one object, my beloved daughter's welfare, I must confess that her admirable conduct and the constant affection she has always shown for me have repaid all my care with interest, making my old age happy.

The only agreeable hours of his old age San Martín owed to his daughter Mercedes and to her two daughters. Of the two granddaughters, Josefa and Merceditas, only one survived her parents, to become the last guardian of her father's museum when her mother died. The will refers to those little girls of his own flesh and blood, directing these bits of advice to their young mother, Mercedes:

I beg you to continue with the same care and industry the education of your daughters, whom I embrace with all my heart, if you wish to have the same happy fortune in your old age that I have had. I make the same commission to your husband, whose honor and probity have not failed to live up to the opinion that I have formed about him, which is a guarantee that he will continue to provide for the happiness of my daughter and granddaughters.

In addition to his granddaughters Josefa and Merceditas, San Martín thought of his relatives in Spain. His parents and two of his brothers had died, but María Helena, his only sister, whom he had not seen since his adolescence, and who was now a widow, still lived there. He dedicated a tender remembrance to her, which shows new affective depths in the noble old man's soul:

It is my express wish that my daughter provide my sister María Helena with a pension of 1,000 francs a year, and at her death a pension of 250 francs to her daughter Petronila, until the latter's death. No other pledge is necessary to secure this gift which I make to my sister and niece than my confidence that my daughter and her heirs will religiously comply with my will.

Upon reaching this point San Martín thought about the son he had wished to have and whom he did not have, and also about the grandson he hoped for and who never came. When Balcarce and Mercedes came to Buenos Aires in 1832 he asked them to take his saber from Mendoza: "for the little grandson I may have . . ." He did not have one. What should he do about the weapon that had served him in his American enterprise? Then he wrote:

The saber that has accompanied me throughout the entire war of South American Independence will be presented to the Most Excellent General of the Argentine Republic, Juan Manuel de Rosas, as a token of the satisfaction that, as an Argentinian, I have felt on seeing the firmness with which he has sustained the republic's honor against the unjust pretensions of the foreigners who tried to humiliate her.

This is the virtuous "paterfamilias," once again standing before history. The elderly Cid, preoccupied with the jewels he must leave his daughters, brusquely remembers his Tizona. This legacy of his saber to Rosas was later to elicit the criticism of the young men who fought against that tyrant of Buenos Aires. But San Martín is not judging the tyrant, because he has never mixed into the internal fights of Argentine politics. That act would also serve Rosas' friends as an argument in the latter's favor, and in such manner Saldías makes use of it in his history of Rosas.

On account of all this the disposition must be explained calmly here, without any intention to quarrel. Rosas was accustomed to write San Martín with a regard which other governors of the Plate never showed toward the exile. Rosas, who had given San Martín's son-in-law a post in the legation in Paris, cited him with praise in his messages to the Legislature, showed interest in his fortune, and decreed him salaries and honors. How could one forget these attentions? But the true and sole reason for the legacy is the one San Martín mentions: Rosas had defended the national integrity twice: once when Buenos Aires was attacked by France, and once when it was blockaded by France and England, basely allied on that occasion.

In a letter from San Martín to Gregorio Gómez ("My dear Goyo"), his best and oldest friend in Buenos Aires, the exile had said in 1839:

I view the circumstances of our unfortunate country with true emotion, and the worst thing of all is that I do not see a ray of hope for the improvement of her fortune. You know how I feel, and consequently I cannot approve the conduct of General Rosas when I see the persecution of the most honorable men of the country. Furthermore, the assassination of Dr. Masa convinces me that the Government of Buenos Aires is based only on violence. In spite of this, I shall never approve that any son of the fatherland should ally himself with a foreign nation to humiliate his country.

This letter summarized the great distinction San Martín made between the internal politics of Rosas, which he condemned, and his external policy, which he applauded.

San Martín's opinions about the aggressions of England and France were expressed when those wars were begun. The paladin of Argentine Independence, the adversary of all conquest or reconquest of Argentine soil by European powers, saw nothing in Rosas' attitude except a patriotic sentiment that is above the war which the unitarians waged against him from Montevideo. He knew that the attitude of the unitarians contained much of ingenuity and desperation. Guido wrote, besides, telling him that commercial interests were being brought into play in Montevideo.

So San Martín willed his saber, not to the governor of Buenos Aires, but to the Confederation's international representative who defended the integrity of the nation's territory, or as it might be termed, the Independence which San Martín founded with that saber.

Now he must decide about Pizarro's Standard. This is the relic of his accomplishments, his only war booty, the possession of which he was proudest. The centuries-old cloth was raveled and discolored. He guarded it with painstaking care and liked to show it to the Americans who came to visit him from time to time. When he died, what would become of the Standard? He would have wished to will it to Buenos Aires, but President Castilla had asked to have it for Peru, at the same time that he ordered the payment of San Martín's pension which was in arrears. How could he refuse him? Not wishing to give up the Standard immediately, he promised it to Peru after his death, and he was true to his word. It appeared very appropriate that the Standard reconquered by him should return to Lima, which doubtless would know how to take care of it. And after having written the preceding clauses, he wrote this additional one:

It is my will that the Standard which the brave Spaniard Don Francisco Pizarro waved during his conquest of Peru shall be returned to that republic.

San Martín's patrimony was scanty enough, as we can see. Where are the bags of pounds which they said he had taken from Peru, and the gold that he had grafted in Chile? Poor old man! All he had was his daughter's subsidy from Argentina, meager military pensions from Peru, and the gifts that his good Spanish friend Aguado made to him. All this inheritance belonged to Mercedes, daughter of his flesh. To America, the daughter of his genius, belonged an ancient banner, his greatest trophy and a liberating saber that never served to usurp any government.

The old man closed and sealed his will, dating it in Paris, and began to await death with wise calm.

Meanwhile his health became worse.

The defect in his vision had dimmed his eyes until he was blind, the final calamity in that existence which had for several years dragged out in silent suffering. The illnesses of his youth had been endured with methodical fortitude, thanks to the loving care of his daughter and the resigned will of the patient. The shortness of breath, the rheumatism, the vertigo were troubles to which the sick man had accustomed himself, or which had abated with alternating periods at the hot baths and in the fresh air of the beach. The nervous crises of fatigue or irritation brought on by his own temperament were separated by long intervals. The old wounds in both his arms, suffered in travel accidents, as well as those which he received at Albuera and San Lorenzo, were now innocuous scars. The fever of Huaura and the cholera of Paris were only unpleasant memories, although he had then been at the point of death. The vomiting of blood which he suffered in Tucumán, Chile, and Peru, accompanied by terrible stomach pains that impelled him to resort to opium, had also lessened in severity. In spite of so many successive sufferings, San Martín reached the age of seventy-two years, vigorous of mind. But he was blind, and this was what saddened him most, although he was rarely heard to complain about it.

In 1848, at the outbreak of the February revolution which provoked so much agitation in Paris, San Martín abandoned his residence at Grand Bourg, removing his family from the dangerous area of turmoil. He sold the house in which he had lived fourteen years and moved to Boulogne-sur-Mer, where he rented the upper floor of a house at No. 5 Grande Street, owned by Dr. Gerard, a French lawyer who was city librarian, and who occupied the lower floor. The owner and the tenant were good neighbors, and they became true friends. San Martín lived in the house at Boulogne for sixteen months. It was his last residence. He brought his furniture there from Grand Bourg and settled down with his daughter and granddaughters.

Concerning those times, he wrote a letter to his Chilean friend General Pinto, the original of which was given to me by Don Gonzalo Bulnes, Pinto's grandson. In this letter he says:

It is essential not to have any illusions about this old continent's true situation: the real struggle which exists today is purely a social one; in a word, the struggle of the have-nots against the haves. Figure out for yourself what such an idea can cause when it infiltrates the lowly masses by means of the harangues in the clubs and the reading of millions of pamphlets. To this propaganda is added the horrible misery of millions of working people, aggravated by the industrial paralyzation, the prospect of a civil, or of a European, war, and finally of national bankruptcy very probably next year, since the estimated deficit for that year is more than four hundred million francs.

In other letters, among them one addressed to Rosas, he insistently made similar observations. What tormented him most was his blindness, especially in the midst of such a cataclysm. He was determined to go to London for an operation on his eyes, and he asked Rosas to allow Balcarce, his son-in-law, an official of the Argentine legation in Paris, permission to accompany him, because without his services as a guide he could not travel. His letters of this period have only the signature in his own hand. His pulse trembled now, and the pen wrote as if sketching in dense shadow.

Once, in other years, the seashore had agreed with him, but he now found the strong winds of the English Channel disagreeable. He had passed the age of seventy, and the old ailments reappeared to plague his ever-suffering body: rheumatism and gastralgia, which only opium eased. His general condition grew worse on account of the nervous disorders caused by the climate, but his pain, and the use of drugs, also contributed their part. The abatement of morale, common to old age, was aggravated by blindness, for, although he had planned since 1848 to be operated on for cataracts, the operation was always delayed. His daughter or granddaughter read the newspapers to him to entertain him.

Nearly every afternoon some friend came to visit him. His son-in-law Balcarce and his neighbor Dr. Gerard tried to distract him with their conversation. Fortunately he maintained complete mental lucidity. His conversation revolved around social conditions in Europe, and his recollections of Spain and America became more closely linked each day in the memory of his past life. A funeral veil covered his eyes, and his voice, energetic in the past, seemed to be weakening. He scarcely ever smoked or drank now, two things he used to enjoy. With his long, bony hand he caressed his granddaughters' youthful brows, and on touching them he felt as though he were already a ghost. . . .

In July 1850 he asked to be taken to Enghien, near Paris, to spend a while at the baths. There he met Félix Frías, an Argentinian, who was a liberal publicist and an enemy of Rosas. They spoke of the distant nation. San Martín recalled the forests of Tucumán and the fruit orchards of Cuyo with a nostalgia that was almost bucolic. Concerning the outlook of emancipated America, which was now suffering the rule of tyrants and dictators, the old man firmly said:

"I cherish a profound faith in the future of those nations."

This word of hope was one of his last political confidences, practically a message to the new generations of America. Death already hovered round about him. He left Enghien early in August, slightly restored by the mineral baths. On August 6, in Boulogne, he went to take a little air in a carriage, unable to go on foot on account of his blindness. On returning home, after having felt the stimulus of the sea air for the last time, his servants helped him to his bed. On the thirteenth the symptoms of exhaustion grew sharper. He suffered pain and foresaw his end, but he did not wish to complain in front of his daughter. When she came near him to fondle him and ask how he felt, he preferred to simulate a smile and respond in French, the language he occasionally spoke with her and which, according to Lafond, the Frenchman, he spoke very well:

". . . C'est l'orage qui mène au port!"

He said it with a tranquil voice: "It is the tempest that blows toward port." Storm of agony at the end of the voyage, and haven of eternity for the ship that was dismasted by its struggle with the wind across the undulating seas of time. It was a desolating phrase for the loved ones who continued living, but for him it was pregnant with poetry and mystic adumbrations. The Holy Scriptures call death a heavenly haven. Thus, on the eve of his death, the stoic soldier spoke as do the poets and saints.

On August 17 he arose with sufficient strength to go into his daughter's rooms, where the blind old man asked that the papers be read to him.

Félix Frías, upon learning of the illness, had come from Paris to be with the family in their anxiety, and it was he who narrated the scene he witnessed in these last hours of the great American.

San Martín took a light lunch and asked to have snuff put in his box to offer his doctor, Dr. Jackson, who would soon arrive. He experienced that false respite which sometimes precedes death.

At two o'clock in the afternoon he suffered a terrible attack in his stomach. There was scarcely time to lift him from his chair and lay him on his daughter's bed in that very room. Dr. Jackson, who had just entered, administered the necessary, but already useless, aid. When the pain was abated, the sick man seemed to become calm, but he was already in the final agony of death. The moribund man half-opened his eyes, and on hearing Balcarce and his daughter talking near him, he made a gesture to his son-in-law and indicated with halting words that he be carried from Mercedes' room so that she might not suffer watching him die. And so, fully conscious, mitigating his family's suffering, sure of himself, San Martín expired at three o'clock in the afternoon of August 17, 1850, in Boulogne-sur-Mer, after an exile of twenty-five years, and after having lived a life of seventy-two years full of labor.

Among those who were with the family in that critical time were Dr. Jackson, Gerard, the lawyer, and Don Francisco Javier Rosales, Chilean chargé d'affaires, a friend and admirer of San Martín who had come to Paris that day to visit him, and who officially communicated the mournful news to his Government:

"He ended his days," says the solemn report, "in the arms of his distraught and virtuous family, with the peace of a righteous man."

When it was night, in the midst of the indifferent city, they prepared the funeral chamber in the house on Grande Street that was plunged into mourning. Two Sisters of Charity came to pray with the daughter and granddaughters for the repose of that incomparable soul. They clasped the hands of the dead man upon his breast and placed a crucifix between them, which was not inappropriate against the heart of that great Christian who had voluntarily sacrificed himself for the salvation of America, in liberty and in justice. The face of the inert San Martín "kept the pronounced features and his severe and respectable character," says someone who saw him. On a table burned two tapers illuminating the body with golden reflections in that chamber of somber corners.

On August 19 the body was enclosed in a triple coffin of cedar, evergreen oak, and tin. The twentieth was the anniversary of San Martín's departure from Valparaiso to Peru with the liberating expedition that was his life's mission of justice. On that day his body was interred in foreign soil more hospitable than that of his own country. His immortal spirit, now itself free, had departed for another expedition across the ocean of shadows toward the haven of eternal justice of which he spoke to his daughter on the eve of his death.

Rosales, the Chilean, and Gerard, the Frenchman, had undertaken all the necessary details pertaining to the city of Boulogne and to the parochial church. They signed the death notice and the burial record. The coffin was left in the Church of Notre Dame. The record then drawn up reads as follows:

Le vingt Aout mil huit cent cinquante a été présenté à l'Eglise en cette paroisse, pour être déposé ensuite provisoirement, dans les caveaux de l'Eglise de Notre Dame, haute ville de Boulogne-sur-Mer, et plus tard être transporté en Amérique, le corps de José de San Martín, brigadier de la Confédération Argentine, capitaine général de la Republique de Chili, généralissime et Fondateur de la liberté du Pérou, né a Yapeyú, province de Misiones (Confédération Argentine) le vingt-cinq février mil sept cent soixante dix-huit, fils du colonel Don Juan de San Martín gouverneur de la dite province Misiones, et de María Francisca Matorras, veuf de Remedios Escalada de la Quintana, décédée à Buenos Aires.

The record concludes with the usual formalities. Two errors had slipped into the facts stated: the mother's name and the father's rank were wrong. But those two well-meaning witnesses could not know all the facts perfectly, neither of them being Argentinian. The French lawyer, Adolfo Gerard, published, two days later, in *L'Impartial,* a Boulogne paper, a moving obituary which was reprinted several times afterwards. The Chilean minister, Rosales, later initiated a subscription among South Americans resident in Europe to erect a monument to San Martín in America, first of the series of statues which were later dedicated to him in both Americas and in Boulogne-sur-Mer. These were the immediate acts of civilian homage following the interment, which by request of the will was carried out without pomp or procession. Peace had finally come for him, although his glorious memory would yet suffer posthumous criticisms because of American ingratitude.

Now that San Martín was dead, his family moved out of their flat on Grande Street and returned to Paris, filled with sorrow at having left their father's remains in a solitary tomb.

The old house at Grand Bourg had been sold by San Martín before he died, and after 1850 the family acquired some property in Brunoy, not far from there, where the son-in-law, his wife, and their two daughters established themselves. In this new residence they gathered together the furniture, papers, and relics of the deceased, consecrating themselves to the private veneration of his memory, while America continued to split up in civil wars.

This property had belonged in remote years to the Marquis de Brunoy and to the La Rochefoucaulds, and it was said that Louis XVI had stayed one night in the house. The title to the marquisate passed to the Duke of Wellington after Waterloo, as a gift of Louis XVIII, and the land was divided. On one of the lots lived the tragedian Talma. Another was acquired by Balcarce. His wife, Doña Mercedes San Martín, restored her father's study, making of it a real sanctuary which, occasionally, was opened to the admiration of visitors. "I still recall her tall and imposing figure, her seductive grace, and the sudden liking which she inspired with the first few words." That is what an Argentinian publicist who visited her in the house of Brunoy wrote about Mercedes. Alberdi, who knew her at Grand Bourg when she was still young, found her to resemble her father, then living.

In 1861 the remains of San Martín were moved from the cathedral of Boulogne-sur-Mer to the church at Brunoy to be deposited in the tomb of his granddaughter, María Mercedes, who had died unmarried the year before. Although the removal was carried out without an official ceremony, his daughter's sentiment caused the coffin to be covered with Pizarro's Standard, because she well knew what that meant to her father's spirit. When this second interment was concluded, the trophy was kept in a rosewood box inscribed as follows:

"The Royal Standard of the Conquistador, Pizarro, presented to the Most Excellent Señor Don José de San Martín, Founder of Peru's Liberty, by the City of Lima, April 3, 1822."

The city of Lima had previously presented him with the proofs of its authenticity, and it was painful to San Martín when it was said that he had stolen the trophy, when the claim was made that it was not authentic, and when the Government of Peru asked for its return.

In his will he had stipulated that after his death this pennant of the conquest should return to Peru. His children complied with San Martín's wish. On the day following the new burial, they gave it to Minister Galvez, Peru's plenipotentiary, in a simple and solemn ceremony which took place in the house at Brunoy.

Besides Minister Galvez, other diplomatic representatives accredited in France came to witness the ceremony: Alberdi of Argentina, Torres Caicedo of Venezuela, Rosales of Chile, Gutiérrez Estrada of Mexico, Calvo of Paraguay, and several South Americans who were traveling in France.

The Standard was spread on a table. The measurements were checked. The Lima document of 1822 was read, and once the relic had been identified it was again placed in its box and tied with a blue-and-white ribbon and sealed with San Martín's seal, and also with the seal of the Peruvian legation. In this manner the presentation was made, a document being drawn up which everyone present signed.

Upon the presentation of the trophy, Balcarce, in his own and in his wife's name, made a brief speech in which he mentioned the testator's wish. Minister Galvez responded: "I have attended the ceremony held in honor of the Protector of Peru with profound emotion. He who assured the emancipation of the River Plate at San Lorenzo and gave Chile her freedom at Chacabuco and Maipú had the glory of preparing Peru's independence and founding, with the abolition of slavery and of the Indians' enforced service, the splendid bases of the nation's civil life. But in his admirable abnegation

San Martín left to other heroes the glory of concluding his immortal enterprise, and hardly was the Peruvian Congress convened, hardly had he received the country's gratitude, when he departed from America, taking as the noblest remembrance of his services Pizarro's Standard, which popular recognition placed in his hands.

"That banner, ladies and gentlemen, deposited for forty years at the illustrious leader's side, and which has covered his ashes, is a precious symbol which has come to combine in a providential fashion the memory of the greatest events in Peru's history. . . . In those forty years the work of the Protector has been consolidated. The liberty he planted has taken deep root, and Peruvian nationhood has been triumphant in the midst of the conflicts attendant to its vast organization. Today when independence is an incontrovertible fact, and the past allows us to look without uneasiness toward the future, Pizarro's banner, symbol of a day of conquest, can be for Peru only a reminder of the civilization which impelled the Old World to fecundate the virgin shores of America.

"So, ladies and gentlemen, this Standard, sanctified upon a tomb where passion is silenced and where only the memory of greatest deeds survives, will be, for the republic in whose name I receive it, the link which unites two epochs of Christian civilization. Peru will receive it enthusiastically and and will see in it an eloquent testimony of the Protector's services.

"I take pleasure in expressing to you, Señor Balcarce, upon receiving from your hands the Standard that has belonged to Pizarro and San Martín, the intense gratitude of Peru, and of my Government, for the sentiments you have expressed in your name and in that of your noble wife."

In the tragedy, *Oedipus,* the chorus consoles the daughter of the blind king on the occasion of her father's death, saying that destiny has granted her good luck in the midst of her ill fortune. The daughter, Antigone, who had shared her father's misfortune, exclaims:

" ". . . that which is not sweet for anyone was sweet for me, when I led him with my hands. Oh, Father, oh dear Father! Thou, whom the eternal shadows of the earth already enfold, wilt never cease being loved by me."

So Mercedes—Antigone—dedicated herself to posthumous worship, and she was the priestess of the paternal glory, the intermediary between home and country. She cherished San Martín's ashes and relics in order to give them to history.

San Martín's daughter, who like her father was an amateur painter, painted on silk a copy of Pizarro's Standard before it was sent to Peru. Years later the relic, which was kept in the Government Palace in Lima, disappeared in a riot. The copy which Mercedes had painted is now preserved in the Museo Histórico Nacional of Buenos Aires, the sole remaining trace of that trophy which symbolized for the city of Lima the transcendent significance of the San Martinian epic.

The news of San Martín's death had reached General Alvear in New York, where he resided as minister of the Argentine Confederation, and this old companion of the voyage on the *Canning* commented upon the mournful news with noble and melancholy words addressed in a letter to General Tomás Guido, the other survivor of the grand enterprise:

I previously wrote to you about the death of General San Martín. I have never forgotten the intimate friendship that united us at the beginning of our revolutionary career, when we went together to serve our country. I am sure that our Government will arrange the removal of this distinguished captain's ashes to Buenos Aires so they may rest in the midst of the people he has defended and has covered with glory by his heroic actions. So, my friend, little by little the number of those men who began the revolution is diminishing, and in a few short years more all will have traveled the same road to seek eternal rest. What torment, grief, and labor the defense of our good cause has cost us! And we must painfully confess that it has not been the enemies of our independence who have caused us to undergo the most exertions and sufferings in that epoch. It has been the inexperience of our own countrymen. Let us forgive all those, my dear General, on the single condition that those of the present will allow us to end in peace and calm the remainder of a tired, sick, and useless life, which can be prolonged very little more in this world, and which in fact is already ending for us.

In 1850, on learning of San Martín's passing, Rosas had ordered his minister, Arana, to write to Balcarce, declaring: "If it is at all possible, proceed to remove the remains of the deceased general to Buenos Aires at the expense of the Argentine Confederation, so they may receive testimony of the appreciation this nation feels for his patriotism, and so that his last request in the matter may be fulfilled." The downfall of Rosas and other internal difficulties delayed the transfer of the sacred remains. Urquiza, in Paraná, decreed for his part the appropriate honors. In 1862, during the presidency of Mitre, the equestrian statue of San Martín was unveiled in Retiro Plaza in Buenos Aires. In 1878, during Avellaneda's presidency, the hero's ashes were brought to the nation and placed in a magnificent urn in the Cathedral. The ceremony was a stirring apotheosis. The last survivors of the San Martinian campaigns, among them the feeble old general Frías and other veterans, attended the public ceremonies and, crying, sang the national anthem in chorus with the people.

Mariano Balcarce, San Martín's son-in-law, minister plenipotentiary of the Argentine Republic in France, died in Paris February 20, 1885, at the age of seventy-seven years, after having fulfilled all the requests his father-in-law had made of him in his will. He had seen his daughter María Mercedes die in France unmarried in 1860, and also his wife Doña Mercedes de San Martín, the hero's virtuous daughter, die February 28, 1875, a white-haired old woman. San Martín's other granddaughter, Doña Josefa Dominga, who had married Don Fernando Guitiérrez Estrada, scion of a noted Mexican family, in Paris in 1861, survived her parents and her sister. She became the sole depository of her illustrious grandfather's relics. Her parents, in fulfillment of San Martín's will, had already sent the great Argentinian's ashes to Buenos Aires, Pizarro's Standard to Lima, and the saber of Maipú to Rosas.

They had then presented San Martín's archives to Mitre, and he had utilized those papers to write his history of the hero and the continental emancipation. In this generous act was expressed the implicit wish of the deceased, who, when he put his papers in order during his exile, had written:

> I cannot overlook the fact that I have a daughter and friends, even though precious few, whom I must satisfy. With this object, and for that which they call glory, I have worked two years in making extracts and arranging documents. I do not do this for self-justification, but so that the deeds and motives upon which my conduct has been founded during the time I have had the misfortune of being a public figure may be verified.

With the presentation by the family of San Martín's archives, no more of his relics remained in the house at Brunoy save the furniture of his bedroom, some books, pictures, and private documents. The Historical Museum of Buenos Aires, under the direction of Don Adolfo Carranza, endeavored to obtain the things that had belonged to San Martín so that they might be dedicated to public veneration. The heirs of Rosas had been prevailed upon to give the saber of Maipú to the Museum when, in 1899, Doña Josefa Dominga Balcarce y San Martín de Gutiérrez Estrada was induced to send, from Paris where she lived, to the Museum in Buenos Aires, where they were to be kept, her grandfather's furniture, a sketch of his bedroom to enable its reconstruction, a portrait of San Martín done in London in 1824 upon his arrival from America, and another painted in Brussels by Mercedes' art teacher in 1827, a copy of Pizarro's Standard painted by the Protector's daughter, and several other mementos. They are now preserved in the National Historical Museum.

The granddaughter reluctantly gave up those objects among which she had lived with the filial devotion taught her by her mother. She cherished them "religiously," and she does not "doubt that they will be duly preserved," she says to Carranza, signing herself as "your very devoted compatriot" in the letter with which she sent them from Paris. San Martín's granddaughter, although born in France, considered herself an Argentinian. And she was so considered by the South Americans who visited her in Brunoy. A lady of simple distinction, she grew old in solitude until she saw her hair turn white, and on April 27, 1924, she died an octogenarian, in Paris, without having left any descendants.

So San Martín's family line was extinguished, and all of it had been worthy of the progenitor. The only daughter, the faithful son-in-law, and the two granddaughters died, like the father, far from that America which the latter had served so well. But they lived to their last day filled with devotion for the fatherland and exemplary veneration for the San Martinian glory. The family were the best witnesses to the virtue that animated the heart of that great man.

The heart of Saint of the Sword today rests in the Cathedral of Buenos Aires, and the memory of the hero serenely illumines the people like a votive **light.**

EPILOGUE

Upon terminating this life of San Martín I feel the necessity of seeking to find, through biographical anecdotes, the hero's spiritual classification. I have told the story of his life from the time his being began to be formed in the loving care of his parents until his progeny were extinguished with the passing of his grandchildren. We already know what he did. Now we ask, who was he?

"A man surrounded by mystery," Gervinus, the historian, has said in describing San Martín. And so, in effect, was this singular man. In the present book I have attempted to rend the veils of mystery which surrounded him. Now we can contemplate San Martín face to face as though we were actually looking into his deep black eyes to penetrate the secret of his very soul.

Many Europeans who knew him personally—Macduff, Haigh, Hall, Miller, Lafond, and Mary Graham—agree in their testimony when they affirm that an impression of superiority emanated from his being, in addition to the physical excellence and intellectual clarity which they likewise attribute to him. Lafond calls him "the American Cincinnatus"; Lord Macduff called him "Emulator of Washington"; Sarmiento dubbed him "Hermes Trismegistus." These are metonymies that define him by comparison to what others, men or myths, were. But San Martín was a person genuinely peculiar, perhaps unique in history. And from this fact proceeds the "mystery which surrounded him," and which we wish to decipher in words, if such a thing is possible.

The first baffling thing about him is his meteoric career in Spain, the ease with which he fights, gaining ranks and friendships in a triumphal rise. A cadet at eleven and a colonel at thirty, decorated at Arjonilla and Bailén, a brilliant military future stretched in front of him in convulsed Europe, when he broke off his career there. That rupture with his mother country, under those circumstances, is his first act of spiritual heroism, and that his compatriots did not comprehend when he presented himself in Buenos Aires to offer his arms to American liberty, is understandable. Suspicion of him appeared immediately. They thought him to be a Spanish spy, and many Argentinians distrusted him.

In the second stage of his life, his epic fame was sung across the Andes, and he astonished people with his strategic insight and his capacity for fulfillment of his plans. It was a great achievement, worthy of a military hero, to have prepared America's most complete army amid the poverty of Cuyo, crossed the desolate mountain range with 5,000 men, and restored liberty in Chile as a consequence of the foreseen victory. His intuition, knowledge, patience, ingenuity, and indefatigable industry in the midst of misery and sickness are as amazing, then, as his knack as a soldier, when, in the midst of general uncertainty, he charted the new course toward the Andes and the Pacific, because he had heard "the voice of destiny calling him." In that stage of his life many distrusted his efforts, attributing them to personal ambition. But there is in San Martín something more that surpasses his genius of insight and his heroic actions.

The crossing of the Andes and the war in Chile were only a road leading toward other horizons in the continental panorama across which his genius moved as though it were an organ of the territory and of the race as a whole. Along this road he traveled to the Pacific in order to enter Lima, ousting merely by his presence the last of the Spanish viceroys. His will, only his will, subtle and intrepid at the same time, achieved the co-operation of Chileans and Argentinians for the expedition of the Pacific, and in this way he fitted out the ships that carried him to Peru. He wished to take Lima without the shedding of blood. The warrior of the Andes tried to avoid having war in Peru. He occupied the coast, incited the mountain people to revolt, sowed the spirit of desertion in the Royalist army and the idea of liberty in the Peruvian people. In this way he vanquished Peru, cradle of the Spanish conquest and the last bastion of the colonial system. This truly magical accomplishment, worthy only of a master of the spirit, seemed to many so incomprehensible that they attributed to the military cowardice of an enterprising soldier, his determination to avoid bloodshed, and his wish to triumph, not over the armies, but over popular opinion.

But the most undeniable mystery of San Martín's life is found in his meeting with Bolívar, in his renunciation of the protectorship of Peru, following Guayaquil, when the last battle of the continental epic was yet to be fought. He retired from Peru after having given the nation its being, founded its liberal institutions, and constituted the National Congress, before which he put aside the insignia of his power. The suitable silence he then maintained gives rise to all kinds of slander. Now we know what his silence hid, and on this account San Martín shines in our eyes, bathed by the light of a sublime virtue, never before seen in any man of arms.

When he came from Spain to Buenos Aires in 1812, he was an apostate in the eyes of Spain, in whose armies he had matured as a soldier. When he went from Cuyo to Chile, abandoning the United Provinces which were anarchy-ridden on account of hate, he was an apostate in the eyes of Argentina, in which country he had recruited his legions. When he left Chile for the shore of Peru and quarreled with Cochrane over the payment of the fleet, he was an apostate in the eyes of Chile, which had lent him her banner. When he retired from Peru, leaving the final battle for Bolívar, he was an apostate in the eyes of that nation which he had founded. And apostate he seemed anew to his compatriots when, upon reappearing like a ghost at the gates of Buenos Aires in 1829, he refused the dictatorship which the two factions engaged in civil strife offered him. He did not brandish his saber to gain power. His mission was the liberation of the continent, and that mission, faithfully fulfilled, explains all his attitudes.

In war he achieved military successes worthy of a great soldier, but what contributes most to his greatness is the abnegation with which he took up his arms. He would be just like other warriors if there had not existed in him that spirit of sacrifice with which he sanctified the sword. He never wielded it to gain power, but only for the liberation of his America, and in the fulfillment of that Promethean mission the bound Titan was breaking the chains that tied him to the past.

He broke first with Spain in order to come to fight for the emancipation of Buenos Aires. He later broke with Buenos Aires to continue his campaign in the Pacific. Then he broke with Dionysiac America to avoid struggles for personal predominance, and finally he departed from American soil to live almost thirty years in exile, and to die in Europe, facing the sea, poor, blind, and alone, pronouncing words of forgiveness and of hope.

The mystery which surrounded him, recalled by Gervinus' phrase, emanates from that capacity for renunciation, because that is what is usually lacking in men of power. He possessed a skill capable of armed victories, but in addition he possessed love. The mystic aureole of his heroism is due to his aptitude for sacrifice. With magnanimous serenity he went down into the abyss filled with the foulest human passions, and he came up out of there wiser and more serene.

There is in San Martín a greater glory than that of having contended with the Mountain and the Sea, or of having conquered, with soldiers which he produced out of nothing, the Spanish arms which had beaten Napoleon, destroying in that act the ancient empire of kings in the New World. That greater glory is his virtue, an exceptional quality in a soldier. It is the virtue of having been able to conquer himself and renounce the promotions, the honors, and the prizes that go with triumph in each of the places where he was victorious; subdue his fleshly desire to such an extent that he did not take the fruits of power, neither the gold nor the luxury, which so many other military conquerors appropriated; overcome adversity when his star was eclipsed, and crown his life in exile, in solitude, and in poverty with the charitable silence of the purest masters of the spirit. To achieve this last he had to pardon abuses, and he knew how to pardon them, perhaps more on account of his love for

America than of his love for men, a love for the land amidst whose primitive passions he was a luminous child of the Sun.

In the South American inferno José de San Martín, in spite of his exemplary life, about which we already know, was called spy, traitor, hypocrite, ambitious, charlatan, inept, cuckold, ignorant, sybarite, sensual, mulatto, coward, drunkard, assassin, and thief. Because such labels were unjust, I have called him "the Saint of the Sword," since the spirit with which he served the men who abused him was true sanctity. Genius deserves glory, not only because of the effort with which it is achieved, but also for the taunts and the troubles which always form the sinister accompaniment of glory.

As his liberating mission was being accomplished, hostilities against him were growing. Beginning silently, they burst out in 1820 when he left Argentina. They grew in the hour of his greatest heroism, after 1822, when he left Peru. They were renewed when he did not wish to accept, in 1829, the dictatorship which his country, blood-stained by civil wars, offered to him.

Colonel Federico de Brandsen, a veteran and cultured French soldier who fought in Peru and who admired San Martín, wrote about him:

In the midst of his glory black envy launched its infernal venom against that great man. Perfidy grasped its daggers, and ingratitude, with a heart of bronze, disturbed the hero's soul. More sensitive than ambitious, he abandons, with tears, the work he had begun. He puts aside the Supreme Power and flees from a land that did not deserve to have him. His retirement was the signal for the unleashing of all the passions. Ignorance, cowardice, presumption, mistakes, excesses, and the crimes which the latter usually engender, insistently assault and undermine the insecure structure of nascent liberty.

The legend of Orpheus, who descends to Avernus in search of Eurydice until he finds her, and who, as he passes by the wild beasts, tames them with the celestial music of his lyre, is an allegory of the heroic life: Eurydice is the soul's freedom, the wild beasts are the baser passions, and the music is the spell of love's harmony.

The Sword, which is usually an instrument of crime when it is moved by egoism, can come to be God's flaming steel in the right hand of the Archangel. That is why there are armed angels. And the name of "Gabriel" means "God's power."

Such a mystery was made visible to men when San Martín appeared to serve his America, serving her like one who had been initiated into the highest truths.

Through the various chronological stages into which his life is divided, one notices the internal unity and a spiritual perfection, because "understanding," "power," and "love" form the crown of wisdom, and he who includes the three in a higher synthesis can be considered master of mankind. José de San Martín applied himself, first of all, to learn who he was and why he had been born, gaining dexterity in the manipulation of the instruments with which he was to realize his mission. He then consummated his enterprise with calculated lucidity of plan and inflexible will in his purpose. And when he had finished his heroic accomplishment, understanding and power enabled him to overcome himself in a silent work of love. Thus this man's conscience perfected itself within him according to the Pythagorean rules of the Pyramid, which is solid worldly reality at its base, sharply ascending along its sides, and the apex of purity at its luminous summit, with the symbols of eternity in its bosom and shifting sands round about.

The hostilities which the winds of paltry rancor raised against him were nothing but sands surrounding his immovable conscience. A man without hereditary prestige or landed property in his native country, he achieved everything by the power of his will. He lacked pecuniary fortune and physical health, but his character conquered all, and he conquered himself. He tasted victory, but he surpassed it with a humility never witnessed in a soldier. Child of the Sun in a Dionysiac continent, hatred entwined its serpents about the indefatigable hero's limbs. He endured sickness, toil, poverty, ingratitude, and slander with impressive resignation. From those fires he emerged purified like the noblest metals, and in that his sanctity consisted, lay sanctity which is indistinguishable from duty and which did not seek either heavenly or worldly rewards.

In this way he refused salaries, promotions, commands, prizes, and honors. Chile presented him with 10,000 pesos and he donated them to a public library. Chile gave him a farm and he consigned its produce to pay for a vaccinator and a woman's hospital. From Europe, while he was poor himself, he ordered his foreman of the Los Barriales farm to feed the poor people of the district with the harvests. On the battlefield at Maipú he embraced the beaten general Osorio. In the jail at San Luis he himself removed the chains from a Royalist prisoner. At the conference of Punchauca he drank a toast to reconciliation with Spain. Such was the virtue of this lay saint.

San Martín fought for thirty consecutive years. The field of his campaign was three continents and three oceans. In his military itinerary he traversed the longest roads and the highest mountains. These things measured in exceptional dimensions the soldier's magnitude. The principal theater of his genius was our [South] America, which now shelters one hundred million souls and which offers fertile soil to European civilizations. Europe's geographical names lend greater prestige, and her battles furnish greater fame, but we ought to overlook the modesty of the theater in which the San Martinian destiny was realized to evaluate his genius in his own conscience and in his mission.

San Martín as soldier found no pleasure in combat, and he planned his campaigns with mathematical precision or with political skill, trying to reach his objectives with the least bloodshed. He did not seek the cajolery of triumph or the fruits of power, and he said that his cause was that of humanity. These circumstances define the moral content of a new kind of heroism. It does not belong to the Homeric tradition, and in it is formed the paladin of "protective force," as he himself said.

A contemporary of Napoleon and Bolívar, he was different from them, and his singular case anticipated what happened following the last European war, when all the belligerents tried to appear as victims of an unjust aggression and none attempted to deify its generals. Joffre in his French retirement after victory is the symbol of this new military sensibility. The esthetic sense of war, which created Alexander, Caesar, and Napoleon, tends to be supplanted by the ethic sense latent in the myths of the revolutionary epic. San Martín is the spiritual and extremely individualistic prototype of that new heroic sensibility. He made use of the necessary arms, but without arbitrariness or sensuality. Upon him rested a moral mandate. For this reason his figure as a military hero projects itself into the silhouette of a civil hero. More attractive than his military deeds is his conscience. His saint's sword reflects, upon being unsheathed, the light of justice.

We do not know what San Martín could have learned in the lodges of Cádiz and London or from his contact with men of Spain, France, and England who were familiar with the esoteric traditions of antiquity in that apocalyptic age that followed the French Revolution and which was the period of his personal apprenticeship. Napoleon himself was considered at the time to be a wizard, and the legends of the Eleusinians, Rosicrucians, and Templars were then in vogue. San Martín was not a wizard, he was a saint, and the Lautaro lodges which he founded in America, and the inflexible silence he maintained about them until his death, the infallible harmony of his thoughts, his words, and his deeds throughout a long existence, the power of his will, and the mystery which they say surrounded his being, suggest to me the belief that he possessed the rules of wisdom, and that he was an agent of extraordinary powers. He himself, upon embarking for Peru, confessed that he was an agent of destiny.

The symbols of all rituals of the spirit are nothing but appeals to man's subconscious mind to create mystic impulses for action. The rituals of all religions, as well as the drama of the ancient rituals of Egypt and Greece, impress the senses with their images and awaken guiding intuitions, giving to individual will a deep ethic sense which comes from the divine. There are extraordinary men who do not need that formalistic ritual because for them the world is, in itself, a drama of symbols and they find in it the key to their own nature and to the destiny of human life. But other men—nearly all men—do not see anything but the exterior of the symbols and make religion and ethics nothing but the practice of a ritual without discovering the transcendent truth which the symbols represent. San Martín was one of those who discover wisdom in the painful learning of experience itself.

If man in general can be the measure of things, each man is the measure of himself. Experience, real or symbolic, does not awaken anything in each of us save what was dormant in our own spirit, and to this the legend of Parsifal alludes, as does the myth of Eurydice, when Parsifal has a spiritual awakening after having shed the blood of the Swan and disarms himself before entering the mystic Temple in which his soul discovers the law of sacrifice and of liberation. We do not know whether San Martín passed through a formalistic ritual in the lodges of Europe, and it perhaps does not interest us, because the ritual and its doctrine lack an essential virtue. Their virtue depends upon the blindfolded neophyte who either does or does not remove his blindfold, according to his own innate possibilities. To progress from darkness to light, to know sorrow and conquer it, to discover, in a word, the meaning of life, the mysteries of Eleusis, which Aeschylus, Plato, Solon, and Pythagoras knew may be useful, but also the world and its symbols and existence with its anguish can be useful for certain exceptional souls, such as Cervantes, Washington, Goethe, and San Martín, who knew the rules of true wisdom. The talent of the latter, a man of few letters, proceeded from his intuition, and his will nurtured itself directly in the silent mind of nature.

On the road to Damascus there comes occasionally to the traveler, as it did for Saul, a lightning flash that rips the seven veils of mystery. At other times, after much peregrination, a Parsifal crosses the obscure heart of the Mountain "where time becomes space" and the spirit is reborn, enlightened. The hour of the lightning flash was, for San Martín, the year 1811, when he broke his pact with the Spanish kings upon discovering who he was, when he said: "One will be what one must, or he will be nothing." The hour of the Mountain experience was, for him, the year 1817, when, upon crossing the Andes, he slept in the snow near desolated Aconcagua, dreaming of his America. At that time he said: "I must follow the destiny that calls me." The hour of the mystic Temple was the year 1822, when at Guayaquil he decided upon his renunciation of love. He then said: "I am, and shall continue to be, in retirement from the world." His soul was ascending, along the paths of sorrow, toward the highest spheres of wisdom. San Martín's dedication of his old age, during his voluntary exile, to the education of his daughter gives us the clue to all his legendary life.

Progressing beyond the blood of cruel extermination motivated by prehistoric hate, the Saint discovers the blood of sacrifice motivated by Christian love. Christ says that he had come to bring war, and he affirmed, when they went to arrest him, that legions of armed angels could be summoned by the sound of his voice. But it is his will to submit to the cross. Only pain teaches men, and only love frees them.

San Martín knew these ineffable facts. His will knew them, because he was a genius of will. The will of geniuses of action, whether heroes or saints, is neither whim, nor phantasy, nor instinct. It is spirit which nurtures itself in the cosmic essence of life. On this account its highest manifestations astonish us with their enigmatic nature and triumph by their brilliance.

The message which San Martín brought to the armies and peoples of America, a message which we must not forget, is summed up in that inspiration of love which opposes to the arbitrary force of the instinct the protective force of the spirit. San Martín expressed it in these words:

"Your duty is to console America. You do not come to conquer, but to liberate peoples. . . ."

"The time of oppression and force has passed: I come to put an end to that epoch of pain and humiliation. . . ."

"I am an instrument of justice, and the cause which I defend is the cause of humanity. . . ."

Thus is deciphered the heroic legend of San Martín, the Saint of the Sword, patriotism's ascetic, illuminated before the bemused eyes of his Dionysiac America by the mystic halo of universal virtue.

NOTES

PART I

Chapter I

1, p. 1. *Criollo:* From the Spanish verb meaning "to be born" and properly applied to persons of Spanish or French blood born outside the homeland. Like Creole, the English form, the word is used as both noun and adjective, as in "criollo saddle," "criollo customs," etc.

2, p. 3. "Clean blood": The old Spanish expression signifying purity of lineage.

3, p. 5. *Arroba:* A familiar unit of weight, averaging twenty-five pounds, although varying considerably with place and time.

4, p. 6. Tala: A variety of urticaceous tree that grows to large size in the Argentine, but for the name of which no English translation exists.

5, p. 7. Tupac Amarú: Indian leader in Peru, whose real name was José Gabrill Condorcanqui (1742(?)–81). Taking the name of an Inca, Condorcanqui led a revolt in 1780 in favor of the Indians. He was captured and brutally executed, but later the reforms for which he fought were nearly all granted.

Chapter II

1, p. 11. Bolívar: The other great Liberator in South American history, whose career from beginning to end was in striking contrast to that of San Martín.

2, p. 15. Benjamin Vicuña Mackenna: Chilean historian and politician (1831–86), a sound scholar who wrote biographies of Sucre, Bernardo O'Higgins, and Diego Portales, also *History of Valparaiso* and *The War with Spain*, all still in Spanish.

Chapter III

1, p. 20. Andrés Bello: Who was born in Venezuela and spent much time in Chile, was one of the greatest of all Criollo authorities on the Spanish language.

2, p. 23. Tomás Guido: Lifelong friend, confidant, and companion-at-arms to San Martín, whose *Memories* form one of the most valuable source books on the Liberator's feats and personality.

3, p. 26. Manuel Belgrano: Argentine general born in Buenos Aires (1770–1820) and educated in Spain. Led the Argentine troops in the early period of the War of Independence and fought in Paraguay, Chile, and Peru. After a series of defeats, he was succeeded by San Martín. He died in Buenos Aires and in Argentina is looked upon with reverence as the initiator of the revolt against Spanish rule.

Chapter IV

1, p. 30. Juan Manuel de Rosas: Argentine dictator (1793–1877) who led an army of gauchos in support of the federalists against the unitarians. He brought his country from chaos to order and ruled with an iron hand. Overthrown by Justo José de Urquiza in 1851, he fled to England and lived in Southampton until his death.

2, p. 30. Goth: A word frequently used of Spaniards in a derogatory sense and applied to this day to Conservatives as contrasted to liberals. The original derivation is obvious.

3, p. 34. Mariano Torrente: Spanish historian (1792–1856) who left his country during the period of the French invasion and lived in Mexico and Cuba. His best-known work is *A General History of the Hispanic-American Revolution,* although he wrote numerous other books.

Chapter V

1, p. 36. Carbonari: Literally charcoal-burners, a secret society organized in Naples by Murat early in the nineteenth century, to oppose foreign rulers. The society gradually merged into the more general movement for the unity of Italy.

2, p. 37. *La Araucana:* The epic poem of Chile, written by Alonso de Ercilla y Zuñiga (1533–94), a Spanish poet, who fought the brave Araucanian Indians and while in prison began the poem that has immortalized them.

3, p. 37. Bernardino Rivadavia: Argentine statesman and diplomat, who fought against the British invasions and was president from 1826 to 1827. He was responsible for widespread reforms, but was finally driven into exile because of his stanch principles of centralization. His period is known as the Age of Rivadavia.

4, p. 39. Bartolomé Mitre (1821–1906): Argentine statesman and writer, opponent of the dictator Rosas, himself dictator and later president, author of the definitive study of San Martín and his epoch.

5, p. 43. Bernardo Monteagudo: One of San Martín's valued aids, who after a long and useful career was assassinated in Lima. He was one of the prime movers in the Argentine War of Independence.

Chapter VI

1, p. 41. Oromí: Argentine leader of the revolutionary period, related to San Martín's wife and referred to frequently in subsequent passages.

2, p. 50. Remeditos, or "little Remedios," a common use of the Spanish diminutive, as in Merceditas for Mercedes, the name of San Martín's daughter.

3, p. 54. Manuela Saenz: Companion of Bolívar, who left her adoring English husband to campaign with her fiery lover and who saved his life in the September conspiracy by holding his would-be assassins at bay while he leaped from a Bogotá balcony, escaping from the city the next day.

Chapter IX

1, p. 74. *Gaucho:* The cowboy of the Argentine pampas, who has given rise not only to many legends, but to a whole school of literature.

2, p. 78. Stamped paper: The *papel sellado* required for practically all legal documents in Latin America.

Chapter X

1, p. 84. O'Higgins and Carrera: Bernardo O'Higgins, Chilean hero in the War of Independence, was the natural son of an Irish nobleman, Ambrosio O'Higgins. He became dictator in Chile in 1817 and remained until 1823, when he was forced into exile. Carrera was one of three brothers and a sister, all stormy petrels and all bitter enemies of San Martín.

2, p. 89. Federation: In South American history, federal and unitarian signify in the first case more or less what we would mean by "confederacy," with the emphasis on states' rights, and in the second a powerful central government. These opposing concepts caused much bloodshed during and after the Wars of Independence.

3, p. 92. Hermes Trismegistus: Hermes Thrice-great, a late name for the Greek god,

NOTES 363

more or less identified here with his Egyptian counterpart Thoth, and the fabled author of Hermetic books, filled with mystical philosophy.

PART II

Chapter I

1, p. 97. William Miller: English soldier (1795–1861) who fought under San Martín in Chile and took a leading part in the liberation of Peru. He was exiled from Peru for supporting Santa Cruz, but returned after twenty years.
2, p. 99. *Maturrangos*, one of many words, such as *gachupines, chapetones,* etc., applied by Criollos to Spaniards and always derogatory, although not necessarily perfectly definite in meaning.

Chapter III

1, p. 123. Admiral Thomas Cochrane: British sailor and nobleman (Lord of Dundonald), who had a long and stormy career at sea and in politics. He took part in the Chilean and Peruvian Wars of Independence in 1818 and subsequently. He quarreled with San Martín, took service with Brazil and later with Greece, and ended his career as admiral of the British fleet.
2, p. 125. Joel Poinsett: North American statesman (1779–1851) sent to Latin America by President Madison to investigate the struggle for independence. He brought the poinsettia plants to the U.S., immortalizing his name.
3, p. 125. Commodore David Porter: American naval officer famous for his exploits in Latin-American waters, commander of the frigate *Essex,* one-time admiral in the Mexican Navy and finally chargé d'affaires in Constantinople.

Chapter VII

1, p. 162. Federal: Cf. Part I, Chapter X, note 2.
2, p. 163. Buenos Aires: Refers to the province, not the city.
3, p. 163. *Chipiras:* Blankets drawn between the legs as a sort of trouser and commonly worn by the gauchos.
4, p. 167. Cf. Chapter V, Part I.

Chapter VIII

1, p. 170. "Each brown pig gets its San Martín.": This is the Spanish way of saying each pig will be killed at the proper moment. Our San Martín was the "brown one" and the pig at the same time, in the twin sense in which the expression is used in the old proverb. But the haughty viceroy, who used the saw, preferred a few days later to send his envoys to the invader.

Chapter IX

1, p. 188. The Saint of the Sword: The title of the biography in Spanish was *El Santo de la Espada.*
2, p. 193. Metallic lord: This refers to Cochrane's seizure of funds when he was unable to collect pay due him and his men. Cf. Part II, Chapter III, note 1.

Chapter X

1, p. 199. Auxiliary troops: In this instance Señor Rojas plainly means reinforcements, as some of the famous grenadiers were included, and they were not auxiliaries by any stretch of the imagination.

2, p. 203. General Tomás Cipriano Mosquera (1798–1878): Famous in Colombian and Latin-American history as military man, political figure, and writer. He was a member of one of the old city of Popayán's earliest and most illustrious families.

3, p. 206. *"El Libertador nos ha ganado de mano"*: "The Liberator [Bolívar] has beaten us to the jump," an expression used in card playing, when the first player (*mano*) wins over a similar hand held by another.

PART III

Chapter I

1, p. 215. Padilla, Bravo, and Maldonado: Heroes of the revolt of "Los Comuneros" in Spain during the reign of Charles V.

Chapter II

1, p. 232. *Matuchos:* Another unpleasant nickname for Spaniards.

Chapter III

1, p. 241. Soleristas: From Pueyrredón, Sarratea, and Soler, three contemporary political leaders.

2, p. 241. *Porteños:* The people of Buenos Aires, "of the port."

3, p. 242. *Cornudo:* In Spanish the word *cornudo* (literally "horned" and signifying cuckold), may when applied to oneself mean nothing worse than unlucky.

Chapter IV

1, p. 250. *Argos* and *El Centinela:* Two well-known newspapers of the period.

2, p. 253. Nitrous: Means that the land had an excessive amount of niter or saltpeter.

3, p. 257. War with Brazil: This war was fought between Brazil and Argentina over that territory called La Banda Oriental, which separates the two countries. Its principal result was the establishment of Uruguay as an independent nation in 1828 as a convenient buffer state.

4, p. 261. Rosas, cf. Part I, Chapter IV, note 1.

Chapter V

1, p. 262. Rodríguez and Rivadavia: Cf. Part I, Chapter V, note 3. Rivadavia served as minister under Governor Rodríguez of Buenos Aires (1820–23), then went as envoy to Great Britain.

2, p. 265. José Gervasio Artigas: Dictator and national hero of Uruguay (1764–1850). The most powerful leader in the Banda Oriental (later Uruguay), he fought off Argentines and Brazilians, but in 1820 was forced to resign and flee to Paraguay, after which Uruguay was conquered by Brazil.

3, p. 271. Unitarians and federalists: Cf. Part I, Chapter X, note 2.

Chapter VI

1, p. 277. Rafael del Riego y Nuñez: Spanish general (1785–1823) who fought the French and later, as a Mason and Liberal, led the revolution of 1812 in Spain, with its repercussions in Latin America. The "Himno de Riego" formerly Spain's national anthem, was first sung at Málaga in 1820.

2, p. 279. $14,000: The reference is to Argentine pesos, not United States dollars.

3, p. 285. Domingo Faustino Sarmiento, 1811–88: Essayist, educator, journalist, and statesman. As President of Argentina, he reformed the entire school system. His book *Facundo* is regarded as one of the greatest ever written in Latin America.

Chapter VII

1, p. 293. Pruvonema's book: This is explained fully in a later reference in this chapter.

2, p. 294. Director Pueyrredón: Following Argentina's War of Independence there was set up a Directorate similar to that of the French revolutionary period.

3, p. 303. *"Arequipa"* etc.: The doggerel is somewhat risqué and perhaps may best be freely translated as follows: "Arequipa [where San Martín landed in Chile] has given its consent. Cuzco [ancient Indian capital, therefore La Indiecita] will soon follow suit. What will Lima do? Why, this old mulatto woman [Lima] will be syringed with a chili [hot pepper]." (Note by C.V.)

4, p. 306. International Bureau of American Republics: This bureau was the forerunner of the present-day Pan American Union.

Chapter VIII

1, p. 308. Alto Peru: Often referred to in the translation as Upper Peru, where much of the fighting in the War of Independence took place. The part of Peru that became Bolivia is a high tableland, hence "Alto."

2, p. 314. Balcarces: The members of this well-known family here referred to are Mercedes, San Martín's daughter, and her husband.

3, p. 319. José María Restrepo: One of Colombia's most distinguished historians.

Chapter IX

1, p. 329. Lapacho: A familiar flowering tree of Argentina and Uruguay

2, p. 332. Garcilaso and Ercilla: The epic poets of Peru and Chile.

3, p. 334. Francisco de Paula Santander: Founder of the Great Colombia (La Gran Colombia), a union of Venezuela, Colombia, and Ecuador, father of democracy and of education in Colombia, and known as "the man of laws."

4, p. 335. Nueva Granada: The viceroyalty made up of what is now Venezuela, Colombia, and a part of Ecuador.

Chapter X

1, p. 341. City of May: The reference is, of course, to Buenos Aires, where the revolution against Spanish rule began on May 25, 1810.

INDEX